T*SQ Transgender Studies Quarterly

Volume 1 ∗ Numbers 1–2 ∗ May 2014

Postposttranssexual

Key Concepts for a Twenty-First-Century Transgender Studies

Edited by Paisley Currah and Susan Stryker

ARTS & CULTURE

NEW MEDIA

BOOK REVIEW

Introduction

SUSAN STRYKER and PAISLEY CURRAH

Welcome to *TSQ: Transgender Studies Quarterly*, which we intend to be the journal of record for the rapidly consolidating interdisciplinary field of transgender studies. Although the field is only now gaining a foothold in the academy, the term *transgender* has a long history that reflects multiple, sometimes overlapping, sometimes even contested meanings. For some, it marks various forms of gender crossing; for others, it signals ways of occupying genders that confound the gender binary. For some, it confers the recognition necessary for identity-based rights claims; for others, it is a tool to critically explore the distribution of inequality. The term *transgender*, then, carries its own antinomies: Does it help make or undermine gender identities and expressions? Is it a way of being gendered or a way of doing gender? Is it an identification or a method? A promise or a threat? Although we retain *transgender* in the full, formal title of this journal, we invite you to imagine the *T* in *TSQ* as standing in for whatever version of *trans-* best suits you—and we imagine many of our readers, like us, will move back and forth among several of them. We call your attention as well to our use of the asterisk (symbol of the open-ended search) in the journal's logo, our hopefully not-too-obscure gesture toward the inherently unfinishable combinatorial work of the *trans-* prefix. Whatever your critical, political, or personal investment in particular trans- terminologies, we hope that you will find—or make—an intellectual home for yourself here.[1]

It is worth pausing to reflect on the historical moment in which *TSQ* has appeared. For starters, as we write this introduction in September 2013, Chelsea Manning, the Wikileaks whistle-blower and "cover girl" of this, our inaugural issue, has just announced her gender transition within the US military prison system. There could be no better illustration of the timeliness or significance of paying careful attention to transgender issues. For some, Manning's decision to announce her transition provoked dismissive accusations of mental illness and narcissistic attention seeking, charges that exemplify a sorry history of pathologizing and stigmatizing transgender phenomena. For others, her transition has drawn focus to the porous and shifting boundaries between some articulations of gay and transgender identity and highlights the evolving, and achieved, nature of identity for us all. And for still others her transition shines a light on transphobic and homophobic oppression within the military, conditions that no doubt bolstered her resolve to disseminate classified documents in order to expose wrongdoing in the inner workings of the US security apparatus. In some quarters, Manning evokes shopworn stereotypes of the transgender figure as subversive, terroristic, dangerous, or pathetic; in others, she redefines courage and patriotism; elsewhere, she exemplifies the principled resistance to state-based repression to which we should all aspire. For some, Manning's transgender status is a random if not bizarre detail in her story, while for others it is the causal explanation on which the entire plot hinges. Whatever one's opinion of Manning's actions, her case raises complex questions about the relationship of transgender identity to issues of state, to moral and political agency, to visions of social justice, and to strategies of social transformation. Her case already exemplifies the inexcusable dearth of transgender-specific medical care in prisons—an unconstitutional "cruel and unusual punishment" routinely suffered by trans people within the carceral system—and adds fuel to trans activist demands within the prison abolition movement. At the very least, in one of the biggest news stories of the decade, she has compelled mass media outlets and the general public to ponder the proper use of pronouns and to grapple with issues of gender self-determination in the absence of medical and legal supports for gender transition. It is virtually impossible, in the wake of the Manning case, to ignore transgender issues or not to have opinions about them.

Moreover, Chelsea Manning represents but one of many contemporary moments of cultural attention to transgender phenomena. As she begins her undoubtedly long ordeal in prison, the most talked-about television program in the United States is the Netflix original series *Orange Is the New Black*, a prison show featuring as a secondary character an African American transgender lesbian, played by African American transgender actress Laverne Cox. The *Wall Street Journal*'s website coverage of Trans*H4CK, a "hackathon" (profiled in the New Media section of this issue) in which "hackers use code to break gender barriers" (fakerapper), exemplifies the increasingly prevalent opportunities for transgender identities and practices to positively represent the entrepreneurial values of flexibility and fluidity within the digital information economy. *Matrix* trilogy codirector Lana Wachowski finally goes public with her long-rumored transition from male to female. The Palm Center, a think tank at University of California, Santa Barbara, announces that it has received a $1.35 million grant to study transgender issues in the military. The Arcus Foundation convenes a national gathering of US transgender rights and advocacy organizations to explore possibilities for increased funding, while the Open Society Institute convenes a similar gathering at the international level. The University of Arizona (which hosts the editorial office of *TSQ*) announces an unprecedented transgender studies faculty cluster hire, with the intention of building a graduate degree program. At the same time, scarcely a day goes by—if one subscribes to the right listservs or visits the right news sites—without encountering a report of deadly violence against a trans person somewhere in the world, which undermines any credible progress narrative on transgender rights and calls for an explanation of how it is that whatever "progress" can be claimed remains so unequally distributed. What might be characterized as the "transgender turn" in recent affairs provides a context for the advent of *TSQ* while simultaneously demanding the in-depth analysis of this turn's conditions of possibility that we hope to provide in these pages in the years to come.

History and Scope of the Field

Arguably, transgender studies was first articulated as a distinct interdisciplinary field in Sandy Stone's foundational "Posttranssexual Manifesto," which she began writing in the late 1980s and first published in 1991. It is in homage to this work of roughly a quarter-century ago that we have called the first issue of *TSQ* "Post-posttranssexual: Key Concepts for a Twenty-First-Century Transgender Studies." Stone's task at the time was to explode the concept of the "transsexual," then often perceived (particularly by the people who lived a transsexual life) as a restrictive category that required gender-changing people to be silent about their personal histories as the price of their access to the medical and legal procedures necessary for their own well-being. Her goal was to break that silence and transform what she called the "textual violence inscribed in the transsexual body" into a critical "reconstructive force" (295). Stone argued that juxtaposing medically constituted transsexual embodiments against the backdrop of culturally intelligible gendered bodies generated "new and unpredictable dissonances" in which "we may find the potential to map the refigured body onto conventional gender discourse and thereby disrupt it." She wanted "to take advantage of the dissonances created by such a juxtaposition to fragment and reconstitute the elements of gender in new and unexpected geometries." Stone's intent was to point past what "transsexual" then meant and to call our attention to new genres of problems "whose potential for *productive* disruption of structured sexualities and spectra of desire has yet to be explored" (296). These genres constitute the domain of transgender studies.

Our task now is to look back, briefly, over the work already conducted in the field of transgender studies before turning our sights toward what the next, postposttranssexual, iteration of that field now seems to hold in store. We are honored to include among the nearly ninety authors who have supplied keywords and key concepts for this inaugural issue of *TSQ* a contribution from Stone herself, in which she proposes an ongoing guerrilla intervention into field formation in order to guard against sterile professionalism at this moment of accelerating institutionalization.

Since at least the nineteenth century, medical, scientific, and legal institutions in Europe and North America have construed individuals who manifest transgender behaviors or characteristics as particular kinds or types of beings whose bodies are thereby rendered susceptible to various sorts of social intervention (consensually or not). In this sense, there has been a "science" of transgender phenomena for more than 150 years, and a voluminous professional and technical literature on transgender topics has existed for many decades. The long-term biopolitical project of cultivating "gender congruence" while eliminating incongruity has achieved a high degree of institutionalization over the past century and a half, including the development of professional organizations, medical standards of care for transgender individuals, a significant body of case law and public policy, peer-reviewed social-scientific publications, and academically affiliated research centers and clinics. Most notable in this regard is the World Professional Association for Transgender Health (WPATH), formerly known as the Harry Benjamin International Gender Dysphoria Association, which publishes the clinically oriented *International Journal of Transgenderism*, this journal's nearest though somewhat distant kin.[2]

The interdisciplinary field of transgender studies that began to emerge more than two decades ago differs from these previous approaches. Unlike the medico-juridical and psychotherapeutic frameworks, it does not merely investigate transgender phenomena as its proper object; it also treats as its archive and object of study the very practices of power/knowledge over gender-variant bodies that construct transgender people as deviant. Transgender studies, in other words, is to the medico-juridical and psychotherapeutic management of transgender phenomena what performance studies is to performance, or science studies is to science. Transgender studies does not, therefore, merely extend previously existing research agendas that facilitate the framing of transgender phenomena as appropriate targets of medical, legal, and psychotherapeutic intervention; rather, it draws upon the powerful contestations of normative knowledge that emerged over the course of the twentieth century from critical theory, poststructuralist and postmodernist epistemologies, postcolonial studies, cultural studies of science, and identity-based critiques of dominant cultural practices emanating from feminism, communities of color, diasporic and displaced communities, disability studies, AIDS activism, and queer subcultures and from the lives of people interpellated as being transgender.

Transgender studies began to take shape as an interdisciplinary field concurrently with the emergence of the term *transgender* itself in the early 1990s, as a broadly inclusive rubric for describing expressions of gender that vary from expected norms. The term came to name a range of phenomena related to deep, pervasive, and historically significant shifts in attitudes toward, and understandings of, what gender itself means and does. The work of the field is to comprehend the nature of these shifts and the new forms of sociality that have emerged from them; it seeks as well to reevaluate prior understandings of gender, sex, sexuality, embodiment, and identity, in light of recent transgender phenomena, from critical perspectives informed by and in dialogue with transgender practices and knowledge formations. As historically new possibilities for gender self-perception and expression emerge, as states reevaluate and sometimes alter their practices of administering gender, as biomedical technologies blur customary boundaries between men and women and transform our mode of reproduction, as bodies and environments collapse into one another across newly technologized refigurations of subjects and objects, transgender studies appears an increasingly vital way of making sense of the world we live in and of the directions in which contemporary changes are trending.

In its narrowest sense, transgender studies revolves around the category "transgender" itself—its history, dissemination, application, uptake, logics, politics, and ongoing definitional and categorical transformations. Indeed, the circulation of the term itself functions as a marker of the deep sociopolitical and cultural shifts with which the field is concerned. Some of the earliest recorded uses of variants of the word *transgender* appear in the United States in the 1960s among self-organized communities of predominantly white, middle-class, male-bodied individuals who persistently expressed feminine comportment, identities, and dress (but please see the keyword entry "transgender" in this issue for fuller documentation of this term's emergence). Such people began describing themselves as "transgenderal," as "transgenderists," or as practicing "transgenderism." Their aim in doing so was to resist medical, psychiatric, or sexological labeling either as "transvestites," which connoted episodic cross-dressing primarily for reasons of erotic gratification, or as "transsexuals," which connoted medicalized bodily transformations of sex-signifying physical attributes through which a permanent legal change of social gender could be accomplished. "Transgender," on the other hand, was meant to convey a nonpathological sense that one could live in a social gender not typically associated with one's biological sex or that a single individual should be able to combine elements of different gender styles and presentations. Thus, from the beginning, the category "transgender" represented a resistance to medicalization, to pathologization, and to the many mechanisms whereby the administrative state and its associated medico-legal-psychiatric institutions sought to contain and delimit the socially disruptive potentials of sex/gender atypicality, incongruence, and nonnormativity.

The new sense of *transgender* as a catchall term for gender variation entrenched itself by the mid-1990s and had great intellectual reach; it gathered together, under a specific term, a broad class of phenomena related to historical shifts in how sex, sexuality, gender, identity, and embodiment are thought to be conjoined and how—and to what ends—they may be reconfigured. On the other hand, the term's very reach allowed it to collapse many forms of difference into a single category, particularly as that term has been used in public health, HIV prevention, international philanthropy, NGOs, and human rights discourse; it often functions reductively to mask and contain differences that need to be distinctly articulated. One critical aspect of transgender studies is to consider the work that the term *transgender* does: tracing the genealogy of "transgender" as a category; documenting and debating the consequences of its rapid deployment in a wide range of contexts; and interrogating the ways in which it can function (sometimes simultaneously) as a pathway of resistance or liberation, as a mechanism for surveillance and control, or as a neutrally descriptive technical term in an analytics of emergent cultural phenomena.

Transgender studies promises to make a significant intellectual and political intervention into contemporary knowledge production in much the same manner that queer theory did twenty years ago. The work of the field is not confined to identitarian concerns any more than queer theoretical maneuvers were confined to the study of gay and lesbian identities. And like queer theory, transgender studies can function in minoritizing as well as universalizing modes. The central tensions in the field are thus structured by a tripartite focus on perspectival knowledge (of anything) gained from living a transgender sort of life; expert knowledge (by anyone) of transgender lives and related matters; and knowledge pertaining to the metacontextual conditions (potentially everything) that inform our contemporary encounter with transgender phenomena. Studying transgender issues is both worthwhile and substantive in its own right and also of significant interest for what it can teach about broader conditions of life.

A particularly rich stream of dialogue within transgender studies pertains to the relationship between *transgender* and *queer* and to the variously intersecting, parallel, and antithetical manners in which these two terms—which acquired their current critical connotations at roughly the same historical moment—are involved with identity politics and subcultural community formations. Another, similarly rich stream of dialogue pertains to the relationship of *transgender* to feminist politics and women's communities, to the extent to which transgender issues problematize the political efficacy of the category "woman," or to the question of which transgender-identified people or practices can be considered a proper subject of feminist activism. Transgender studies likewise engages with studies of masculinity and men, both disseminating and analyzing a politically significant array of alternative masculinities.

There are certainly individuals who call themselves "transgenders" (noun), or who think of themselves as "transgendered" (adjective), or who see their particular categories or modes of self-expression or self-identification as falling somewhere under a collective transgender umbrella. Transgender exists, and we can study it, as we can study any social phenomena, from disciplinary, interdisciplinary, and transdisciplinary perspectives. The field thus concerns itself with the full life content of such people—the accounts they offer of themselves and their world; their visions of the past and of futurity; their material histories and concrete social organization; the art they make and the literature they write; their activist campaigns and political struggles; their health and illnesses; their spirituality and religious beliefs; their forms of community; their experience of the life cycle, of interpersonal relationships, of kinship, and of institutions; their erotic lives, inner lives, domestic lives, and working lives; the way they represent themselves and are represented by others.

Transgender studies also examines the relationship of an attributed transgender status to other categories of personal and collective identity. Particularly in the United States, transgender is often considered part of an imagined LGBTIQ (lesbian, gay, bisexual, transgender, intersex, queer) community, and transgender studies consequently attends to the cultural politics of this identitarian grouping—especially given the complex discursive slippages among notions of homosexuality (same-sex attraction), intersexuality (biologically mixed sex status), and transsexuality (transposition of sexed body and gendered identity). Parsing the sometimes fine-grained distinctions between these categories can have important consequences within such contemporary policy debates as marriage equality, military service, employment nondiscrimination, public accommodations, and healthcare access.

Transgender has been correlated, too, often through acts of epistemological violence, with past and present terms drawn from nonanglophone cultural traditions around the world (mahu, sworn virgin, female husband, bakla, eunuch, hijra, travesti, berdache, and so on). The perils and potentials of the "transgender" rubric are most evident in such transnational contexts, particularly those that traverse global North/South and East/West divides. Naming differences from dominant configurations of modern Eurocentric categories of sex, gender, sexuality, embodiment, and identity in different cultures or contexts, assigning meaning or moral weight to such difference, and exploiting that difference according to the developmental logic of commercial and territorial expansion, of colonialism and capitalism, has been a central feature of Western societies for half a millennium. Attention to "transgender phenomena"—to anything that calls attention to the contingency and variability of sex/gender statuses through difference from expected forms—can thus be considered an intrinsic aspect of modern occidental knowledge production, deeply related to pervasive and persistent forms of political and economic domination, rather than a recent innovation.

Understanding the dissemination of *transgender* as a term that originated among white people within Eurocentric modernity necessarily involves an engagement with the political conditions within and through which that term circulates. Because transgender can be imagined to include all possible variations from an often unstated norm, it risks becoming yet another project of colonization—a kind of Cartesian grid imposed on the globe—for making sense of human diversity by measuring it within a Eurocentric frame of reference, against a Eurocentric standard. Even in the highly self-reflexive and well-intentioned act of trying to establish a critical space for the interrogation of transgender phenomena worldwide with this journal, we have made errors of judgment and execution that have inadvertently deepened real and trenchant inequities and injustices in the geopolitical, linguistic, and racial distribution of privilege and power, which we truly regret. And yet we nevertheless aver that transgender *can* function as a rubric for bringing together, in mutually supportive and politically productive ways, gender-marginalized people in many parts of the world, who experience oppression because of their variance from socially privileged expressions of manhood or womanhood. Transgender can operate both as a practice of decolonization that opens new prospects for vitally necessary and radically democratic social change and as a vector for the perpetuation of colonialist practices. We feel that decolonizing the transgender imaginary is of such crucial importance to the future elaboration of the field that the second issue of *TSQ* will focus entirely on this question.

Transgender studies promises new transdisciplinary and interdisciplinary perspectives while also posing methodological questions for various academic disciplines. Transgender can, for example, be a useful neologism for interrogating the past. While it would be anachronistic to label a previous era's departures from currently normative expressions of gender as "transgender" in an identitarian sense, there is another sense in which *transgender* as a critical term demarcates a conceptual space within which it becomes possible to (re)name, (dis)articulate, and (re)assemble the constituent elements of contemporary personhood in a manner that facilitates a deeply historical analysis of the utter contingency and fraught conditions of intelligibility of all embodied subjectivity. It can be used to pose new comparative questions about gender difference over geographic space as well over as historical time, between languages and cultures, or between one organization of kinship and another. It can challenge us to develop new models of what counts as mental health or physical well-being and to understand that social institutions such as the family can take many forms and encompass many kinds of members.

Perhaps most importantly, the field encompasses the possibility that transgender people (self-identified or designated as such by others) can be subjects of knowledge as well as objects of knowledge. That is, they can articulate critical knowledge from embodied positions that would otherwise be rendered pathological, marginal, invisible, or unintelligible within dominant and normative organizations of power/knowledge. As is similarly the case in such fields of intellectual activism as race and ethnicity studies, disability studies, feminist studies, and other areas of inquiry that seek to dismantle social hierarchies rooted in forms of bodily difference, the critique of knowledge that operates within transgender studies has an intricate and inseparable connection to broader movements for social justice and social transformation.

Finally, transgender does not simply critique present configurations of power/knowledge; it is engaged with all manner of unexpected becomings, oriented toward a future that, by definition, we can anticipate only imperfectly and never fully grasp. Transgender studies offers fertile ground for conversations about what the posthuman might practically entail (as well as what, historically, it has already been). The field engages with the radically transformative implications of contemporary and prospective biomedical technologies of the body as well as with critical questions about the boundaries between human and nonhuman animals or between nonliving and living materiality. It ponders many of the same philosophical questions about the embodied nature of consciousness that arise in the neurocognitive sciences, robotics, and studies of artificial intelligence. As such, transgender studies is emerging as a vital arena for exploring the evolving edge of our species-life at a historical moment of rapid technological and environmental change that calls into question some of our most fundamental notions of what human life means and may come (or cease) to be.

The Political Economy of Transgender Knowledge Production

We would like to be transparent about the economics behind the making of *TSQ*. It takes a great deal of labor and money to establish a new journal. By launching *TSQ* and committing to publishing four issues a year, Duke University Press will be taking on significant production costs for design, copyediting, proofing, typesetting/compositing, ad sales, shipping, marketing and advertising, manuscript tracking, permissions and rights clearances, journal sales, managing editorial and author correspondence, and many other kinds of labor and services. According to projections from our colleagues at the Press, in the best-case scenario the Press will have about $200,000 in outlays before *TSQ* breaks even around its fifth year. To offset that risk, the press asked us to raise a minimum of $100,000 to underwrite some of those costs. That is not a negligible sum, but when one realizes all that is involved in getting a new journal into circulation, it is not an unreasonable amount of money, either. Spread out over the five-year start-up period, it represents only about $20,000 a year—in other words, less than you would pay an editor in the United States working half-time with benefits.

At the time of writing, we have made a lot of progress toward our fundraising goals. Our most generous supporter has been the University of Arizona, which has already contributed about $35,000 from various sources as part of its unprecedented initiative to become the institutional home of transgender studies in the academy. We have also received contributions from the departments and programs of some of our editorial board members as well as from the board members themselves, all of whom we gratefully acknowledge in the list of founding supporters published in this issue (see "Supporters of *TSQ*"). We reached out to five major foundations with a history of giving to trans causes, but sadly, none of them funded us. We then turned to crowd funding and launched a Kickstarter campaign in May 2013. We are aware of some criticisms of crowd-sourced fundraising, particularly criticism of it as a technique of neoliberalism, helping shift costs from service providers to consumers in ways that increase profits and decrease benefits. We agree with this critique of neoliberal justifications for the individualization of responsibility in the name economic efficiency, but we find it more applicable to public and corporatized sectors of the economy than to a voluntary-participation activity such as our campaign. Nevertheless, we have heard that crowd-sourced fundraising for *TSQ* is a mechanism for taking money from poor, marginalized trans people of color and using it for the benefit of privileged white academics while ultimately turning it into profit for an elite university press. We are also aware of, however, and find persuasive, arguments in favor of grassroots fundraising as a mechanism for broader-based participation in social change activism—including knowledge work—that reduces corporate and non-profit foundation leverage in transformational movements while simultaneously creating greater accountability to grassroots communities.

Getting the word out through social media, our own contacts, and those of the journal's editorial board, we asked potential Kickstarter supporters to make an investment "in the next stage in the development of transgender studies" by helping "create a first-rate platform for publishing peer-reviewed transgender-related scholarship" (*TSQ: Transgender Studies Quarterly* 2013). This crowd-sourcing campaign generated tremendous excitement about the journal (for most supporters, it was the first time they had heard of us) as well as a little rancor. By the end of our thirty-day campaign, we had exceeded our goal of $20,000, raising $24,752 from 404 individuals. About $3,500 of that came from ten higher-end donors, some of them quite wealthy, who each gave in the $200–$1500 range. Nearly half the amount raised came from 86 people who gave between $100 and $200 each; based on name recognition, we assume that most of these individuals are academics, professionals, and members of the coeditors' families. Contributors at these levels, as well as the $75 level, received premiums in the form of steeply discounted transgender studies books and DVDs that were available to the editors. Most donors—230 of them, to be exact—gave $10 or $25 each to have their names listed on our website or in the first issue of *TSQ* as founding supporters. We welcome their contributions, gratefully acknowledge them, and vow to do our best to keep *TSQ* relevant to this grassroots constituency. Thus far, including the Kickstarter campaign, we have secured about $60,000 in total funding for *TSQ* and have another $40,000 to raise in the next few years. We appreciate Duke's confidence in our ability to do so and in launching the journal before we have every dollar in the bank.

TSQ is not the first journal required to provide start-up funds for its launch, and in the age of declining library budgets and increasing institutional subscription prices—especially in the sciences—it will not be the last. In fact, our commitment to raise funds for the journal not only ensured that it would come into existence after years of planning, it also ensured that the individual issue price would be relatively affordable, with annual subscription rates of only $28 for students, $45 for individuals, and a range of $175 to $205 for institutions, depending on whether the subscription is electronic only, print only, or print plus electronic. We felt particularly strongly about print accessibility. Many presses are now moving away from the cumbersome and expensive process of printing journals, but not everyone who might want to read *TSQ* will have an institutional affiliation that gives them access to the e-journal format. Because each issue of the journal addresses a particular theme, every volume of *TSQ* will consist of four (or three, if there is a double issue) book-length works on transgender studies appearing each year, and we think there will be demand for single-issue purchases as well as regular subscriptions. A print version will allow us to sell single issues in independent bookstores as well as through online booksellers. In the final analysis, print journals simply cost more to produce than those limited to distribution on digital platforms, but we think in this instance the additional cost is justified.

The logic and language of economics saturate the foregoing paragraphs: investment, costs and prices, labor, production, marketing, demand, selling—indeed, we might well have used "brand" when referring to Duke's prestigious reputation. During our Kickstarter campaign, a few individuals contacted us to ask why we had decided not to join the open-access revolution and self-publish *TSQ* as a free online-only journal. Why, they wanted to know, must the purity of critical scholarship, or the works of art the journal will feature, be sullied by involvement in the transactions of the (putatively nonprofit) academic marketplace? Why raise money for this "privilege"? *TSQ* is not an athletic shoe or a new soft drink, after all, but a venue for the transmission of new trans knowledges—why should its contents not circulate freely to the people who need them most?

Unfortunately, the project of *TSQ* is not transgender knowledge per se; it is transgender knowledge *production*. No matter how idealistic we would like to be about the work we do as academics and editors, putting ideas into intellectual circulation cannot be separated from the quotidian activity that goes into making a journal. Indeed, the very distinction between an "immaterial" world of cultural and artistic practices and the material, economic world of capital, of buying and selling, as Pierre Bourdieu reminds us, is itself a product of the bourgeois subject and its "double-entry accounting," which, through its "dissimulation or, more precisely, *euphemization*" of what is at stake, invents a "pure, perfect universe of the artist and the intellectual" that masks the economic practices that subtend it (1986: 242). There are no disinterested, noneconomic forms of exchange (arts, culture, education) untethered to the economic realm of labor, capital, and the production of commodities. Even if we had decided to self-publish *TSQ*, we would not have been able to avoid the costs of the labor and services required to produce it. Rather than pay trained workers at the Press to design, print, and distribute *TSQ*, we would have to do much of this specialized work ourselves (as well as the never-ending fundraising to pay for it). And that, for us, was an untenable proposition that would take us away from our own right livelihood as scholars.

There is yet another reason we chose not to take the DIY route to publication. There are innumerable trans-oriented blogs, zines, community forums, gatherings, or other outlets through which self-produced transgender knowledges already circulate. We celebrate this flourishing realm of cultural production while seeking to add to it a different kind of transgender knowledge, one that circulates with a different kind of legitimation, with different effects of power, within systems of power that we cannot readily escape simply because we critique them.

Knowledge production is an activity that, again following Bourdieu, results in the accumulation of a particular form of capital: cultural or symbolic capital. Until now, transgender studies has appeared as a disjointed series of ephemeral happenings and artifacts—conferences, edited collections, and special issues of disciplinary journals—with very little cultural capital. With the launch of *TSQ*, we hope to secure transgender studies as an established field of inquiry. We want the academic job search committees who now look askance at files from job applicants who work in trans studies to take those applicants more seriously. When independent scholars, graduate students, and untenured academics publish their cutting-edge original research in *TSQ*, we want that line on their curriculum vitae to count for more. We want to help scholars working in the academy to advance up the tenure and promotion ladder. Because we believe that theoretical and scholarly work has consequences outside the academy, however much that work needs to be done according to conditions within the academy, we want the work published in the journal to help change how and what people think about transgender issues. We want to do that not only by publishing new content or more data but by providing more space for new frameworks that help make a different kind of sense of transgender phenomena. We do this not metaphorically but literally, by creating the real estate, the page counts and word counts of a peer-reviewed journal, within which these frameworks can be elaborated to an unprecedented extent. We want to cultivate a space where critical conversations can be ongoing, not episodic, where it is not the case that every article needs to rehash foundational concepts for uninitiated readers. Journals are the terrain on which contests of ideas are waged, won, and lost, with consequences that can reverberate both within and outside the academy. We simply need more ground to stand on.

The kind of cultural capital we seek to build cannot simply be conjured out of thin air. It is produced through an intricate and often self-reinforcing mesh-work of social relationships, money, and institutional affiliations. Financial capital and cultural capital cannot be neatly disentangled, which is why a degree from Harvard is "worth more" (and costs more) than a degree from most other institutions. To best wield the power of cultural capital for transgender studies, *TSQ* must follow the norms and standards of academic publishing, including adhering to the peer-review process and listing on its masthead an editorial board filled with accomplished and well-credentialed scholars. Given the newness and precariousness of our field, the vulnerabilities often attached to transgender lives, and the potential for transgender studies to stage an intervention in knowledge-production that has real-world consequences, we also felt the need for the imprimatur of a prestigious university press. We are glad that journals from traditional disciplines and established interdisciplinary fields have accumulated enough cultural capital to move to the open-access environment. At the present time, transgender studies does not have that luxury. We are determined to pro-duce a journal that demands to be taken seriously, because we undertake our work with the utmost seriousness. We recognize that not everyone will agree with or accept our decisions. As *TSQ* moves forward, we sincerely hope that those who would have done things differently nevertheless will become involved in the platform we are trying to create and will work toward their own vision of what this journal, and this field, can become.

Structure and Content

TSQ's editorial team is unpaid except for the graduate student worker who serves as editorial assistant. There are two general coeditors, who are contracted with Duke University Press to serve (potentially renewable) five-year terms. *TSQ* has a large editorial board comprising roughly two dozen scholars across all ranks, many topical and geographical areas of specialization, and several language competencies (though most work in the US and Canadian anglophone academy). While slightly fewer than half of the founding board members are people of color, a slight majority of the board's membership falls somewhere on the transgender spectrum. Our initial selection of the editorial board was designed to address many different diversity concerns simultaneously, including the need to recruit as many tenured and tenure-track academic professionals as possible. As a result, the composition of the board—including the general editors—tends to reproduce some of the existing structural inequalities that make it easy for white, English-speaking, masculine-presenting people to be overrepresented within the academy and for the global North and West to be privileged over the global South and East. As the journal and the field continue to develop, as a more diverse pool of transgender studies scholars move into tenure-track professorships, and as *TSQ* editors rotate off their service on the board, we trust that the editorial structure will become even more diverse than it already is.

Each issue of *TSQ* will be devoted to a special topic or theme. Following the current key words and concepts issue and the forthcoming issue on decolonizing the transgender imaginary, the next few issues will be devoted to quantitative methods and population-based studies, to arts and cultural production, and to such other topics as animal studies, higher education, archives, sex classification, surgery, translation, and sinophone studies. We invite our readers to submit proposals for future issues. Each issue should have a two- or three-member editorial team. To ensure continuity of editorial vision while encouraging new perspectives and approaches, at least one representative from the editorial board will serve as an additional guest editor. The general coeditors will be responsible for the overall consistency, quality, and direction of the journal.

Although published by Duke University Press, the editorial office for *TSQ* currently runs out of the University of Arizona. In addition to accessing the journal through Duke's website, please also visit *TSQ*'s editorial page at lgbt.arizona.edu/TSQ-main, where you will find current calls for papers and enhanced content for selected issues. In addition, we hope to use that space to host a lively forum about scholarship published in the journal as well as broader discussions of transgender studies and of trans issues more generally.

The inaugural issue of *TSQ*, featuring nearly ninety short keyword contributions as well as this extensive introduction, is different from our usual format. Typically, each issue of *TSQ* will include a brief foreword by the general editors, the guest editorial team's introduction to the issue, several feature articles, and a few of several recurring sections: book, arts and culture, and new media reviews; documents and images; opinion pieces; interviews; annotated bibliographies; translations; and fashion. Not every recurring section will appear in every issue. For this first issue, because the general editors are also serving as the issue editors, we are combining the forward and the introduction; because there are so many individual articles, we are offering only a general overview of the contents rather than a more detailed commentary.

Our goal in launching *TSQ* with a special double issue on keywords and concepts is to showcase the breadth and complexity of the field. With contributions from emerging academics, community-based writers, and senior scholars, we hope that a curated collection of very short pieces will provide evidence of both the field's already established depth and maturity and its irreverent youthful vitality. Even so, it is an impossible task to adequately document the full scope of the field—that will be work for *TSQ* to pursue in the years ahead, without hope of completion. We nevertheless trust that readers will find not only a compelling if somewhat partial snapshot of where the field seems to us to be right now but will also be inspired by its very incompleteness to imagine new ways of working within transgender studies, to see new ways for trans studies to connect to an evolving set of topics, and to find unexpected resonances with other concerns and fields of study.

When we published our initial call for contributions for "Postposttranssexual: Key Concepts for a Twenty-First-Century Transgender Studies," we really had no idea what sorts of work we would receive. We could not, however, be more delighted with the outcome. Some of the submissions—like Vic Muñoz's entry "Tatume," which discusses a native American squash—offer a deep and resilient resistance to the entire project of mapping the field terminologically. Muñoz refuses to pick a term and define it; rather, in discussing the qualities of a squash, he begins to reveal poetically a different relationship between acts of naming and imaginings of ownership, between lands and the peoples who occupy them and sustain themselves upon its products. In doing so, the very articulation of a transgender conceptual vocabulary becomes framed by questions of displacement, diaspora, conquest, and colonization. This is indeed the ground—the stolen ground—upon which all of our work proceeds and from which, like Muñoz, we must now cultivate a future that can deliver justice to the violence of this past. Other authors offered equally poetic, if sometimes more whimsical, creative riffs on such words and concepts as *nature*, *hips*, *perfume*, *sickness*, *translation*, or the jaw-breaking neologism *transxenoestrogenesis*.

If we had a template lurking in the backs of our minds for what the first issue of *TSQ* might look like, it was Raymond William's *Keywords*: *A Vocabulary of*

Culture and Society, which traced the shifting usage over time of a hundred or so words to show how our very ability to conceptualize social organization and the cultural field was produced by a history of ideological struggle. Some of the entries in *TSQ* definitely seem to draw inspiration from that approach, such as Julian Carter's deft exposition of the concept *transition* or David Valentine's of *identity*. Others, like David Getsy's take on *capacity*, reveal not so much a critical history embedded in certain keywords but rather words with as yet unrealized critical potentials for the field. Some contributions take existing terms from canonical thinkers (Foucault, Deleuze, and Guattari are current favorites, with Marx and Freud not far behind) and develop the significance for transgender studies of such key concepts as *the state, biopolitics, normal, capital, line of flight, nomad science,* and *revolution*. Others offer overviews of well-known methodologies (psychoanalysis, for example, or phenomenology) and demonstrate their applicability within transgender studies. Some suggest how trans issues play out in various fields—media studies, sports studies, sinophone studies, or childhood studies— and some, like Jasbir Puar's entry on *disability* and Heather Love's on *queer*, map the productive tensions between trans studies and other interdisciplines. Still other contributions function as encyclopedia entries on currently relevant topics: cultural competency, depathologization, surgery, pornography, human rights, and revisions to the International Classification of Diseases. And given that transgender studies involves the critical interrogation of emergent social phenomena, it is no wonder that many of the terms we have chosen to publish invoke identity categories that are only now coming into wider visibility or that have actually been coined with *TSQ* in mind: *transableist, transbutch, somatomorph,* and *x-jendā*, to name but a few. In some cases, we doubled up on the keywords, accepting submissions for both *child* and *childhood, cisgender* and *cisgenderism, psychoanalysis* and *psychoanalytic*. In doing so, we intended to signal that one map of the field could never be enough and that the work these concepts do depends in part on how and where they circulate. We wish we had time and space enough to give a shout-out to every entry and every author, but we simply do not, though we are proud to include them all.

We should close by mentioning the recurring features that round out our first issue. In our first book review section, Regina Kunzel assesses the raft of recent anthologies and special journal issues devoted to transgender studies, which offer further evidence of critical mass the field is now achieving. Doran George reviews the transgender performance scene in San Francisco for our arts and culture section. And *TSQ* interviews Kortney Ryan Ziegler about Trans*H4CK, his hackathon for transgender social justice, for our new media section. Thanks to them all, as well as to section editors A. Finn Enke, Eliza Steinbock and Tobias Raun, for their work on their respective sections.

These thanks, of course, are but the beginning of a long and seemingly ever-lengthening list. We also need to thank Erich Staib, journal acquisitions editor at Duke, and all his colleagues there, for believing in this project and for working with us to bring it to fruition: Rob Dilworth, Mike Brondoli, Sue Hall, Cason Lynley, Jocelyn Dawson, Kim Steinle, Charles Brower, Joel T. Luber, Cynthia Gurganus, Terri Fizer, Diane Grosse, and Bonnie Perkel. Thanks to Aren Aizura and Ben Singer for their work as managing editors in the very early stages of getting this journal off the ground, as well as to Abe Weil, who is providing editorial assistance now. Laura Alexander, Jenny Carrillo, and Heather Hiscox of Alexander-Carrillo Consulting in Tucson coordinated our successful Kick-starter campaign. The staff at the University of Arizona Institute for LGBT Studies helped in innumerable ways with administering our fundraising efforts and developing our website: John Polle, Tom Buchanan, Rachel Nielsen, Lisa Logan, Laura Caywood-Barker, and Cherie McCollum Parks. University of Arizona Provost Andrew Comrie deserves high praise for his visionary support of transgender studies, as do Dean J. P. Jones, of the College of Social and Behavioral Sciences, and Gender and Women's Studies Head of Department Monica J. Casper. We thank the hundreds of individual and institutional donors, listed elsewhere, who have contributed to the advent of this journal. We thank the members of our editorial board and our section editors, also listed elsewhere, for their hard volunteer work. We thank the authors included here as well as those who submitted work we were unable to publish for one reason or another. We thank the generation of thinkers and activists and community members who came before us and upon whose shoulders we stand and our colleagues and students, without whom transgender studies would not exist. Last but certainly not least, we thank our respective families for the love and support they have offered each of as we have jointly undertaken the daunting but rewarding task of launching *TSQ: Transgender Studies Quarterly*.

Notes

1. While many of us use "trans studies" in casual conversation, we decided not to call this simply a journal of trans studies, because it either seems too unspecific for general or formal usage or would entail addressing a wide range of trans- phenomena other than those involving gender.

2. Portions of the scope and history section of the introduction have been coauthored by Aren Aizura as well as Paisley Currah and Susan Stryker. These portions are drawn from the initial journal proposal, drafted when Aizura was managing editor, and have been reworked so many times that precise attribution is no longer possible. Altered, edited, or expanded versions of some parts of this text have appeared in "Transgender Studies 2.0" (Stryker and Aizura 2013) as well as in Stryker's afterword to Howard Chiang's *Transgender China* anthology (2013).

References

Bourdieu, Pierre. 1986. "The Forms of Capital." In *Handbook of Theory and Research for the Sociology of Education*, ed. J. Richardson, 241–58. New York: Greenwood.

fakerapper. Photograph ("Hackers Use Code to Break Gender Barriers," *Wall Street Journal* [September 16, 2013]). Instagram. instagram.com/p/eU8TrIKbfo (accessed October 15, 2013).

Stone, Sandy. 1991. "The *Empire* Strikes Back: A Posttranssexual Manifesto." In *Bodyguards: The Cultural Politics of Gender Ambiguity*, ed. Julia Epstein and Kristina Straub, 280–304. New York: Routledge.

Stryker, Susan. 2013. Afterword to *Transgender China*, ed. Howard Chiang, 287–92. New York: Palgrave.

Stryker, Susan, and Aren Z. Aizura. 2013. "Transgender Studies 2.0," introduction to *The Transgender Studies Reader 2*, ed. Susan Stryker and Aren Z. Aizura, 1–12. New York: Routledge.

TSQ: Transgender Studies Quarterly. 2013. "Kickstarter Campaign." www.kickstarter.com/projects /tsq/tsq-transgender-studies-quarterly (accessed December 17, 2013).

Abstract This section includes eighty-six short original essays commissioned for the inaugural issue of *TSQ: Transgender Studies Quarterly*. Written by emerging academics, community-based writers, and senior scholars, each essay in this special issue, "Postposttranssexual: Key Concepts for a Twenty-First-Century Transgender Studies," revolves around a particular keyword or concept. Some contributions focus on a concept central to transgender studies; others describe a term of art from another discipline or interdisciplinary area and show how it might relate to transgender studies. While far from providing a complete picture of the field, these keywords begin to elucidate a conceptual vocabulary for transgender studies. Some of the submissions offer a deep and resilient resistance to the entire project of mapping the field terminologically; some reveal yet-unrealized critical potentials for the field; some take existing terms from canonical thinkers and develop the significance for transgender studies; some offer overviews of well-known methodologies and demonstrate their applicability within transgender studies; some suggest how transgender issues play out in various fields; and some map the productive tensions between trans studies and other interdisciplines.

Abjection

ROBERT PHILLIPS

Abjection refers to the vague sense of horror that permeates the boundary between the self and the other. In a broader sense, the term refers to the process by which identificatory regimes exclude subjects that they render unintelligible or beyond classification. As such, the abjection of others serves to maintain or reinforce boundaries that are threatened.

This term can be used to think of the instability of gendered and/or sexed bodies—especially those occupied by transgender individuals—which are at the center of academic debates surrounding queer, feminist, and trans subjectivity. Drawing on a psychoanalytic reading of subjective identity as a defensive construction and on the French literary obsession with monsters, psychoanalyst and linguist Julia Kristeva develops the term *abjection* in *Powers of Horror: An Essay on Abjection* (1982).

Abjection literally means "to cast out," yet Kristeva's theorization plays with this definition by recognizing that in the context of marginalized subjects, abjection goes beyond "casting out" and becomes a more interactive process through which the boundaries of the self are protected by rejecting whatever "does not respect borders, positions, rules. The in-between, the ambiguous, the composite" (4). In other words, it renders problematic any assumption regarding the fixity of the borders separating subjects from objects and self from other.

Abjection, as Kristeva describes it, "disturbs identity, system, order" (ibid.) and encompasses a kind of borderline uncertainty—ambiguous, horrifying, and polluting. Transgendered bodies, then, especially when viewed as physical bodies in transition, defy the borders of systemic order by refusing to adhere to clear definitions of sex and gender. The abject can thus serve as a cleaving point of abstruseness and unease—separating, pathologizing, and psychologizing trans subjectivity. The anxiety at the root of this unease with transgender subjectivity can be traced back, in part, to a fear of the ambiguous.

Judith Butler employs Kristeva's concept of abjection to discuss the often problematic embodiment of sexuality and gender. Specifically, Butler explores how normative heterosexual identities are circumscribed via a process that rejects and excludes "figures of homosexual abjection" (1993: 103). Like homosexual subjectivities, transgender subjectivities challenge heteronormative understandings of gender, sex, bodies, embodiment, and (dis)ability. Heteronormative subjects, then, can come to feel threatened, because in order to maintain their own tenuous subjectivity, they must simultaneously identify with the abject others whom they are also required to reject (ibid.: 113). In a similar manner, Nico Besnier (2004) draws on Kristeva's formulation of abjection in his analysis of transgender Tongan men whose gender practices make them socially illegible. Despite the strategic negotiation of social relations with their fellow Tongans, many transgender Tongan men found themselves excluded from the multitude of mainstream social relationships that would usually afford them protection.

While historically the term has had a negative connotation, groups that have traditionally been thought of as marginal are reclaiming their difference and embracing their abjection. Trans activists have taken up abjection as a constructive political strategy, which can disrupt and confound long-standing systems of power that are sustained by the methodical exclusion, repression, and silencing of certain others. Abjection, Kristeva wrote, "draws me toward the place where meaning collapses" (1982: 2). It is in this liminal space where the subject experiences a crisis of meaning in which transformation is possible—the difference between internal and external becomes unclear, and in the process, conditional identity is stripped away to reveal a queer object. In this sense the notion of embracing abjection is epitomized by Susan Stryker's essay "My Words to Victor Frankenstein above the Village of Chamounix: Performing Transgender Rage" (1994), in which she connects her own transsexual body with the figure of Frankenstein's monster. Stryker acknowledges and welcomes her abjection when she declares, "I am a transsexual, and therefore I am a monster" (240). Through this declaration, she is reclaiming the word *monster* in order to relieve it of its power; but more importantly, abjection becomes a tool with which to further challenge and problematize conventions of socially constructed gender categories.

In David Halperin's formulation of abjection (2007), the promiscuous behavior of some gay men has come to threaten the "normalization" of "gayness" and alienate the concomitant goal of equality. While Halperin specifically addresses gay men, his ideas may also be applied to trans subjects. He argues that it is becoming increasingly commonplace for many gay men to mimic a desexualized heterosexual existence consisting of married, monogamous couplings and to emphasize their normativity in order to appear acceptable to others. Yet, as Halperin argues, by acknowledging and welcoming the abjection that accompanies their subjectivity and subsequently taking advantage of the moments when meaning collapses, marginalized subjects (including transgender individuals and gay men) can question the hegemonic forces that seek their oppression and in the process regain control of the signification of their subjectivity.

In modern literature, the abject is a prominent feature in the work of writers such as Jean Genet and Marcel Jouhandeau.

Robert Phillips lectures on anthropology and women's and gender studies at the University of Manitoba. His book *Little Pink Dot: Technology, Sexuality, and the Nation in Singapore* is forthcoming.

References

Besnier, Nico. 2004. "The Social Production of Abjection: Desire and Silencing among Transgender Tongans." *Social Anthropology* 12, no. 3: 301–23.

Butler, Judith. 1993. *Bodies That Matter: On the Discursive Limits of "Sex."* New York: Routledge.

Halperin, David. 2007. *What Do Gay Men Want?* Ann Arbor: University of Michigan Press.

Kristeva, Julia. 1982. *Powers of Horror: An Essay on Abjection.* Translated by Leon S. Roudiez. New York: Columbia University Press.

Stryker, Susan. 1994. "My Words to Victor Frankenstein above the Village of Chamounix: Performing Transgender Rage." *GLQ* 1, no. 3: 237–54.

DOI 10.1215/23289252-2399470

Adolescence

GABRIELLE OWEN

The idea of adolescence is a relatively recent social category, emerging in the late nineteenth century alongside medicolegal notions of homosexuality and the concept of inversion, which conflates gay or lesbian desire with trans phenomena. While the word *adolescence* dates back to the fifteenth century in English and can be found to designate a stage of human life through the seventeenth and eighteenth centuries, adolescence begins to function later in medical discourse and early psychology as a type of person, one who can be shaped and directed away from perceived social ills, such as homosexuality and prostitution, and toward social aims such as marriage and reproduction. By the turn of the century, G. Stanley Hall's *Adolescence* (1904) claimed that adolescence was the key to the advancement of civilization, the developmental moment of state intervention that would propel humankind into the next stage of evolutionary history.

We might understand the idea of adolescence as a mechanism of Foucault's biopower, a technology of self put into the service of the nation-state. One of the ways in which biopower regulates and disciplines trans phenomena is by locating them in the presumably pliable stage of adolescence, where state intervention appears to be developmentally natural and necessary. In the mid-nineteenth century, both childhood and adolescence became intense sites of disciplinary anxiety and control (Foucault 1978). Parents, doctors, and teachers were instructed to watch for the warning signs of degeneracy, disease, mental illness, and criminal tendencies. Emerging institutions of medicine, psychology, and education deployed childhood and adolescence to construct institutional knowledge and to establish authority and expertise. For example, it is adolescence that allows Freud to claim "complete certainty" about the cause of homosexuality in a young woman (1955: 147), and Krafft-Ebing similarly uses childhood and adolescent behavior to explain various kinds of trans phenomena in *Psychopathia Sexualis* (1894). In these contexts, adolescence serves a narrative function. It becomes the moment of subjective fluctuation before the presumed stability of adulthood (Kristeva 1995); and as such, it constructs the narrative inevitability of a normative adulthood.

Adolescence constructs and reifies adulthood as the stage of life when selfhood is final, established, known. And so the idea of adolescence contains transition, movement, and change in which the perceived turbulence of puberty is loaded with meanings about the discovery of self. Adolescence is constructed as the moment that gendered *becoming* occurs. And yet this developmental narrative is one we impose on experience, locating moments of transition, change, and rebellion in adolescence and locating moments of arrival, stability, and conformity in adulthood. Transgender phenomena suggest a much more varied and complex range of possibilities for bodily experience and gendered subjectivity, drawing our attention to the contingency of any subjective arrival whether it be normative or trans-identified.

Transgender and queer perspectives put pressure on the developmental narrative of adolescence, speaking instead of the queer child who might grow sideways (Stockton 2009), or of the reordering or rejection of developmental sequence itself (Halberstam 2005), or of the liberatory potential for naming the self at any point in the prescribed sequence (Bornstein 1995, 2006). Trans embodiment disrupts and denaturalizes the developmental narrative of adolescence, revealing it for what it is—sometimes a story we have been told and sometimes a story of our own making. And yet adolescence persists as the ideological container for the trans phenomena that permeate all human experience. Adolescence functions simultaneously as a site of discovery and disavowal, sustaining assumptions about what childhood was and what adulthood should be, manufacturing narrative coherence for moments of arrival, and creating distance for moments of contradiction, contingency, or change. The work of transgender theory unravels adolescence along with fixed notions of gender identity, sexuality, and selfhood. But trans embodiment suggests also the possibility of reconstruction, revision, and remaking outside the developmental imperative.

Gabrielle Owen teaches gender studies and children's literature at the University of Nebraska–Lincoln. Recent publications include "Queer Theory Wrestles the 'Real' Child: Impossibility, Identity, and Language in Jacqueline Rose's *The Case of Peter Pan*" (*Children's Literature Association Quarterly*, fall 2010).

References

Bornstein, Kate. 1995. *Gender Outlaw: On Men, Women, and the Rest of Us*. New York: Vintage.
———. 2006. *Hello Cruel World: One-Hundred and One Alternatives to Suicide for Teens, Freaks, and Other Outlaws*. New York: Seven Stories.
Foucault, Michel. 1978. *An Introduction*. Vol. 1 of *The History of Sexuality*. Translated by Robert Hurley. New York: Vintage.
Freud, Sigmund. 1955. "The Psychogenesis of a Case of Homosexuality in a Woman." In *The Standard Edition of the Complete Psychological Works of Sigmund Freud*, vol. 18, ed. and translated by James Strachey, 145–72. London: Hogarth.

Halberstam, Judith. 2005. *In a Queer Time and Place: Transgender Bodies, Subcultural Lives*. New York: New York University Press.

Hall, G. Stanley. 1904. *Adolescence: Its Psychology and Its Relations to Physiology, Anthropology, Sociology, Sex, Crime, Religion, and Education*. 2 vols. New York: Appleton.

Krafft-Ebing, Richard von. 1894. *Psychopathia Sexualis*. Translated by Charles Gilbert Chaddock. Philadelphia: Davis.

Kristeva, Julia. 1995. *New Maladies of the Soul*. New York: Columbia University Press.

Stockton, Kathryn Bond. 2009. *The Queer Child; or, Growing Sideways in the Twentieth Century*. Durham, NC: Duke University Press.

DOI 10.1215/23289252-2399479

Archive

K. J. RAWSON

The basic meaning of *archive*—a repository that houses historical artifacts—has been continually expanded by metaphoric uses of the term invoking "any corpus of selective collections and the longings that the acquisitive quests for the primary, originary, and untouched entail" (Stoler 2009: 45). The intersections of transgender phenomena and the archive thus involve both a material dimension (the collecting, maintaining, and accessing of transgender historical materials in a physical repository) and a theoretical dimension (the power dynamics, political motives, epistemological function, and affective currents of any archival project).

Physical archives have always contained traces of transgender phenomena, albeit with varying degrees of intentionality. Prior to the development of "transgender" as a discrete identity, a variety of state-sponsored materials—dress code laws, police documents, immigration reports, homicide records—provide a glimpse of the troubled meetings between gender-nonconforming people and the social and legal mechanisms that have attempted to define, control, and dictate gender norms. Other historical artifacts collected in various archives—personal letters, photographs, keepsakes, ephemera—offer fragmented glimpses into the day-to-day lives of people who transgressed gender boundaries before such practices were coalesced around transgender identity and community. Such traces of early transgender history are closely intertwined with the history of sexuality; indeed, as early lesbian and gay archives emerged in the United States in the 1970s, their collections included trans-related materials.

While LGBT-specific archives have continued to collect transgender materials, and more general archives have also developed transgender collections, transgender-specific archives have also emerged as an independent effort. The first exclusively transgender archival collections began in the 1980s with the National Transgender Library and Archive (NTLA) in Georgia and the Trans-Gender Archive at the University of Ulster in Northern Ireland (both collections have since been donated to other archives). Since 2007, two additional transgender-specific archival collections have emerged: the Houston Transgender Archive and the Transgender Archives at the University of Victoria. The proliferation of digital technologies has also enabled new archival practices in cyberspace, where a range of new genres (blogs, vlogs, podcasts, social media, forums, wikis) have materialized, decentralizing established archives as the single and authoritative epicenter of transgender history (Rawson 2013).

This ongoing development of the material practice of transgender archiving is inextricable from its theoretical dimension, which accounts for the purpose, political function, and effects of such collections. Transgender-specific archives function as "a technology of identity" (Rohy 2010: 354): as the central collection parameter, "transgender" becomes legitimated as an identity through the rich historical lineage that the archive evidences. Far from a neutral or objective record of the past, a transgender archive is thus a rhetorical institution that is intentionally adapted to an audience for a particular persuasive purpose.

Yet transgender phenomena prove quite challenging to the archive. The very site of transgender experience—the body—cannot be captured by the historical fragments collected in an archive because of the irreducible distance between historical objects and the lives they come to represent (Arondekar 2009). As a result of archival memory's separation of "the source of 'knowledge' from the knower," the archive fails to capture much embodied and ephemeral memory (Taylor 2003: 19). In its radical recontextualization of historical materials, the archive emerges as a discrete object of selection and representation that always involves silences and exclusions. This cycle of inclusion and exclusion, of representation and misrepresentation, is the permanent shadow of any trans archival project, even digital ones; while transgender archives fight historical neglect, silences, and misrepresentations, the selection and discrimination involved in archiving creates a residual silencing of others. And what of the history that is hoped to be forgotten? Transgender people who transition their gender presentation may feel betrayed by the archive's stubborn and insistent refusal to forget. Thus, while archiving transgender materials is important for community and personal identity formation, political advocacy, and historical memory, it should be treated as a powerful mechanism of memory and identity with far-reaching impacts.

K. J. Rawson is an assistant professor in the Department of English at the College of the Holy Cross. With Eileen E. Schell, he coedited *Rhetorica in Motion: Feminist Rhetorical Methods and Methodologies* (2010); his scholarship has also appeared in *Archivaria, Enculturation,* and several edited collections.

References

Arondekar, Anjali. 2009. *For the Record: On Sexuality and the Colonial Archive in India.* Durham, NC: Duke University Press.

Rawson, K. J. 2013. "Rhetorical History 2.0: Toward a Digital Transgender Archive." *Enculturation,* May 28. enculturation.gmu.edu/toward_digital_transgender_archive.

Rohy, Valerie. 2010. "In the Queer Archive: *Fun Home.*" *GLQ* 16, no. 3: 340–61.

Stoler, Ann Laura. 2009. *Along the Archival Grain: Epistemic Anxieties and Colonial Common Sense.* Princeton, NJ: Princeton University Press.

Taylor, Diana. 2003. *The Archive and the Repertoire: Performing Cultural Memory in the Americas.* Durham, NC: Duke University Press.

DOI 10.1215/23289252-2399488

Asterisk

AVERY TOMPKINS

The asterisk (*), or star, is a symbol with multiple meanings and applications that can mark a bullet point in a list, highlight or draw attention to a particular word or phrase, indicate a footnote, or operate as a wildcard character in computing and telecommunications. In relation to transgender phenomena, the asterisk is used primarily in the latter sense, to open up *transgender* or *trans* to a greater range of meanings. As Sevan Bussell (2012), a blogger and advocate for using *trans**, has explained, "The asterisk came from internet search structure. When you add an asterisk to the end of a search term, you're telling your computer to search for whatever you typed, plus any characters after." Though *trans** has appeared sporadically in print and online for several years, discussions of this new nomenclature began appearing regularly in online gender-community spaces only around 2010.

Although *transgender* has been used since the early 1990s as an umbrella term to cover the widest possible range of gender variation, it is now understood in some circles to represent only binary notions of transness and to refer only to trans men and trans women rather than to those who contest the gender binary (Killermann 2012). Proponents of adding the asterisk to trans argue that it signals greater inclusivity of new gender identities and expressions and better represents a broader community of individuals. *Trans** is thus meant to include not only identities such as transgender, transsexual, trans man, and trans woman that are prefixed by trans- but also identities such as genderqueer, neutrios, intersex, agender, two-spirit, cross-dresser, and genderfluid (ibid.).

Ironically, typing "trans*" into a search engine yields only results that include the trans- prefix, thereby reinscribing the very conceptual limitations of trans being argued against by those who advocate using the asterisk. We therefore must consider how the asterisk may have a more multifaceted theoretical application. Recalling the variety of ways in which the asterisk can function, *trans** blends the symbol's wildcard function with its use as a figurative bullet point in a list of identities that are not predicated on the trans- prefix formulation. Similarly, starring *trans* draws attention to the word, indicating the possibility of a deeper meaning than the prefix itself might suggest. Finally, the asterisk may act as a footnote indicator, implying a complication or suggesting further investigation. In this sense, the asterisk actually pushes beyond the trans- prefix and opposes it as the only legitimate way to refer to trans* identities and communities.

Avery Tompkins is a visiting assistant professor at Transylvania University, where he teaches courses in sociology, gender studies, and first-year writing. He is the author of "'There's No Chasing Involved': Cis/Trans Relationships, 'Tranny Chasers,' and the Future of a Sex-Positive Trans Politics" (*Journal of Homosexuality*, 2014).

References

Bussell, Sevan. 2012. "Why We Use the Asterisk." *Candiussell Corner*, October 2. candiussellcorner
.blogspot.com/2012/10/why-we-use-asterisk-sevan.html.

Killermann, Sam. 2012. "What Does the Asterisk in 'Trans*' Stand for? And Why Should I Use It?" *It's Pronounced Metrosexual.* itspronouncedmetrosexual.com/2012/05/what-does-the -asterisk-in-trans-stand-for (accessed August 28, 2013).

DOI 10.1215/23289252-2399497

Asylum

TRISTAN JOSEPHSON

Asylum is a key immigration strategy for transgender subjects migrating to the United States. As individuals who are frequently rejected by their families and who are especially vulnerable (and often especially visible) members of their communities, trans migrants have few options to access documented status. Routinely depicted as the side door to immigration, asylum allows subjects who are explicitly barred from immigrating, or who are marginalized by the heteronormative family unification bias of the 1965 Immigration and Nationality Act, to enter and/or become legally documented in the United States. As a particular form of immigration, the process of asylum involves the actual movement of trans bodies across national borders as well as shifts in the legal status and relationship of trans migrants to the US state.

Asylum law and policy developed in the post–World War II period and was codified in the United States with the passage of the Refugee Act of 1980. The Act adopted the United Nations' definition of a refugee—which also applies to asylum seekers—as anyone who is fleeing persecution or who has a "well-founded fear" of persecution "on account of" race, religion, nationality, membership in a particular social group, or political opinion (INA §101(a)(42)(A)). Of these five grounds, membership in a particular social group provides the best basis for claims by trans asylum seekers. There is no statutory definition for what qualifies as membership in a particular social group, but *Matter of Acosta* (19 I & N Dec. 211, 233 (BIA 1985)) described it as "a group of persons all of whom share a common, immutable characteristic." Only shared and unchangeable characteristics that form a fundamental part of an individual's identity or conscience are considered to constitute that individual as a member of a particular social group. This immutability requirement exists in tension with how feminist and transgender studies have theorized gender and sex as socially constructed and as historically and culturally contingent. Trans asylum seekers must posit their sexual and gender identities as essential and fixed, even as their sexed and gendered embodiment may be shifting. The requirement highlights the legal strategies necessary for asylum seekers to make themselves legible to asylum adjudicators by practicing a kind of strategic essentialism.

Several federal court decisions have dealt with trans and gender-nonconforming asylum seekers. The first published asylum cases dealing with trans subjects did not explicitly acknowledge the categories of transsexual or transgender, so trans asylum seekers had to draw on already established legal categories of gender and sexuality to build their claims. The earliest published case was *Geovanni Hernandez-Montiel v. INS* (225 F.3d 1084 (9th Cir. 2000)), in which Geovanni Hernandez-Montiel, a teenaged female-identified migrant from Mexico, was awarded asylum as a "gay man with a female sexual identity." This case established that a trans individual who could frame gender identity in terms of sexual identity could constitute a particular social group. Two later federal court decisions—*Luis Reyes-Reyes v. Ashcroft* (384 F.3d 782 (9th Cir. 2004)) and *Francisco Ornelas-Chavez v. Alberto Gonzalez* (458 F.3d 1052 (9th Cir. 2006))—also recognized this particular social group. *Nancy Arabillas Morales v. Alberto Gonzalez* (472 F.3d 689 (9th Cir. 2007)) was the first published case in which an asylum seeker's claim was based directly on a transsexual identity (and the first in which the female-identified applicant was referred to with female pronouns).

Asylum both makes clear the failings of dominant legal paradigms to account for trans subjects and reveals how legal categories emerge to regulate trans subjects. Simultaneously, however, asylum opens up other ways of thinking about trans subjects and identities that push against the reification of the categories of transsexual and transgender in the law and in cultural forms. For example, despite its shortcomings as a case for trans asylum seekers, *Hernandez-Montiel v. INS* actually acknowledges the links between sexuality and (trans) gender identity. Many trans people do not experience sexuality and gender identity as mutually exclusive and/or contradictory categories. Yet definitions of transgender developed within academic scholarship as well as within public policy and social services tend to stabilize and homogenize dominant notions of transgender to the exclusion of other gender and sexual identities (Valentine 2007). Somewhat paradoxically, *Hernandez-Montiel v. INS* troubles these theorizations of transgender within the United States and highlights how the category of transgender is produced as a category of knowledge and management in legal and social realms.

Tristan Josephson received his PhD in cultural studies from the University of California, Davis, in 2013 and is currently teaching as a lecturer at Sonoma State University and San Francisco State University. His research and teaching interests include queer and feminist theory, trans studies, and critical legal theory. He is working on a book manuscript titled "On Transits and Transitions: Mobility, Displacement, and Trans Subjectivity in the United States." His article "Trans Citizenship: Marriage, Immigration, and Neoliberal Recognition in the United States" is forthcoming in *Law, Culture and the Humanities*.

Reference

Valentine, David. 2007. *Imagining Transgender: An Ethnography of a Category.* Durham, NC: Duke University Press.

DOI 10.1215/23289252-2399506

Becoming

T. GARNER

Becoming is a highly productive concept in transgender studies and in theoretical perspectives on the body in general because of its capacity to provide a way of reconsidering the nature of the body and body modification. In particular, it has the potential to undermine the accusation that trans bodies are unnatural or constructed.

With its origins in the Greek philosophy of Heraclitus and Aristotle, in which it is an ontological concept that describes change and movement in opposition to the stasis of being, the notion of becoming is fundamental to poststructuralist, feminist theories of the body, such as the work of Rosi Braidotti (2000, 2002), Judith Butler (1993, 1999), Elizabeth Grosz (1994, 2011), and Margrit Shildrick (2002), where it is used as a way of undermining the dichotomies of nature/culture, body/technology, and self/other.

Much of their usage draws on Gilles Deleuze and Félix Guattari's ([1972] 1983, [1980] 1987) notion of becoming, which provides a destabilization of being and the structures of power associated with it. Here, becoming is both an onto-logical and an ethical position that involves movement from stable, "molar" entity to indeterminable, "molecular" nonidentity, extending beyond the limits of domi-nant corporeal and conceptual logics.

"Neither a sacralised inner sanctum, nor a pure socially shaped entity, the enfleshed Deleuzian subject is rather an 'in-between': it is a folding-in of external influences and a simultaneous unfolding outwards of affects," as Braidotti describes in her articulation of "neo-materialism" (2000: 159). In other words, the affective body of becoming "is as much outside itself as in itself—webbed in its relations—until ultimately such firm distinctions cease to matter" (Seigworth and Gregg 2010: 3).

In Donna Haraway's (2003, 2008) critique of Deleuze and Guattari's notion of "becoming-animal"—which, despite its potential for moving beyond bounded entities, remains to some extent grounded in them—"becoming-with" provides a reconsideration of the nature of multispecies development. In this understanding, species do not merely encounter and react to each other but engage in a process of becoming-with.

It is Australian scholar Nikki Sullivan who takes up the concept of becoming most effectively in relation to transgender bodily practices. In Sullivan's formulation, becoming is a process applied to all forms of embodiment, not to flatten out differences but to highlight the fact that "all bodies mark and are marked" (2006: 561). She asks us "to rethink the ways in which bodies are entwined in (un)becoming rather than presuming that they are simply mired in being unless they undergo explicit, visible and transformational procedures" (ibid).

Consider transgender body modification, one of those "explicit, visible and transformational procedures" to which Sullivan refers. The trans body is that which is marked, that which is becoming (strange or other), always situated in opposition to the original body, which is uncritically associated with being (natural). In contrast, for Sullivan, being is becoming; the nature of the body is always already constructed.

An engagement with the notion of becoming brings into focus the borders between and within bodies, both individual and political, because it is these demarcations that shape bodies and their (trans)formations. Fundamentally an interrogation into the operations of power (and resistance), this perspective makes visible the technologies, within both discourse and practice, through which bodies and borders become possible.

This approach repudiates an individualized conception of the body and the self; there is no "us versus them," always "us and them (and them . . .)," to the extent that none of these terms is intelligible without the others. It undermines the concepts of bodily integrity and wholeness as it necessitates a consideration of the "intra-active" character of materiality—the idea that "things" do not precede their interactions but emerge through them (Barad 2007). As such, it opens up the possibility of a posthumanist ontology.

T. Garner is an instructor in the Department of Gender, Sexuality, and Women's Studies at Simon Fraser University and the community organizer of the British Columbia Poverty Reduction Coalition. Hir research is at the intersection of queer and transgender theory, critical studies of health and pathology, and new media studies. Recent works include "Chest Surgeries of a Different 'Nature'" (*Annual Review of Critical Psychology*, 2014) and "(De)Pathologization: Transsexuality, Gynecomastia, and the Negotiation of Mental Health Diagnoses in Online Communities" in *Critical Inquiries: Theories and Methodologies for Social Justice in Mental Health* (forthcoming).

References

Barad, Karen. 2007. *Meeting the Universe Halfway: Quantum Physics and the Entanglement of Matter and Meaning.* Durham, NC: Duke University Press.

Braidotti, Rosi. 2000. "Teratologies." In *Deleuze and Feminist Theory*, ed. I. Buchanan and C. Colebrook, 156–72. Edinburgh: Edinburgh University Press.

———. 2002. *Metamorphoses: Towards a Materialist Theory of Becoming.* Cambridge: Polity.

Butler, Judith. 1993. *Bodies That Matter: On the Discursive Limits of "Sex."* New York: Routledge.

———. 1999. *Gender Trouble: Feminism and the Subversion of Identity* New York: Routledge.

Deleuze, Gilles, and Félix Guattari. (1972) 1983. *Anti-Oedipus: Capitalism and Schizophrenia.* Translated by R. Hurley, M. Seem, and H. R. Lane. Minneapolis: University of Minnesota Press.

———. (1980) 1987. *A Thousand Plateaus: Capitalism and Schizophrenia.* Translated by Brian Massumi. Minneapolis: University of Minnesota Press.

Grosz, Elizabeth. 1994. *Volatile Bodies: Toward a Corporeal Feminism.* Sydney: Allen and Unwin.

———. 2011. *Becoming Undone: Darwinian Reflections on Life, Politics, and Art.* Durham, NC: Duke University Press.

Haraway, Donna. 2003. *The Companion Species Manifesto: Dogs, People, and Significant Otherness.* Chicago: Prickly Paradigm.

———. 2008. *When Species Meet.* Minneapolis: University of Minnesota Press.

Seigworth, Gregory J., and Melissa Gregg. 2010. "An Inventory of Shimmers." In *The Affect Theory Reader*, ed. Melissa Gregg and Gregory J. Seigworth, 1–25. Durham, NC: Duke University Press.

Shildrick, Margrit. 2002. *Embodying the Monster: Encounters with the Vulnerable Self.* London: Sage.

Sullivan, Nikki. 2006. "Transmogrification: (Un)Becoming Other(s)." In *The Transgender Studies Reader*, ed. Susan Stryker and Stephen Whittle, 552–64. New York: Routledge.

DOI 10.1215/23289252-2399515

Bio/logics

SARI M. VAN ANDERS

Biologism is the belief that biological factors are both deterministic to and the essence of specific human phenomena, including identity categories like race/ethnicity, socioeconomic status, and gender/sex (a useful term for simultaneously denoting physiological and social processes). However, there are multiple forms of biologism (van Anders, Caverly, and Johns, forthcoming), especially related to understandings of gender/sex and trans in legal spheres (Allen 2007–8; Cruz 2010; Stirnitzke 2011). I call these "bio/logics" (B/L): implicit and/or explicit reasoning guides informed by features thought to be natural, corporeal, evolved, and material (e.g., sex over gender). B/L en masse locate gender/sex in one true natural form that can only be authenticated by others. Identifying different types of B/L highlights the cultural situatedness of even biologic sex (Cruz 2010; Kessler 1998; Fausto-Sterling 2000). Moreover, delineating B/L's heterogeneous technologies highlights how they can differentially inform ideas, rules, and laws in ways that have major implications for inclusionary and exclusionary practices around gender/sex and trans.

Interior bio/logics (iB/L) refer to a hierarchy in which the most essential features of gender/sex are seen to be the most biologic, and the most biologic are the most *interior*: the most deeply embedded in the body and the least changeable or malleable. For example, though hair, genes, hormones, nails, gonads, and genitals are all corporeal, natural, and material, iB/L privilege genes as the most interior, followed by gonads over genitals, and hormones over hair or nails. iB/L remain a major foundation for legal definitions of gender/sex within case law (van Anders, Caverly, and Johns, forthcoming). Because of the intransigence of genes (an iB/L trump), iB/L make little room for legal recognition of gender/sex transitions. Surgical alteration of genitals only serves to reinforce iB/L, in that genitals are not a definitive marker of gender/sex precisely because they can be altered.

Newborn bio/logics (nB/L) exteriorize gender/sex in a corporeal, displayable body with medical authority naturalizing sex and therefore surgico-medical authority *re*naturalizing sex. Specifically, a medical professional's cursory genital observation instantiates gender/sex at birth, and nB/L reinstantiate gender/sex at transition by recapitulating the newborn process, necessitating surgical modification of genitals for the updated genital observation. With nB/L, only genital features observable in newborns are allowed to be sex markers, thus invalidating the use of nonbiologic but material sex demarcations that might be used in adulthood. nB/L undergird the reliance on surgico-medical authority for legal requirements to change gender/sex designations on US birth certificates over features like self-identification, lived experiences, counseling, or even hormone therapy (Currah and Moore 2009; Greenberg 2000; Markowitz 2008; Spade 2008; van Anders, Caverly, and Johns, forthcoming) because these latter features cannot be made visible in newborns via cursory visual examinations (Kessler and McKenna, 1978). The use of contemporary sex-related technologies reinforce nB/L: they are employed in newborns only to resolve nondefinitive genital observations or to infer "true" gender/sex for surgical "correction" (Dreger 1998; Fausto-Sterling 2000; Kessler 1998).

Trace bio/logics (tB/L) reflect a biologic trajectory whereby corporeal features that influence later sex development are privileged as determinants of gender/sex. In contrast to iB/L, where the most *interior* features are the most deterministic of gender/sex, tB/L denote gender/sex *starting points* as the most definitive. Gonads and genitals are thought to be immutably present regardless of removal or absence, and the "trace" might operate in several ways. It might be material, as with hormones: once-gonads (ovaries; testes) release hormones in utero and postnatally in ways that affect sex/ual development. Or the trace might be heteronormatively conceptual, as with genitals: born-penises are meant to penetrate, born-vaginas to be penetrated (and born-vulvas to be ignored). tB/L underlie some current case law regarding legal definitions of gender/sex, as the once-presence of biologic sex markers like gonads, genitals, or uteruses at an early point is privileged over the current presence or absence of these same markers (van Anders, Caverly, and Johns, forthcoming).

Sari M. van Anders is an assistant professor of psychology and women's studies and affiliate faculty in neuroscience, reproductive sciences, and science, technology, and society at the University of Michigan. Recent works include "Beyond Masculinity: Testosterone, Gender/Sex, and Human Social Behavior in a Comparative Context" (*Frontiers in Neuroendocrinology*, August 2013) and "Nomenclature and Knowledge-Culture; or, We Don't Call Semen 'Penile Mucus'" (*Psychology and Sexuality*, forthcoming).

References

Allen, J. 2007–8. "Quest for Acceptance: The Real ID Act and the Need for Comprehensive Gender Recognition Legislation in the United States." *Michigan Journal of Gender and Law* 14, no. 2: 169–99.

Cruz, David B. 2010. "Getting Sex 'Right': Heteronormativity and Biologism in Trans and Intersex Marriage Litigation and Scholarship." *Duke Journal of Gender Law and Policy* 18, no. 1: 203–22.

Currah, Paisley, and Lisa J. Moore. 2009. " 'We Won't Know Who You Are': Contesting Sex Designations in New York City Birth Certificates." *Hypatia* 24, no. 3: 113–35.

Dreger, Alice D. 1998 *Hermaphrodites and the Medical Invention of Sex.* Cambridge, MA: Harvard University Press.

Fausto-Sterling, Anne. 2000. *Sexing the Body: Gender Politics and the Construction of Sexuality.* New York: Basic Books.

Greenberg, Julie, A. 2000. "When Is a Man a Man, and When Is a Woman a Woman?" *Florida Law Review* 52, no. 4: 745–68.

Kessler, Suzanne J. 1998. *Lessons from the Intersexed.* New Brunswick, NJ: Rutgers University Press.

Kessler, Suzanne J., and Wendy McKenna. 1978. *Gender: An Ethnomethodological Approach.* New York: Wiley.

Markowitz, Stephanie. 2008. "Note: Change of Sex Designation on Transsexuals' Birth Certificates: Public Policy and Equal Protection." *Cardozo Journal of Law and Gender* 14: 705–30.

Spade, Dean. 2008. "Documenting Gender." *Hastings Law Journal* 59, no. 1: 731–842.

Stirnitzke, Audrey C. 2011. "Transsexuality, Marriage, and the Myth of True Sex." *Arizona Law Review* 53, no. 1: 285–320.

van Anders, Sari M., Nicholas L. Caverly, and Michelle M. Johns. Forthcoming. "Newborn Bio/Logics and Legal Definitions of Gender/Sex for US State Documents." *Feminism and Psychology.*

DOI 10.1215/23289252-2399524

Biometrics

NICHOLAS L. CLARKSON

The events of September 11, 2001, offered a rationale for expanding and legitimizing surveillance practices already in use or under development in the United States. Biometrics—technologies that measure the body, often with the intent of identifying individuals[1]—featured significantly in that expansion. While full-body scanners at airport security checkpoints have been the most prominent face of this expansion for many US residents, other biometric technologies, such as fingerprint scans, iris and retinal scans, facial and hand geometry analyzers, and gait signature analysis, among others, also feature in security discussions and practices. Proponents of these technologies often argue that objective computer analyses provide better security than human agents while avoiding the liability of racial profiling. However, cultural critics of biometrics have argued that these machines are "infrastructurally encoded" with assumptions about race, gender, and ability and thereby continue to enforce bodily norms consistent with profiling practices (Pugliese 2007, 2010).

The analog antecedents of contemporary digitized biometrics highlight the legacy of biometrics as techniques of subjugation.[2] For example, British colonists used fingerprinting to distinguish Indian subjects, whom British officers could not otherwise tell apart (Pugliese 2007: 120). Furthermore, practices of measuring the body arose from the racist science of anthropometry, a branch of physical anthropology that sought to determine intelligence, for example, through a system of cranial measurements. These cranial measurements were used to support arguments that white men were more intelligent and civilized than women and the "other races" (Pugliese 2007; Amoore and Hall 2009; Magnet 2011). Though anthropometry is widely discredited, biometrics researchers continue to cite anthropometric methods (Magnet 2011: 39). Sir Francis Galton's use of the term *biometry* additionally highlights the connection between anthropometry and contemporary biometrics. In 1910, Galton used this term to describe the process of collecting measurements in service of anthropometric hypotheses.[3]

Though practices of measuring the body have a long history, the contemporary meaning of *biometrics* appeared in the early 1980s. The *Oxford English Dictionary*'s first noted use of the term appeared in *American Banker* in 1981, in which authors hoped that biometrics would prove useful for unspecified "banking operations."[4] This is consistent with Kelly Gates's (2011) claim that biometric surveillance systems proliferated in tandem with neoliberal reforms before their exponential expansion under the rubric of "homeland security."

In the midst of the continuing proliferation of biometric technologies, transgender theory and trans bodies provide a unique vantage point from which to critique such developments. In particular, when trans bodies confound body scanners and individuals with dark skin tones reveal the racialized calibrations of facial geometry analysis, we are reminded that gender and race remain central to contemporary identity projects in spite of claims to the contrary by the biometrics industry.[5] Gates argues that biometric systems respond to the need to bind identities to bodies while our identity information supposedly circulates untethered through computer networks. Because our vocabularies of gender and race have such limited ability to provide useful information about an individual, one might think that attempts to secure identities to bodies would be minimally invested in gender or race. Nevertheless, manufacturers persistently encode normative assumptions about gender and race into biometric systems even as they claim to produce objective technologies.

Beyond the utility of trans bodies for highlighting the gendered and raced assumptions of biometrics, it is also crucial for the lives of transpeople that we continue to investigate and theorize these developments. As Dean Spade emphasizes in *Normal Life* (2011), the most vulnerable transpeople are the ones most exposed to mechanisms of surveillance. Biometrics are not only deployed to protect expensive, privatized resources (such as banking assets); these techniques are frequently imposed upon the most vulnerable populations in the most coercive relationships. This includes mandated fingerprint scanning for welfare recipients, retinal and fingerprint scanning for prisoners, and fingerprint scanning for migrants to the United States through the Department of Homeland Security's US-VISIT program (Magnet 2011; Department of Homeland Security 2013). For trans theory, then, biometrics are a focal point for examining the biopolitical nexus of gendered, raced, and sexualized concerns. Exploring the connections between our experiences of biometrics and those of other, similarly targeted groups reveals the bodily norms encoded into and enforced by these technologies.

Nicholas L. Clarkson is a PhD candidate in gender studies at Indiana University. His dissertation investigates regulation of gender, race, and sexual norms in contemporary US identity documentation policy and airport security practices.

Notes

1. The *Oxford English Dictionary* (*OED*) defines "biometrics": "The use of unique physical characteristics (fingerprints, iris pattern, etc.) to identify individuals, typically for the purposes of security," as well as "the physical characteristics that can be so used" (*Oxford English Dictionary Online*, s.v. "biometrics," accessed December 3, 2012, www.oed.com).

2. Shoshana Amielle Magnet (2011: 52–53) draws a distinction between analog biometrics (such as bertillonage and ink fingerprinting) and contemporary digital biometrics.

3. The *OED* quotes Galton's 1901 use of "biometry" as follows: "The primary object of Biometry is to afford material that shall be exact enough for the discovery of incipient changes in evolution which are too small to be otherwise apparent." Following the Galton quote, the *OED* offers an example from the journal *Animal Biology* in 1927: "When we take the averages of large numbers . . . we find a strong average resemblance, due to heredity, between parent and offspring, or between brothers and sisters. The science of biometry deals with studies of this sort" (*Oxford English Dictionary Online*, s.v. "biometry," accessed December 3, 2012).

4. Ibid.

5. Joseph Pugliese (2007) has noted that the cameras photographing faces to be analyzed for facial geometry patterns are calibrated to the optimal exposure for the reflectivity of white skin. This means that for those with very dark skin, the computer sometimes cannot detect a face in the photograph. Additionally, the makers of fingerprint scanners

have argued that the fingers of some Asian women cannot be read by these devices due to their supposedly insufficient fingerprint ridges.

References

Amoore, Louise, and Alexandra Hall. 2009. "Taking People Apart: Digitised Dissection and the Body at the Border." *Environment and Planning D: Society and Space* 27: 444–64.

Department of Homeland Security. "Learn about Biometric Identification (US-VISIT)." www .dhs.gov/how-do-i/learn-about-biometric-identification-us-visit (accessed August 28, 2013).

Gates, Kelly A. 2011. *Our Biometric Future: Facial Recognition Technology and the Culture of Surveillance*. New York: New York University Press.

Magnet, Shoshana Amielle. 2011. *When Biometrics Fail: Gender, Race, and the Technology of Identity*. Durham, NC: Duke University Press.

Pugliese, Joseph. 2007. "Biometrics, Infrastructural Whiteness, and the Racialized Zero Degree of Nonrepresentation." *Boundary 2* 34, no. 2: 105–33.

———. 2010. *Biometrics: Bodies, Technologies, Biopolitics*. New York: Routledge.

Spade, Dean. 2011. *Normal Life: Administrative Violence, Critical Trans Politics, and the Limits of Law*. Cambridge, MA: South End.

DOI 10.1215/23289252-2399533

Biopolitics

SUSAN STRYKER

The term *biopolitics* dates to the early twentieth century (Lemke 2011), but it is only in Michel Foucault's work from the 1970s forward that the concept (sometimes denominated by him as *biopower*) begins to be considered a constitutive aspect of governance within Eurocentric modernity (Foucault 1978, 1997, 2004). Biopolitics, generally speaking, describes the calculus of costs and benefits through which the biological capacities of a population are optimally managed for state or state-like ends. In its Foucauldian formulation, the term refers specifically to the combination of disciplinary and excitatory practices aimed at each and every body, which results in the somaticization by individuals of the bodily norms and ideals that regulate the entire population to which they belong. In Foucauldian biopolitics, the individualizing and collectivizing poles of biopower are conjoined by the domain of sexuality, by which Foucault means reproductive capacity as well as modes of subjective identification, the expression of desire, and the pursuit of erotic pleasure. Sexuality, in this double sense of the biological reproduction of new bodies that make up the body politic as well as the ensemble of techniques that produce individualized subjectivities available for aggregation, supplies the capillary space of power's circulation throughout the biopoliticized *populus*.

To accept Foucault's account of sexuality's biopolitical function is to encounter a lacuna in his theoretical oeuvre: the near-total absence of a gender analysis. This is perhaps unsurprising given the anglophone roots of the gender concept, which was developed by the psychologist John Money and his colleagues at Johns Hopkins University in the 1950s during their research on intersexuality, and which was only gradually making its way into the humanities and social science departments of the English-speaking academy in the 1970s when Foucault was delivering his first lectures on biopolitics in France (Germon 2009; Scott 1986). Yet as an account of how embodied subjects acquire behaviors and form particularized identities and of how social organization relies upon the some-times fixed, sometimes flexible categorization of bodies with differing biological capacities, gender as an analytical concept is commensurable with a Foucauldian perspective on biopolitics.

Gendering practices are inextricably enmeshed with sexuality. The identity of the desiring subject and that of the object of desire are characterized by gender. Gender difference undergirds the homo/hetero distinction. Gender conventions code permissible and disallowed forms of erotic expression, and gender stereo-typing is strongly linked with practices of bodily normativization. Gender sub-jectivizes individuals in such a manner that socially constructed categories of personhood typically come to be experienced as innate and ontologically given. It is a system filled with habits and traditions, underpinned by ideological, religious, and scientific supports that all conspire to give bodies the appearance of a natural inevitability, when in fact embodiment is a highly contingent and reconfigurable artifice that coordinates a particular material body with a particular biopolitical apparatus. Approached biopolitically, gender does not pertain primarily to questions of representation—that is, to forming correct or incorrect images of the alignment of a signifying sex (male or female) with a signified social category (man or woman) or psychical disposition (masculine or feminine). Gender, rather, is an apparatus within which all bodies are taken up, which creates material effects through bureaucratic tracking that begins with birth, ends with death, and traverses all manner of state-issued or state-sanctioned documentation practices in between. It is thus an integral part of the mechanism through which power settles a given population onto a given territory through a given set of adminis-trative structures and practices.

Transgender phenomena—anything that calls our attention to the contingency and unnaturalness of gender normativity—appear at the margins of the biopolitically operated-upon body, at those fleeting and variable points at which particular bodies exceed or elude capture within the gender apparatus when they defy the logic of the biopolitical calculus or present a case that confounds an administrative rule or bureaucratic practice. Consequently, transgender phenomena constantly flicker across the threshold of viability, simultaneously courting danger and attracting death even as they promise life in new forms, along new pathways.

Bodies that manifest such transgender phenomena have typically become vulnerable to a panoply of structural oppressions and repressions; they are more likely to be passed over for social investment and less likely to be cultivated as useful for the body politic. They experience microaggressions that cumulatively erode the quality of psychical life, and they also encounter major forms of violence, including deliberate killing. And yet, increasingly, some transgender subjects who previously might have been marked for death now find themselves hailed as legally recognized, protected, depathologized, rights-bearing minority subjects within biopolitical strategies for the cultivation of life from which they previously had been excluded, often to the point of death.

The criterion for this bifurcation of the population along the border of life and death is *race*, which Foucault (1997: 254) describes as "the basic mechanism of power." Certainly, trans bodies of color (particularly if they are poor and feminized) are disproportionately targeted by the death-dealing, "necropolitical" operations of biopower (Mbembe 2003), while bodies deemed white are more likely to experience viability. However, Foucault critically disarticulates race and color to enable a theorization of racism capable of doing more than pointing out that people of color tend to suffer more than whites, and this theorization is particularly useful for transgender studies.

Foucault (1997: 80) understands racism as an artificial biologization of social, cultural, linguistic, or economic differences within a supposedly biologically monist population—that is, as a selective evolutionary process of "speciation" through which new kinds of social entities that are considered biologically distinct from one another emerge. The racism through which biopower operates can be described as a "somatechnical assemblage" (Pugliese and Stryker 2009: 2–3) that brings together a hierarchizing schema of values and preferences, sets of life-affirming or death-making techniques that enact those values and preferences, and a variety of phenotypic, morphological, or genitative qualities and characteristics associated with individual bodies, upon which those techniques operate. Race and racism are therefore broadly understood as the enmeshment of hierarchizing cultural values with hierarchized biological attributes to produce distinct categories of beings who are divided into those rendered vulnerable to premature death and those nurtured to maximize their life. Race thus construed conceptually underpins the biopolitical division not only of color from whiteness but of men from women, of queers from straights, of abled-bodied from disabled, and of cisgender from transgender, to the extent that a body on one side of any of these binaries is conceptualized as biologically distinct from a body on the other side. The caesura, or break, that race introduces into the body politic allows the population to be segmented and selected, enhanced or eliminated, according to biological notions of heritability, degeneracy, foreignness, differentness, or unassimilability—all in the name of "defending" society and making it "pure."

Contemporary transgender identities, populations, and sociopolitical movements exemplify this process of biopolitical racialization. Biopower constitutes transgender as a category that it surveils, splits, and sorts in order to move some trans bodies toward emergent possibilities for transgender normativity and citizenship while consigning others to decreased chances for life. Recent work in transgender studies addressing this biopolitical problematic includes Dean Spade 2011, Toby Beauchamp 2009, Aren Z. Aizura 2012, and C. Riley Snorton and Jin Haritaworn 2013. A critical theoretical task now confronting the field is to advance effective strategies for noncompliance and noncomplicity with the biopolitical project itself.

Susan Stryker is associate professor of gender and women's studies and director of the Institute for LGBT Studies at the University of Arizona and serves as general coeditor of *TSQ: Transgender Studies Quarterly*. Her most recent publication is *The Transgender Studies Reader 2* (coedited with Aren Z. Aizura, 2013), winner of the 2013 Ruth Benedict Book Prize.

References

Aizura, Aren Z. 2012. "The Persistence of Transgender Travel Narratives." In *Transgender Migrations: The Bodies, Borders, and Politics of Transition*, ed. Trystan T. Cotton, 139–56. New York: Routledge.

Beauchamp, Toby. 2009. "Artful Concealment and Strategic Visibility: Transgender Bodies and US State Surveillance after 9/11." *Surveillance and Society* 6, no. 4: 356–66.

Foucault, Michel. 1978. *An Introduction*. Vol. 1 of *The History of Sexuality*. New York: Pantheon.

———. 1997. *Society Must Be Defended: Lectures at the Collège de France, 1975–1976*. New York: St. Martin's.

———. 2004. *Security, Territory, Population: Lectures at the Collège de France, 1977–1978*. New York: Palgave Macmillan.

Germon, Jennifer. 2009. *Gender: A Genealogy of the Concept*. New York: Palgrave Macmillan.

Lemke, Thomas. 2011. *Biopolitics: An Advanced Introduction*. New York: New York University Press.

Mbembe, Achille. 2003. "Necropolitics." *Public Culture* 15, no. 1: 11–40.

Pugliese, Joseph, and Susan Stryker. 2009. "The Somatechnics of Race and Whiteness." *Social Semiotics* 19, no. 1: 1–8.

Scott, Joan. 1986. "Gender: A Useful Category for Historical Analysis." *American Historical Review* 91, no. 5: 1053–75.

Snorton, C. Riley, and Jin Haritaworn. 2013. "Trans Necropolitics: A Transnational Reflection on Violence, Death, and the Trans of Color Afterlife." In *Transgender Studies Reader 2*, ed. Susan Stryker and Aren Z. Aizura, 66–76. New York: Routledge.

Spade, Dean. 2011. *Normal Life: Administrative Violence, Critical Trans Politics, and the Limits of Law.* Brooklyn, NY: South End.

DOI 10.1215/23289252-2399542

Brain Imaging

C. ARMES GAUTHIER

Brain imaging technologies aid in systematic evaluation of biological, behavioral, and environmental systems. The methods used to conduct this research attempt to gather data representing structures, function, or activity. The visual monitor shows structures and activation based on how the brain interacts with the environment. Such observations illuminate how certain parts of the brain function contingently upon specific stimuli. The ethical stakes of studies into sexual dimorphism and gender identity in particular are quite high in the context of state policy informed by such research (see Fleck 1979; Fine 2010; Fausto-Sterling 1985a, 1985b).

To date, no consistent evidence of brain-based sexual dimorphism exists, in part because there are no stable criteria that distinguish sexes reliably or concretely (Fausto-Sterling 1985a). Despite this fact, the theory of sexual dimorphism remains entrenched within Western culture. Experiments are designed around brain organization theory, which posits that the brain is a sexually dimorphic structure prior to birth and lends itself to the sexual differences people experience in their lives—which is not supported by existing data (Jordan-Young 2010: 21). Rebecca Jordan-Young's pivotal book on brain and sex-hormone–based gender research, "Brainstorm: The Flaws in the Science of Sex Differences" (2010), aptly describes various design and methodological problems in the studies discussed. The book explains the language barrier across fields for defining terms of gender, sex, and sexual orientation and critically evaluates brain organization theory as a widely used framework to conduct research (12–18). Jordan-Young calls for a departure from brain organization theory, with its poor experiment design, and for a genuine exploration of the complex nature of sex, gender, and sexuality (3, 9).

The studies reviewed for this introduction to transgender phenomena utilize brain imaging in conjunction with sex-hormone measurements to explore multiple questions: to determine if transsexuals are "born this way," to ascertain which brain structures are markers of gender identity, and to evaluate how hormones influence specific brain structures. Underlying these overarching questions is a renewed discussion of sexuality with regard to gender identity and biological sex.

Unsurprisingly, the transsexual is identified as a set of unidirectional pathologies as described in the American Psychiatric Association's *Diagnostic and Statistical Manual of Mental Disorders* (*DSM*), displaying neuropsychological abnormalities and existing in the wrong body. There is no serious consideration given to the experiences of these individuals, rather than their inherent transsexualism, in shaping their brains. The brain structures in transsexuals are scrutinized prior to and during hormonal transition, mediated through structural and functional imaging methods that may illustrate that the deviance in transsexual activation patterns and/or microstructures examined is distinct from those of individuals of their biological sex and much closer to those of individuals who share their gender identity. After extensive statistical analysis and a complex process of meaning making (see Alač and Hutchins 2004; Dumit 2004) out of the images on the visual monitor, most studies determine that there are similarities in brain structures and activation patterns between transsexuals prior to hormone therapy (HT) and subjects who share their gender identity. Changes after HT are usually found not to be attributable to the differences in brains prior to HT (see Luders et al. 2009; Rametti et al. 2011; Zhou et al. 1995; Van Goozen et al. 2002; Swaab 2004; Garcia-Falgueras and Swaab 2008; Miles, Green, and Hines 2006; La Torre, Grossman, and Piper 1976; Haraldsen et al. 2003; Prince 2005; and Sullivan 2008). The results and conclusion of inherent transsexuality, sans the hormonal transition aspect, mirror Simon LeVay's (1993: 120–24) earlier work in which he located structural and functional differences between self-identified gay men's brains and those of heterosexual men, noting that the structures were similar to those of presumably heterosexual women.

Currently the trajectory of this research is a retelling of the same predominant concepts with different subjects and still lacks proper scientific acumen. What is needed is not new data to support current theories but, rather, new theories that support the data gathered. Critically utilized for understanding sexual dimorphism, gender identity, and sexual orientation, the brain imaging of transgender phenomena is a fertile site for reimagining concepts of embodiment (Salamon 2010).

C. Armes Gauthier is an alumnus of the University of California, San Diego, with degrees in cognitive science, neuroscience, and critical gender studies. Gauthier is currently exploring somatic education in terms of embodiment, integrative health, and healing at IPSB College and the University of California, San Diego, Center for Mindfulness.

Note

This article is based on my thesis, written under the direction of Lisa Cartwright. Gratitude for support from Lisa Cartwright, PhD; Cristina Visperas; Kaya DeBarbaro, PhD; Ang[e] Moore; friends, lovers, family, especially Cathy.

References

Alač, Morana, and Edwin Hutchins. 2004. "I See What You Are Saying: Action as Cognition in FMRI Brain Mapping Practice." *Journal of Cognition and Culture* 4, no. 3: 629–61.

Dumit, Joseph. 2004. *Picturing Personhood: Brain Scans and Biomedical Identity.* Princeton, NJ: Princeton University Press.

Fausto-Sterling, Anne. 1985a. *Myths of Gender: Biological Theories about Women and Men.* New York: Basic Books.

———. 1985b. "Sex and the Single Brain: Addendum to the Second Edition." In Fausto-Sterling, *Myths of Gender*, 223–70.

Fine, Cordelia. 2010. *Delusions of Gender.* New York: Norton.

Fleck, Ludwig. 1979. *Genesis and Development of a Scientific Fact.* Chicago: University of Chicago Press.

Garcia-Falgueras, A., and D. F. Swaab. 2008. "A Sex Difference in the Hypothalamic Uncinate Nucleus: Relationship to Gender Identity." *Brain* 131, no. 12: 3132–46.

Haraldsen, I., et al. 2003. "Sex-Sensitive Cognitive Performance in Untreated Patients with Early Onset Gender Identity Disorder." *Psychoneuroendocrinology* 28, no. 7: 906–15.

Jordan-Young, Rebecca. 2010. *Brainstorm: The Flaws in the Science of Sex Differences.* Cambridge, MA: Harvard University Press.

La Torre, R. M., I. Grossman, and W. E. Piper. 1976. "Cognitive-Style, Hemispheric Specialization and Tested Abilities of Transsexuals and Non-transsexuals." *Perceptual and Motor Skills* 43, no. 3: 719–22.

LeVay, Simon. 1993. *The Sexual Brain.* Cambridge, MA: MIT Press.

Luders, Eileen, et al. 2009. "Regional Gray Matter Variation in Male-to-Female Transsexualism." *NeuroImage* 46, no. 4: 904–7.

Miles, C., R. Green, and M. Hines. 2006. "Estrogen Treatment Effects on Cognition, Memory, and Mood in Male-to-Female Transsexuals." *Hormones and Behavior* 50, no. 5: 708–17.

Prince, C. V. 2005. "Homosexuality, Transvestism, and Transsexuality: Reflections on Their Etiology and Differentiation." *International Journal of Transgenderism* 8, no. 4: 17–20.

Rametti, Guiseppina, et al. 2011. "White Matter Microstructure in Female to Male Transsexuals before Cross-Sex Hormonal Treatment: A Diffusion Tensor Imaging Study." *Journal of Psychiatric Research* 45: 199–204.

Salamon, Gayle. 2010. *Assuming a Body: Transgender and Rhetorics of Materiality*. New York: Columbia University Press.

Sullivan, Nikki. 2008. "The Role of Medicine in the (Trans)Formation of 'Wrong' Bodies." *Body and Society* 14, no. 1: 105–16.

Swaab, D. F. 2004. "Sexual Differentiation of the Human Brain: Relevance for Gender Identity, Transsexualism, and Sexual Orientation." *Gynecological Endocrinology* 19, no. 6: 301–12.

Van Goozen, Stephane H. M., et al. 2002. "Organizing and Activating Effects of Sex Hormones in Homosexual Transsexuals." *Behavioral Neuroscience* 116, no. 6: 982–88.

Zhou, Jiang-Ning, et al. 1995. "A Sex Difference in the Human Brain and Its Relation to Transsexuality." *Nature* 378, no. 6552: 68–70.

DOI 10.1215/23289252-2399551

Brown Bois

VAN BAILEY

The term *brown boi* is rooted in the founding of the nonprofit organization the Brown Boi Project. The term serves as a sociocultural identity and a call to social action. B. Cole, founder of the Brown Boi Project, discovered that mentorship, connection, and the power of language were ways to connect queer people of color from common lived experiences. While completing research in graduate school, B. Cole discovered that masculine-identified people of color were using various labels to describe their identity. For example, individuals were using terms such as *two-spirit*, *AG* (aggressive), *dom* (dominant), *stud*, *macha*, *boi*, *trans**, and *butch* to describe their sexual, gender, and lived identities. Thus B. Cole coined *masculine of center* as an umbrella term to include all gender-nonconforming masculine people of color. The term is elaborated in the Project's mission statement: "Masculine of Center (MoC), in its evolving definition, recognizes the cultural breadth and depth of identity for lesbian/queer womyn and gender-nonconforming/trans people who tilt toward the masculine side of the gender spectrum" (Brown Boi 2010). The term *masculine of center* reaches beyond identification and commonality and calls for social action and change. Social action and change are needed to reteach healthy notions of brown bois' relationship to masculinity. Understanding holistic health and unpacking masculinity only assist brown bois in moving toward a gender justice framework for social change. Gender justice holds brown bois accountable to challenge the structural imbalances of masculinity and femininity (Brown Boi 2012). The organization strives to generate a gender-inclusive framework that includes a practice of nonoppressive masculinity rooted in self-love, honor, community, and collaboration with feminine-identified people, particularly women and girls (ibid.).

The Praxis of Self-Love and Social Change

In 2010, after creating the term *masculine of center*, B. Cole was inspired to tap into community resources, including discovering dynamic community partners, to create the concept of the brown boi. A brown boi seeks to impact the lives of straight and queer boys/bois of color through a culturally based gender-trans-formative leadership approach that cultivates strength, learning, and account-ability (Brown Boi 2012). Much of the existing research regarding boys/bois of color in learning environments is rooted in racialized norms. These norms are created in how we understand race and its reproduction through lived and observed behavior. However, there is a lack of knowledge about how gendered behavior as it relates to masculinity impacts learning for boys/bois of color (Shepard et al. 2011). The organization desires to create a new conversation regarding gender in people of color communities. Masculinity holds structural power regardless of what body it inhabits. Boys/bois of color allowed to acknowl-edge their strengths can in turn accept their privileges through in-depth personal exploration, mentorship, and connection to community. Self-love allows for the dismantling of shaming around privilege and strength and in turn pushes indi-viduals to be accountable for their privileges. Gender-transformative learning inspires masculine-of-center people to realize their full potential through self-actualization. Feminine-identified people are included through actions of love that reimagine healthy masculinities. This self-actualization acknowledges struc-tural power and misogyny, disarms shame, and encourages emotive connection and community accountability (Brown Boi 2012). The Brown Boi Project is a praxis of transgender studies and leadership development.

Transgender studies must continue to expand the conversations of race, gender, and masculinity in order to transform leadership development strategies. Brown bois are at the crux of theory and practice. They are trained leaders who embark on the journey of love and self-work in order to dismantle systems of harm, including institutions that perpetuate misogyny. Brown bois are more than members of a nonprofit organization; they are leaders in the movement to dis-mantle traditional notions of masculinity, a movement that includes all women in gender and racial justice movements.

Van Bailey, EdD, is the inaugural director of the Office of BGLTQ Student Life at Harvard College and a member of the Brown Boi Project.

References

The Brown Boi Project. 2010. "Mission and Core Values." www.brownboiproject.org/mission _core_values.html (accessed November 29, 2012).

———. 2012. "Toward Healthy and Whole: Rethinking Gender and Transformation for Bois of Color." October. www.brownboiproject.org/BBP%20Toward%20Healthy%20and %20Whole.pdf.

Shepard, Samuel, et al. 2011. "Masculine Norms, School Attitudes, and Psychosocial Adjustment among Gifted Boys." *Psychology of Men and Masculinity* 12, no. 2: 181–87.

DOI 10.1215/23289252-2399560

Capacity

DAVID J. GETSY

A capacity is both an "active power or force" and an "ability to receive or maintain; holding power."[1] A capacity manifests its power as potentiality, incipience, and imminence. Only when exercised do capacities become fully apparent, and they may lie in wait to be activated.

Transgender capacity is the ability or the potential for making visible, bringing into experience, or knowing genders as mutable, successive, and multiple. It can be located or discerned in texts, objects, cultural forms, situations, systems, and images that support an interpretation or recognition of proliferative modes of gender nonconformity, multiplicity, and temporality. In other words, transgender capacity is the trait of those many things that support or demand accounts of gender's dynamism, plurality, and expansiveness.

The dimorphic model of sex and the binary account of gender—not to mention the assertion of their static natures—are never adequate ways of knowing the sophisticated and divergent modes of existence people enact. Such strictures always encode their own possibilities for collapse and deconstruction, and transgender capacity erupts at those moments when such reductive norms do not hold.

The most important feature of transgender capacity is that it can be an unintended effect of many divergent decisions and conditions. That is, a transgender critique can be demanded of a wide range of texts, sites, systems, and objects—including those that would at first seem unrelated to transgender concerns and potentialities. A capacity need not be purposefully planted or embedded (though of course it may be), and it does not just result from the intentions of sympathetic or self-identified transgendered subjects. It may emerge at any site where dimorphic and static understandings of gender are revealed as arbitrary and inadequate. Transgender phenomena can be generated from a wide range of positions and competing (even antagonistic) subjects, and it is important to recognize that a transgender hermeneutic can and should be pursued at all such capacitating sites.

The usefulness of this concept is primarily methodological and is meant as a tool for resisting the persistent erasure of the evidence of transgender lives, gender diversity, nondimorphism, and successive identities. Its questions are valid to many areas of scholarly inquiry, including such different fields as biology, sociology, and economics. It is a retort to charges of anachronism and a reminder to search widely for the nascence of transgender critique. With regard to historical analysis, transgender capacity poses particularly urgent questions, since it is clear that there is a wealth of gender variance and nonconformity that has simply not been registered in the historical record. Without projecting present-day understandings of transgender identities into the past, one must recognize and make space for all of the ways in which self-determined and successive genders, identities, and bodily morphologies have always been present throughout history as possibilities and actualities.[2] Dimorphic and static definitions of gender and sexual difference obscure such diversity and facilitate the obliteration of the complex and infinitely varied history of gender nonconformity and strategies for survival. To recognize transgender capacity is not to equate all episodes of potential but rather to allow the recognition of their particularity and to resist the normative presumptions that have enforced their invisibility.

Transgender epistemologies and theoretical models fundamentally remap the study of human cultures. Their recognition of the mutable and multiple conditions of the apparatus we know as gender has wide-ranging consequences. That is, once gender is understood to be temporal, successive, or transformable, all accounts of human lives look different and more complex. It would be a mistake to limit this powerful epistemological shift to clearly identifiable trans topics and histories. While transgender subjects and experience must remain central and defining, the lessons of transgender critique demand to be applied expansively.

Across the disciplines, there is much evidence of the limitations of static and dimorphic models of genders, identities, and relations. One must search for and be attentive to transgender capacities in both expected and unexpected places. Tracking them is a hermeneutical rather than an iconographic task, and the conceptual space of gender transformability erupts anywhere that dimorphism is questioned, mutability becomes a value, or self-creation becomes a possibility. While they are most readily located in the study of the representation of human bodies and experiences, transgender capacities can be located in such topics as abstract art, rhetorical forms, digital cultures, technologies of complex systems, economic ecologies, and histories of scientific discovery. In these areas and beyond, there are innumerable forms and modes of transgender capacity still to be found, imagined, or realized.

David J. Getsy is Goldabelle McComb Finn Distinguished Professor and chair of the Department of Art History, Theory, and Criticism at the School of the Art Institute of Chicago. His most recent book, *Abstract Bodies: Sixties Sculpture in the Expanded Field of Gender*, is forthcoming in 2015.

Notes

1. *Oxford English Dictionary Online*, s.v. "capacity," accessed December 16, 2013, www.oed.com.
2. An important statement of the problem and a defining methodological position on addressing it (to which this account of transgender capacity is indebted) is J. Jack Halberstam's discussion of "perverse presentism" in *Female Masculinity* (1998: 50–59).

Reference

Halberstam, J. Jack. 1998. *Female Masculinity*. Durham, NC: Duke University Press.

DOI 10.1215/23289252-2399569

Capital

DAN IRVING

Capital refers to a dynamic social relationship emerging from the capitalist private property form and subsequent exploitative labor relations. Capital's fundamental principle is wealth accumulation through profit. The distribution of wealth throughout society is contingent on what is advantageous to those with capital, or the power to shape social relations. The ways in which proprietary and exploitative logics materialize on macro and micro levels cannot be predetermined and depend on national and local particularities. Capital's operational specificities are characterized through its functioning as part of assemblages of power relations including colonialism, nation, gender, and sexuality (Joseph 2002: 14).

Propelled by a perpetual need for growth, capital is characterized by continuous movement. It cannot be contained within narrow territorial, productive, or categorical borders. While capital is a global force, its lines of flight are nonlinear (Browning and Kilmister 2006: 71) and indeterminate. Discursively, ownership and exploitation logics exceed class as a social location and economic site of commodity production and consumption. The politics of transgender representation in Canada exemplify how ownership, entitlement, and the appropriation of labor extend beyond arenas understood as capitalist. The space taken up by, and extended to, "successful" trans middle-class professionals to set the agenda for and to be representative of trans movements erases the labor performed by racialized transsexual and two-spirit people—many of whom were women working as prostitutes—to ensure better lives for marginalized populations.

Capital constantly subsumes activities that have often been outside competitive market relations (Browning and Kilmister 2006: 147; Negri 2008: 4). In fact, capital(ist) discourses permeate our immaterial social and cultural worlds in ways that impact reproductive and intimate relations (Negri 2008) and shape desire (Browning and Kilmister 2006: 135). Critical scholars of neoliberalism—capital's current regime of accumulation—emphasize market society where nearly all aspects of life privilege individualism, privatization, and competition.

How capital mediates subject formation is a key debate that continues to enrich research concerning trans embodiments, experiences, and resistance (Spade 2012; Aizura 2009; Irving 2008). Within neoliberal society, the ontological functioning of capital has reconstructed "homo economicus" (Foucault 2008). Antisocial and alienating discourses stressing sole proprietorship, industriousness, innovation, productivity, and investment govern the fashioning of individuals as "entrepreneurs of the self" (Rose 1990). Autonomy is celebrated, as people are personally responsible for honing themselves to be physically, spiritually, and emotionally fit to engage and excel in competitive free-market relations.

Freedom and democracy are linked to one's ability to participate in competitive productive relations. Individuals become human capital. This concept indicates ways in which oppressed and marginalized groups are interpolated into capital(ist) "common sense" relations. As sole proprietor of oneself, one is encouraged to acquire the education, skills, and experiential knowledge necessary to increase competitive advantage within *all spheres* of market society (Foucault 2008). Care of the self is an element of exploitative relations, since labor is re-created as an affective, intellectual, and communicative activity, a "creation of being" (Negri 2008: 222). Akin to corporate actors, many transgender activists work to achieve recognition for trans and two-spirit–identified people through promoting images of them as rational active subjects. It is understood that such acknowledgment from state and society will most likely ensure the vitality of trans subjects as well as the well-being of their families and communities. The logics that comprise capital as a social relation, as well as the ways in which capital intertwines with other power relations, are hidden from view; however, by analyzing "possessive individualism" (Macpherson 1962), certain dimensions of capital can be uncovered.

Capital continuously maneuvers to normalize exploitative relationships, to naturalize private property relations (e.g., whiteness as property), and to steadily erode common, collective, and cooperative spaces. Despite the fact that only a few actually own private property (the "1 percent"), whiteness as property refers to the expectations of power and control held by whites in US society (Harris 1993). Like racialized others, the majority of whites are forced to sell their labor to those with capital; however, their elevated sociocultural and political status shapes their unreflective claims to privilege ("We deserve to live in a safe neighborhood," for example). Trans activist efforts to remove Gender Identity Disorder from the American Psychiatric Association's *Diagnostic and Statistical Manual*, 4th ed., and to include "gender identity" in nondiscrimination and hate-crimes laws are two additional examples.

Given global economic crises, escalating rates of un(der)employment, and declining economic growth, an increasing number of people are rendered abject as surplus populations. Members of surplus populations are denigrated in language reflective of capital as worth-less, unproductive, unfit, backward, risky, and/or inflexible and are subsequently blamed for their social and often literal deaths. Given that racialized, queer, and trans people are overrepresented within the category of surplus, it is imperative that research within transgender studies problematize discourses of sex and gender self-determination, geopolitical dimensions of transitioning medically, and trans rights struggles.

"Trans-" (Stryker, Currah, and Moore 2008) methods can enrich the formation of resistance strategies. While nearly impossible to see in its totality, capital is a whole system (Jameson 2011: 3, 6) of scattered economic practices (Gibson-Graham 2006: 2) framing social orders. Like sex and gender, capital(ism) is an historical phenomenon that is neither naturally dominant nor self-containing (ibid.: 54). Capital's continuous movement to legitimize itself reveals moments at which it falters or fails. It is within these spaces that it can be disrupted (Browning and Kilmister 2006: 136) as monstrous others labor to cultivate the diverse relations of solidarity necessary for transitioning into "new economic becomings" (Gibson-Graham 2006: 60).

Dan Irving is an assistant professor of human rights and coordinates the Sexuality Studies Minor Program in the Institute of Interdisciplinary Studies at Carleton University. His work is published in the *Transgender Studies Reader 2* and *Sexualities*. He is the coeditor (with Rupert Raj) of *Trans Activism in Canada: A Reader* (forthcoming).

References

Aizura, Aren. 2009. "The Romance of the Scalpel: 'Race,' Labour, and Affect in Thai Gender Reassignment Clinics." In *Queer Bangkok: Twenty-First-Century Markets, Media, and Rights*, ed. Peter A. Jackson, 143–62. Hong Kong: University of Hong Kong Press.

Browning, Gary, and Andrew Kilmister. 2006. *Critical and Post-critical Political Economy*. New York: Palgrave MacMillan.

Foucault, Michel. 2008. *The Birth of Biopolitics: Lectures at the College de France, 1978–1979*. New York: Palgrave Macmillan

Gibson-Graham, J. K. 2006. *A Postcapitalist Politics*. Minneapolis: University of Minnesota Press.

Harris, Cheryl. 1993. "Whiteness as Property." *Harvard Law Review* 106, no. 8: 1710–91.

Irving, Dan. 2008. "Normalized Transgressions: Legitimizing the Transsexual Body as Productive." *Radical History Review*, no. 100: 38–59.

Jameson, Fredric. 2011. *Representing Capital: A Reading of Volume 1*. London: Verso.

Joseph, Miranda. 2002. *Against the Romance of Community*. Minneapolis: University of Minnesota Press.

Macpherson, C. B. 1962. *The Political Theory of Possessive Individualism: From Hobbes to Locke*. Oxford: Oxford University Press.

Negri, Antonio. 2008. *Empire and Beyond*. Cambridge: Polity.

Rose, Nicholas. 1990. *Governing the Soul: The Shaping of the Private Self*. London: Routledge.

Spade, Dean. 2012. *Normal Life: Administrative Violence, Critical Trans Politics, and the Limits of Law*. Boston: Southend.

Stryker, Susan, Paisley Currah, and Lisa Jean Moore. 2008. "Introduction: Trans-, Trans, or Transgender?" *Women's Studies Quarterly* 36, no. 3–4: 11–22.

DOI 10.1215/23289252-2399578

Cataloging

KATELYN ANGELL and K. R. ROBERTO

The United States Library of Congress (LC) plays a pivotal role in naming and categorizing the information that informs and describes human life both within the country and internationally. Because of the power imbued in this responsibility, the language used must accurately reflect the people whose identities are at stake. In recent years, librarians have begun to analyze the subject headings assigned to transgender studies works (Roberto 2011; Johnson 2010; Adler 2009), an initiative aimed at ensuring that linguistic representation reproduces lived experiences. Critical engagement with the way in which information is organized and named is important not just to librarians but to everyone, because how people are described is how they will be perceived.

A brief description of standard cataloging protocol will lay the groundwork for a discussion of transgender studies topics within information organization. In order for people to quickly and efficiently locate the most pertinent resources on a particular topic, library catalogs and databases generally include a controlled vocabulary. This consists of a list of terms used to categorize the materials in the catalog. These terms are called subject headings, and they enhance a user's experience by allowing the user to locate the most relevant items on a topic within a single, powerful search. Each item in the catalog is generally assigned between one and six subject headings (Library of Congress 2009).

Beginning in 1898 (Stone 2000), LC incorporated subject terms into its cataloging practice, titling this controlled vocabulary Library of Congress Subject Headings (LCSH). LCSH is both the oldest and biggest subject heading system in the world (Anderson and Hofmann 2006), its reach extending far beyond US borders. A project undertaken in the late 1990s revealed that twenty-four out of eighty-eight national libraries on six continents use LCSH within their national bibliographies (Heiner-Freiling 2000). An additional twelve countries, including Estonia and the Czech Republic, use either translated or modified versions of LCSH. These statistics demonstrate the staggering influence that LC exercises over classification of the world's information, as cataloging decisions made by US librarians affect information seekers across the globe.

Regardless of its popularity, LCSH is nonetheless just one of many controlled vocabularies. Another large country with a similarly robust cataloging system is China. In 1980 Chinese librarians developed the celebrated Chinese Thesaurus, which includes well over 100,000 terms (Zhang 2004). It is essential to note the existence of a multitude of smaller, often discipline-specific controlled vocabularies. LC (2013) maintains a list of about 300 specialized controlled vocabularies used around the world to organize information. Three of the vocabularies on this list pertain directly to the classification of queer topics, indubitably created as a viable alternative to traditional vocabularies such as LCSH.

Despite the practicality and effectiveness of a ubiquitous system of subject headings, LCSH is not without its share of historical criticism regarding the language used to describe items in its collection (Fischer 2005; Olson 2000; Berman 1971). For decades information professionals concerned with problematic and/or biased subject headings have been working to either edit existing headings or create new terms that do not fall prey to what Hope A. Olson defines as "cultural supremacy of the mainstream patriarchal, Euro-settler culture" (2000: 69).

Unfortunately, LCSH's terminology for transgender studies works tends to fall squarely into Olson's concept of cultural supremacy. The heading "Transsexuals" was created in 1985 and "Transvestites" in 1989. As Johnson notes, "Female-to-male transsexuals" was created in 2002, but "Male-to-female transsexuals" was only established in 2006, following "the intervention of contributing Subject Authority Cooperative Program (SACO) librarians" (2010: 668), who were not employed by LC.

The situation turns especially problematic when discovering subject headings for transgender concepts that fall outside transsexual boundaries. After "the continued contestation of its meaning . . . Transgender people" was finally established as a subject heading in May 2007 (ibid.: 666, 667), but the specificities of transgender people's possible identities are neither especially salient nor easily construed. Melissa Adler and K. R. Roberto both note the conspicuous lack of any subject terms for genderqueer persons, with the former specifically mentioning that "Genderqueers" was proposed as an addition to LCSH in 2006 and was seemingly ignored (Adler 2009: 310); the concepts of agender and multigender suffer from similar invisibility.

The established subject terminology for drag performers is criticized by numerous authors for its lack of accurate and sensitive language (Johnson 2010: 672–73; Adler 2009: 321; Roberto 2011: 57–58). Instead of assigning "Drag kings" or "Drag queens," LCSH requires the use of "Male impersonators" and "Female impersonators," respectively; the explanatory note for "Female impersonators" states that the heading is to be used for "works on men who impersonate women, generally for purposes of comic effect. . . . Works on persons, especially males, who assume the dress and manner of the opposite sex for psychological gratification, are entered under Transvestites" (Library of Congress 2012). In Roberto's words,

"Calling drag performers 'impersonators' emphasizes artifice over intent; it creates a hierarchical structure where drag performance is less important than the gender being 'imitated' (2011: 58). One possible explanation for these discrepancies is that, unlike gay, lesbian, and bisexual topics in LCSH, transgender topics have not benefited from decades of advocacy work by information professionals to create finely detailed terminology (Greenblatt 2011).

Presently there are several avenues available to anyone wishing to alter or create terms within LCSH. LC's Subject Authority Cooperative Program (SACO), situated within their Program for Cooperative Cataloging, encourages participating libraries to propose subject headings. Nonmembers can also suggest subject headings using LC's Subject Authority Proposal Form (Library of Congress 2011). While there is no guarantee that LC will make the suggested changes, these options are presently the most realistic means of improving subject heading nomenclature.

Other people choose to work outside mainstream cataloging practices, developing new controlled vocabularies in an attempt to classify and document their own identities and experiences. For example, in 1997 a Netherlands-based queer history archive created the *Queer Thesaurus*, a bilingual Dutch/English and English/Dutch vocabulary devoted to LGBTQ and queer topics (van der Wel 2011). *Queer Thesaurus* boasts more than three thousand terms and could easily be translated to other academic and community archives seeking an appropriate controlled vocabulary. Awareness of such knowledge and tool kits results in a united front of stakeholders committed to optimal linguistic representation and empowerment.

Katelyn Angell is a reference and instruction librarian at Long Island University, Brooklyn Campus. Her research interests include information literacy instruction, feminist and gender studies, and the organization of information.

K. R. Roberto is a doctoral student in the Graduate School of Library and Information Science at the University of Illinois at Urbana-Champaign.

References

Adler, Melissa. 2009. "Transcending Library Catalogs: A Comparative Study of Controlled Terms in Library of Congress Subject Headings and User-Generated Tags in LibraryThing for Transgender Books." *Journal of Web Librarianship* 3, no. 4: 309–31. doi:10.1080/19322900903341099.

Anderson, James D., and Melissa A. Hofmann. 2006. "A Fully Faceted Syntax for Library of Congress Subject Headings." *Cataloging and Classification Quarterly* 43, no. 1: 7–38. doi:10.1300/J104v43n01_03.

Berman, Sanford. 1971. *Prejudices and Antipathies: A Tract on the LC Subject Heads Concerning People.* Metuchen, NJ: Scarecrow.

Fischer, Karen S. 2005. "Critical Views of LCSH, 1990–2001: The Third Bibliographic Essay." *Cataloging and Classification Quarterly* 41, no. 1: 63–109. doi:10.1300/J104v41n01_05.

Greenblatt, Ellen. 2011. "The Treatment of LGBTIQ Concepts in the Library of Congress Subject Headings." In *Serving LGBTIQ Library and Archives Users: Essays on Outreach, Service, Collections, and Access,* ed. Ellen Greenblatt, 212–28. Jefferson, NC: McFarland.

Heiner-Freiling, Magda. 2000. "Survey on Subject Heading Languages Used in National Libraries and Bibliographies." *Cataloging and Classification Quarterly* 30, no. 1: 189–98. doi:10.1300/J104v29n01_13.

Johnson, Matt. 2010. "Transgender Subject Access: History and Current Practice." *Cataloging and Classification Quarterly* 48, no. 8: 661–83. doi:10.1080/01639370903534398.

Library of Congress. 2009. "Workshop Slides" (PowerPoint link). loc.gov/catworkshop/courses/basicsubject/index.html (accessed November 29, 2012).

———. 2011. "Subject Authority Proposal Form." loc.gov/aba/pcc/prop/proposal.html (accessed December 1, 2012).

———. 2012. "Library of Congress Authorities." authorities.loc.gov (accessed December 2, 2012).

———. 2013. "Subject Heading and Term Source Codes." loc.gov/standards/sourcelist/subject.html (accessed July 9, 2012).

Olson, Hope A. 2000. "Difference, Culture, and Change: The Untapped Potential of LCSH." *Cataloging and Classification Quarterly* 29, no. 1–2: 53–71. doi:10.1300/J104v29n01_04.

Roberto, K. R. 2011. "Inflexible Bodies: Metadata for Transgender Identities." *Journal of Information Ethics* 20, no. 2: 56–64. doi:10.3172/JIE.20.2.56.

Stone, Alva T. 2000. "The LCSH Century: A Brief History of the Library of Congress Subject Headings, and Introduction to the Centennial Essays." *Cataloging and Classification Quarterly* 30, no. 1: 1–15. doi:10.1300/J104v29n01_01.

van der Wel, Jack. 2011. "IHLIA—Making Information on LGBTIQ Issues in the Past and the Present Accessible and Visible." In Greenblatt, *Serving LGBTIQ Library and Archives Users,* 158–61.

Zhang, Wenxian. 2004. "The Development and Structure of the Chinese Thesaurus for Subject Indexing." *International Information and Library Review* 36, no. 1: 47–54. doi:10.1016/j.iilr.2003.10.001.

DOI 10.1215/23289252-2399587

Child

TEY MEADOW

What is a transgender child? These days, it depends on whom you ask.

A relatively new social form, we see no references to transgender children prior to the mid-1990s. Previously confined to medical and psychiatric discourses and labeled "effeminate boys" and "masculine girls," children who transgress gender norms in their surrounding social contexts were understood primarily as inverts and more recently as protohomosexuals (Bryant 2006; Sedgwick 1991). In the early twenty-first century, however, multiple constituencies are vying to define the terms of the transgender child and to secure explanations of the etiology, prevalence, and characteristics of this emergent identity group.

The first generation of parents actively supporting and facilitating gender nonconformity in their children wasted no time forging local, national, and international communities. From the advocacy organizations they form to the blogs, websites, and listservs they populate, they are devising their own collective answers to that question. Some parents use the term *transgender* only in reference to children who have made social and/or medical transitions from one gender category to the other (Brill and Pepper 2008); others ascribe to the more conventional notion of the transgender umbrella and seek to loop in kids across the spectrum of gender fluidity. These labeling processes are not merely symbolic. They mirror a series of difficult decisions families face: Will they facilitate social transitions for their very young children? Will they seek out and endure the stress and expense of providing gender-confirming medical care for adolescents? How will they explain their child to relatives, to other parents, to social service agencies and schools? Is it possible, and what would it mean, to make the "wrong" decisions?

The psychiatrists and physicians who treat these youths and families also seek more secure and reliable mechanisms for determining which children are truly transgender, which will become gay or lesbian, and which may exhibit no gender nonconformity at all later on. Over the last two decades, professionals have developed specialized clinics for treating gender-nonconforming children, and parents and children often submit to a vast battery of tests as a condition of their treatment. An international consortium of gender experts collaborated on producing standardized measures for gender, along with a robust research agenda that includes theorizing the causes, incidence, and developmental trajectories of atypical childhood gender behaviors and identities. It appears that while puberty-blocking hormone therapies offer relief to many children, these and other, newer medical technologies simultaneously exert their own normalizing pressures to order, taxonomize, and measure gender transgressions.

Older transgender adults initially resisted the efforts of the parent activists and advocates who first began agitating for support from schools and doctors in the late 1990s and early 2000s, fearing political repercussions from the public endorsement of social transition for young children. While many have since come out in support of gender-nonconforming children and their families, trans adults must cope with the deeply different trajectories and life chances of the smallest gender outlaws. Some of these children may elect to be stealth (maintain total privacy about their gender histories) as adults; some may never identify openly as transgender; many will never go through their natal puberties or retain childhood memory books filled with pictures that do not mirror their gender identities as adults. For these reasons, this new generation may have wider latitude to dis-identify with transgender history and with those who came before them.

A central paradox animates all of these efforts to define the transgender child. While most adults understand gender development teleologically, they still struggle with whether and how to distinguish childhood self-knowledge from adult identity. They labor to determine if gender is ever fluid or stable, unfinished or finished, a property of the self or a creation of the outside world. Woven through these projects are countless other questions: Politically and personally, what does it mean to label a particular child transgender? If what an assigned male child tells you is that she *is* a girl, does the term *transgender* truly represent her personal identity? Does it represent a shift in social category, or is it merely a signifier of how other people understand her history? Is a significantly gender-nonconforming or masculine girl transgender if she still identifies as a girl? Is being transgender distinct from being a "blend" (Brill and Pepper 2008: xiv), a "gender prius," "gender creative," "gender independent" (Ehrensaft 2011), or any of the host of other new terms for gender fluidity in children? Do these words even demarcate a particular form of personhood, or do they simply rebrand deviance while implying that the vast majority of children are safely gender normative? Fundamentally, do we, the adults, get to decide the answers to these questions?

Tey Meadow is a Cotsen Postdoctoral Fellow at the Princeton Society of Fellows. She is currently at work on a book about the first generation of families raising transgender children.

References

Brill, Stephanie, and Rachel Pepper. 2008. *The Transgender Child: A Handbook for Families and Professionals.* San Francisco: Cleis.

Bryant, Karl. 2006. "Making Gender Identity Disorder of Childhood: Historical Lessons for Contemporary Debates." *Sexuality Research and Social Policy* 3, no 1: 23–39.

Ehrensaft, Diane. 2011. *Gender Born, Gender Made: Raising Healthy Gender Nonconforming Children.* New York: The Experiment.

Sedgwick, Eve Kosofsky. 1991. "How to Bring Your Kids Up Gay." *Social Text* 29, no 1: 18–27.

DOI 10.1215/23289252-2399596

Childhood

CLAUDIA CASTAÑEDA

In many societies, the child is constituted as a body that is always in the process of becoming, moving from birth to maturation, from infancy to adulthood. Childhood becomes the time-space in which the human begins as an unfinished entity that undergoes a specifically developmental and so also normatively progressive trajectory of bodily and social transformation whose endpoint is completion as an adult. Gender plays a central role in this process: while the child's gender is fixed at (or before) birth and read off from the body's genitals (as well as chromosomes and hormones), the child must also *become* fully gendered as an (adult) man or woman through development. The developmental process works through a system of normalization, furthermore, such that the child's development may proceed along either normal or pathological lines. Since normal development is not guaranteed, the child becomes the site of tremendous cultural investment with regard to all developmental processes, including that of gender.

Transgender childhood bears the mark of the simultaneously fixed and molten status of the child and child-body with regard to gender development and of the child's normalization as well. For a child to claim a transgender status (or for an adult to claim transgender status for a child) is difficult because the child is always already seen as incomplete, as not yet fully formed; its gender is not fully mature, and the child is also seen as not fully capable of knowing its own gender. At the same time, precisely because of this not-yet-complete status, the child is especially *subject to* scrutiny with regard to its gender: does it have a normal gender, is it showing all the necessary signs that match expectations derived from ways of seeing and knowing the body? Transgender childhood becomes a threat to normative gender development and so to (normal) gender itself; if gender can shift away from the expected normal binary of male and female associated with particular bodily signs, then how can we know the gender of any child-body? And yet at the same time, because of its presumed malleability, the child-body also becomes one that can be put back on course when it deviates from the norm. It becomes a recuperable transgender body in a way that the adult transgender body cannot, because the latter is already fully formed.

Nowhere is this more evident—if somewhat counterintuitively so—than in the medicalization of transgender children. At present, there are two main (often sequential) medical treatments for transgender children: hormone suppression therapy and cross-sex hormone therapy, administered at the onset of puberty (Spack et al. 2012). From within medical discourse, the primary and explicitly identified benefit of these treatments designed specifically for persons in the state of childhood is their reversibility. Hormone suppression therapy puts the pubertal process "on hold" while cross-sex hormones begin a partial process of transition that can be halted up to a point without permanent cross-sex effects. In other words, the phenomenon of transgender childhood has been subjected to medicalization in which the not-yet status of the child remains central: in one case, the child cannot possibly know its gender for sure and must be put "on hold" until it reaches a more fully adult state of reason; while in the other, the young person is allowed to transition bodily, but only to the degree that the process may be reversed should a different state of reason take shape with maturity. In contrast, surgical options are not available to children before a certain age precisely because they are not reversible. The approved treatments reconstitute the child in gendered terms as a not-yet entity, in which the potential for "normal" gendering must be maintained through reversibility.

Conversely, both of these forms of early intervention and treatment for transgender children ensure that the marks of the first gendering (as male or female) become as invisible as possible: whereas adult bodily transitions cannot alter gender-coded characteristics that mark the transgender body, such as height in male-to-female transsexuals (tall coded as male, shorter coded as female), early hormonal treatment may avoid such markers altogether (the male-to-female child will never grow as tall as otherwise would have occurred, for example). Such interventions in childhood can also avoid surgeries that those who transition as adults might otherwise undertake (such as shaving the Adam's apple or breast removal). Thus transgender childhood constitutes a pathological instance of childhood *and* gender simultaneously—there is "something wrong" with the child *through* its gender, but early medical interventions can make that gender normal without a trace of its past pathology. Because of the child's broader social subordination (ageism), the medical treatment of transgender children more likely constitutes a new site of bodily subjection *to* normalizing gender regimes than a site of greater freedom. Still, it is always possible for transgender childhood to become a site of possibility for new, nonnormative, or resistant transgender subjectivities.

Claudia Castañeda is senior scholar in residence in the Institute for Interdisciplinary Studies at Emerson College. She is the author of *Figurations: Child, Bodies, Worlds* (2002).

Reference

Spack, Norman P., et al. 2012. "Children and Adolescents with Gender Identity Disorder Referred to a Pediatric Medical Center." *Pediatrics* 178, no. 3: 418–25. doi:10.1542/peds.2011-0907.

DOI 10.1215/23289252-2399605

Cisgender

B. AULTMAN

The term *cisgender* (from the Latin *cis-*, meaning "on the same side as") can be used to describe individuals who possess, from birth and into adulthood, the male or female reproductive organs (sex) typical of the social category of man or woman (gender) to which that individual was assigned at birth. Hence a cisgender person's gender is on the same side as their birth-assigned sex, in contrast to which a transgender person's gender is on the other side (trans-) of their birth-assigned sex.

   Cisgender emerged from trans* activist discourses in the 1990s that criticized many commonplace ways of describing sex and gender. The terms *man* and *woman*, left unmarked, tend to normalize cisness—reinforcing the unstated "naturalness" of being cisgender. Thus using the identifications of "cis man" or "cis woman," alongside the usage of "transman" and "transwoman," resists that norm reproduction and the marginalization of trans★ people that such norms effect. Furthermore, though "nontransgender" is a synonym for cisgender, the term came under criticism for the negative quality of its identity description as the state of being the opposite of transgender. Cisgender can be thought of as a positive identification of a non-trans★ identity.

"Cisgender," when used appropriately, helps distinguish diverse sex/gender identities without reproducing unstated norms associated with cisness. For example, instead of simply saying "man" or "woman," one would use "cis woman" or "trans man" in much the same way one would use "black woman" or "white man" (Stryker 2008). Finally, as a substitute for "nontransgender," "cisgender" can be viewed as a way of including transgender as a categorical equal in the complex way we identify as sexed and gendered human beings.

However, not all scholars agree on this last point. Some argue that "cisgender" still retains some of the normalizing implications that "nontransgender" possessed. Although attempting to remove the difference associated with transness by adopting "cisgender," the term seems to place normativity entirely on the side of cisness—and thus reinforce the difference of transness (Enke 2013). Although emerging out of the language of trans★ activism for equality, "cisgender" does not necessarily do the job it was intended to do—to help position transgender people as equals to their cisgender peers by disrupting the assumptions implied in our language. However inadvertently, "cisgender" may still subtly reaffirm the "naturalness" of being born with certain sexed characteristics (Enke 2013).

B. Aultman is a PhD student in political science at the Graduate Center of the City University of New York. His interests exist at the intersection of American politics, law, and gender/trans★ studies. He has published two book chapters on American political institutions in *Importing Democracy* (2010).

References

Enke, A. Finn. 2013. "The Education of Little Cis: Cisgender and the Discipline of Opposing Bodies." In *The Transgender Studies Reader 2*, ed. Susan Stryker and Aren Z. Aizura, 234–47. New York: Routledge.

Stryker, Susan. 2008. *Transgender History*. Berkeley, CA: Seal.

DOI 10.1215/23289252-2399614

Cisgenderism

ERICA LENNON and BRIAN J. MISTLER

Cisgenderism refers to the cultural and systemic ideology that denies, denigrates, or pathologizes self-identified gender identities that do not align with assigned gender at birth as well as resulting behavior, expression, and community. This ideology endorses and perpetuates the belief that cisgender identities and expression are to be valued more than transgender identities and expression and creates an inherent system of associated power and privilege. The presence of cisgenderism exists in many cultural institutions, including language and the law, and consequently enables prejudice and discrimination against the transgender community.

The pervasive nature of cisgenderism creates, designates, and enforces a hierarchy by which individuals are expected to conform and are punished if they do not. This hierarchy includes rigid beliefs and rules about many aspects of gender, including gender identity, expression, and roles. Individuals who do not conform to these rules are seen as deviant, immoral, and even threatening. In turn, prejudice, discrimination, and even violence are viewed as justifiable in order to protect and preserve this very system that benefits those in power who created it.

Use of the term *cisgenderism* is slowly increasing in the literature (see, e.g., Ansara and Hegarty 2012). Historically, the term *transphobia* has been utilized more often in the literature and common discourse. However, despite this greater utilization, "transphobia" addresses fear of trans-identified individuals instead of capturing the critically central and evidently flawed assumptions that underlie the pervasive cultural system of prejudice and discrimination directed toward the transgender community. Other terms have also been updated to more accurately reflect similarly biased worldviews, including a shift from the use of "homophobia" to reflect antigay prejudice and stigma to the use of "heterosexism" (Herek 2004: 15). This shift originated out of an argument that "homophobia" denoted an inherent assumption that antigay prejudice was based largely on fear and in turn did not describe the underlying "cultural ideology" that leads to biased attitudes and behaviors (ibid.: 16).

It is similarly important to distinguish cisgenderism from the use of the term *sexism*. As the name implies, sexism is present when the oppression is rooted in the perceived sex that was assigned at birth. With sex being limited to two dichotomous categories (male and female), *sexism*, inherently, is also a limited term that does not encompass oppression rooted in a spectrum of identities that extends beyond a dichotomous category assigned at birth. In contrast, cisgenderism focuses on oppression that is rooted in one's perceived gender identity, which can be more fluid than sex assigned at birth. Gender identity, in contrast with sex, refers to a person's innate, deeply felt psychological identification of their gender, which again may or may not correspond to the person's designated sex at birth. In addition, the term *sexism* is associated with power and privilege aligned with "maleness," as it focuses on men, and that which is masculine, as being valued above women and that which is deemed feminine. In turn, cisgenderism expands the oppression that is captured by capturing not only the power and privilege associated with being male but also the power and privilege of identifying as someone whose gender identity aligns with assigned sex at birth. As an example, the actions of a cisgender woman refusing to assist in the change of a policy that would permit gender-nonspecific housing or gender-neutral restrooms on a college campus would not be able to be classified under the term "sexism," but such actions would be able to be captured under "cisgenderism." Consequently, *cisgenderism* is a less restrictive term and captures a greater sense of oppression that exists. As such, the growing use of the term more accurately reflects a specific and pervasive cultural and systemic ideology. This in turn offers researchers, the transgender community and allies, and society at large a tool for continued discourse toward deeper transformation.

Erica Lennon is a staff psychologist in the Counseling Center at the University of North Carolina at Charlotte and specializes in working with LGBTQ students, including, in particular, members of the trans* community. Recent publications include the coauthored "Breaking the Binary: Providing Effective Counseling to Transgender Students in College and University Settings" (*Journal of LGBT Issues in Counseling*, 2010).

Brian J. Mistler is associate dean of students at Ringling College of Art and Design in Sarasota, Florida. Recent publications include the coauthored "Breaking the Binary: Providing Effective Counseling to Transgender Students in College and University Settings" (*Journal of LGBT Issues in Counseling*, 2010).

References

Ansara, Y. Gavriel, and Peter Hegarty. 2012. "Cisgenderism in Psychology: Pathologising and Misgendering Children from 1999 to 2008." *Psychology and Sexuality* 3, no. 2: 137–60.

Herek, Gregory, M. 2004. "Beyond 'Homophobia': Thinking about Sexual Prejudice and Stigma in the Twenty-First Century." *Sexuality Research and Social Policy* 1, no. 2: 6–24.

DOI 10.1215/23289252-2399623

Cross-Dresser

MIQQI ALICIA GILBERT

Cross-dressing, in its contemporary Western sense, is the wearing of clothing not belonging to one's birth-designated sex. This simple (and simplistic) definition belies a raft of social, psychological, and philosophical issues. According to the various editions of the American Psychiatric Association's *Diagnostic and Statistical Manual, transvestic disorder* applies to a heterosexual male who receives erotic stimulation from wearing women's clothing. However, *cross-dresser*, the preferred term, requires for its existence a set of very strong institutional precepts the violation of which must be societally condemnable.

The first requirements involve the instantiation and supervision of a strong bi-gender system such as we have in our culture. More, there needs be a social or formal set of standards for gendered appearance that distinguish between the two genders and, ipso facto, the two sexes. These are required in order to make the idea of cross-dressing coherent. Were there no limitations or restrictions on what an individual could wear, there would be no cross-dressing. Indeed, while cross-dressing has a long history going back to ancient times—for example, in Rome and India (Bullough and Bullough 1993: 3–112)—it has always been present and has gone through different levels of prohibition (Stryker 2008: 17–18). While some cultures, including India, the Philippines, Thailand, and some aboriginal tribes, have a space and role for cross-dressing members though often without really embracing it, contemporary Western cultures by and large do not tolerate it. In cultures where the prohibition is strong, there are two requirements: first, a strict bi-gender system, and second, a prohibition, legal and/or social, against gender "impersonation."

Cross-dressing covers a huge range and can go from donning one or two items of women's clothing, usually undergarments, for the purposes of arousal and masturbation, to spending days or weeks living and performing as a woman. It is quite remarkable that these widely different activities fall under the same umbrella. Often a cross-dresser, especially one with experience, will receive little or no sexual frisson from cross-dressing and certainly will not maintain a state of arousal during the entire episode. Indeed, as the cross-dresser matures, the sexual aspect diminishes and an interest in the growth and development of one's "woman-self" increases. What I have called the "committed cross-dresser" is interested in discovering more about his her-self and exploring his feminine side than he is about sexual release (Gilbert 2000: 2). Put simply, what may begin as a fetish need not end there. V. L. Bullough and B. Bullough (1993: 212) cite Havelock Ellis's objection to the term *transvestite* (and presumably *cross-dresser*) as putting too much focus on clothing, whereas a great many cross-dressers care at least as much if not more about the social role of the woman they portray. For this reason, I would urge the term *cross-gender* over *cross-dresser*.

Females as well as males have been involved in cross-dressing, but there is often a different judgment laid upon them. Women who have passed as soldiers have often been praised and applauded, though not uniformly (as for example in the case of Jeanne d'Arc). The Western patriarchal subordination of women means, on one hand, that it makes sense for a woman wanting freedom from oppression to try to pass as a man; but, on the other hand, she may well be attacked for trying to rise above her "rightful" place. Men, on the other hand, have no such justification, since by cross-dressing in a patriarchal society they are placing themselves lower on the power ladder, a move that is specifically against the very idea of masculinity and hence traitorous.

Nonetheless, the question remains as to the source of the disapprobation in our culture. Why should there be such societal angst regarding the person, woman or man, who wants to sometimes appear as the "opposite" gender? Stephen Ducat points out that taboos exist when there is an attraction to an activity that society wants to stem. "Unlike incest, cross-dressing, or exhibitionism," he points out, "there is no taboo against having sex with cheese" (Ducat 2004: 29). His point is that no one wants to have sex with cheese, and, if someone does, no one else cares. This points to the attraction of males to femininity, to the temporary abandonment of the responsibilities and burdens of masculinity as construed societally. The bi-gender system outlines rigid rules of behavior for each gender, and not everyone is comfortable in their assigned role all the time.

Contemporary western society is slowly making room for and improving the lot of the transsexual. More laws are being eased, and more accommodation made, though there is still very far to go. The cross-dresser, however, receives little protection or benefit from these advances, because the cross-dresser, unlike the transsexual, is in constant violation of the bi-gender regime. He or she is not seeking admission into the non–birth-designated sex but only a temporary visa, so to speak, one good for several hours or a few days, confounding many social constituencies. Transsexuals often view cross-dressers as dilettantes, wannabes, or unsophisticated amateurs. The fact that a huge number of transsexuals began their life as cross-dressers seems immaterial. Feminists often deride cross-dressers for picking and choosing those parts of femininity they want and ignoring the rest, a charge not always without merit but one that certainly does not apply across the board. Cis-women often find cross-dressers interesting, while men become very uncomfortable.

The bottom line is that in Western Euro-American cultures there is a sense in which the cross-dresser, especially the out cross-dresser, is the true gender outlaw. Of all the members of the transgender community, broadly understood as those who defy the identity of birth-designated sex with lived gender, she or he refuses one gender and moves back and forth at will, thereby demonstrating the constructed and essentially artificial nature of the bi-gender dichotomy. Unfortunately, the censure laid on cross-dressers keeps the majority firmly in the closet where they are politically unable to become the sort of force needed by the transgender movement. Should the walls between the genders weaken and become more permeable, it is the cross-dresser who will demonstrate that one can have more than one gender.

Miqqi Alicia Gilbert (aka Michael A. Gilbert) is professor of philosophy at York University in Toronto, Canada. His book *Arguing with People* is forthcoming.

References

Bullough, V. L., and B. Bullough. 1993. *Cross Dressing, Sex, and Gender*. Philadelphia: University of Pennsylvania Press.

Ducat, Stephen. 2004. *The Wimp Factor: Gender Gaps, Holy Wars, and the Politics of Anxious Masculinity*. Boston: Beacon.

Gilbert, Michael A. 2000. "The Transgendered Philosopher." *International Journal of Transgenderism* 4, no. 3: 1–16. www.iiav.nl/ezines/web/ijt/97-03/numbers/symposion/gilbert.htm.

Stryker, Susan. 2008. *Transgender History*. Berkeley, CA: Seal.

DOI 10.1215/23289252-2399632

Cultural Competency

WILLY WILKINSON

As an outcome of the lack of cultural competency about transgender and gender-nonconforming populations, transgender people have experienced significant barriers to full access in many spheres of society and have consequently experienced discrimination, harassment, and violence (Grant et al. 2011). *Cultural competency* refers to the ability to understand, communicate with, and effectively interact with diverse populations, and it can be measured by awareness, attitude, knowledge, skills, behaviors, policies, procedures, and organizational systems. *Culture* is defined as "the integrated pattern of thoughts, communications, actions, customs, beliefs, values, and institutions associated, wholly or partially, with racial, ethnic, or linguistic groups, as well as with religious, spiritual, biological, geographical, or sociological characteristics" (Office of Minority Health 2013). Cultural groups can include people who share racial and ethnic affiliations, linguistic characteristics, generation, geographic residence, socioeconomic status, physical ability or limitations, sex, sexual orientation, gender identity and expression, and other characteristics, and they can be population groups that share a defined set of cultural expressions and expectations. Transgender cultural competency is imperative across the board for improved health, social service, legal, faith-based, employment, and educational outcomes.

The phrase "multicultural competence" first surfaced in a mental health publication by psychologist Paul Pedersen in 1988, a decade before "cultural competence" came into popular use. While health care institutions were the first to promote the concept of cultural competency, and undoubtedly continue to be the most common field that recognizes the need, all fields can benefit from a cultural competency perspective. Behavioral health, public health, social services, educational institutions, criminal justice, law enforcement, faith-based organizations, government services, employers, and other organizations, businesses, and institutions can certainly improve their knowledge, skills, behaviors, policies, and procedures to create a welcoming and nondiscriminatory environment for transgender and gender-nonconforming individuals and families.

Rather than a body of knowledge that can be learned in an afternoon workshop, training series, or course, cultural competency is a lifelong process of engagement. Critiques of the concept of cultural competency highlight concerns that people sometimes view the work as short term or that power imbalances are not examined, instead preferring the term "cultural humility," which emphasizes self-evaluation and nonpaternalistic approaches (Tervalon and Murray-Garcia 1998).

Indeed, intersectionality, or multiple systems of oppression and discrimination (Wikipedia 2013a), exists for many transgender people. Systematic injustice and inequality occur not just based on gender identity and expression but also within overlapping experiences of race, gender, socioeconomic class, ability, sexual orientation, health status, linguistic capability, migration, and other characteristics. Transgender cultural competency requires recognition and commitment to genuinely understanding and working to address the multiple parameters that impact so many transgender lives. Within this framework of intersectionality, transgender cultural competency involves an understanding of terms, identities, and concepts associated with transgender and gender-nonconforming communities, including utilizing culturally appropriate language and behavior for addressing and working with transgender populations; broadening understanding of the myriad socioeconomic, health, and legal issues that transgender people face; and developing and implementing culturally appropriate systems and service approaches for working with transgender individuals and families.

Cultural competency issues are addressed worldwide through many avenues for an array of audiences. In 2000, the US Department of Health and Human Services, Office of Minority Health, first introduced the National Culturally and Linguistically Appropriate Services (CLAS) Standards—fourteen mandates, guidelines, and recommendations for health care organizations to develop language access services and organizational systems for more culturally competent care (Office of Minority Health 2001). Since the original CLAS Standards focused fairly exclusively on racial and ethnic diversity, LGBT-specific CLAS standards were later developed independently to recommend that substance abuse organizations (but transferable to other entities) implement the following: LGBT-inclusive policies and procedures, LGBT training as part of larger diversity training, LGBT-inclusive forms and oral language used in assessment and interventions, a welcoming and inclusive climate, and linkages with local LGBT resources and communities so that appropriate referrals can be made for LGBT clients (LGBT Constituency Committee and LGBT TRISTAR 2008). In April 2013, the fifteen Enhanced CLAS Standards were released with a much broader definition of culture (including gender identity and sexual orientation for the first time) as well as an expanded approach to the intended audience beyond health care institutions (Office of Minority Health 2013).

On a global level, approaches to transgender cultural competency issues are informed by the economic situation, legal issues, and whether there is a historical cultural framework for understanding trans and gender-nonconforming people. Organizations in their respective locales as well as such far-reaching organizations as Global Action for Trans Equality, University of California, San Francisco, Center of Excellence for Transgender Health, American Jewish World Service, and others are working to support trans human rights around the world. Many countries are addressing transgender cultural incompetence in health care. In Kampala, Uganda, where it is illegal to be gay or associate with gay people, with trans people considered to be "gay" (Wikipedia 2013b), activists are working to ensure that trans people are not turned away from the emergency room at the local hospital and that they can establish relationships with doctors who are willing to treat them (Kopsa 2012). The organization Gender DynamiX in Cape Town, South Africa, is working to improve competence in the police force (Gender DynamiX 2013), while South Africa, Chile, several European countries, and others are educating government agency workers who handle identification changes (Shlasko, pers. comm., August 2, 2013). In Argentina, where the 2012 landmark Gender Identity Law enabled trans people to change their identification documents without medical intervention and access transition-related care through public and private health insurance, the organization Nadia Echazú works to improve trans access to education and employment beyond the sex industry (Baird 2013). In locales such as Thailand, India, Pakistan, and the Yucatan region of Mexico, where there is an indigenous tradition of gender diversity, stigma and marginalization persist throughout society, yet not the level of cultural incompetence at which providers are unaware of the existence of trans people. Finally, in locations with dire economic conditions, where basic survival is paramount and primary health care is not available to poor trans people, health care institutions are not necessarily the first priority with regard to addressing cultural incompetence. Indeed, approaches vary around the world, with Europe relying almost exclusively on a medical model, while much of the global South relies on a human rights model (Shlasko, pers. comm., August 2, 9, 2013).[1]

It is essential for health service providers (including medical, mental health, substance abuse, and other public health professionals), government agencies, educators (preschool, K-12, and college level), and others to understand the complex array of identities and expressions that transgender and gender-nonconforming people represent. This includes people who identify as male or female as well as people who identify as something between or beyond male and female. It is also important to understand the various ways in which trans and gender-nonconforming people want to be addressed and to be equipped to successfully navigate appropriate name and pronoun use. Also key is the ability to respectfully obtain this information when it is unclear what is appropriate and to recover gracefully when a mistake is made.

Trainees in transgender cultural competency benefit from a firm grasp of social and medical transition, including the routes and barriers to transition-related care for transgender and gender-nonconforming people. It is important to understand how underlying factors of low socioeconomic status, limited health care access, lack of family acceptance, partner and community discomfort, discrimination in employment and housing, legal challenges, and medical conditions including HIV/AIDS can make medical transition challenging to pursue. Indeed, the lack of coverage for transition-related care under most health insurance plans for what are often cost-prohibitive procedures contributes to significant financial hurdles.

In the United States, many jurisdictions prohibit discrimination based on gender identity and expression in public accommodations such as health services. Organizations, government services, and educational institutions can develop trans-inclusive policies and procedures to identify, respond to, and appropriately serve this population. They can update their written forms to ascertain and document transgender status; implement trans-inclusive policy for gender-specific environments including restrooms, locker rooms and shower facilities, housing accommodations, dress code, support groups, and urinalysis; and develop clearly written nondiscrimination policies that specifically protect against discrimination based on gender identity and expression. Systems should be in place to address grievances and poor-quality treatment so that staff persons can receive additional training and/or appropriate sanctions if necessary.

School district policies for accommodating trans and gender-nonconforming students, such as the one developed in Toronto, Canada, recommend systems that emphasize dignity, respect, privacy, safety, and curriculum integration in educational settings free of bullying, harassment, and discrimination (Toronto District School Board 2011). In addition, K-12 schools can support students with transgender family members through celebration of diversity of all kinds, staff training, and LGBT affinity groups. Colleges and universities can support transgender and gender-nonconforming students by incorporating transgender issues into the curriculum across fields and providing trans-affirming academic, social, medical, and mental health programs. A resource has recently been developed to document trans-inclusive policies and practices at American college and university campuses (TONI Project 2012).

Many are confused about how to navigate social interactions and work with individuals with complex, nonbinary identities. They may work with transgender clients, patients, and students with multiple concerns such as immigration issues, limited dominant language capability, cross-cultural differences, unemployment, unstable housing and homelessness, mental health concerns, substance abuse, HIV/AIDS, hepatitis, and other medical conditions, to name a few. Challenging scenarios can be addressed by researching Internet resources, developing effective partnerships with colleagues who serve this population, and getting training from experts in the field of transgender cultural competency. With awareness, compassion, attention to knowledge and skills development, and a commitment to updating organizational systems, health service providers, educators, government agencies, law enforcement, faith-based organizations and others throughout society can build the capacity of their organizations to create nondiscriminatory service environments for transgender individuals and families.

Willy Wilkinson, MPH, is an award-winning writer and public health consultant who has trained and advised close to three hundred community health organizations, businesses, and educational institutions on how to provide equal access for LGBT populations. His publications include "Working with Transgender Persons" (*Psychiatric Times*, September 2012) and contributions in the forthcoming *Trans Bodies, Trans Selves* and *Manning Up*. His memoir *Born on the Edge of Race and Gender: A Voice for Cultural Competency* is also forthcoming.

Note

1. The "medical model" refers to the concept that trans people are entitled to medical care and legal identity document change based on medical diagnoses. The "human rights model" refers to the concept that trans people are entitled to basic human rights so that they can participate fully in society, as in, for example, the Yogyakarta Principles (2007), a "universal guide to human rights which affirm binding international legal standards with which all states must comply" with regards to sexual orientation and gender identity.

References

Baird, Vanessa. 2013. "Trans Revolutionary." *New Internationalist Magazine*, no. 463. newint.org /features/2013/06/01/argentina-transgender-rights (accessed October 21, 2013).

Gender DynamiX. 2013. "Know Your Rights—Changes to SAPS Standard Operating Procedures." www.genderdynamix.org.za/know-your-rights-changes-to-saps-standard-operating -procedures/ (accessed August 9, 2013).

Grant, Jaime M., et al. 2011. "Injustice at Every Turn: A Report of the National Transgender Discrimination Survey." National Center for Transgender Equality and National Gay and Lesbian Task Force. transequality.org/PDFs/NTDS_Report.pdf (accessed October 21, 2013).

Kopsa, Andy. 2012. "A Day in Kampala." With Clare Byarugaba. akopsa.wordpress.com/2012/09/05 /a-day-in-kampala/ (accessed August 9, 2013).

LGBT Constituency Committee and LGBT TRISTAR. 2008. "Best Practices Report: Standards for Culturally Responsive Services for Sexual and Gender Variant Clients and Communities: Substance Abuse Treatment and Prevention Programs in California." www.adp.ca.gov /Advisory/CC/pdf/LGBT_Standards.pdf (accessed October 21, 2013).

Office of Minority Health. 2001. "National Standards on Culturally and Linguistically Appropriate Services in Health Care." Washington, DC: US Department of Health and Human Services. minorityhealth.hhs.gov/assets/pdf/checked/finalreport.pdf (accessed October 21, 2013).

———. 2013. "National Standards for Culturally and Linguistically Appropriate Services in Health and Health Care: A Blueprint for Advancing and Sustaining CLAS Policies and Practice." Washington, DC: US Department of Health and Human Services. www .thinkculturalhealth.hhs.gov/Content/clas.asp (accessed October 21, 2013).

Pederson, Paul. 1988. *A Handbook for Developing Multicultural Awareness.* Alexandria, VA: American Association for Counseling and Development.

Tervalon, Melanie, and Jann Murray-Garcia. 1998. "Cultural Humility versus Cultural Competence: A Critical Distinction in Defining Physician Training Outcomes in Multicultural Education." *Journal of Health Care for the Poor and Underserved* 9, no. 2: 117–25. communitypartners.org/TCWF/HA2013/Cultural_Humility_article.pdf.

TONI Project: Transgender On-Campus Non-discrimination Information. 2012. National Center for Transgender Equality. www.transstudents.org (accessed October 21, 2013).

Toronto District School Board. 2011. "TDSB Guidelines for the Accommodation of Transgender and Gender Non-Conforming Students and Staff." www.tdsb.on.ca/Portals/0/AboutUs /Innovation/docs/tdsb%20transgender%20accommodation%20FINAL_1_.pdf.

Wikipedia. 2013a. "Intersectionality." en.wikipedia.org/wiki/Intersectionality (accessed August 2, 2013).

———. 2013b. "LGBT Rights in Uganda." en.wikipedia.org/wiki/LGBT_rights_in_Uganda (accessed August 9, 2013).

Yogyakarta Principles. 2007. *The Application of International Human Rights Law in Relation to Sexual Orientation and Gender Identity.* www.yogyakartaprinciples.org/principles_en .pdf (accessed October 21, 2013).

DOI 10.1215/23289252-2399641

Depathologization

AMETS SUESS, KARINE ESPINEIRA, and PAU CREGO WALTERS

Trans[1] people have long been defined as pathological. To this day, gender transition processes are classified as mental disorders in diagnostic manuals, such as the American Psychiatric Association's *Diagnostic and Statistical Manual of Mental Disorders* (*DSM*) and the World Health Organization's *International Statistical Classification of Diseases and Related Health Problems* (*ICD*). Meanwhile, trans people are exposed worldwide to dynamics of stigmatization, discrimination, social exclusion, and transphobic violence, including forms of physical and institutional abuse. Within the context of the current revision processes of the diagnostic manuals mentioned above, in recent years an international activism for trans depathologization has emerged, with former activist initiatives and critical trans academic discourses as precedents. Relevant aspects inherent to activist-academic depathologization discourses include the questioning of the current diagnostic classification of gender transitions, the demand of a recognition of trans rights, among them legal and health rights, the revision of the trans health care model, and the claim of an acknowledgment of gender/body diversity.

An example of an activist initiative focused on trans depathologization is STP, International Campaign Stop Trans Pathologization: an international platform that involves the participation of activist groups, organizations, and networks worldwide. STP coordinates the annual International Day of Action for Trans Depathologization every October, an event during which demonstrations and other activities in support of trans depathologization take place in many cities of different world regions.

Within a multiple field of contextually specific forms of trans depathologization activisms worldwide, STP demands the removal of current classifications that understand gender transitions as mental disorders in the *DSM* and the *ICD*. This demand is based on the observation of structural interrelations between dynamics of psychiatrization, discrimination, and transphobia and on an acknowledgment of the negative effects that a psychiatric classification has on the citizenship rights of trans people. The contemporary model of trans health care is criticized for limiting trans people's decisional autonomy by the imposition of an evaluation process and for reducing the diversity of gender transition processes and health care paths through the triadic model of diagnosis, hormone treatment, and surgery. The frequent requirements of a gender-transition–related diagnosis, hormone therapy, and, in some countries, genital surgery, sterilization, and divorce in order to attain legal gender recognition are denounced as contradicting fundamental human rights recognized by the Yogyakarta Principles (2007) and other international resolutions. Furthermore, trans depathologization activism seeks to gain a broader social recognition of gender/body diversity (STP 2012a, 2012b, 2013).

Indeed, the trans depathologization framework introduces a paradigm shift in the conceptualization of gender identities: from conceiving gender transition as a mental disorder to recognizing it as a human right and expression of human diversity. From this perspective, the conflict is not situated in the individual trans person but in a society characterized by transphobia and gender binarism. Thus the contemporary concept of trans(s)exuality is analyzed as a culturally and historically specific construction. Furthermore, the ethnocentric and neocolonialist character of Western-biased psychiatric classifications is put into question for rendering invisible the cultural diversity of gender expressions and identities worldwide and for imposing an exclusive framework of conceiving gender diversity. Trans depathologization discourses include awareness of the diversity of gender conceptualizations, expressions, and trajectories worldwide as well as the presence of context-specific circumstances and priorities within international trans activism.

A central issue in discussions about trans depathologization is the question of how to introduce a depathologization perspective without risking access to trans health care. Given that in some health care contexts, illness-based diagnostic categories are the requisite for public coverage of transition-related health care, there is a fear that depathologization would put access to these health care services at risk, thus fostering social inequalities in the access to trans health care. Trans depathologization activism conceives the right to depathologization and the right to health care as two fundamental human rights, suggesting various strategies in order to facilitate access to state-covered trans health care within a depathologization framework. These include the proposal of a nonpathologizing reference in the *ICD* that understands transition-related health care as a process not based on mental disorder or illness as well as the elaboration of a human rights–based framework for state-funded coverage of transition-related health care (STP 2012a, 2013). Most recently, the approval of the Argentinian Gender Identity Law in June 2012 created a precedent for legal gender recognition and public coverage of trans health care from a human rights perspective.

In the academic context, throughout the last decades an emerging trans scholarship has ruptured the traditional discursive exclusion of trans people from academia, thereby contributing critical revisions of pathologization dynamics in health care, social, legal, and academic contexts as well as new theoretical frameworks and conceptualizations (see, among others, Missé and Coll-Planas 2010; Stryker and Whittle 2006; Thomas, Espineira, and Allessandrin 2013). In addition, trans artists have created new imaginaries for gender/body diversity beyond the binary.

Depathologization discourses are related to a postmodern/poststructuralist deconstruction of dichotomous models, a questioning of medicalization and psychiatrization processes in Western society, postcolonial discourses, and discussion of health care models based on participation, social determinants of health, and human rights perspectives.

Finally, it is important to note that trans depathologization discourses do not conceive depathologization as only a trans-specific issue. The questioning of cis/heteronormativity and gender binarism, as well as the demand of a broader social recognition of gender/body diversity, is considered an important issue for all people. The current pathologization of gender transition processes is perceived as part of the structural violence inherent to the social gender order. It is also relevant to highlight the link between the demand of trans depathologization and a broader questioning of Western psychiatric classification systems and practices. Therefore, the depathologization perspective opens up potential alliances with other critical theoretical reflections and social movements, among them intersex, body diversity, and antipsychiatry discourses and activisms.

Amets Suess is a sociologist and trans activist who works as a researcher and teacher at the Andalusian School of Public Health, Granada, Spain. He is a collaborating author in the anthology *El género desordenado: Críticas en torno a la patologización de la transexualidad* (2010) among other publications.

Karine Espineira holds a PhD in information and communication sciences from the University of Nice Sophia Antipolis. She is the author of *La transidentité: De l'espace médiatique à l'espace public* (2008) and coeditor of *La Transyclopédie* (2012), *Transidentités: Histoire d'une dé pathologisation* (2013), and *Identités intersexes: Identités en débat* (2013).

Pau Crego Walters is an independent scholar in the field of trans health rights with a focus on de/pathologization discourses in relation to trans embodiments and subjectivities. He is a contributing author of *La Transyclopédie* (2012) and *Trans Bodies, Trans Selves* (2014).

Notes

The authors are members of the coordination team of STP, International Campaign Stop Trans Pathologization.

1.   In this text, the term *trans* refers to individuals who engage in gender expressions, trajectories, or identities different from the gender assigned at birth. The term *trans(s) exuality* is used to refer both to transsexuality as describing the current medical model of gender transition and to an activist reappropriation of the term, expressed by using the spelling *transexuality* (Valentine 2007). The use of these concepts takes into account their Western character, which may not correspond to culturally diverse forms of gender transition processes in different parts of the world.

References

Missé, Miquel, and Gerard Coll-Planas, eds. 2010. *El género desordenado: Críticas en torno a la patologización de la transexualidad.* Barcelona and Madrid: Egales.

STP, International Campaign Stop Trans Pathologization. 2012a. *Reflections on the ICD Revision Process from a Depathologization and Human Rights Perspective.* www.stp2012.info /STP2012_Reflections_ICD.pdf (accessed November 1, 2013).

———. 2012b. *Reflections on the SOC-7.* www.stp2012.info/STP2012_Reflections_SOC7.pdf (accessed November 1, 2013).

———. *Reflections from STP regarding the ICD revision process and the publication of the DSM-5.* www.stp2012.info/STP_Communique_August2013.pdf (accessed November 1, 2013).

Stryker, Susan, and Stephen Whittle, eds. 2006. *The Transgender Studies Reader.* New York: Routledge.

Thomas, Maud-Yeuse, Karine Espineira, and Arnaud Alessandrin, eds. 2013. *Transidentités: Histoire d'une dépathologisation. Cahiers de la Transidentité N⁰ 1, Observatoire des Transidentités.* Paris: L'Harmattan.

Valentine, David. 2007. *Imagining Transgender: An Ethography of a Category.* Durham, NC: Duke University Press.

Yogyakarta Principles. 2007. *The Application of International Human Rights Law in Relation to Sexual Orientation and Gender Identity.* www.yogyakartaprinciples.org/principles_en .pdf (accessed November 1, 2013).

DOI 10.1215/23289252-2399650

Disability

JASBIR K. PUAR

Although trans and disability identity discourses each have histories that traverse the second half of the twentieth century, both experienced a period of intensification in the early 1990s that advanced new strategies for the recuperability of previously abjected forms of bodily difference. This periodization signals a broader late twentieth-century shift in practices of social visibility, recognition, and economic utility. Specifically, the emergence of "disability" and "trans identity" as intersectional coordinates required exceptionalizing both the trans body and the disabled body in order to convert the debility of a nonnormative body into a form of social and cultural capacity, whether located in state recognition, identity politics formations, market economies, the medical industrial complex, academic knowledge production, or subject positioning (or all of the above). While the exceptional disabled body can overcome its limits, the trans body can potentially rehabilitate itself.

Historically and contemporaneously, the nexus of disability and trans has been fraught, especially for trans bodies that may resist alliances with people with disabilities in no small part because of long struggles against stigmatization and pathologization that may be reinvoked through such affiliations. But stigmatization is only part of the reason for this thwarted connection, for, as Dan Irving

(2008) and Aren Aizura (2011) separately argue, neoliberal mandates regarding productive, capacitated bodies entrain trans bodies to recreate an abled body not only in terms of gender and sexuality but also in terms of economic productivity and the development of national economy.

For the most part, at this point in time the potential alliance politics of trans disability are seemingly perceived only in terms of the intersectional "trans-disabled subject" or the "disabled trans subject." Eli Clare (2013), a trans man with cerebral palsy, has perhaps generated the most material on the specific episte-mological predicaments of the "disabled trans" subject or the "trans disabled" subject, providing a much-needed intersectional analysis. Clare writes of the ubiquity of this sentiment: "I often hear trans people—most frequently folks who are using, or want to use medical technology to reshape their bodies—name their trans-ness a disability a birth defect" (262). Here Clare emphasizes the trans interest in a cure for the defect, a formulation that has been politically pro-blematized in disability rights platforms, reinforces ableist norms, and alienates potential alliances (ibid.).

Intersectionality, however, provides only one method of thinking about the relationship between trans and disability. Often the intersectional subject gets tokenized or manipulated as a foil such that the presence of this subject actually then prohibits accountability toward broader alliances. Such approaches produce these intersectional subjects from which people can disavow their responsibility and implicated interface while maintaining that the representational mandate for diversity has been satisfied—in other words, a gestural intersectionality that can perform a citational practice of alliance without actually doing intersectional research or analyses.

More interesting to me is the question of what kinds of assemblages appear before and beyond intersectionality that might refuse to isolate trans and dis-ability as separate and distinct conceptual entities. What kinds of political and scholarly alliances might potentiate when each acknowledges and inhabits the more generalized conditions of the other, creating genealogies that read both entities as implicated within the same assemblages of power rather than as intersecting at specific overlaps? For example, there is an instructive history of the ways in which trans and disability have been conceptually and socio-juridically segregated from one another, along a trajectory that moves from the 1990 Americans with Disabilities Act (ADA) to the present moment of trans hailing by the US state,[1] that merits rethinking in ways that reassemble difference and highlight shared debt to more generalizable material processes.

The explicit linkages to the trans body as a body rendered either disabled or rehabilitated from disability have been predominantly routed through debates about gender identity disorder (GID). Arriving in the American Psychiatric

Association's *Diagnostic and Statistical Manual*, third edition (*DSM*-III) in 1980, on the heels of the depathologization of homosexuality (*DSM*-II, 1974), GID was eliminated in the *DSM*-5 released in May 2013 and replaced with "gender dysphoria." These complex debates have focused largely on a series of explicit inclusions and exclusions of GID in relation to the *DSM* and the 1990 ADA. The inclusion of GID in the *DSM* and its specific focus on childhood behavior was largely understood as a compensatory maneuver for the deletion of homosexuality, thus instating surveillance mechanisms that would perhaps *prevent* homosexuality. In contrast, the notable inclusion of the specific *exclusion* as a disability in the ADA of GID not resulting from physical impairments—couched in an exclusionary clause that included transvestitism, transsexuals, pedophilia, exhibitionism, voyeurism, and "other sexual disorders" as well as completely arbitrary "conditions" such as compulsive gambling, kleptomania, pyromania, and use of illegal drugs—was largely understood, unlike the specific exclusion of homosexuality, as a commitment to the entrenchment of pathologization of GID.[2]

Noting that the ADA "unequivocally" endorses the use of *DSM*-IV in recognizing conditions of disablement, Kari Hong argues that the exclusion not only works to disqualify certain "conditions" from consideration as disabilities but also "isolate[s] [these] particular conditions from medical authority" (2002: 123) Ultimately, states Ruth Colker (2004), Congress sacrificed these excluded groups in order to protect another "minority" group: individuals with HIV. This move of course insists upon problematic bifurcations, perhaps strategically so, between individuals diagnosed with GID and individuals diagnosed with HIV. Consequently, Kevin M. Barry (2013, 1) argues, "The ADA is a moral code, and people with GID its moral castaways."

In essence, this exclusion operates to relegate the labor capacities of the transsexual body as unfit for integration into work forces. Further, the ADA redefines standards of bodily capacity and debility by insisting that the reproduction of gender normativity is integral to the productive potential of the disabled body. Finally, the disaggregation, and thus the potential deflation of political and social alliances, of homosexuality, transsexuality, and the individual with HIV, is necessary to the solidification of this gender normativity that is solicited in exchange for the conversion of disability from a debility to a capacity. The modern seeds of what Robert McRuer and Nicole Markotič (2012: 167) call "crip nationalism" are evident here, as the tolerance of the "difference" of disability is negotiated through the disciplining of the body along other normative registers of sameness—in this case, gender and sexuality.

Part of the oscillation between intersectionality and assemblage is to methodologically move beyond the mutual interruptions of theory X by theory Y and vice versa. Such mutual interruptions are themselves symptoms of the liberal deployment of intersectionality, implicitly based on the assumption of the equality of each vector to the other and the absence of each in the other. The focus here is not on epistemological correctives but ontological irreducibilities, irreducibilities that transform the fantasy of discreteness of categories not through their disruption but rather through their dissolution via multiplicity.

To enact such a project moves from questions such as What is disability? and What is trans? toward What does disability do? What does trans do? For the latter question one could point to other endeavors at similar efforts to articulate trans as a force that impels indeterminate movement rather than as an identity that demands epistemological accountability or as a movement between identities. Susan Stryker, Paisley Currah, and Lisa Jean Moore (2008) explicate the "trans-" (trans-hypen) in the sociopolitical; Jami Weinstein (2012) develops the notion of "transgenre," Mel Chen (2012) articulates trans as movements of speciation. Gilles Deleuze and Félix Guattari's (1987) use of "transsexuality" opens to a fluid spectrum of possibility: trans as a motion, not an identity, and trans as a continuum of intensity, not identity.

How might we assemble trans and disability such that rather than cohering as new transnormativities, they do not strive to manifest wholeness or to invest in the self as coherent and thereby reproduce liberal norms of being? Susan Stryker and Nikki Sullivan (2009: 61) argue that "individual demands for bodily alteration are also, necessarily, demands for new forms of social relationality—new somatechnological assemblages that ethically refigure the relationship between individual corporealities and aggregate bodies." This formulation, then, of new somatechnologies that refuse the individualizing mandate of neoliberal paradigms of bodily capacity and debility in favor of articulating greater connectivities between "aggregate assemblages of bodies" is precisely the goal of crafting convivial political praxis.

Jasbir K. Puar is associate professor of women's and gender studies at Rutgers University. She is the author of *Terrorist Assemblages: Homonationalism in Queer Times* (2007). Her book *Affective Politics: States of Debility and Capacity* is forthcoming.

Notes

1. Susan Stryker calls this transnormative citizenship (pers. comm., August 2, 2013).
2. The text in the ADA reads:
   Sec. 12211. Definitions
   (a) Homosexuality and bisexuality
   For purposes of the definition of "disability" in section 12102(2) of this title, homosexuality and bisexuality are not impairments and as such are not disabilities under this chapter.

(b) Certain conditions

Under this chapter, the term "disability" shall not include

(1) transvestism, transsexualism, pedophilia, exhibitionism, voyeurism, gender identity disorders not resulting from physical impairments, or other sexual behavior disorders;

(2) compulsive gambling, kleptomania, or pyromania; or

(3) psychoactive substance use disorders resulting from current illegal use of drugs. (Americans with Disabilities Act of 1990, 42 U.S.C. § 12208 [1990])

References

Aizura, Aren. 2011. "The Romance of the Amazing Scalpel: 'Race,' Labour, and Affect in Thai Gender Reassignment Clinics." In *Queer Bangkok*, ed. Peter A. Jackson, 143–62. Hong Kong: Hong Kong University Press.

Barry, Kevin M. 2013. "Disabilityqueer: Federal Disability Rights Protection for Transgender People." *Yale Human Rights and Development Law Journal* 16, no. 1: 1–50.

Chen, Mel. 2012. *Animacies: Biopolitics, Racial Mattering, and Queer Affect.* Durham, NC: Duke University Press.

Clare, Eli. 2013. "Body Shame, Body Pride: Lessons from the Disability Rights Movement." In *The Transgender Studies Reader 2*, ed. Susan Stryker and Aren Z. Aizura, 261–65. New York: Routledge.

Colker, Ruth. 2004. "Homophobia, HIV Hysteria, and the Americans with Disabilities Act." *Journal of Gender, Race, and Justice* 8, no. 1: 33–34.

Deleuze, Gilles, and Félix Guattari. 1987. *A Thousand Plateaus: Capitalism and Schizophrenia.* Translated by Brian Massumi. Minneapolis: University of Minnesota Press.

Hong, Kari. 2002. "Categorical Exclusions: Exploring Legal Responses to Health Care Discrimination against Transsexuals." *Columbia Journal of Gender and Law* 11, no. 1: 88–126.

Irving, Dan. 2008. "Normalized Transgressions: Legitimizing the Transsexual Body as Productive." *Radical History Review*, no. 100: 38–59.

McRuer, Robert, and Nicole Markotić. 2012. "Leading with Your Head: On the Borders of Disability, Sexuality, and the Nation." In *Sex and Disability*, ed. Robert McRuer and Anna Mollow, 165–82. Durham, NC: Duke University Press.

Stryker, Susan, and Nikki Sullivan. 2009. "King's Member, Queen's Body: Transsexual Surgery, Self-Demand Amputation, and the Somatechnics of Sovereign Power." In *Somatechnics: Queering the Technologisation of Bodies*, ed. N. Sullivan and S. Murray, 49–36. Aldershot, UK: Ashgate.

Stryker, Susan, Paisley Currah, and Lisa Jean Moore. 2008. "Introduction: Trans-, Trans, or Transgender?" *WSQ: Women's Studies Quarterly* 36, no. 3–4: 11–22.

Weinstein, Jami. 2012. "Transgenres and the Plane of Gender Imperceptibility." In *Undutiful Daughters: New Directions in Feminist Thought and Practice*, ed. Henriette Gunkel, Chrysanthi Nigianni, and Fanny Söderbäck, 155–68. New York: Palgrave Macmillan.

DOI 10.1215/23289252-2399659

Error

YETTA HOWARD

"Error," in twentieth-century medical and scientific discourse, is bound up with diagnosing and understanding trans identifications in terms of wrong embodiment, or a FAAB/MAAB (female-assigned-at-birth/male-assigned-at-birth) body perceived within dominant biomedical perspectives as a mistake or as at odds with one's gender and bodily identity. Accordingly, trans-as-error functions in tandem with rubrics of identificatory, mental, and bodily disorders that have historically included nonheterosexual identities and intersexed bodies. As T. Benjamin Singer discusses in his work on photography, the medical gaze, and the trans-health model, trans as pathology—hence as an error to be corrected—has injurious ethical effects that usher in misunderstandings about nonnormatively embodied identities (2006: 602). By the late twentieth and twenty-first centuries, a range of trans identifications continue to be recognized via such notions of error, yet gender theorists and creative practitioners persist in reconceptualizing error as a mode of inhabitation and incorporation—so that "error" ultimately describes the movement away from a normatively transcendent model of embodiment. In *The Female Grotesque*, Mary Russo writes of female bodies as constituted "in error" and provides ways to think about the exclusions set up by feminist politics through a critique of social conformity (1995: 10–12). While the category of female has been associated with the grotesque other, so too have trans bodies become emblems of mutation and freakiness; but trans artists have, in the contemporary era, embraced such characterizations as an oppositional approach to inhabitation and cultural production.

These embodied aesthetics of error are readily apparent in photographer Del LaGrace Volcano's *Sublime Mutations* (2000), his collection of photographs that integrates vulgarity, disposability, and bodily flaws as explorations of transmasculine allure and value (Volcano 2012: 5–6; Halberstam 2005: 114–15). Emphasizing transfeminine embodiment, Zackary Drucker's confrontational video and performance art approaches "error" as a framework of transgressive desire and antinormativity. Her film *You will never, ever be a woman. You must live the rest of your days entirely as a man, and you will only get more masculine with each passing year* (2008) aggressively reroutes and displaces transphobic rhetoric designating transfemininities as bad copies of cis femininities by showing two transwomen whose insults at each other culminate in sex. Invoking the psychoanalytic assessment of female embodiment as lack, Drucker's performance piece *The Inability to Be Looked at and the Horror of Nothing to See* (2009) gets the "nothing to see" "wrong" by displaying nonclassifiably female genitals that visibly show through women's underwear while audience members pluck visibly "errant" hair from the artist's body. Such rethinking of trans embodiment is also presented in Marie Losier's documentary *The Ballad of Genesis and Lady Jaye* (2011), which features Genesis P-Orridge, known mainly for the 1970s industrial noise-music project Throbbing Gristle's use of broken instruments and manipulation of nonmusical objects for sound. In their Orlan-inspired "Pandrogyne" project, P-Orridge and lover Lady Jaye undergo a series of surgeries remaking themselves as invariably "wrong" versions of each other. The association of "error" with "trans" therefore develops as a radically productive misalignment of the positive/negative binary required by contemporary queer politics of the body.

Yetta Howard is an assistant professor in the Department of English and Comparative Literature at San Diego State University. She is completing a book, "Ugly Differences," and is at work on a new project called "Erratic Erotics."

References

The Ballad of Genesis and Lady Jaye. 2011. Directed by Marie Losier. New York: New Yorker Films.

Halberstam, Judith. 2005. *In a Queer Time and Place: Transgender Bodies, Subcultural Lives.* New York: New York University Press.

Russo, Mary. 1995. *The Female Grotesque: Risk, Excess, and Modernity.* New York: Routledge.

Singer, T. Benjamin. 2006. "From the Medical Gaze to *Sublime Mutations*: The Ethics of (Re) Viewing Non-Normative Body Images." In *Transgender Studies Reader*, ed. Susan Stryker and Stephen Whittle, 601–20. New York: Routledge.

Volcano, Del LaGrace. 2000. *Sublime Mutations.* Tübingen: Konkursbuch Verlag Claudia Gehrke.

———. 2012. "Artist Statement." *Archive: The Journal of the Leslie-Lohman Museum of Gay and Lesbian Art*, no. 43: 5–6.

DOI 10.1215/23289252-2399668

Feminism

SALLY HINES

Emerging in the 1960s, second-wave feminism was one of the first academic fields to respond to the growing public awareness of modern Western transgender practices. Transgender raises questions about the relationship between "sex" and gender role and identity, issues that have long been central to feminist thought. On a theoretical, political, and cultural level, however, feminist scholars have often been hostile to transgender practices (see, for example, Raymond 1980; Jeffreys 1997; Greer 1999). The publication of Janice Raymond's thesis, *The Transsexual Empire*, in 1980 established a radical feminist approach to transgender that was to significantly affect the dominant feminist position for succeeding decades. Raymond's argument is that sex is chromosomally formed and thus secured at birth. From this perspective, gender is seen as an expression of biological sex, with the categories of sex and gender codependent. Raymond's standpoint led to a radical feminist reading of transsexuality as a genetic male practice fashioned by a patriarchal medical system. Moreover, fuelled by the insistence that female biology or female socialization makes one a feminist, the place of trans people within feminist communities became disputed.

In her seminal book *Gender Trouble* (1990), Judith Butler brought attention to how dominant understandings—including those of radical feminism—of sex, gender, and sexuality followed, and by turn reinforced, a "heterosexual matrix." In contrast, Butler theorizes sex, gender, and sexuality as distinct though potentially overlapping categories, an approach that has proved significant for accounting for divergent gendered identities and expressions. Butler's work was influential in the development of queer feminism during the 1990s, which led to a more productive feminist engagement with transgender. The emphasis on "difference" within queer theory went beyond the prevailing notion of trans people as a homogenous group to recognize distinct trans identities and practices (Hines 2005). In viewing *all* gendered and sexual identities as socially constructed, queer theory aims to dissolve the naturalization and pathologization of perceived "minority" identities.

The writing of trans activists was central to challenging antitransgender feminism. For example, Sandy Stone (1996), Leslie Feinberg (1996), and Julia Serano (2007) offered explicit critiques of the rejection of trans people from feminism. Likewise, scholars working within the interdisciplinary area of transgender studies have drawn out intersecting areas of concern between feminism and transgender, challenging the exclusion of trans people from feminist communities. Henry Rubin, for example, argues for a dialectical rather than identity-based employment of embodiment to enable a feminist approach to take account of "differently located bodies which appear similar in form" (Rubin 1996: 7–8). This may allow for "a way of knowing that can provide me(n) with a feminist viewpoint, and that is not generated out of a woman's experience of her body. Instead, it is generated out of subjectively located struggle" (ibid.).

Emi Koyama's recent discussion of "transfeminism," which expresses the feminist concerns of trans women, shows how trans politics enables contemporary feminism to move beyond the confines of gendered binary feminism in order for feminist and trans communities to develop productive alliances: "Transfeminism is not merely about merging trans politics with feminism, but it is a critique of the second wave feminism from third wave perspectives" (2003: 2). This approach has been incorporated into contemporary feminist and queer activist communities—often discussed as representing a "third wave" of feminism—which are increasingly accepting of a multiplicity of gendered identities and representations that are not fixed to biological sex.

Sally Hines is the director of the Centre for Interdisciplinary Gender Studies, University of Leeds. Her research interests are in the areas of gender, sexuality, intimacies, the body, citizenship, and recognition. These areas are brought together in her body of work on transgender. Her latest book is *Gender, Diversity, Citizenship, and Recognition: Towards a Politics of Difference* (2013).

References

Butler, Judith. 1990. *Gender Trouble: Feminism and the Subversion of Identity*. New York: Routledge.

Feinberg, Leslie. 1996. *Transgender Warriors: Making History from Joan of Arc to Dennis Rodman*. Boston: Beacon.

Greer, G. 1999. *The Whole Woman*. London: Random House.

Hines, S. 2005. "'I Am a Feminist but . . .': Transgender Men, Women, and Feminism." In *Different Wavelengths: Studies of the Contemporary Women's Movement*, ed. J. Reger, 57–78. New York: Routledge.

Jeffreys, S. 1997. "Transgender Activism: A Feminist Perspective." *Journal of Lesbian Studies* 1, no. 3–4: 55–74.

Koyama, Emi. 2003. "Transfeminist Manifesto." In *Catching a Wave: Reclaiming Feminism for the Twenty-First Century*, ed. R. Dicker and A. Piepmeier, 1–15. Boston: Northeastern University Press.

Raymond, Janice. 1980. *The Transsexual Empire*. London: Women's Press.

Rubin, H. 1996. "Do You Believe in Gender?" *Sojourner* 21, no. 6: 7–8.

Serano, Julia. 2007. *Whipping Girl: A Transsexual Woman on Sexism and the Scapegoating of Femininity*. Berkeley, CA: Seal.

Stone, Sandy. 1996. "The *Empire* Strikes Back: A Posttranssexual Manifesto." In *Body Guards: The Cultural Politics of Sexual Ambiguity*, ed. K. Straub and J. Epstein, 280–304. New York: Routledge.

DOI 10.1215/23289252-2399677

Film

HELEN HOK-SZE LEUNG

What Counts as a Trans Film?

This deceptively simple question has provoked heated discussion among festival programmers, film critics, and even filmmakers. Is a trans film one that features self-identified trans characters or characters that viewers would recognize as trans? One made by trans filmmakers or starring trans actors, regardless of content? Does it have to be meant for trans viewers, have a trans aesthetic, or just be open to trans interpretations? Who decides which of these criteria are important, in what contexts, and for what reasons? This last consideration—of the discourse around a film—is perhaps the most significant: when and why a film is talked about as a "trans film" tells us a lot about the current state of representational politics and community reception as well as trends and directions in film criticism.

Sibling Rivalry

Susan Stryker once quipped that transgender studies is queer theory's "evil twin" who "willfully disrupts the privileged family narratives that favor sexual identity labels . . . over gender categories" (2004: 212). The notion of trans cinema bears a similar sibling relation to that of queer cinema. Films that feature gender variance have always had a significant place in queer cinema, but considerations of trans issues have tended to be subsumed under the focus on sexuality. The recent emergence of transgender film festivals provides one corrective to this problem.[1] The family feud over queer versus trans approaches to specific films has at times divided communities but also inspired constructive conversations. For example, the furor over lesbian perspectives on *Boys Don't Cry* (dir. Kimberly Peirce, 1999) that fail to honor Brandon Teena as a trans subject (Pratt 2005: 173–74; Halberstam 2005: 89–92) or the debate on the hostile queer reception of Cheng Dieyi's cross-gender embodiment in *Farewell My Concubine* (dir. Chen Kaige, 1993; see Leung 2010: 46) shows how film can spark rigorous discussion about the boundary and relation between *queer* and *trans* as interpretive categories.

Critically Trans

The growth of trans-centric approaches in film criticism has contributed to more diverse ways of "seeing" trans on-screen. Analyses of stereotypes (Ryan 2009) expose the media dynamics that result in limiting and transphobic representations. Going beyond identity politics, adventurous critical approaches include the theorizing of transgender as a form of relationality between characters on-screen (Halberstam 2005: 92–96), the exploration of how cinema depicts bodily transformative procedures such as theatrical training and martial arts as forms of "trans practice" (Leung 2010: 94–106), and the examination of cinematic affect and trans aesthetics (Steinbock 2011). While textual analyses dominate the field, there are also important recent efforts to conduct theoretically sophisticated and empirically grounded studies of trans audience and community reception (Williams 2012).

Trans Auteurs

On the production side, the most exciting development is an emergent wave of trans-identified filmmakers, most notably in North America, whose works are committed not only to telling stories meant consciously for a trans or trans-literate audience but also to aesthetic and genre experimentation. For example, Jules Roskam's *Against a Trans Narrative* (2009) critiques medicalized narratives of transsexuality as well as the dominant self-narration of trans-masculine subjects. Morty Diamond's *Trans Entities: The Nasty Love of Papì and Wil* (2008) is a form of "docu-porn" that redresses mainstream pornography's exploitative representation of trans people while challenging the absence of sexuality in the documentary genre. Kimberly Reed's *Prodigal Sons* (2008) displaces the story of her own gender transition with a poignant exploration of her brother's story of mental illness and adoption history. These filmmakers are trans auteurs in the sense that they consciously construct a complex relation between their trans identification and their aesthetic signature on screen.

Trans by Any Other Name?

Concerns have been expressed over the predominantly Western framework of trans studies that fails to account for forms of embodiment and identity that lie outside its purview (Roen 2006; Towle and Morgan 2006). The same challenge faces the study of trans cinema: How should we approach films that feature gender variance in contexts outside or predating the Western discursive history of "trans"? Should we speak instead of a *kathoey* cinema from Thailand that has produced such films as *Iron Ladies* (dir. Yongyoot Thongkongtoon, 2000) and *Beautiful Boxer* (dir. Ekachai Uekrongtham, 2004)? How should we approach the genre of films featuring premodern forms of cross-dressed embodiment in traditional theaters across East Asia, such as *Farewell My Concubine* and *The King and the Clown* (dir. Joon-ik Lee, 2005)? How do we speak of subjectivities that do not neatly differentiate between same-sex desire and cross-gender identification, like that of the protagonist in *The Blossoming of Maximos Oliveros* (dir. Auraeus Solito, 2005)? Engaging with these questions even as they query the parameters, limits, and raison d'être of trans film studies remains a challenging but crucial undertaking.

Helen Hok-Sze Leung is an associate professor of gender, sexuality, and women's studies at Simon Fraser University. She is the author of *Undercurrents: Queer Culture and Postcolonial Hong Kong* (2008) and *Farewell My Concubine: A Queer Film Classic* (2010).

Note

1.   The impact of transgender film festivals warrants more attention in film festival scholarship, which, as evidenced in a bibliography developed by the Film Festival Research Network (2013), is focused predominantly on queer film festivals.

References

Film Festival Research Network. 2013. "9.1.1 LGBT/Queer Film Festivals." www.filmfestival research.org/index.php/ffrn-bibliography/9-specialized-film-festivals/9-1-identity-based -festivals/9-1-1-lgbt-queer-film-festivals (accessed October 24, 2013).

Halberstam, Judith. 2005. *In A Queer Time and Place*. New York: New York University Press.

Leung, Helen Hok-Sze. 2010. *Farewell My Concubine: A Queer Film Classic*. Vancouver: Arsenal Pulp.

Pratt, Minnie Bruce. 2005. *S/he*. Boston: Alyson.

Roen, Katrina. 2006. "Transgender Theory and Embodiment: The Risk of Racial Marginalization." In *The Transgender Studies Reader*, ed. Susan Stryker and Stephen Whittle, 656–65. New York: Routledge.

Ryan, Joelle Ruby. 2009. "Reel Gender: Examining the Politics of Trans Images in Film and Media." PhD diss., Bowling Green University.

Steinbock, Eliza. 2011. "Shimmering Images: On Transgender Embodiment and Cinematic Aesthetics." PhD diss., University of Amsterdam.

Stryker, Susan. 2004. "Transgender Studies: Queer Theory's Evil Twin." *GLQ* 10, no. 2: 212–15.

Towle, Evan B., and Lynn M. Morgan. 2006. "Romancing the Transgender Native: Rethinking the 'Third Gender' Concept." In Stryker and Whittle, *Transgender Studies Reader*, 666–84.

Williams, Jonathan R. 2012. "Trans Cinema, Trans Viewers." PhD diss., University of Melbourne.

DOI 10.1215/23289252-2399686

Gender Self-Determination

ERIC A. STANLEY

> I am Miss Major, none of this Ms. shit. I am not a liberated woman. I'm a transgender woman and I'm working on becoming liberated as we speak.
> —Miss Major, *Captive Genders: Trans Embodiment and the Prison Industrial Complex*

Gender self-determination is a collective praxis against the brutal pragmatism of the present, the liquidation of the past, and the austerity of the future. That is to say, it indexes a horizon of possibility already here, which struggles to make freedom flourish through a radical trans politics. Not only a defensive posture, it builds in the name of the undercommons a world beyond the world, lived as a dream of the good life.[1]

Within at least the US context, the normalizing force of mainstream trans politics, under the cover of equality, operates by consolidation and exile. Or put another way, through its fetishistic attachment to the law and its vicissitudes, mainstream trans politics argues for inclusion in the same formations of death that have already claimed so many. This collusion can be seen in the lobbying for the addition of "gender identity" to federal hate crimes enhancements. While the quotidian violence many trans people face—in particular trans women of color—is the material of daily life, this push for the expansion of the prison-industrial complex through hate crimes legislation proliferates violence under the name of safety.

Legislative and semilegislative apparatuses from the United Nations and NGOs to local governance have begun to include similar language around "gender equity." Champions of such moves might cite the Yogyakarta Principles (2007), which are the findings of a human rights commission convened to foreground

"Sexual Orientation and Gender Identity" globally, or such recent decisions as that of the Australian government to add a third gender option of "X" to their passports as signs of progress. However, an ethic of gender self-determination helps us to resist reading these biopolitical shifts as victories. Here the state and its interlocutors, including at times trans studies, work to translate and in turn confine the excesses of gendered life into managed categories at the very moment of radical possibility.[2]

To begin with the "self" in the wake of neoliberalism might seem a dangerous place to turn a phrase, especially one that is suggested to offer such radical potentiality—and perhaps it is. After all, the "self" in our contemporary moment points most easily toward the fiction of the fully possessed rights-bearing subject of Western modernity, the foil of the undercommons. However, here it is not the individual but a collective self, an ontological position always in relation to others and dialectically forged in otherness, that is animated. The negation of this collective self, as relational and nonmimetic, is the alibi for contemporary rights discourse, which argues that discrete legal judgments will necessarily produce progressive change. Rather than believe that this is an oversight of the state form, critics of human rights discourse remind us that this substitution is a precondition of the state's continued power.

Antagonistic to such practices of constriction and universality, gender self-determination is affectively connected to the practices and theories of self-determination embodied by various and ongoing anticolonial, Black Power, and antiprison movements. For Frantz Fanon and many others, the violence of colonialism and antiblackness are so totalizing that ontology itself collapses; thus the claiming of a self fractures the everydayness of colonial domination. The Black Panther Party for Self Defense echoed a similar perspective in their 1966 *Ten Point Plan*. Self-determination, for the Panthers and for many others, is the potentiality of what gets called freedom. Connecting these histories, "gender self-determination is queer liberation is prison abolition" was articulated by the gender and queer liberation caucus of CR10, Critical Resistance's tenth anniversary conference in 2008 (The CR10 Publications Collective, 2008: 7).

To center radical black, anticolonial, and prison abolitionist traditions is to already be inside trans politics.[3] From STAR's (Street Transvestite Action Revolutionaries) alliance with the Young Lords in New York City and the recent organizing against US drone attacks led by trans women in Sukkur, Pakistan, to Miss Major's words that anoint this essay, these forms of gender self-determination, even if left unnamed, argue that national liberation and the overthrow of colonial and carceral rule must be grown together with gender liberation (see Littauer 2012).

Gender self-determination opens up space for multiple embodiments and their expressions by collectivizing the struggle against both interpersonal and state violence. Further, it pushes us away from building a trans politics on the fulcrum of realness (gender normative, trans, or otherwise) while also responding to the different degrees of harm people are forced to inhabit. As a nonprescriptive politics, its contours cannot always be known in advance—it is made and remade in the process of its actualization, in the time of resistance and in the place of pleasure. Becoming, then, as Gilles Deleuze might have it—or more importantly, as Miss Major lives it (Stanley and Smith 2011)—is the moment of gender self-determination: *becoming liberated as we speak.*

Eric A. Stanley is a President's Postdoctoral Fellow in the Departments of Communication and Critical Gender Studies at the University of California, San Diego. Eric is an editor of *Captive Genders: Trans Embodiment and the Prison Industrial Complex* (2011) and has published articles in *Social Text*, *Women and Performance*, and *American Quarterly*.

Notes

1. I am here using Fred Moten and Stefano Harney's concept of the "undercommons" to point toward the commons as relation and nonplace. For more, see Moten and Harney 2004.
2. For more on the category of work of the state, see Dean Spade 2011.
3. This is a point that Che Gossett (2014) helps us collectively remember.

References

Black Panther Party for Self Defense. 1966. "The Ten Point Plan." www.blackpanther.org /TenPoint.htm (accessed January 7, 2014).

The CR10 Publications Collective, ed. 2008 *Abolition Now! Ten Years of Strategy and Struggle against the Prison Industrial Complex.* Oakland, CA: AK.

Gossett, Che. 2014. "We Will Not Rest in Peace: AIDS Activism, Black Radicalism, Queer and/or Trans Resistance." In *Queer Necropolitics*, ed. Jin Haritaworn, Adi Kuntsman, and Silvia Posocco. London: Routledge.

Littauer, Dan. 2012. "LGBT Global News 24–7." *Gay Star News*, August 2. www.gaystarnews.com /article/pakistan-trans-activists-protest-against-us-drone-strikes020812.

Moten, Fred, and Stefano Harney. 2004. "The University and the Undercommons: Seven Theses." *Social Text* 22, no. 2: 79.

Spade, Dean. 2011. *Normal Life: Administrative Violence, Critical Trans Politics, and the Limits of Law.* Brooklyn, NY: South End.

Stanley, Eric A., and Nat Smith, eds. 2011. *Captive Genders: Trans Embodiment and the Prison Industrial Complex.* Oakland, CA: AK.

Yogyakarta Principles. 2007. *The Application of International Human Rights Law in Relation to Sexual Orientation and Gender Identity.* www.yogyakartaprinciples.org/principles_en .pdf (accessed November 1, 2013).

DOI 10.1215/23289252-2399695

Guerrilla

SANDY STONE

I get to write this, and you get to read it, because this journal exists. It's an altogether astonishing moment. Beginnings are delicate times when the foundation stones of the edifice you're building are still visible; maybe if we take a look around now, we can save ourselves some trouble later.

The "Posttranssexual Manifesto" asserts that the essence of posttranssexuality is subversion. We operate by undermining essentialist feminist discourses that reify binarism under other names, and the author asks the trans community to take up arms in that effort by asserting the primacy of self-declaration—by "reading oneself aloud." This could be, and frequently is, misread as simply "coming out." But reading oneself aloud is never as simple as making-visible; it also implies writing oneself into the selfsame discourses by which one is written—burrowing in and virally disrupting the smoothness and closure on which power depends.

The meta of that description could well be an operational definition of post-posttranssexuality: asserting the vision that guides our acts and drives us forward, while simultaneously refusing closure on any single discourse of our own manifold discourses that, in their enticing collisions and rebounds and fungible resonances, constitute, somewhere near their center of mass, the presumptive subject of this journal. It's holding those concepts in productive tension—the quixotic effort of articulating structure while refusing closure and insisting on situation—that, I think, defines our discipline and our fragile moment.

And we're very early in that moment. Keep in mind that *no one working in transgender studies has a degree in transgender studies*. That's how close to the origin of our discipline we are. This is the way zeroth-generation disciplines work. The value in that particular fact for us is that trans studies is still coalescing. We don't yet have a canon or a bunch of old folks telling us what the field is or what counts as its discourse and who gets to say stuff about and within it. But soon enough we will, as surely as the night follows the day, and you can count on that.

The trajectory for discipline building is well understood. In Phase One, individuals, geographically scattered and usually unaware of each other, generate the rough ideas of what will become the discipline.

In Phase Two, others become aware of this work and may become aware of each other. They may form working groups at conferences devoted to other topics, or they may just hang out in each other's hotel rooms and jam about possible white papers.

In Phase Three, a few people with the necessary energy and drive come together, geographically or, as is more usual, virtually, and organize the first publications, meetings, and, later, conferences. This is the point when the larger, nascent protocommunity first begins to become self-aware and when the loose constellation of ideas that gravitate around this not-quite-existent collection of individuals begins to take shape.

In Phase Four, the general description and usually the name of the discourse achieve a level of acceptance among "TradAcs" (traditional academics). This varies from place to place, as TradAcs are exquisitely conscious of how legitimacy works and are quick to separate legitimized disciplines from the rest; it has always appeared to this author that what drives this fervent defense of disciplinary boundaries is a combination of a certain schadenfreude coupled with a nagging sense of the fragility of the identity of one's own discipline, particularly in the social sciences.

Phase Four is where we are now. To some extent it's a fragile moment, but it is also heady and bursting with possibilities. And, though it's not yet fully formed and its goals not yet fully articulated, it's also the discipline's peak moment. Believe it or not, it's all downhill from here. Which is why I'm asking you to pay attention, because what happens next is that some grad students somewhere read this journal or look at a conference program, and instead of saying to themselves, "Wow, this wonderful stuff can help me change the world," they say, "Hey, maybe this stuff can help me get a job." Thus begins the transition from revolutionary action to commodification. Next thing you know, you've got disciplinary jargon—not because it helps clarify the discourse but because it makes your work less approachable by people in neighboring disciplines and thereby makes your discipline more special.

So let's think about the two words at the heart of this disciplinary moment: *transgender* and *studies*.

Aside from its indexicality in simultaneously defining and calling into being a sociopolitical class, *transgender*—a word that has existed for less than twenty years—still, and with great immediacy, evokes fungibility and transgression; the irruption of the trans episteme into the smooth fabric of sociality and theory, still fresh as it is, possesses enormous power for positive change. With that in mind, let's look beyond trans as a sociopolitical positionality and developing demographic, and let's think about how to use the power that we, by fighting and surmounting the forces that oppose our claiming our own selves, come to literally embody.

How will—can, should—*trans* engage *studies*? *Studies* is an institutional concept, meant in part to maintain a certain distance between observer and observed, to preserve objectivity—or, at minimum, to afford plausible deniability. *Studies* is the institution's way of saying that the work proceeds in a detached and impartial manner. Yet we have barely begun, really, to explore how powerful trans—born in the joy and pain of living bodies and fully engaged in the world—can be.

Understand, then, the peril that freights this moment. *Dulce et decorum est*: "sweet and fitting it is,"[1] this moment when our feisty, nasty selves, saturated with change and flushed with success, meet the institutional rewards and requirements of transitioning from a movement to a discipline. What is gained, what lost?

My stakes in our nascent community, and in writing this, are, long after transgender studies has become an academic commodity, to encourage us to keep thinking like revolutionaries. From its oldest foundations, the present-day academy is designed to be terminally conservative, and it carries out that mission by creating future academics in its image. By virtue of this very narrow slice of time in which we now exist and work, we have so far avoided being digested by some academic institution and turned into its own flesh. It's not easy to avoid that singularly unpleasant fate, not least because it's so seductive; and, to be honest, not everyone wants to avoid it. In fact, my real audience for this little essay is almost vanishingly small. But it's certainly not zero.

How do we go about nurturing Beginner's Mind? (And here to some extent I'm plagiarizing myself, because lately I've been pondering this and have written about it once or twice [Stone 2013].)

First: Find your own voice. This is not merely Job Number One; it's really your only job. If you do nothing else, ever, than survive the struggle to find your own voice, you have still fulfilled a primal life goal, and everything else that happens flows from that pluripotent act. In the beginning is your word. Finding your voice is the deeper meaning underlying the hoary mythoids that saturate Western storytelling. Speaking yourself disrupts both society's and culture's stupendous drive to speak you. Eventually there are balances and inflection points to be found between speaking and being spoken, because in living fully in the world one does both; but at the inception, stick with speaking. You have a lifetime to figure out the balance.

Second: Announce your stakes. If you speak from your heart about what really matters *to you*, then the work and your love for it will follow. It is extremely important—crucial—that from the very beginning your work flows from your own stakes in the discourse. If you hold back, the chances are much greater that you'll settle for less than your best efforts, and it's only through your best efforts that you raise the power it takes to change the world.[2]

This is by no means a popular view. In the Advanced Communication Technologies Laboratory (ACTLab) at the University of Texas at Austin, in which we practiced these ideas as our normal way of doing business, I was frequently accosted by graduate students from other universities who said, "That's not how we do things. I intend to do whatever they tell me to until I get tenure. Then maybe I can do something worthwhile." And that's the last you ever hear of them. Forget "how we do things." Think how *you* do things.

Finally: Be wary of discussing postmodernity from within the modernist paradigm. Because it subverts binarism, refuses closure, and foregrounds multiplicity, trans is a postmodern discourse; yet, perforce, *studies* assumes writing in a language saturated with binarism, closure, and the idea of wholeness that Brian Massumi (1992: 3) translates as molarity;[3] Audre Lorde ([1984] 2007) pointed out that the master's tools will never dismantle the master's house. How to deploy Trans discourse to disrupt modernist critique? We can do better.

Regarding transgender, my worst-case scenario was waking up at about age sixty and realizing *I hadn't done it*—never taken the risk, nor surmounted the fear, nor become who I knew I really was. Which was worse, then: being safe or being me?

Extend that to academia.

Be an academic guerrilla. It won't be easy. In fact, it's virtually guaranteed to be painful, exhausting, and humiliating, but what you gain from sticking with it is your work . . . and your life, by which I mean your ability to fully inhabit your own narrative. Hey, all it takes is all you've got. And isn't that what life is all about?

Allucquére Rosanne "Sandy" Stone is professor emerita and founding director of the Advanced Communication Technologies Laboratory (ACTLab) and the New Media Initiative at the University of Texas at Austin. She is considered a founder of the academic discipline of transgender studies.

Notes

1. The complete line from Horace's *Odes* (III.2.13) is "Dulce et decorum est pro patria mori" (How sweet and fitting it is to die for one's country). The author of this essay hopes the reader sees the irony in this context.
2. OK, as Steve Jobs put it, maybe we settle for just making a dent in the universe. But speaking for myself, "change the world" is not just bloviation; I do really believe that if we do not think in those terms, we are not doing our job.
3. I cannot unpack that in the space I have here; my point is that a critique of multiplicity from a molar perspective is meaningless because the discourses do not intersect.

References

Lorde, Audre. (1984) 2007. "The Master's Tools Will Never Dismantle the Master's House." In *Sister Outsider: Essays and Speeches*, 110–14. Berkeley, CA: Crossing Press.

Massumi, Brian. 1992. *A User's Guide to Capitalism and Schizophrenia: Deviations from Deleuze and Guattari*. Cambridge, MA: MIT Press.

Stone, Sandy. 2013. Foreword to *Feminist and Queer Information Studies Reader*, ed. Patrick Keilty and Rebecca Dean, xii–xvi. Sacramento, CA: Litwin Books.

DOI 10.1215/23289252-2399704

Handmade

JEANNE VACCARO

The handmade is a methodological orientation. It calls for a reconsideration of how we read the body—as text, interpretation of surface, excavation of depth, or dimensional record. To differently value the quantitative event and harness sensory perceptive data, the handmade generates evidence, collectively shared, that we cannot observe by the logics of diagnosis. How, for example, might we access still forms of motion or elastic temporalities? Many gestures of alignment—of making a body in relation to the social—are durational patterns and accidental and unconscious shapes. The handmade confronts the time of event and achievement to illuminate the everyday as a site of value for transgender politics and takes seriously the ordinary feelings and textures of crafting transgender life.

If we are to dislodge transgender from the event of its medicalization and meditate, alternatively, on the handmade dimensionality of experience, what might transgender come to mean? The labor of making transgender identity is handmade: collective—made with and across bodies, objects, and forces of power—a process, unfinished yet enough (process, *not* progress); autonomous choreography; free; do-it-yourself; nongeometrical transformation; freeform. The handmade is a haptic, affective theorization of the transgender body, a mode of animating material experience and accumulative felt matter. As bodily feeling and sensation transform flesh parallel to diagnostic and administrative forces, a handmade orientation foregrounds the work of crafting identity. The material properties of soft and pliable forms of emotional life, skin elasticity, scar tissue, cellular organization, and bodily capacity and dimension operate as a corrective to the limited categories of surface/depth and before/after. Density and texture yield felt knowledge. Labor congeals as residual emotion. Transgender life is made and remade as matter, identity, politics. The handmade generates new evidence of what a body and its difference might be.

Deploying ideas of craft—too frequently dismissed as low art, skilled labor, or "women's work"—the handmade connects transgender to collective process and quotidian aesthetics. Craft is a conceptual limit, categorically unlike the sublime; in Immanuel Kant's ([1790] 2000) aesthetic judgment, it is mere purpose, effect. Maligned in Renaissance hierarchies of liberal and mechanical arts, craft evokes the remunerative, utilitarian, ornamental, and manual labor and laborers—the feminine, ethnic and "primitive." A philosophy that subordinates labor, the manual, and the sense of touch to abstraction, rationality, and the sense of sight operates in a political economy of devaluing bodies. Alternatively, Theodor Adorno theorizes aesthetic function and autonomy as dialectic of fine and applied arts: "Freedom from purpose and purposefulness can never be absolutely separated from one another" ([1965] 1979: 38). In these uneven historical accumulations of value written between bodies and objects, the hand and handmade compel a generative turn to the material. As the material is marginalized by discursive forms of legibility, the performative dimensions of craft privilege the politics of the hand, that which is worked on, and the sensory feelings and textures of crafting transgender identity.

Jeanne Vaccaro is the Andrew W. Mellon Postdoctoral Fellow in Sexuality Studies at the University of Pennsylvania. She is the editor of "The Transbiological Body," a special issue of *Women and Performance: A Journal of Feminist Theory* (2010).

References

Adorno, Theodor. (1965) 1979. "Functionalism Today." *Oppositions* 17, no.: 37–41.
Kant, Immanuel. (1790) 2000. *Critique of the Power of Judgment*. Edited by Paul Guyer. Translated by Paul Guyer and Eric Matthews. Cambridge: Cambridge University Press.

DOI 10.1215/23289252-2399713

Hips

ERICA RAND

Hips contribute to gender expression, attribution, pleasure, policing, frustration, misery, erotics, and joy. They can seem hopelessly immutable in structure or malleable in shape and meaning. They involve purported universals and entrenched particularities, bringing formidable barriers and giddy hope to projects of gender signification.

Hips occupy a place in the unfortunate system of classification that enshrines hierarchized biological features as the essence of sex. Hips are called a "secondary sex characteristic" because they likely widen during estrogen-heavy puberties. Hormones shape gender in the bone. Fat accumulations magnify differences. Colloquialisms exaggerate them. Women have hips, we say; men do not. People become pears or apples.

Yet where bone meets fat, supposed biological destiny meets notions of agency as discipline. A minute on your lips, forever on your hips: hips can signal feminine excess or the insufficient restraint of people brown, "ethnic," zaftig, poor. Vernacular usage also marks biology as inconsistent, unreliable. Adjectives that commonly modify hips have -*like* suffixes, gendering affinity rather than essence, although the two may line up. "Womanly hips" usually attaches to people labeled women, but implies that not all people labeled women have them. Some, instead, have "boyish hips," a phrase that also exists largely to describe people labeled female. (Thus, while "womanly hips," to some, means "childbearing hips," pregnant people, their hips, or both may not be womanly gendered.) Boyish hips often have a showy public presence: in fashion, sport, or when Angie Harmon's hips (and the way she wears her pants) make a butch/femme romance of *Rizzoli and Isles* (TNT 2010–). "Girlish hips," by contrast—except on self-identified girls—live the quieter life of man-tits, as shamefully feminizing fat.

Hips in motion present more evidence for inspection. It is common wisdom that hips can betray you—reveal you or turn on you, sometimes simultaneously. They can show your desires (a staple of porn and the dance floor), your gender, your self. They may swish, switch, or sway as if they could not do otherwise—as if queer, femme, or hot mama were essential identities, uncontrollable moving forces. Or they can display you through haltedness. "My hips just don't move that way," offered in despair, pride, relief.

When it comes to hips, all of the following can matter: the right belt, the right hormones (endogamous, exogamous); stomach, shoulders, thighs, and butt; muscle, food, training; the uniform, the outfit; spandex, padding; disposable income for all of the above; ideas about essence, affinity, and culture working their way separately or together. (I am a natural with that hula hoop. What is that about? Or not about?) The stakes include gender attribution and gendered pleasures. Maybe I want a soft curve or vertical hardness when you put your hands on my hips just so. The wrong hips can be anguish; the right hips divine. "Hips don't lie," Shakira says (Shakira et al. 2006). That depends on what you mean by "lying" and your means to make hips speak for you.

Erica Rand is Whitehouse Professor of Art and Visual Culture and of Women and Gender Studies at Bates College. Her recent publications include "Beyond the Special Guest: Teaching 'Trans' Now," a special issue of *Radical Teacher*, coedited with Shana Agid (winter 2012), and *Red Nails, Black Skates: Gender, Cash, and Pleasure on and off the Ice* (2012).

Reference
Shakira, et al. 2006. "Hips Don't Lie." From Shakira: *Oral Fixation*, vol. 2. Epic.

DOI 10.1215/23289252-2399722

Human Rights

CARSTEN BALZER/CARLA LAGATA

The human rights perspective is a relatively new field for advocacy toward equality for trans and gender-variant people on the global level.

As a recurrence of the horrors of World War II, on December 10, 1948, the Universal Declaration of Human Rights was adopted by the United Nations General Assembly with a count of forty-eight votes (with more than thirty votes from global South and East countries) to none, with only eight abstentions, mostly Soviet Union countries (Yearbook of the United Nations 1948–49: 535). The declaration states, among other things, that "all human beings are born free and equal in dignity and rights" (Universal Declaration of Human Rights: Article 1) and that "everyone is entitled to all the rights and freedoms set forth in this Declaration, without distinction of any kind, such as race, colour, sex, language, religion, political or other opinion, national or social origin, property, birth or other status" (ibid.: Article 2). The historian Samuel Moyn, however, argues that "even in 1968, which the UN declared 'International Human Rights Year,' such rights remained periphal as an organizing concept and almost non-existent as a movement," and that only "over the course of the 1970s, the moral world of Westerners shifted, opening a space for the sort of utopianism that coalesced in an international human rights movement that never existed before" (Moyne 2010: 2, 1). In this context, concerns regarding the dangers of a new kind of colonialism or imperialism were raised.[1]

Whereas in the 1990s the Western concepts "homosexuality" or "sexual orientation" were put on the agenda by international LGB(T) movements, which focused on UN human rights organs (Kollman and Waites 2009: 5)—a process that also led to controversial debates[2]—the inclusion of the concept "gender identity," referring to the concerns of gender-variant and trans people, still had to wait until the next century.[3] It was not before the first decade of the new millennium that a significant change could be observed in the perception and articulation of the concerns of gender-variant/trans people on a global scale. This change can be described as a paradigm shift in the perception and framing of the concerns of gender-variant/trans people. The hitherto dominant and globalized Western medical-psychiatric perspective, which defines gender-variant/trans people as a deviation of an apparently natural binary gender order and thus pathologizes and stigmatizes them[4] is being challenged by a new set of discourses (and engagements) (Balzer 2010).

This new perspective is centered on the social and legal situation of gender-variant/trans people, which is marked by severe human rights violations. On a global scale, these violations encompass, among others: severe forms of hate violence, including hate killings, rape, and torture; criminalization and prose-cution of so-called cross-dressing, so-called cross-gender behavior, and gender reassignment surgery; and prosecution that especially targets trans/gender-variant people without legal basis or based on legislation and legal measures designed for other purposes, such as antiprostitution, antihomosexuality, loitering, or nuisance laws. In addition, several forms of structural and state-sponsored dis-crimination have resulted from decades of Western dissemination of patholo-gizing/stigmatizing discourses (Balzer and Hutta 2012). The new understanding conceives of gender-variant/trans people as equal members of society in the context of the universality of human rights and puts the focus on the human rights violations.

A key indicator of this paradigm shift has been the reception of the Yogyakarta Principles on the Application of International Human Rights Law in relation to Sexual Orientation and Gender Identity, which were drafted and signed by thirty-one international experts (half of them coming from the global South and East) in 2006 in the Indonesian city of Yogyakarta. In the context of the above-mentioned paradigm shift, Principle 18 (Protection from Medical Abuses) is especially important: "No person may be forced to undergo any form of medical or psychological treatment, procedure, testing, or be confined to a medical facility, based on sexual orientation or gender identity. Notwithstanding any classifications to the contrary, a person's sexual orientation and gender identity are not, in and of themselves, medical conditions and are not to be treated, cured or suppressed" (Yogyakarta Principles 2007). The Yogyakarta Principles were cited soon after by United Nations bodies, national courts, and national governments as well as international bodies like the Organization of American States, the Council of Europe, and the European Union. A further key indicator has been the historical UN Human Rights Council resolution on June 17, 2011, the first resolution on sexual orientation and gender identity. The resolution, which was submitted by South Africa along with Brazil, recognized the systematic human rights violations to which LGBT people are subjected worldwide. The paradigm shift is also having an impact on the reform of the *International Classification of Diseases and Related Health Problems* by the World Health Organization in the 2010s (Eisfeld 2014). An indicator of this paradigm shift on the national level is the Argentinean Gender Identity Law, implemented in 2012, which is thoroughly based on a human rights discourse rather than on a medical discourse and therefore is seen as the global best-practice example in regard to legal gender recognition.

Simultaneously, in the 2000s, the rise of new regional and international gender-variant/trans people's movements, networks, and organizations, such as Red Latinoamericano y del Caribe de Personas Trans (2004), Transgender Europe (2005), Pacific Sexual Diversity Network (2007), Asia Pacific Transgender Network (2008), and Global Action for Trans Equality (2010) could be observed, as along with the emergence of a global gender-variant/trans people's movement (Balzer and Hutta 2012). Here it is important to note that the shift toward a human rights paradigm of trans issues and the transnationalization of trans activism have been mutually strengthening.

However, with these significant successes and victories come new challenges. These are external challenges, such as the danger of a backlash stimulated by states and institutions under the discourse of "traditional values," as well as internal challenges such as the need to overcome the dominance of Western discourse, concepts, and practices of gender-variant/trans people's global human rights activism.

Carsten Balzer/Carla LaGata is the senior researcher at Transgender Europe (TGEU) and lead researcher of the "Transrespect versus Transphobia Worldwide" project. S_he is coauthor of *Transrespect versus Transphobia Worldwide—A Comparative Review of the Human-Rights Situation of Gender-Variant/Trans People* (2012).

Notes

1. The philosopher and subaltern studies scholar Gayatri Chakravorty Spivak, for instance, argued that "the idea of human rights, in other words, may carry within itself the agenda of a kind of social Darwinism—the fittest must shoulder the burden of righting the wrongs of the unfit—and the possibility of an alibi . . . for economic, military, and political intervention" (2004: 524).
2. For instance, the sociologist Matthew Waites demanded that "those allied to a broadly conceived 'global queer politics', including many individuals in pro-LGBT, pro-queer and human rights NGOs, legal practitioners, and political activists, need more vigorously to conceptualize, define and situate the concepts—and contest their meanings" (Waites 2009: 153). The sociologists Dana Collins and Molly Talcott point to the dominance of Western concepts and practices and argue that "transnational queer movements embody more profound aspirations in that they do not limit the meaning of queer liberation to singular identity politics or rights-restraining institutions" (Collins and Talcott 2011: 577).
3. The demands and critiques regarding the dominance of Western concepts and practices mentioned above also apply here.
4. This Western medical-psychiatric perspective was already challenged by trans academics and activists as well as by the emergence of the new discipline of transgender studies in Europe and North America in the 1990s. See, for example, Stryker 2006.

References

Balzer, Carsten. 2010. "Eu acho transexual é aquele que disse: 'Eu sou transexual!' Reflexiones etnológicas sobre la medicalización globalizada de las identidades trans a través del ejemplo de Brasil." In *El género desordenado: Críticas en torno a la patologización de la transexualidad*, ed. Miquel Missé and Gerard Coll-Planas, 125–40. Barcelona: Egales Editorial.

Balzer, Carsten, and Jan Simon Hutta. 2012. *Transrespect versus Transphobia Worldwide—A Comparative Review of the Human-Rights Situation of Gender-Variant/Trans People*. With Tamara Adrián, Peter Hyndal, and Susan Stryker. Berlin: Flyeralarm. www.transrespect -transphobia.org/en_US/tvt-project/publications.htm (accessed June 10, 2013).

Collins, Dana, and Molly Talcott. 2011. " 'A New Language That Speaks of Change Just as It Steps toward It': Transnationalism, Erotic Justice, and Queer Human Rights Praxis." *Sociology Compass* 5, no. 7: 579–90.

Eisfeld, Justus. 2014. "*International Statistical Classification of Diseases and Related Health Problems*." TSQ 1, no. 1–2: 107–110.

Kollman, Kelly, and Matthew Waites. 2009. "The Global Politics of Lesbian, Gay, Bisexual, and Transgender Human Rights: An Introduction." *Contemporary Politics* 15, no. 1: 1–17.

Moyne, Samuel. 2010. *The Last Utopia: Human Rights in History*. London: Belknap.

Spivak, Gayatri Chakravorty. 2004. "Righting Wrongs." *South Atlantic Quarterly* 103, no. 2–3: 523–81.

Stryker, Susan. 2006. "(De)Subjugated Knowledges: An Introduction to Transgender Studies." In *The Transgender Studies Reader*, ed. Susan Stryker and Stephen Whittle, 1–18. New York: Routledge.

The Universal Declaration of Human Rights. United Nations. www.un.org/en/documents/udhr (accessed June 10, 2013).

Waites, Matthew. 2009. "Critique of 'Sexual Orientation' and 'Gender Identity' in Human Rights Discourse: Global Queer Politics beyond the Yogyakarta Principles." *Contemporary Politics* 15, no. 1: 137–56.

Yearbook of the United Nations, 1948–49. "Social, Humanitarian, and Cultural Questions." unyearbook.un.org/1948-49YUN/1948-49_P1_CH5.pdf (accessed June 10, 2013).

Yogyakarta Principles. 2007. *The Application of International Human Rights Law in Relation to Sexual Orientation and Gender Identity*. www.yogyakartaprinciples.org/principles_en.pdf (accessed June 10, 2013).

DOI 10.1215/23289252-2399731

Identity

DAVID VALENTINE

"Identity" is two-faced. It is used to represent both intrapsychic states and relational processes: It can be claimed to be both socially constructed and transhistorically essential, a being and a doing, ascribed and attained, made in language and exceeding language, simultaneously intensely private and biographical, a locus for political struggle, and the focus state power. It is formed along multiple historically formed social vectors we call gender, class, race, sexuality, and so on, but it is also, simply, about one's own experience here and now. Judith Butler (1990), Michel Foucault ([1980] 1990), and others have argued forcefully that identity is a product of modern power, arising as a reaction to the demand that the subject identify hirself in the context of modern systems of biopolitical governance, and as such is a site of knowledge production—about the other and about the self. But, as Butler argues, subjective experience rendered as identity elides the biopolitical and contextual conditions of its production, which is precisely what enables its subjective experience as essential and transhistorical, a key modality for the work of biopower.

However, identity has another dual character that underpins the contrasts outlined above: it is both a vernacular and an analytic concept. A descendent of Enlightenment and Romantic concepts, central to modern biopower, and a focus of scholarly attempts at de-essentialization, *identity* circulates also—inevitably, Butler shows—as the modern Western folk theory of essential self. In a direct assault on the use of identity as a trope in social scientific analyses, Rogers Brubaker and Frederick Cooper (2000) argue that identity always (by force of its vernacular currency) implicitly smuggles stable subject positions into critical social scientific analyses—especially along the axes of race, gender, and sexuality—even as scholars argue against such essentialisms. That is, as Brian Massumi (2002) points out, the indexical connotations of identity as fixed and stable follow social theorists into their deconstructive texts.

So what then might we, as analysts, learn from those who do *not* have a socially speakable identity in the vernacular sense—that is, those whose subjective experiences are not (yet) hailed by forms of biopower that require a response from the subject? This counterintuitive question emerged during online research with cisgendered men about their sexual attraction to preoperative or nonoperative transgender women (I refer to them as men who have sex with transgender women, or MSTW). Joanne Meyerowitz (2002) shows how, in the heyday of mid-twentieth-century transsexual medicine, doctors had to be convinced of a transsexual woman's postsurgical heterosexual identity as the central sign of "true" transsexual identity. It is surprising, then, how little attention has been paid to transgender people's cisgendered sexual partners and *their* identities; a comprehensive review of this literature would be possible in a regular journal-length article. Almost universally, however, the extant literature focuses almost entirely on the identity dilemmas of cisgendered partners in *existing* relationships with people who come out as transgender, especially the partners of MTF (male-to-female) transgender-identified people (some exceptions are Devor 1997; Mauk 2008).

In short, there is very little discussion of cisgendered women or men who actively eroticize transgender embodiment (i.e., what would usually be referred to as their "sexual identity"). If the latter have any kind of name, it is "admirer" or "tranny chaser," terms that are broadly used about these men but almost universally rejected by MSTW study participants. Instead, in focus groups and interviews, MSTW actively sought normative terms that did not invoke "identity" per se to describe themselves: "The term I truly prefer is gentleman," wrote one, another suggesting "normal." When pushed to talk explicitly about sexual identity, MSTW almost unanimously called themselves "heterosexual" or "bisexual," though a very specifically configured bisexuality. One participant wrote: "Bisexuality doesn't suit me," because it implies attraction to men and women. "I'm not attracted to men at all, only women and transwomen." Almost all the men we interviewed denied homosexual identity, arguing that the object of their desire was *femininity*, irrespective of their partner's embodiment.

However, the dilemma for the men is that their desire for feminine-identifying sexual partners who have penises is culturally conceivable only in terms of closeted homosexuality; indeed, even the transwomen we interviewed frequently made this claim. MSTW participants, recognizing this, expressed dissatisfaction with "labeling" and the possibility of homosexual identification: "Why is it that when a man likes a transwoman that he has to be labeled something?" one complained. The answer is, of course, that sexuality is, as Foucault ([1980] 1990) has argued, perhaps the most elemental form of identity in the modern West. But the men's claims that sex with transwomen was an element of their heterosexuality or just something that they *did* (two common claims) are not conceivable in the vernacular terms of identity, and it is identity that is seen as the outcome of sexual desire and practice.

I would argue, then, that MSTW do not have an identity in that the power of genital determination makes their desires conceivable (and hailable) only as "homosexuality," a possibility they reject. Of course, they are still assimilable into the narrative power of sexual identity through that hailing, but the configuration of bodies, body parts, and language introduces an interruption into the hailing process. Indeed, I would suggest that the dearth of complex discussion of MSTW desire in the scholarly literature derives precisely from the fact that they cannot be accounted for in these vernacular/biopolitical terms, and so their erotic projects must be either ignored, dismissed, or explained away, even by critical scholars who seek to undermine identity as an agent of biopower. That is, MSTW are not "outside" power; rather, the demand of power for easy recognition through the hetero/homo–male/female binary complex is interrupted by the unexpectedness of these embodied and subjective arrangements.

Brubaker and Cooper claim that it is not clear why human social practices and meanings around self and other should at all be conceptualized as producing identity as their end goal (2000: 6). As I have argued, the reason is that identity is key to biopower's naturalized vernacular, a vernacular that MSTW desire interrupts, even if just for a moment. One task for transgender studies, then, I argue, is to exploit this interruption and dispense with identity as an analytic trope, for even when we show it to be contingent and multiple (or combat it by calling on affect or history or culture), its vernacular meanings are powerful indexical remainders that draw on the systems of power we seek to open up. Identity fails when there is complexity: but surely it is the case that all humans have lifeworlds too complex to be accounted for by the restrictive ontologies of identity and its implication in biopolitical systems of power. Jettisoning "identity" may, indeed, be necessary in order to open up the full consequences of its role in shaping modern selves, a task for which transgender studies is well suited.

David Valentine is an associate professor of anthropology at the University of Minnesota. He is the author of *Imagining Transgender: An Ethnography of a Category* (2007).

Note

The research on which this essay is based draws on the NICHD-sponsored project, Gender Identity and HIV Risk II, Walter Bockting, principal investigator. I thank Walter Bockting, Jamie Feldman, and Bean Robinson for allowing me to participate in this project.

References

Brubaker, Rogers, and Frederick Cooper. 2000. "Beyond 'Identity.'" *Theory and Society* 29, no. 1: 1–47.

Butler, Judith. 1990. *Gender Trouble: Feminism and the Subversion of Identity*. New York: Routledge.

Devor, Aaron. 1997. *FTM: Female-to-Male Transsexuals in Society*. Bloomington: Indiana University Press.

Foucault, Michel. (1980) 1990. *An Introduction*. Vol. 1 of *The History of Sexuality*. Translated by Robert Hurley. New York: Vintage.

Massumi, Brian. 2002. *Parables for the Virtual: Movement, Affect, Sensation*. Durham, NC: Duke University Press.

Mauk, Daniel. 2008. "Stigmatized Desires: An Ethnography of Men in New York City Who Have Sex with Non-operative Transgender Women." PhD diss., Columbia University.

Meyerowitz, Joanne. 2002. *How Sex Changed: A History of Transsexuality in the United States*. Cambridge, MA: Harvard University Press.

DOI 10.1215/23289252-2399749

International Statistical Classification of Diseases and Related Health Problems

JUSTUS EISFELD

The *International Statistical Classification of Diseases and Related Health Problems* (*ICD*) is, as the name states, a collection of diseases and health problems compiled by the World Health Organization (2012). At the same time, it is also the basis for payments for health care in virtually all countries in the world. And therein lies the problem for trans★ people.[1]

The current edition, *ICD*-10, lists "Gender Identity Disorders" in the section covering "Disorders of Adult Personality and Behaviour," in the chapter "Mental and Behavioural Disorders." Other disorders that can affect trans★ people and that are listed in the same section are "Disorders of Sexual Preference" and "Psychological and Behavioural Disorders Associated with Sexual Development and Orientation." As many trans★ activists have pointed out, trans★ people's identities are not diseases and should not be pathologized (GATE 2012a; Winters 2008, 2012a, 2012b; STP, International Campaign Stop Trans Pathologization 2012). At the same time, some trans★ people want and need access to trans★-specific healthcare. This is one issue that comes up again and again in research on problems faced by trans★ people: access to healthcare, and especially access to transition-related healthcare (Winter 2012; Grant et al. 2011; Council of Europe 2011; Motmans 2009; Kisia and Wahu 2010; Whittle, Turner, and Al-Alami 2007; Keuzenkamp 2012; Bones Rocha et al. 2009; Alisheva, Aleshkina, and Buhuceanu 2007; Human Rights Commission Te Kāhui Tika Tangata 2007).

These needs are a seeming contradiction; the *ICD* is a gateway for some trans★ people to access rights such as funded transition-related healthcare, which relies on an *ICD* code, while preventing others (or even the same people) from accessing other rights, because the *ICD* acts as a gatekeeper, such as with access to legal gender recognition, which is often dependent on a diagnosis of gender identity disorder (Balzer and Hutta 2012, Transgender Europe 2012). A best-practice model solving the seeming contradiction at the national level is the Argentinian Gender Identity Law, especially Articles 4 and 11.[2]

On top of that is the critique of the view of trans* people's transition-related healthcare needs as a disorder versus a variation of the human race that may or may not need medical attention. As large parts of the medical field are based on the assumption of disorder (as the *International Classification of Disorders* certainly is), this is a continuing ideological struggle between, on one hand, the label "disorder" with the usual power imbalance that accompanies it (doctors get to put the label of disorder on patients, for example—and never the other way around), and on the other hand, criticism of that imbalance from critical health care voices and users of health services.

The current diagnostic codes used for trans* people are also subject to abuse: in some countries (for example, Norway [Helsedirektoratet 2012]), only trans* people diagnosed with the code F64.0, "Transsexualism," are allowed to access treatment, while others (for example, people diagnosed with F64.8—"Other Gender Identity Disorders") are not. The diagnosis itself can take bizarre forms; for example, a month-long hospitalization in a mental health hospital (Insight NGO 2010).

One of the most challenging issues is the very need to include trans* health issues in the next *ICD* edition, *ICD*-11. That inclusion must be a reference or a set of references not based in illness and, at the same time, able to create a path to health care, public or private insurance coverage, and legal recognition of trans* people's identities.

Taking into account this last and seemingly unavoidable connection between diagnosis and health care coverage, other questions arise: what kind of diagnosis would be needed?

There are several, sometimes conflicting, demands on what a future *ICD* code must be able to achieve. On one hand, it must be phrased in neutral language to be usable in places where transphobia in health cost reimbursements is rampant, where any reference to trans* issues could lead to an automatic exclusion of the procedure or the person from coverage. On the other hand, in other places, trans*-specific codes are either needed for legal gender recognition or could be useful for scientific purposes (i.e., research into side effects or long-term effects of hormone use). A code must be broad enough to cover those trans* people who need access to specific services while procedures get refined and needs may change over time, yet it must not be so broad as to cover all trans* people irrespective of their actual need for health care. Some codes also need to give clues for treatment to those doctors who are willing to help trans* people but do not know how.

In order to fulfill all these requirements, GATE (Global Action for Trans* Equality) proposed what we called a starfish model, which we described as a decentralized system of codes that can be used together or independently, depending on the local situation (GATE 2012a). We named it for the starfish, which has a decentralized nervous system. Essentially, a trans*-specific code would be placed in a section of the *ICD* that also houses uncomplicated pregnancy and other factors influencing health and health status. This code would then refer out to other, non–trans*-specific codes in, for example, the endocrinologic and genito-urinary parts of the *ICD*, codes that could be used for trans* people but also for other patients. One example would be "Testosterone Deficiency" or "Absence/Presence of Vagina." These nonspecific codes could be used either as stand-alone codes or in combination with the trans* specifier, depending on the local conditions.

Justus Eisfeld is a codirector of GATE—Global Action for Trans* Equality. He is coauthor of *The State of Trans* and Intersex Organizing: A Case for Increased Support for Growing but Under-Funded Movements for Human Rights* (2013).

Notes

I would like to acknowledge the work of GATE's codirector Mauro Cabral in developing many of the concepts on which this text is based as well as his help in drafting this text and his leadership in GATE's work on the *ICD* reform. Furthermore, I would like to thank the members of GATE's *ICD* working group for their critical thinking and input in GATE's work.

1. The international trans* organization Global Action for Trans* Equality (GATE) uses the term *trans** to name those people who identify themselves in a different gender than that assigned to them at birth and/or those people who feel they have to, prefer to, or choose to present themselves differently from the expectations associated with the gender role assigned to them at birth—whether by clothing, accessories, cosmetics, or body modification. This includes, among many others, people who identify as transsexual and transgender, transvestite, travesti, hijra, cross-dresser, fa'afafine, two-spirit, no gender, third sex, or genderqueer. The term *trans** should be understood as a political umbrella term that encompasses many different and culturally specific experiences of embodiment, identity, and expression. The asterisk aims to make its open-ended character explicit.

2. A translation of the law was provided by GATE (2012b).

References

Alisheva, Djamilya, Julia Aleshkina, and Florin Buhuceanu. 2007. *Access to Health Care for LGBT People in Kyrgyzstan*. New York: Open Society Institute.

Balzer, Carsten, and Jan Simon Hutta, eds. 2012. *Transrespect versus Transphobia Worldwide: A Comparative Review of the Human-Rights Situation of Gender-Variant/Trans people*. Berlin: Transgender Europe.

Bones Rocha, Kátia, et al. 2009. "La atención a la salud en Brasil a partir de la percepción de travestis, transexuales y transgéneros." *Forum: Qualitative Social Research* 10, no. 2, art. 28. nbn-resolving.de/urn:nbn:de:0114-fqs0902281.

Council of Europe. 2011. *Discrimination on Grounds of Sexual Orientation and Gender Identity in Europe*. Strasbourg: Council of Europe Publishing.

GATE—Global Action for Trans* Equality. 2012a. *It's Time for Reform: Trans* Health Issues in the International Classification of Diseases.* transactivists.org/2012/05/20/94 (accessed December 10, 2012).

———. 2012b. "English Translation of Argentina's Gender Identity Law as Approved by the Senate of Argentina on May 8, 2012." globaltransaction.files.wordpress.com/2012/05/argentina -gender-identity-law.pdf (accessed September 6, 2013).

Grant, Jaime M., et al. 2011. *Injustice at Every Turn: A Report of the National Transgender Discrimination Survey.* Washington, DC: National Center for Transgender Equality and National Gay and Lesbian Task Force.

Helsedirektoratet. 2012. *Gjennomgang av behandlingstilbudet til transseksuelle og transpersoner.* Letter to Helse- og omsorgsdepartementet. October 1.

Human Rights Commission Te Kāhui Tika Tangata. 2007. *To Be Who I Am: Report of the Inquiry into Discrimination Experienced by Transgender People / Kia noho au ki tōku anō ao: He Pūrongo mō te Uiuitanga mō Aukatitanga e Pāngia ana e ngā Tāngata Whakawhitiira.* Auckland: Human Rights Commission Te Kāhui Tika Tangata.

Insight NGO. 2010. "Situation of Transgender Persons in Ukraine." Kiev: Insight NGO.

Keuzenkamp, Saskia. 2012. *Worden wie je bent. Het leven van transgenders in Nederland.* The Hague: Sociaal en Cultureel Planbureau.

Kisia, Andiah, and Milka Wahu. 2010. *A People Condemned—The Human Rights Status of Lesbians, Gays, Bisexual, Transgender, and Intersex Persons in East Africa 2009–2010.* Nairobi: UHAI.

Motmans, Joz. 2009. *Being Transgender in Belgium: Mapping the Social and Legal Situation of Transgender People.* Brussels: Institute for the Equality of Women and Men.

STP, International Campaign Stop Trans Pathologization. 2012. "Manifesto." stp2012.info/old/en /manifesto (accessed December 10, 2012).

Transgender Europe. 2012. "First Mapping of Legal and Health Care Situation of Trans People in 58 Countries." www.transrespect-transphobia.org/en_US/mapping.htm (accessed December 10, 2012).

Whittle, Stephen, Lewis Turner, and Maryam Al-Alami. 2007. *Engendered Penalties: Transgender and Transsexual People's Experiences of Inequality and Discrimination.* Wetherby, UK: Communities and Local Government.

Winter, Sam. 2012. *Lost in Transition: Transgender People, Rights, and HIV Vulnerability in the Asia-Pacific Region.* Bangkok: UNDP.

Winters, Kelley. 2008. *Gender Madness in American Psychiatry: Essays from the Struggle for Dignity.* Dillon, CO: Booksurge.

———. 2012a. "Third Swing: My Comments to the APA for a Less Harmful Gender Dysphoria Category in the DSM-5." GID Reform Weblog. gidreform.wordpress.com/2012/06/19 /third-swing-my-comments-to-the-apa-for-a-less-harmful-gender-dysphoria-category -in-the-dsm-5 (accessed December 10, 2012).

———. 2012b. "An Update on Gender Diagnoses, as the DSM-V Goes to Press." GID Reform Weblog. gidreform.wordpress.com/2012/12/05/an-update-on-gender-diagnoses-as-the -dsm-5-goes-to-press (accessed December 10, 2012).

World Health Organization. 2012. "*ICD*-10 Version:2010." *International Statistical Classification of Diseases and Related Health Problems.* apps.who.int/classifications/icd10/browse/2010/en (accessed December 10, 2012).

DOI 10.1215/23289252-2399740

Intersex

IAIN MORLAND

Sometimes individuals are born with genital, genetic, or hormonal characteristics that some people find confusing. From this phenomenon of "intersex," a range of claims and counterclaims have flowed regarding sexual difference, medicine, gender, and identity.

Intersex was coined in 1915 by the zoologist Richard Goldschmidt to describe moths with atypical sex characteristics (Stern 1967: 156). The definition was soon extended to encompass several types of human "hermaphroditism," but the latter word remained in circulation as a medical diagnosis throughout the twentieth century. Intersex is often popularly conflated with ambiguous genitalia—external sexual anatomy that cannot be easily described as entirely female or male, such as a larger-than-typical clitoris. However, for clinicians, an intersex diagnosis can refer also to attributes that are not apparent on the body's surface, including XXY sex chromosomes or indifference to the hormones that produce effects connotative of masculinity. What such intersex diagnoses have in common is the medicalization of a failure to classify the body as one of two sexes. That such a failure would be problematic is not obvious, nor is its medicalization; nonetheless, medical treatment of intersex is standard practice in the West. Treatment typically begins in childhood, even in infancy. It can extend over a lifetime in the case of hormonal interventions or repeated genital surgeries, despite assurances from generations of clinicians that the latest medical techniques will eradicate intersex before an individual is aware of it.

Within the last decade, medical guidelines have shifted to recommend psychological support and disclosure by default (Hughes et al. 2006: 154), but the extent to which these guidelines have been put into practice remains disappointingly unclear. After all, seminal clinical protocols from the 1950s made similar recommendations, yet led to decades of secrecy toward patients. The older protocols fostered a tenacious belief among many doctors and parents that genital surgery is a kind of preemptive psychological treatment, on the grounds that an individual's sense of gender will follow from the experience of having a dichotomously sexed anatomy. Several assumptions were implicit in this belief—that having an unambiguous and univalent gender is desirable; that it is better not to reflect consciously on the formation of one's gender; and, in turn, that early medical treatment can promote healthy gender development by averting conscious reflection on the formation of one's gender and its relationship (if any) to one's sexual anatomy. Taking these assumptions to their extreme, some clinicians have even argued that parents who fail to arrange early genital surgery for their sexually ambiguous offspring are guilty of child neglect (Rossiter and Diehl 1998: 61).

The architect of the traditional treatment protocols, psychologist John Money, was also an influential advocate of elective genital surgery for transsexual individuals. Consequently, an unresolved contradiction existed between Money's insistence that gender always develops in response to one's sex anatomy during childhood and his recognition that for transsexual individuals, gender develops divergently from the expectations set by one's anatomy (Diamond 1999: 1022). This contradiction facilitated the emergence during the late 1950s and early 1960s of a medical consensus over intersex treatment, for it gave Money's gender theory the fashionable appearance of being "interactional" in its refusal to polarize nature and nurture. Really, it was a theory composed of irreconcilable propositions (Downing, Morland, and Sullivan, forthcoming).

Nevertheless, the significance of Money's theory and its implications for clinical practice cannot be overstated, because the term *gender* itself was coined by him. It was a response to learning about an individual whose genital appearance was "feminine" due to intersex development and who was a doctor, husband, and father by adoption (Money 1973: 397). The ostensible discrepancy between this individual's masculine position in language and his sexual anatomy inspired Money to find a word for the former that reflected its difference from the latter. Money chose *gender* because the word connoted the arbitrariness of sexed pronouns in linguistics. Strangely, though, in the very article in which Money first used *gender* in its new sense, he also unveiled his signature recommendation that the treatment of intersex should eliminate any such discrepancy between an individual's gender and genitalia (1955: 254, 257).

Of course, one need not choose between an account of gender as determined by genital appearance and gender as an effect of language. I would say, following Michel Foucault's analysis of sexuality (1978: 155), that gender names one of many ways in which power—including medical power—grips bodies to produce individuals who are at once constrained and enabled by norms. To claim to belong (or not) to a gender is to orient oneself normatively in relation to others, seeking recognition for behaviors, attributes, and sensations that one regards as important, rather than to make a descriptive claim about one's genitalia. However, Money neither liked nor understood Foucault's work (Money 1998: 106–7), and to this day, medical sexology remains largely disengaged from relevant debates in the humanities over gender and the constitution of the self.

For instance, one large clinical team has asserted that medicine's task during the neonatal period is "to select a gender able to match the individual identity (II) of the child (which is invisible during this period), the social identity (SI) (which is the way 'society' looks at the individual and the only tangible identity approachable after birth) and the behavioural identity (BI), which is not formed yet" (Vidal et al. 2010: 312). This vague enterprise—where something invisible is aligned with something unformed in order to match something social (and where the enclosure of "society" in quotation marks suggests a lack of precision around that term too)—is not an acceptable rationale for medical treatment, especially where such treatment is irreversible. It is unscientific also, insofar as its success cannot be measured, merely inferred from the retrospective presumption that treatment has foreclosed "unbearable situations for the parents and the child" (ibid.).

I recognize that some parents of intersex infants are anxious to prevent, for example, people peering over their shoulders at their child's genitalia during diaper changing (Gough et al. 2008: 500). Yet it is surely never appropriate to scrutinize the genitalia of another person's child. The way to stop such behavior is to shame those who do it rather than to perform surgery. Treatment shames the child by suggesting that the problem is not the uninvited act of looking but the anatomy that is seen. Here is another key reason why the medicalization of intersex is a fundamentally erroneous project: it mistakes social norms and their transgression for properties of bodies, which can be modified or disambiguated through clinical interventions. But ambiguity is an interpretation, not a trait; and one cannot do surgery on a norm.

Further, the efforts by clinicians and families to eliminate intersex have traditionally entailed the strenuous production of silences—about hospital visits, scars, parental fears, injections, and even years of childhood—that actively create intersex as a state of strangeness rather than securing its removal from discourse. The experience of treatment as simultaneously objectionable and ineffective has been a central complaint of the intersex rights movement since its inception in the early 1990s (Chase 1998: 197–203). Consequently, activists have reappropriated intersex as an identity. To identify as intersex is to assert both that treatment does not work, insofar as medical interventions amplify the strangeness of one's intersex attributes, and that treatment should not be done at all, insofar as it discriminates against individuals on the basis of immutable characteristics. Such activism reveals that power never wholly grips or disciplines the body but produces opportunities for resistance to medicalization.

A collaborative effort in 2005 by patient advocates and clinicians to replace the medical terms *intersex* and *hermaphrodite* with *disorders of sex development* has highlighted the inseparability of power and resistance. To some commentators, the new nomenclature has usefully refocused doctors' attention on those phenomena that, unlike gender, can benefit demonstratively from medical intervention—such as a reduction in the risk of gonadal tumors or the facilitation of fertility. To others, the phrase *disorders of sex development* has nullified the advances made in the name of intersex activism and cast as disordered or disabled those individuals for whom intersex remains an identity (Reis 2007: 538). These contrasting outcomes are not mutually exclusive. Moreover, *intersex* continues to circulate among patient activists and humanities scholars. To exaggerate the capacity of medicine to determine the meaning of sexual atypicality would amplify medical power even while seeking to resist it.

In the context of trans studies, both intersex and transsexuality raise the question of what kind of body one needs to have in order to claim membership in a gender and whether a person's sense of belonging to a gender is colored by the experience of living in a body that has been touched by medical technology. Sometimes intersex and transsexuality have been construed as complementary examples of gender's construction—where the former shows gender's assemblage by force, and the latter its alteration by free will. But that analysis assumes the success of most intersex treatment and fails to account for the continuity of identity experienced by many trans individuals before and after medical treatment. Encounters with medicine neither cause trans people to change gender nor cause intersex individuals to acquire gender in the first place. Future scholarship might situate medical claims to treat intersex within the emerging canon of failure studies and help to divert academic and activist critiques of intersex medicine from that same disillusioning destination.

Iain Morland, PhD, has published more than a dozen scholarly essays on the ethics, psychology, and politics of intersex. He edited the *GLQ* issue "Intersex and After" (2009) and is coauthor with Lisa Downing and Nikki Sullivan of *Fuckology: Critical Essays on John Money's Diagnostic Concepts* (forthcoming).

References

Chase, Cheryl. 1998. "Hermaphrodites with Attitude: Mapping the Emergence of Intersex Political Activism." *GLQ* 4, no. 2: 189–211.

Diamond, Milton. 1999. "Pediatric Management of Ambiguous and Traumatized Genitalia." *Journal of Urology* 162, no. 3: 1021–28.

Downing, Lisa, Iain Morland, and Nikki Sullivan. Forthcoming. *Fuckology: Critical Essays on John Money's Diagnostic Concepts.* Chicago: University of Chicago Press.

Foucault, Michel. 1978. *The Will to Knowledge.* Vol. 1 of *The History of Sexuality.* Translated by Robert Hurley. Harmondsworth: Penguin.

Gough, Brendan, et al. 2008. "'They Did Not Have a Word': The Parental Quest to Locate a 'True Sex' for Their Intersex Children." *Psychology and Health* 23, no. 4: 493–507.

Hughes, Ieuan A., et al. 2006. "Consensus Statement on Management of Intersex Disorders." *Journal of Pediatric Urology* 2, no. 3: 148–62.

Money, John. 1955. "Hermaphroditism, Gender, and Precocity in Hyperadrenocorticism: Psychologic Findings." *Bulletin of the Johns Hopkins Hospital* 96, no. 6: 253–64.

———. 1973. "Gender Role, Gender Identity, Core Gender Identity: Usage and Definition of Terms." *Journal of the American Academy of Psychoanalysis* 1, no. 4: 397–402.

———. 1998. *Sin, Science, and the Sex Police: Essays on Sexology and Sexosophy.* Amherst, NY: Prometheus.

Reis, Elizabeth. 2007. "Divergence or Disorder? The Politics of Naming Intersex." *Perspectives in Biology and Medicine* 50, no. 4: 535–43.

Rossiter, Katherine, and Shonna Diehl. 1998. "Gender Reassignment in Children: Ethical Conflicts in Surrogate Decision Making." *Pediatric Nursing* 24, no. 1: 59–62.

Stern, Curt. 1967. *Richard Benedict Goldschmidt, 1878–1958.* Washington, DC: National Academy of Sciences.

Vidal, Isabelle, et al. 2010. "Surgical Options in Disorders of Sex Development (DSD) with Ambiguous Genitalia." *Best Practice and Research Clinical Endocrinology and Metabolism* 24, no. 2: 311–24.

DOI 10.1215/23289252-2399758

Islam and Islamophobia

RÜSTEM ERTUĞ ALTINAY

In the Qur'an, the rules of permissible social conduct are organized according to a dimorphic gender paradigm. The only verse that references nonnormative gender is in a passage regulating Muslim women's social encounters with men (Qur'an 24:31). The verse states that women need not follow the usual rules of modesty when in the presence of male attendants who are free of sexual desires and who employ bodily and linguistic codes generally associated with women (Haneef 2011: 101). Female-to-male transgenderism is mentioned only in the hadith (sayings and acts ascribed to the prophet Mohammad), which contains several examples of transphobia, such as: "Narrated by Abu Hurairah: The Apostle of Allah cursed the man who dressed like a woman and the woman who dressed like a man" (Imam Abu Dawud, bk. 027, no. 4087).

Feminist and queer interpretations of Islam counter such transphobic, homophobic, and patriarchal elements in the hadith by contesting its reliability as a source of Islamic knowledge and jurisprudence. Some scholars attempt to resolve the conflict between what has been interpreted as the acceptance of transgender people in the Qur'an versus the explicit transphobia of the hadith by attributing different motivations to transgender expression: on one hand, it may be possible simply to acknowledge an innate (God-given) gender identity, while on the other hand it may be necessary to condemn a deliberate deviation from gender norms for the purpose of transgressing Islamic rules of conduct—particularly for engaging in forbidden sexual behavior (Haneef 2011: 101). Accordingly, while a desexualized transgender subject may enjoy a certain level of social acceptance, those who express a purportedly deviant sexual desire are highly stigmatized, particularly if they engage in what is perceived as same-sex intercourse. It is worth noting that male and female same-sex desires and practices have different historical genealogies in Islam (Najmabadi 2011: 536–37), and in most sociohistorical contexts male same-sex practices have been stigmatized and criminalized more severely. As Afsaneh Najmabadi argues for the case of contemporary Iran, this stigma also affects many transwomen's lives (ibid.: 536).

Unlike sex *assignment* operations for congenital intersex conditions, which are generally considered to be legitimate, sex *reassignment* operations for transgender people are more controversial in Islam. In Islamic bioethics, persons have only limited autonomy over their own bodies, which are understood to have been given to them in trust by their creator, Allah. Within this paradigm, sex reassignment operations are forbidden to the extent that they are framed as self-inflicted physical injuries or unnecessary cosmetic procedures that have long-term negative effects on the patient's physical and psychological well-being. The main opponents of reassignment procedures are Sunni jurists who argue that such operations amount to a repudiation of Allah's will and that they constitute a form of deceit (Haneef 2011: 102–3). The proponents of the procedure, primarily Shi'ah imams and a minority of Sunni jurists, emphasize the Islamic principle that "necessity overrides prohibition" (ibid.). These proponents typically employ a pathologizing discourse to argue that sex reassignment operations are not cosmetic procedures but, rather, necessary treatments to cure a legitimate medical condition. This framework has been particularly influential in Shi'ah-dominated Iran, where medical sex reassignment is subsidized by the state and bears a complex relationship to the heteronormalization of people with same-sex desires and practices (Najmabadi 2011: 534–35).

Transsexuality's complicated status in Iran is frequently represented in the West by the reductive caricature of a Muslim fundamentalism that forces gays to change sex; it thereby offers a prime example of the orientalism and Islamophobia, so prevalent among Western LGBT communities, against which many Muslim trans and queer people have to contend. Nationalist discourses that frame

Islam and Islamicate societies as uniquely transphobic, homophobic, ignorant, and backward serve the myth of Western exceptionalism and legitimize various forms of violence and oppression—from military intervention in the Middle East to racial profiling of Arabs and Muslims in Europe and the United States.

Similar Islamophobic discourses also exist in the Middle East and its diaspora, particularly among secularist and/or non-Muslim communities. The most debated example of the phenomenon is the practice of "pink-washing" in Israel. Israel maintains relatively LGBT-friendly social policies, which it advertises internationally to project an image of itself as a liberal haven in a Middle East dominated by phobic and reactionary Islamic forces. This tolerant, democratic, and progressive image is then used to counter criticism of Israel's repressive actions toward Palestine (Puar 2011). As a result, the problems experienced by LGBT people living in Islamicate contexts become instrumentalized to serve their oppression.

Leftist activist, academic, and public debates on LGBT normativity, nationalism, and conservatism tend to focus on Israeli pink-washing, post-9/11 border securitization and surveillance in the United States, and antimigrant sentiment in Europe, in order to rhetorically mobilize Muslim LGBT people as the victims of these practices and policies. Nevertheless, conservative discourses also exist in various forms among Muslim LGBT communities, ranging from anti-Semitism and sectarianism to militarism and ultranationalism. As demonstrated by the case of Bulent Ersoy, the popular Turkish trans diva whose public acceptability has been predicated on her embrace of conservative notions of Muslim Turkish womanhood, Muslim trans identities and subjectivities emerge within complex sociopolitical dynamics. As is the case elsewhere, they may operate on one level as a strategy for surviving a phobic context, while on another level they perpetuate forms of oppression at the expense of other individuals and communities (Altınay 2008).

Gender and sexuality play central regulatory roles in everyday life in Islam, including the embodied codes of worship. Hence, having a trans subjectivity necessarily shapes the experience of Islam for trans people. To gain insights into this dynamic experience, it is important to acknowledge the intersectional diversity inherent in the category of the Muslim transgender subject. Understanding Islam and Islamophobia in the context of transgender studies requires us to analyze how new subject positions emerge and how they become available to trans bodies under specific sociohistorical and political circumstances. It is necessary not simply to understand Islam but to understand Islam within broader matrices of power, in entanglement with other disciplinary mechanisms and meaning-making paradigms.

Rüstem Ertuğ Altınay is a doctoral candidate in the Department of Performance Studies at New York University. His articles on gender, sexuality, and the politics of embodiment in Turkey have been published in various peer-reviewed journals and edited volumes.

References

Altınay, Rüstem Ertuğ. 2008. "Reconstructing the Transgendered Self as a Muslim, Nationalist, Upper-Class Woman: The Case of Bulent Ersoy." *Women's Studies Quarterly* 36, no. 3–4: 210–29.

Haneef, Sayed Sikandar Shah. 2011. "Sex Reassignment in Islamic Law: The Dilemma of Transsexuals." *International Journal of Business, Humanities, and Technology* 1, no. 1: 98–107.

Imam Abu Dawud. 1990. *Sunan Abu Dawud*. Translated by Ahmad Hasan. New Delhi: Kitab Bhavan.

Najmabadi, Afsaneh. 2011. "Verdicts of Science, Rulings of Faith: Transgender/Sexuality in Contemporary Iran." *Social Research* 78, no. 2: 533–56.

Puar, Jasbir. 2011. "Citation and Censorship: The Politics of Talking about the Sexual Politics of Israel." *Feminist Legal Studies* 19, no. 2: 133–42.

The Qur'an. 2005. Translated by M. A. S. Abdel Haleem. Oxford: Oxford University Press.

DOI 10.1215/23289252-2399767

LGBT

ZEIN MURIB

The ubiquitous use of the LGBT initialism across various social, academic, and political discursive contexts in the United States suggests that the constitutive categories of lesbian, gay, bisexual, and transgender are equivalent, informed by similar experiences, and, as such, appropriate to collapse into a single category: LGBT. This brief analysis of LGBT, or what Dean Spade (2004: 53) incisively dubs "LGB-fake-T," highlights the ways in which its consolidation and subsequent circulation produce troubling exclusions and marginalizations when it is taken to represent a cohesive collection of identities and political interests.

Denaturalizing the presumed coherence of LGBT requires attention to how the constitutive categories of lesbian, gay, bisexual, and transgender have been linked to concepts of gender and sexuality. Joanne J. Meyerowitz (2002), in her history of transsexuality in the United States, traces the processes through which doctors after World War II began to theorize sex as biological, gender as socially shaped, and sexuality as desire.[1] Nan Boyd's 2003 history of queer San Francisco furnishes a useful analysis of how these theoretical distinctions between gender and sexuality later influenced assimilationist lesbian and gay political groups, some of which made concerted efforts to align their respective identities exclusively with private expressions of same-sex desire (i.e., sexuality) and away from public expressions of nonnormative gender. The emergence of a seemingly bounded transgender category in the 1990s that attends these increasingly rigid conceptualizations of gay and lesbian categories is compellingly argued by David Valentine (2007) to enable imagining gender variance outside the categories of lesbian and gay, the result of which was the construction of white, gender-nor-mative lesbian and gay subjects, a construction that poses transgender people, butches, queens, cross-dressers, working-class bar-goers, queer people of color, and all combinations thereof as deviant, or other.

It is from this brief overview that the question of how LGBT began to circulate arises. During the late 1990s and early 2000s, some transgender activists in the United States argued that they ought to be included in the mobilizations of mainstream lesbian and gay political groups. They cited the policing of normative femininity and masculinity as the roots of the discrimination that they were fighting, the violence of which is equally directed at transgender people, lesbian women, and gay men. In response, and perhaps seeing the value of demonstrating a commitment to diversity and inclusion within a liberal, rights-based political context, various lesbian and gay groups amended their titles and mission statements to claim that they serve the lesbian, gay, bisexual, and transgender, or LGBT, communities.

Though some consider LGBT utopian in its commitment to inclusion and representation, its widespread use has also been subject to strong critiques that depart from the position that listing lesbian, gay, bisexual, and transgender identities in the LGBT initialism poses them as discrete, ordered categories. For instance, Susan Stryker (2008: 148) argues that listing "T" with "LGB"—and at the end, no less—locates transgender as an orientation. In other words, LGBT priv-ileges the expression of sexual identity over gender identity, the result of which is the conflation of transgender with desire rather than with expressions of gender that inflect sexuality. The paradox of LGBT, then, is that although the inclusion of transgender alongside lesbian, gay, and bisexual opened up new political alliances across these groups, it also closed off possibilities for coalitions with different political groups—such as activists fighting for immigrant rights who face con-cerns over documentation that are similar to those of transgender people—by naturalizing sexuality as the similarity that binds lesbian, gay, bisexual, and transgender groups together.

Zein Murib is a PhD candidate in political science at the University of Minnesota whose dissertation traces the historical and political processes through which "LGBT" evolved as a political identity category in the United States between 1970 and 2010.

Note

1.   The relationship of sexuality to gender has been actively taken up by feminists and queer theorists as well. See Judith Butler's "Against Proper Objects" (1994) and "*GLQ* Forum: Thinking Sex/Thinking Gender" (2004).

References

Boyd, Nan Alamilla. 2003. *Wide-Open Town: A History of Queer San Francisco to 1965.* Berkeley: University of California Press.

Butler, Judith. 1994. "Against Proper Objects." *differences* 6, no 2: 1–26.

"The *GLQ* Forum: Thinking Sex/Thinking Gender." 2004. *GLQ* 10, no. 2: 211–312.

Meyerowitz, Joanne J. 2002. *How Sex Changed: A History of Transsexuality in the United States.* Cambridge, MA: Harvard University Press.

Spade, Dean. 2004. "Fighting to Win." In *That's Revolting! Queer Strategies for Resisting Assimilation*, ed. Mattilda Bernstein Sycamore, 47–53. Berkeley, CA: Soft Skull.

Stryker, Susan. 2008. "Transgender History, Homonormativity, and Disciplinarity." *Radical History Review*, no. 100: 145–57.

Valentine, David. 2007. *Imagining Transgender: An Ethnography of a Category.* Durham, NC: Duke University Press.

DOI 10.1215/23289252-2399776

Lines of Flight

MATT FOURNIER

Line of flight, a term developed by Gilles Deleuze and Félix Guattari in *A Thousand Plateaus* (1987), designates an infinitesimal possibility of escape; it is the elusive moment when change happens, as it was bound to, when a threshold between two paradigms is crossed. "Line of flight" is Brian Massumi's English translation of the French "ligne de fuite," where "fuite" means the act of fleeing or eluding but also flowing, leaking (1987: xvii). Gender dysphoria is one such moment of leakage, when the face you see in the mirror is not a face for you anymore, when a supposedly familiar landscape is blurred by the transposition of gender-signifying marks from one millieu to another, when the socially determined coordinates of familiarity-identity-gender no longer add up to a legible (legitimate) pattern, when materiality itself escapes the frame of representation, because this frame is built on gender binarism.

The philosophy at work in *A Thousand Plateaus* is, according to Deleuze and Guattari, a "geophilosophy": a system with no verticality, no transcendence, and, most of all, no binarism—only space, a perpetually redesigned space, structured by various and contingent power apparatuses (13–15). Applied to the gender/transgender spectrum, their perspective allows us to navigate gender as a geography, as a landscape, with its gridded plains, its wastelands, its hidden underground; and to percieve gender transition as a move—that is, as a political move, a strategic or tactical move, a move in a game-space—and as movement itself, a displacement between the established plateaus of gender. Even though Deleuze and Guattari never frontally addressed the possibility of apprehending gender and sexuality in terms of geophilosophy, their understanding of spatiality, with its ability to describe and to critique power apparatuses, may prove productive in regard to gender politics. In *Tendencies* (1993), Eve Kosofsky Sedgwick reasserts the kinship between queer and transitivity: etymologically, "queer" means "across," "oblique"; it seems crucial for "trans" to maintain the same disruptive impact.

The endless process described by Deleuze and Guattari as territorialization (where power apparatuses stabilize and encode planes of consistencies), derritorialization (disruption and transcoding of these planes of consistencies), and reterritorialization (such as the emergence of a new state after a revolution) offer a useful model for thinking about gender. In contemporary paradigms, both gender and "gender identity" are understood (and tested) as planes of consistencies; that is, as stable dispositives or "plateaus." The maleness or femaleness of individual bodies is measured through scales and ranges: your testosterone level places you among men or women, as do the answers you provide to multiple-choice tests. Gender is a question of numbers—though of course these numbers are inscribed in a discourse relying on "nature," so that uncommon ranges are labeled "unnatural." Wrong numbers have to be corrected so that the individual (the subject?) can reenter the ranges of normality—a process similar to the "coding" inherent to territorialization. Coding, in Deleuze and Guattari's perspective, is always "trans-coded," that is, deviated from its recurring schemes, its territory, and carried away toward a line of flight.

Gender disruptions open up the space between plateaus, the uncodified smooth space where affective intensities, not language, matter. Trans people know very well how aleatory it is to pass, how random the reading of the signs can be: a few more facial hairs, a shirt more or less open, a slightly uncontrolled voice, and you are on the other side. The product of particular intensities—your body processing hormones, clothing, surgery, moods, environnement—becomes a pattern of signs, read through social patterns re/territorializing transgender bodies. Though Massumi insists that a line of flight "has no relation to flying," its English translation nevertheless suggests an Icarian fugue, an escape too glorious to have already happened but still there, open, somewhere between "right now" and the closest future.

Matt Fournier is a teaching associate in the Department of Romance Studies at Cornell University and a PhD candidate at the University of Vincennes-Saint-Denis. His recent publications include "Wendy Delorme's War Machines" (*L'Esprit Créateur*, Spring 2013) and "Another Map on the Wall: Deleuze, Guattari, and Freeman at the Iron Curtain" (*Journal of Postcolonial Writing*, Spring 2014).

References

Deleuze, Gilles, and Félix Guattari. 1987. *A Thousand Plateaus: Capitalism and Schizophrenia.* Minneapolis: University of Minnesota Press.

Massumi, Brian. 1987. "Notes on the Translation and Acknowledgments." In Deleuze and Guattari, *A Thousand Plateaus*, xvii–xx.

Sedgwick, Eve Kosofsky. 1993. *Tendencies.* Durham, NC: Duke University Press.

DOI 10.1215/23289252-2399785

La Loca

MELISSA M. GONZÁLEZ

Loca, possibly derived from the classical Arabic word for "stupid," means "crazy" when used as an adjective in Spanish. The feminine noun *la loca* can describe not only a crazy woman but also a gender-nonconforming homosexual man. While the noun *loca* is roughly analogous to terms like *sissy* or *(flaming) queen*, and Spanish speakers use it transnationally to describe particularly "effeminate" homosexual men, different regions also employ other meanings. Specifically, Argentines and Uruguayans sometimes use the term to describe trans- or cis-women sex workers, while Cubans sometimes use it to describe promiscuous ciswomen.[1] Regardless of its specific application, the term consistently signals some form of feminine gender nonnormativity and can be used in a derogatory sense. Scholars of gender and sexuality in the West and its colonies will note how the term *loca* reflects parallels in the biopolitical management of both craziness and homosexuality, two subjectivities that have been historically relegated to a position of otherness. On the other hand, joining the long list of terms that began as insults but have been re-signified by minorities, the noun *loca* is used not only *for* but also *by* gender-nonconforming homosexual people born as men. The various meanings of *loca* are of particular importance for transgender studies, especially when considering newer iterations of the term in Latin America that expand its usual usage, bringing it closer in meaning to something like the term *genderqueer*.

Translating *la loca* poses noteworthy challenges. On one hand, it is crucial when dealing with transnational phenomena to respect the untranslatability of some dimensions of local difference and to avoid Anglocentricity. On the other hand, translations can not only aid cross-cultural understanding but also help us perceive some commonalities in gender and sexuality enabled by globalized capitalism. In the late twentieth and early twenty-first centuries, for example, global capitalism has enabled the inclusion of white (and *criollo* [of European descent] in Latin America), masculine, bourgeois gay men in the imagined communities of many nations as rights-bearing citizen-consumers. Meanwhile, although nonnormatively gendered and transgender subjects have still been pre-dominantly treated as spectacles of otherness, abject subjects, and/or victims of

violence, there have also been increasing opportunities for transgender normativity via state and legal recognition—as with Argentina's Gender Identity Law.
Nonnormatively gendered subjects who resist or fail at homo- and gender-normative assimilation, however, are still excluded from the imagined community of
the nation and are both less visible and more vulnerable to erasure.

Pedro Lemebel, a Chilean author and performance artist who identifies as
a *loca*, has become famous for making perspicacious and scathing critiques of the
contemporary, homonormative forms of gayness that cast nonnormative femininity as shameful. Lemebel's usage of the term *loca* describes homosexual people
whose femininity crosses the boundaries of their assigned male gender because
they wear makeup and/or accessories traditionally reserved for women—such as
shawls and heels—and interchangeably use both masculine and feminine pronouns. While some people in Latin America self-identify as or equate terms like
trans and *loca*, a few others, like Lemebel, identify primarily as *loca*, and not as
trans, *transexual*, *travesti*, *trava*, or *transgénero* (the latter being a direct translation of the English term *transgender*, a term that is increasingly used in Latin
America, mostly in academic and legal conversations).

In a 2000 interview, Lemebel describes the vulnerability of a marginalized
loca identity in a capitalist context: "I think that in the future homosexuality will
be a practice between men; as for that technicolor, that iridescence that holds in its
symbolic wings the thinking of oneself as *loca*, it will disappear, only to fall into
that neo-fascist concept of macho with macho. In that sense there will be a tri-
umph of capitalist homosexuality" (Lemebel 2000; my translation). The ability to
conceive of oneself as *loca*, Lemebel asserts, will inevitably fall prey to an all-
consuming capitalist homosexuality that suppresses gender nonnormativity.
Although Lemebel has championed the specificity of a *loca* identity, his interviews
and other writings make very clear his nonessentialist and strategic view of
identity as well as his melancholic embrace of its temporality.

Melissa M. González is an assistant professor of Hispanic studies at Davidson College. Her most
recent article is the coauthored "Orthodox Transgressions: The Ideology of Cross-Species,
Cross-Class, and Inter-racial Queerness in Lucía Puenzo's Novel *El niño pez* (*The Fish Child*)"
(*American Quarterly*, September 2013).

Note

1.   *Diccionario de la lengua española*, s.v. "loco," lema.rae.es/drae/?val=loca (accessed
        October 26, 2013).

Reference

Lemebel, Pedro. 2000. "Entrevista a Pedro Lemebel." By Andrea Jeftanovic. *Revista Lucero.* www
.letras.s5.com/archivolemebel.htm (accessed November 15, 2012).

DOI 10.1215/23289252-2399794

Medieval

KARL WHITTINGTON

Medieval conjures multiple meanings for contemporary readers: an outmoded or unenlightened viewpoint, a realm of fantasy fairytales, or the medieval S/M aesthetic of torture, dungeons, and chains. Academic scholars of medieval culture (here defined as Europe between 500 and 1400 CE) balance such associations carefully, often relying on the period's otherness to draw readers in but then endeavoring to reverse the readers' expectations. Any characterization of a single gender politics of medieval Europe would necessarily be reductive, ironing out the tensions and contradictions inherent in any historical period. But too few scholars are aware of the rich range of materials that medieval studies can offer to transgender history, from the usual twin poles of feminist inquiry (understanding the roots and mechanisms of oppression but also the moments when it was fought or overcome) to everything in between.

The Middle Ages offers neither an entirely retrograde comparison to our own politics (despite its characterization by the Bilerico Project, a prominent blog, as the period of "The Rise of Hatred" [Allen 2008]) nor an alternative cultural model to strive for. For some scholars, the Middle Ages were a time when anatomical sex was largely disconnected from gender; Thomas Laqueur's "one-sex" model is the most famous instance, arguing that premodern philosophers posited variations on a single sex rather than a binary system, a characterization that could theoretically be formulated as more progressive than our own (Laqueur 1990).[1] But for the most part, the violent realities of life as a gender-nonconforming person dominate trans histories of the medieval world. I will briefly sketch a few of the most interesting recent trends in medieval studies that can contribute to transgender histories and point to directions of possible future research. Because sources pointing to "life on the ground" are so difficult to find, in this essay I focus largely on broader theoretical or conceptual issues. An effort will be made to introduce period terms that relate to transgender studies, but I will also use modern terminology that can help identify and explain practices and ideas that certainly existed, though by other names.

Since the concept of the transgender person did not exist in the Middle Ages, scholars instead investigate concrete medieval subjects that relate to the issue, such as intersexuality, cross-dressing, and the medical alteration of the sexed body, all of which are discussed in primary sources. Early Christian exegetes read a hermaphroditic subtext in the biblical creation of man and woman both "in God's image" and in the creation of the female body out of the male (DeVun 2008). That these ideas were later refuted throughout the Middle Ages only suggests that they remained powerful. But the first centuries of Christianity also provide extensive accounts of medieval people leading actual transgender lives. Numerous records describe medieval holy women "becoming male" (*apandro* in Greek) both in appearance and "in soul," sometimes in secret and other times quite openly (Anson 1974: 7, 8).[2] Medieval conceptions of gender necessitated that such crossings were possible only for women; in becoming male, these women were moving closer to an ideal that was always masculine, while any instances of men becoming women were condemned or met with confusion (Bullough 1999). Most scholars focus on the social, material, or spiritual gains for women who lived as men, but this ignores the accounts' possible transgender subtext; many Christian women would have wanted to climb to higher (male) spiritual and social spheres, but only a few actually donned male clothing, entered monasteries, or married other women. Medieval texts offer admiring accounts of these women (passing FTM [female-to-male] cross-dressers, in modern terms), and these texts constitute one of the most concrete possibilities for seeing the subjectivity and desires of actual medieval transgender people in action. In contrast, such stories in the later Middle Ages were primarily the domain of fiction; the thirteenth-century *Roman de Silence* tells the story of Silence, a girl raised as a boy so that she could inherit her family's estate (Lurkhur 2010). In a deliciously modern twist, the allegorical characters of "nature" and "nurture" fight for control of her mind and body; she ultimately is revealed as a woman and marries a king (but only after she is seduced by the former queen, who took her for a man). Silence's struggle over her identity offers to the modern reader the possibility of glimpsing "what concepts of transsexuality remain when the surgeon and clinician are eliminated"—a kind of John/Joan case without the doctors and therapists (221).

Anatomical intersexuality was another major interest of medieval philosophers, medical writers, and theologians (who called it "hermaphroditism" in the Ovidian tradition, *Hermaphroditus* being the mythical child of Hermes and Aphrodite). In some of these texts we find discussions of intersexuality that appear morally neutral, for instance in anatomical descriptions of women's "seven-lobed uterus," where the three "cells" on the right create boys, the three on the left girls, and the one in the center intersex persons (Cadden 1993: 202–3; see also Jacquart and Thomasset 1988: 22–29; Rubin 1994). Other medieval medical theorists explained the creation of a "masculine woman" or "effeminate man" (*femina virago* or *vir effeminatus*) in terms of the relative strength of the male and female seeds that came together at conception (Cadden 1993). But while medical writers often adopted neutral language in describing intersexuality, legal and theological writers were preoccupied with finding ways to assign such people to a discrete gender. Interestingly, intersex persons were sometimes allowed to decide for themselves which sexual/marital role to adopt; the crucial point was that such decisions could not be unmade—the sin was in deviation from or inversion of one's gender, whether it was clear from birth or chosen later (Nederman and True 1996: 513; see also Olsen 2011).

Beyond these practical or medical contexts of intersexuality, medieval authors were also fascinated with an abstract or allegorical sphere, with theorizing a body that is "not only a midpoint between opposites, but . . . holds contraries in stasis and conversation" (DeVun 2008). The hermaphrodite, alternately described as a true fusion of male and female or as a "doubling" of two people in one body, was used as a metaphor for all kinds of philosophical processes of change, transition, or fusion (most interestingly, perhaps, in writings on alchemy). Such texts return us to a core issue of the historical study of sexual difference—the split between theory and practice. The celebration of fluidly sexual or sexually fused bodies in an alchemical treatise, or the admiration of a religious woman who "became male," may tell us little about the actual lives of people whose genital sex was either ambiguous or did not align with their gender identity. But these texts are nonetheless a vital record of transgender ideas circulating in the past; we must not conflate them with the experience of actual bodies, but the historical realm of fiction and fantasy is also the domain of contemporary transgender studies.

We have only scratched the surface of the possibilities for a medieval transgender studies—other subjects under investigation include figures like Joan of Arc, fascination with bearded female saints, cross-dressing in the theater, eunuchs, intersexual grammar and language, the gender-crossings of the carnival, and the complex queerness of the Christic body (see Feinberg 1996; Warner 1981; Kuefler 1999; Lochrie 1997). Discussions of the "medieval" can also extend beyond Europe; while the term originated in Europe, one increasingly reads and hears about histories of "medieval Islam" or "medieval Japan," for example. It is not always clear how many of the rich variety of connotations that the word carries are brought along into these new contexts, but in many cases it is applied to cultural moments that are conceived of as somehow culturally analogous to "medieval"

Europe; it is not a purely temporal designation. Future research should continue to flesh out these views of medieval worlds rife with contradiction—between theory and practice, fantasy and reality, violence and play.

Karl Whittington is assistant professor of art history at the Ohio State University, where he teaches European medieval art and architecture. His articles have appeared in *Gesta, Different Visions, Kunstlicht,* and *Studies in Iconography,* and his first book, *Body-Worlds: Opicinus de Canistris and the Medieval Cartographic Imagination* (2014), was recently published by the Pontifical Institute of Mediaeval Studies.

Notes

1.   A number of books have taken up Laqueur's theory, both in support and criticism. The most well-known critiques are Joan Cadden 1993 and Katharine Park and Robert Nye 1991.

2.   The key source on the subject is still John Anson 1974. See also Valerie Hotchkiss 1996, Elizabeth Castelli 1991, Margaret Miles 1991 (esp. chap. 2), and Kari Vogt 1993.

References

Allen, Mercedes. 2008. "The Rise of Hatred (the Middle Ages)." *The Bilerico Project* (blog). www .bilerico.com/2008/02/transgender_history_the_rise_of_hatred_t.php (accessed December 9, 2013).

Anson, John. 1974. "The Female Transvestite in Early Monasticism." *Viator,* no. 5: 1–32.

Bullough, Vern. 1999. "Cross Dressing and Gender Role Change in the Later Middle Ages." In *The Handbook of Medieval Sexuality,* ed. Vern Bullough and James Brundage, 223–42. New York: Routledge.

Cadden, Joan. 1993. *Meanings of Sex Difference in the Middle Ages.* Cambridge: Cambridge University Press.

Castelli, Elizabeth. 1991. "I Will Make Mary Male: Pieties of the Body and Gender Transformation of Christian Women in Late Antiquity." In *Body Guards: The Cultural Politics of Gender Ambiguity,* ed. Julia Epstein and Kristina Straub, 29–49. New York: Routledge.

DeVun, Leah. 2008. "The Jesus Hermaphrodite: Science and Sex Difference in Premodern Europe." *Journal of the History of Ideas* 69, no. 2: 193–218.

Feinberg, Leslie. 1996. *Transgender Warriors: Making History from Joan of Arc to RuPaul.* Boston: Beacon.

Hotchkiss, Valerie. 1996. *Clothes Make the Man: Female Cross Dressing in Medieval Europe.* New York: Garland.

Jacquart, Danielle, and Claude Thomasset. 1988. *Sexuality and Medicine in the Middle Ages.* Cambridge: Polity.

Kuefler, Matthew. 1999. "Castration and Eunuchism in the Middle Ages." In Bullough and Brundage, *Handbook of Medieval Sexuality,* 279–306.

Laqueur, Thomas. 1990. *Making Sex: Gender and the Body from the Greeks to Freud.* Cambridge, MA: Harvard University Press.

Lochrie, Karma. 1997. "Mystical Acts, Queer Tendencies." In *Constructing Medieval Sexuality*, ed. Karma Lochrie, Peggy McCracken, and James Schultz, 180–200. Minneapolis: University of Minnesota Press.

Lurkhur, Karen. 2010. "Medieval Silence and Modern Transsexuality." *Studies in Gender and Sexuality* 11, no. 4: 220–38.

Miles, Margaret. 1991. *Carnal Knowing*. New York: Vintage.

Nederman, Cary, and Jacqui True. 1996. "The Third Sex: The Idea of the Hermaphrodite in Twelfth-Century Europe." *Journal of the History of Sexuality* 6, no. 4: 497–517.

Olsen, Glenn. 2011. *Of Sodomites, Effeminates, Hermaphrodites, and Androgynes: Sodomy in the Age of Peter Damian*. Toronto: Pontifical Institute.

Park, Katharine, and Robert Nye. 1991. "Destiny is Anatomy." *New Republic*, February 18.

Rubin, Miri. 1994. "The Person in the Form: Medieval Challenges to Bodily Order." In *Framing Medieval Bodies*, ed. Sarah Kay and Miri Rubin, 100–22. Manchester, UK: Manchester University Press.

Vogt, Kari. 1993. "Becoming Male: A Gnostic, Early Christian, and Islamic Metaphor." In *Women's Studies of the Christian and Islamic Traditions*, ed. Kari Elisabeth Børresen and Kari Vogt, 217–42. Dordrecht, the Netherlands: Kluwer Academic.

Warner, Marina. 1981. *Joan of Arc: The Image of Female Heroism*. Berkeley: University of California Press.

DOI 10.1215/23289252-2399803

Microaggressions

SONNY NORDMARKEN

Microaggressions are commonplace, interpersonally communicated, "othering" messages related to a person's perceived marginalized status (Pierce et al. 1977; Sue 2010). These denigrations are often active manifestations of derogatory stereotypes. Invisible to many deliverers and recipients, they reproduce oppression on the interpersonal level. Examining microaggressions lays bare distinct ways in which gender as a dynamic system of power takes shape in trans and gender-nonconforming people's everyday lives.

Microaggressions are routine in social interaction; all social actors deliver them. These often unconscious and unintentional messages manifest as brief, unthinking slights, snubs, insults, or other indignities, frequently embedded within a stream of communication (Sue 2010). They are verbal, nonverbal, and environmental, and they can appear in facial expressions, body language, terminology, representation, or remarks. Microaggressions can be confusing to receive, difficult to notice, pinpoint, or recognize, and particularly challenging to address (ibid.). Recipients feel microaggressions' cumulative impact in stress and somatic effects comparable to those caused by a catastrophically traumatic event (ibid.). Some common effects are: chronic health problems and persistent feelings of alienation, anxiety, anger, depression, fear, hypervigilance, fatigue, hopelessness and/or suicidality (Goldblum et al. 2012; Grossman and D'Augelli 2007; Kosciw et al. 2010; Pauly 1990; Schrock, Boyd, and Leaf 2009).

Trans and gender-nonconforming people encounter microaggressions in a number of realms in their everyday lives, such as workplaces and public restrooms, and from family members, friends, therapists, medical providers, security workers, and strangers (Kidd and Witten 2008). Microaggressors express a perception of otherness, which they may associate with one or more characteristics such as disability, race, gender, or class. Some microaggressions are related to a perceived transness or gender nonconformity. For instance, microaggressors scrutinize, exoticize, sexualize, or fetishize trans people (Nadal, Skolnik, and Wong 2012; Serano 2007), using such terms as "tranny," "she-male," "he-she," or "chicks with dicks"; asking gender- and sex-related questions about a person's body, genitalia, identity, or history; expressing concern about a trans person interacting with children; implying that gender-affirmation surgeries constitute "mutilation" or that trans people are "mentally ill" or "freakish"; approaching non–sex-worker trans women for paid sex; offering intended compliments such as "you turned out so cute" or "I never would have known"; evaluating a person's gender presentation; exposing a person's trans identity (Nordmarken 2012). Many of these actions reflect erroneous, dehumanizing stereotypes about trans people that are represented in news stories, films, and other media (Serano 2007). Thus microaggressions maintain cis-sexism, or the idea that trans people are inferior to and less authentic than cisgender (non-trans) people (ibid.).

Besides manifesting stereotypes, many microaggressions targeting trans and gender-nonconforming people are active manifestations of conventional ways of thinking about gender. Due to the dearth of accurate information on transgender phenomena in public circulation, microaggressors misunderstand or misinterpret trans and gender-nonconforming people's gender identities, invalidating their experiences of reality and at times conflating sexual nonnormativity with gender nonnormativity. Microaggressors address trans people with incorrect gender pronouns, call them by former names, inquire about their "real" identity, ask them to explain their gender identity, and deny or fail to acknowledge their pronouns, name, or identity (Nadal, Skolnik, and Wong 2012; Nordmarken 2012; Nordmarken and Kelly, forthcoming). This "misgendering" takes place because microaggressors assume that they have the ability to know a trans person's "true" identity and that their perception of a trans person is more valid than the trans person's own self-knowledge—what Julia Serano calls "gender entitlement" (2007: 9). Gender entitlement and the cultural conflation of sexed anatomy and gender identity result in a rhetoric of deception, where microaggressors cast trans people as "deceivers" or "pretenders" who "hide" what microaggressors imagine are trans people's "true selves" (Bettcher 2007). Some microaggressors intend to legitimate trans people's identities but, problematically, assume that all trans people are the same (Nadal, Skolnik, and Wong 2012). They might apply the "wrong body" narrative to those who do not experience their gender in such a way (Nordmarken and Kelly, forthcoming).

Microaggressors may communicate disgust, dismissal, apprehension, confusion, shock, surprise, skepticism, disbelief, agitation, or other discomfort when noticing or being alerted to a person's transness. They can become defensive when corrected or reminded about their misuse of pronouns (Nadal, Rivera, and Corpus 2010). They may stare, do double takes, avoid eye contact or proximity, look away, laugh, or become silent (Nordmarken 2012, 2014; Nordmarken and Kelly, forthcoming). They may make excuses for or apologize excessively for misgendering, drawing more attention to and drawing out the uncomfortable interaction (Nordmarken 2012); conversely, they may deny that they have communicated something cis-sexist or transphobic or they may deny that cis-sexism and transphobia exist (Nadal, Skolnik, and Wong 2012). Regardless of intention, microaggressive behaviors often indicate that individuals perceive difference, communicating othering messages.

Although many trans people encounter microaggressions, they have varied experiences. Various institutionalized oppression systems, such as sexism, racism, poverty, and ageism exacerbate the impact of transphobia. Across trans populations, multiply marginalized groups encounter the most discrimination. Socioeconomically disadvantaged trans people experience the highest rates of discrimination and violence (Lombardi et al. 2001). Trans people of color encounter more discrimination than white trans people, and African American trans people encounter the most of all racial groups (Grant et al. 2011). Trans women and other trans-feminine people contend with trans-misogyny, or a combination of transphobia, cis-sexism, and misogyny (Serano 2007). They thus encounter particular kinds of gendered microaggressions that certain trans men and trans-masculine people avoid. For example, in the workplace, employers tend to demote or fire transitioning trans women or dock their pay, while they tend to support transitioning trans men, incorporating them into patriarchal social hierarchies (Schilt 2010; Schilt and Wiswall 2008). Ageism also intensifies trans people's vulnerabilities. Trans youth and elders whose families reject them face homelessness and/or abuse at the hands of their caregivers (Denny 2007; Witten and Eyler 1999; Witten and Whittle 2005).

The translation of stereotype into action can have far-reaching, overtly oppressive, systemic effects, from pathologization to murder. A complete picture of the subjugation trans people contend with is beyond the scope of this article, but a brief overview follows. The idea that trans people are mentally ill is institutionalized in psychiatric texts such as the *Diagnostic and Statistical Manual of Mental Disorders* (American Psychiatric Association 2013) and thus also in medical and legal transition routes. Many social institutions and sites of social life, such as medical systems, workplaces, families, and religious communities openly exclude trans people (Flynn 2006; Grant et al. 2011). State programs and institutions, such as public medical systems, prisons, and immigration detention centers, host regular harassment and abuse, refuse trans people services, and, at times, host violence (Benson 2008–9; Gehi and Arkles 2007; Howe, Zaraysky, and Lorentzen 2008; Namaste 2000; O'Day-Senior 2008; Spade 2011). In addition, trans individuals face harassment, threats, and violence on the street and in other public spaces (Kidd and Witten 2008). While overt denigrations are not microaggressions, they represent the systemic effects of *unacknowledged injustice*, maintaining an institution of cis-sexism and a cis-normative culture that privileges and normalizes cisgender experiences. Thus the invisibility of microaggressions and other cis-sexist actions plays a significant role in maintaining the power of the dominant gender system.

Sonny Nordmarken is a doctoral candidate in sociology at the University of Massachusetts, Amherst. His dissertation examines affect and power in trans people's everyday interactions. He is author of "Becoming Ever More Monstrous: Feeling Transgender In-Betweenness" (*Qualitative Inquiry*, January 2014) and, with Reese C. Kelly, "Limiting Transgender Health: Administrative Violence and Microaggressions in Healthcare Systems" in *Left Out: Health Care Issues Facing LGBT People* (forthcoming).

References

American Psychiatric Association. 2013. *Diagnostic and Statistical Manual of Mental Disorders.* 5th ed. Arlington, VA: American Psychiatric Publishing.

Benson, Christi Jo. 2008–9. "Crossing Borders: A Focus on Treatment of Transgender Individuals in U.S. Asylum Law and Society." *Whittier Law Review* 30, no. 1: 41–66.

Bettcher, Talia Mae. 2007. "Evil Deceivers and Make-Believers: On Transphobic Violence and the Politics of Illusion." *Hypatia* 22, no. 3: 43–65.

Denny, Dallas. 2007. "Transgender Identities and Bisexual Expression: Implications for Counselors." In *Becoming Visible: Counseling Bisexuals across the Lifespan*, ed. B. Firestein, 268–84. New York: Columbia University Press.

Flynn, Taylor. 2006. "The Ties That [Don't] Bind: Transgender Family Law and the Unmaking of Families." In *Transgender Rights*, ed. Paisley Currah, Richard M. Juang, and Shannon P. Minter, 32–50. Minneapolis: University of Minnesota Press.

Gehi, Pooja S., and Gabriel Arkles. 2007. "Unraveling Injustice: Race and Class Impact of Medicaid Exclusions of Transition-Related Health Care for Transgender People." *Sexuality Research and Social Policy: Journal of NSRC* 4, no. 4: 7–35.

Goldblum, Peter, et al. 2012. "The Relationship between Gender-Based Victimization and Suicide Attempts in Transgender People." *Professional Psychology: Research and Practice* 43, no. 5: 468–75.

Grant, Jaime M., et al. 2011. "Executive Summary: Injustice at Every Turn: A Report of the National Transgender Discrimination Survey." Washington, DC: National Center for Transgender Equality and National Gay and Lesbian Task Force. www.thetaskforce.org/reports _and_research/ntds (accessed August 22, 2013).

Grossman, A. H., and A. R. D'Augelli. 2007. "Transgender Youth and Life-Threatening Behaviors." *Suicide and Life-Threatening Behavior* 37, no. 5: 527–37.

Howe, C., S. Zaraysky, and L. Lorentzen. 2008. "Transgender Sex Workers and Sexual Transmigration between Guadalajara and San Francisco." *Latin American Perspectives* 35, no. 1: 31–50.

Kidd, Jeremy, and Tarynn Witten. 2008. "Transgender and Transsexual Identities: The Next Strange Fruit—Hate Crimes, Violence, and Genocide against the Global Trans-Communities." *Journal of Hate Studies* 6, no. 1: 31–63.

Kosciw, J. G., et al. 2010. *The 2009 National School Climate Survey: The Experiences of Lesbian, Gay, Bisexual, and Transgender Youth in Our Nation's Schools.* New York: GLSEN.

Lombardi, Emilia L., et al. 2001. "Gender Violence." *Journal of Homosexuality* 42, no. 1: 89–101.

Nadal, Kevin L., David Rivera, and Melissa Corpus. 2010. "Sexual Orientation and Transgender Microaggressions: Implications for Mental Health and Counseling." In *Microaggressions and Marginality: Manifestation, Dynamics, and Impact*, ed. Derald Wing Sue, 217–40. New Jersey: Wiley.

Nadal, Kevin L., Avy Skolnik, and Yinglee Wong. 2012. "Interpersonal and Systemic Microaggressions toward Transgender People: Implications for Counseling." *Journal of LBGT Issues in Counseling* 6, no. 1: 55–82.

Namaste, Viviane. 2000. *Invisible Lives: The Erasure of Transsexual and Transgender People.* Chicago: University of Chicago Press.

Nordmarken, Sonny. 2012. "Everyday Transgender Emotional Inequality: Microaggressions, Micropolitics, and Minority Emotional Work." Paper presented at the annual meeting of the American Sociological Association, Denver, August 20.

———. 2014. "Becoming Ever More Monstrous: Feeling Transgender In-Betweenness." *Qualitative Inquiry* 20, no. 1: 37–50.

Nordmarken, Sonny, and Reese Kelly. Forthcoming. "Limiting Transgender Health: Administrative Violence and Microaggressions in Healthcare Systems." In *Left Out: Health Care Issues Facing LGBT People*, ed. Vickie Harvey and Teresa Housel. Lanham, MD: Lexington Books.

O'Day-Senior, Dana. 2008. "The Forgotten Frontier? Healthcare for Transgender Detainees in Immigration and Customs Enforcement Detention." *Hastings Law Journal* 60, no. 2: 453–77.

Pauly, Ira B. 1990. "Gender Identity Disorders: Evaluation and Treatment." *Journal of Sex Education and Therapy* 16, no. 1: 2–24.

Pierce, Chester M., et al. 1977. "An Experiment in Racism: TV Commercials." *Education and Urban Society* 10, no. 1: 61–87.

Schilt, Kristen. 2010. *Just One of the Guys? Transgender Men and the Persistence of Gender Inequality*. Chicago: University of Chicago Press.

Schilt, Kristen, and Matthew Wiswall. 2008. "Before and After: Gender Transitions, Human Capital, and Workplace Experiences." *B.E. Journal of Economics and Policy* 8, no. 1: 1–26.

Schrock, Douglas, Emily M. Boyd, and Margaret Leaf. 2009. "Emotion Work in the Public Performances of Male-to-Female Transsexuals." *Archives of Sexual Behavior* 38, no. 5: 702–12.

Serano, Julia. 2007. *Whipping Girl: A Transsexual Woman on Sexism and the Scapegoating of Femininity*. Emeryville, CA: Seal.

Spade, Dean. 2011. *Normal Life: Administrative Violence, Critical Trans Politics, and the Limits of Law*. Brooklyn, NY: South End.

Sue, Derald Wing. 2010. *Microaggressions and Marginality: Manifestation, Dynamics, and Impact*. Hoboken, NJ: Wiley.

Witten, T. M., and Stephen Whittle. 2005. "TransPanthers: The Graying of Transgender and the Law." *Deakin Law Review* 9, no. 2: 503–22.

Witten, T. M., and A. E. Eyler. 1999. "Hate Crimes and Violence against the Transgendered." *Peace Review* 11, no. 3: 461–68.

DOI 10.1215/23289252-2399812

Monster

ANSON KOCH-REIN

The monster is an ambivalent figure recurring in trans* discourse. When trans* people are cast as less than human, the monster (and the creature from Mary Shelley's *Frankenstein* in particular) is often the metaphor of choice. 1970s separatist feminist Mary Daly (1978) and Janice G. Raymond (1979) used the image of Frankenstein's monster to depict trans* women's surgically modified bodies as dangerous and unnatural; similar depictions circulate in crime shows ("*Ch-Ch-Changes*" 2004) and Hollywood films (*The Silence of the Lambs* [dir. Jonathan Demme, 1991]). The varied transphobic uses of the monster trope often draw on ideas of physical monstrosity to uphold their naturalization of binary sex and gender.

In a world where the monster is circulating as metaphoric violence against trans* people, reclaiming such a figure faces the difficulty of formulating resistance in the same metaphorical language as the transphobic attack. Moreover, as a figure of difference, the monster appears in racist, ableist, homophobic, and sexist discourses, making its use especially fraught. Still, we cannot simply dismiss the monster for its history or injurious potential. It is precisely the monster's ambivalent ability to speak to oppression and negative affect that appeals to trans* people reclaiming the monster for their own voices.

Trans* metaphorizations of the monster draw from implications of monstrosity way beyond the idea of monstrous bodies. Sometimes trans* authors describe the embodiment before a desired medical transition as a monstrous experience. More often, however, trans* references to the monster are a way of addressing feelings of gender dysphoria and alienation rather than characteristics of a body. In addition, the trans* monster is claimed as a site of agency that negotiates a queerly complex relationship to nature, origin narratives, and language. In her seminal piece "My Words to Victor Frankenstein above the Village of Chamounix," Susan Stryker ([1994] 2006) uses the eloquent monster of *Frankenstein* to interpret trans* embodiment and rage against a culture that naturalizes the sexual binarism and denies gendered recognition to trans* people. Transgender studies, rather than refuting the attribution of monstrosity, has called for its embrace to restructure the world in such a way that it makes livable what is now deemed monstrous gender (see, e.g., Hale 1998).

The monster, then, is a central figure in representations of trans*, serving widely divergent narratives of transphobic insult and trans* resistance alike.

Anson Koch-Rein is a PhD candidate in the Graduate Institute of the Liberal Arts at Emory University. His dissertation, "Mirrors, Monsters, Metaphors: Transgender Rhetorics and Dysphoric Knowledge," is scheduled for completion in spring 2014.

References

"Ch-Ch-Changes." 2004. Episode of *CSI*, dir. Richard J. Lewis. Paramount. November 18.

Daly, Mary. 1978. *Gyn/Ecology: The Metaethics of Radical Feminism*. Boston: Beacon.

Hale, C. Jacob. 1998. "Tracing a Ghostly Memory in My Throat: Reflections of Ftm Feminist Voice and Agency." In *Men Doing Feminism*, ed. Tom Digby, 99–129. New York: Routledge.

Raymond, Janice G. 1979. *The Transsexual Empire: The Making of the She-Male*. New York: Teachers College Press.

Stryker, Susan. (1994) 2006. "My Words to Victor Frankenstein above the Village of Chamounix: Performing Transgender Rage." In *The Transgender Studies Reader*, ed. Susan Stryker and Stephen Whittle, 244–56. New York: Routledge.

DOI 10.1215/23289252-2399821

Nature

OLIVER BENDORF

I am driving across the tawny plains of Nebraska, imagining nature launching a marketing campaign aimed at transgender folks. Nature: No Therapist's Letter or Passport Required! I like to think that nature's marketing executive would pass over trans metaphors that engage nature in clichéd ways: "trapped," the metamorphic butterfly, a rare bird. Talk to me about a winged rabbit or an eight-legged turtle or a bucktoothed squirrel. Freaks of nature, biodiversity—I am thinking about what these concepts really mean, how transgender studies and nature can begin to shed some light.

What is natural, anyway? Nature matters for transgender studies because of how we map (and are mapped) along boundaries of inside and out, natural and unnatural. Bats are a protected species, but that did not stop my landlord from killing one when it would not "stay outside where it belongs!" Where do we belong?

Transgender studies can shepherd us beyond "tired gendered portrayals of earth-mother-goddess nature" (Beyer 2010) and toward re-genderings of natural space. It is Camp Ida, in Tennessee. It is in urban parks, like San Francisco. It is me last summer, when I squatted to piss behind a log cabin and my packer fell on the dirt. If a packer falls out in the forest and no one is around to see it, am I still trans? Nature: The Original Gender-Neutral Bathroom.

What does a transgender pastoral look like? What does trans do to our visions of country life and green space? A transgender pastoral may be verdant and bucolic, but the reality is occasionally interrupted by transphobes, cunning or dumb, who howl and leave their scat.

And yet my Google search for "transgender pastoral" yields only results about ministry care for transgender folks. Nature, transgender, and this idea of care: who is caring for whom? What will transgender studies do with the environment, pumped up with chemicals these days, its roof on fire? Nature: Not Hormone Free, Either. I want to know what transgender studies will say on environmental education research and vice versa.

I am still driving across Nebraska, thinking about trans ecologies. I am watching a chain of geese across the sky, several V formations linked together, and I think about all the trans people I know who have flocked to San Francisco and those who have not. Transgender studies might find a bridge between critical theory, landscape ecology, and animal behavior to think about how we form communities and navigate vulnerability in metropolitan and rural areas (Ingram 2010). Nature: If

You Lived Here, You'd Be Home Already. Transgender studies can create a discourse in which nature is not the cisgender space it has been made out to be. I mean links between transgender and nature that are, for once, not just about our genitals, though they can be about that too. I want theoretical critique and art and song about species (McWhorter 2010) and biodiversity and evolution and instinct and habitat.

When was the first time you saw nature and knew it as yourself? In a tornado? On the wings of a camouflaged moth? Nature is something the nimbus says to the spotted cow, and we are trans inside of it. Nature: Relax, You'll Look Good Here. I went into nature to try to find the Bellbird (Anderson-Minshall 2012), but I only found myself. The Bellbird has feather patterns deemed female but a distinctly masculine call. I could say I know how it feels, but I do not, because *trans* is our species' word, not the Bellbird's. We are wild animals still learning how to wield our tool of language, sometimes too dull, sometimes too sharp. Nature is something the blade of grass hollers up to Orion's Belt, and we are still trans inside of it.

I got tired of learning masculinity from humans, so I studied the male wren, building his nest twig by twig, singing a sweet song to attract a mate, feeding his young via beak. I studied the barred owl, solitary witness calling out to others from his perch high up in an old burr oak, his hoot more oxygen than my bound lungs are able to manage. I learned from three little dairy goat boys, castrated, never to be angry bucks. My masculinity is a cross-species "biomimicry," cherry-picked day to day (Nature: There's Something for Everyone), and whether this makes me natural or unnatural, I cannot say.

Oliver Bendorf is a master's degree candidate in library and information studies at the University of Wisconsin–Madison, where he recently earned his MFA in poetry. His book *The Spectral Wilderness* was chosen for the 2013 Wick Poetry Prize and is forthcoming.

References

Anderson-Minshall, Diane. 2012. "The World's First Transgender Bellbird Discovered in New Zealand." *Advocate*, October 17. www.advocate.com/society/coming-out/2012/10/17/first -transgender-bellbird-discovered-new-zealand.

Beyer, Tamiko. 2010. "Notes towards a Queer::Eco::Poetics." Doveglion Press. November 29. www .doveglion.com/2010/11/notes-towards-a-queerecopoetics-by-tamiko-beyer.

Ingram, Gordon Brent. 2010. "Fragments, Edges, and Matrices: Retheorizing the Formation of a So-Called Gay Ghetto through Queering Landscape Ecology." In *Queer Ecologies: Sex, Nature, Politics, Desire*, ed. Catriona Mortimer-Sandilands and Bruce Erickson, 254–83. Bloomington: Indiana University Press.

McWhorter, Ladelle. "Enemy of the Species." In Mortimer-Sandilands and Erickson, *Queer Ecologies*, 73–101.

DOI 10.1215/23289252-2399830

Nomad Science

HILARY MALATINO

"Nomad science" is a concept that appears in the twelfth plateau ("1227: Treatise on Nomadology—the War Machine") of Gilles Deleuze and Félix Guattari's *A Thousand Plateaus* (1987: 361), counterposed to a companionate concept coined "state science." These terms offer two distinct, incommensurable ways of thinking about bodily matter and embodied form. Nomad science emphasizes the malleable, fluid, and metamorphic nature of being, while state science conceptualizes being as solid, essential, and unchanging. Given the antiessentialist focus of nomad science, it is a particularly helpful concept in thinking transgender, transsexual, and gender-nonconforming modes of embodiment, particularly those that exceed or actively contest medical understandings of trans* identity. Conversely, state science is a useful heuristic for considering the medical and psychiatric pathologization of trans* and gender-nonconforming subjects.

Nomad science is in dense dialogue with Deleuze and Guattari's theorization of nomadology. Nomadology is the study of wandering subjectivities, of beings that drift from predetermined or normative paths, particularly those paths determined and regulated by apparatuses of the state. For Deleuze and Guattari, nomadism is a form of life that is shaped by continual embarkation on lines of flight—that is, modes of escape, moments of transformation, ways of becoming other-than-normative, and ways of acting in excess of, or insubordinately in relationship to, repressive forces. Lines of flight have the capacity to *deterritorialize*, to undo, to free up, to break out of a system or situation of control, fixity, or repression.

Nomad science, by extension, concerns itself with experiments and inventions that are fundamentally deterritorializing, while state science is, by counterpoint, fundamentally *reterritorializing*. To territorialize an entity is to set and define its limits, to organize component parts into a coherent whole determined by a specific end. Deleuze and Guattari write that "state science continually imposes its form of sovereignty on the inventions of nomad science" (1987: 365); in other words, state science imposes a particular logic of organization on nomadic beings, curtailing and taming the creative inventiveness of these beings.

Deleuze and Guattari outline the salient aspects of this imposition: state science privileges the fixed over the metamorphic; it seeks to establish transhistorical, universally true theories rather than exploring specific, singular instances; in doing so, it fetishizes the eternal, the stable, and the constant, and it thus develops fixed, immutable, and essential understandings of being. State science is incapable of conceptualizing beings as they are caught up in fluid processes of becoming.

Fluids are known for their malleability, their capacity for transformation, their capacity to adjust and recalibrate at the molecular level; when one investigates fluid phenomena, one asks what a fluid is doing in a given situation, interaction, or milieu. That is, one focuses on *the hows and whys of transformation*. When investigating solids, on the other hand, very different properties are assumed, and these assumed properties generate very different sets of questions. Solids are firmly delimited entities. They have stable boundaries rather than blurred or porous ones; they exist as beings unto themselves. Thus a science concerned with solids tends to also be concerned with establishing the characteristics that make delimited entities *what they are*. Unlike dealing with fluids, where the emphasis is on transformation, with solids the emphasis falls on questions of essence that seek to establish attributes that render a solid what it is through contradistinction with what is not.

It is important to bear in mind that Deleuze and Guattari insist on understanding this alternative view of materiality as a science. This is because they propose a formal conceptual system consisting of a set of theorems that help elicit a different understanding of embodiment. They propose a series of rules of thumb (rather than laws—eschewing the juridical language of conventional scientific practice) that enable one to encounter the physical world anew, and to counter the hidebound cognition of materiality enforced by state science.

The tactic of establishing essence through contradistinction is central to the medical pathologization of trans* and gender-nonconforming subjects, which utilizes this tactic to produce gender stereotypes used in the diagnoses of gender identity disorder and gender dysphoria. These stereotypes are necessary to the functioning of the state science of diagnosing gender difference; they are utilized to establish dyadic essences of gender that are then codified within diagnostic criteria. Although the medicalization of gender nonconformance has led to development of guidelines and protocols for transition and would thus seem to be linked to a more fluid conception of gender, these practical protocols are nevertheless built upon conservative typologies of maleness and femaleness. They are not concerned with transition as a (potentially always unfinished) process but rather with the creation and suturing of firmly delimited, discrete, and binarily gendered entities. A nomad science of transition, however, would focus on the specific, resistant, and creative ways in which trans* and gender-nonconforming subjects reinvent and reconstruct themselves in manners irreducible to the medical logic of transition.

We can track a resonant preoccupation with thinking embodiment beyond static, dimorphic understandings of gender in a number of foundational texts in trans* studies. Susan Stryker asserts, early in her career, that trans* bodies should be understood as in excess of what is commonly understood as natural and that they therefore destabilize "the foundational presupposition of fixed genders upon which a politics of personal identity depends" (1994: 238). Sandy Stone, similarly, takes issue with the narrative of transsexuality offered by clinicians and calls for a counternarrative of embodiment, writing that "for a transsexual, as a transsexual, to generate a true, effective and representational counterdiscourse is to speak from outside the boundaries of gender, beyond the constructed oppositional nodes which have been predefined as the only positions from which discourse is possible" (1991: 300). This shared conception of trans* embodiment as in excess of conventional understandings of materiality has its afterlives in contemporary criticisms of the regulatory mechanisms of trans* diagnosis and medical treatment. Dean Spade has written extensively on this topic (2003, 2006, 2011), as has Lucas Cassidy Crawford, who utilizes the conceptual vocabulary of Deleuze and Guattari to think about trans embodiment as a kind of "affective deterritorialization" rather than a way of "coming home" to one of two ideal gender types (2008: 134).

Hilary Malatino is the assistant director of women's studies at East Tennessee State University. Her recent publications include "The Waiting Room: Ontological Homelessness, Sexual Synecdoche, and Queer Becoming" (*Journal of Medical Humanities*, June 2013) and "Utopian Pragmatics: Bash Back! and the Temporality of Radical Queer Action," in *A Critical Inquiry into Queer Utopias* (2013).

References

Crawford, Lucas Cassidy. 2008. "Transgender without Organs? Mobilizing a Geo-affective Theory of Gender Modification." *Women's Studies Quarterly* 36, no. 3–4: 127–43.

Deleuze, Gilles, and Félix Guattari. 1987. *A Thousand Plateaus*. Minneapolis: University of Minnesota Press.

Spade, Dean. 2003. "Resisting Medicine/Remodeling Gender." *Berkeley Women's Law Journal* 15, no. 1: 15–37.

———. 2006. "Mutilating Gender." In *The Transgender Studies Reader*, ed. Susan Stryker and Stephen Whittle, 315–32. New York: Routledge.

———. 2011. *Normal Life: Administrative Violence, Critical Trans Politics, and the Limits of Law*. Boston: South End.

Stone, Sandy. 1991. "The *Empire* Strikes Back: A Posttranssexual Manifesto." In *Body Guards: The Cultural Politics of Gender Ambiguity*, ed. Julia Epstein and Kristina Straub, 280–304. New York: Routledge.

Stryker, Susan. 1994. "My Words to Victor Frankenstein above the Village of Chamounix: Performing Transgender Rage." *GLQ* 1, no. 3: 237–54.

DOI 10.1215/23289252-2399839

Normal

ELIZABETH STEPHENS

Unlike other key terms in transgender studies, there is no comprehensive critical genealogy of the concept of "normal" or "normality." Recently, a number of studies have examined particular episodes in this history: Creadick (2010) and Adams (1997) have looked at the postwar years, while Warner (1999) has examined the late twentieth century. Despite the lack of a long history of normality, however, critiques of normality occupy a central position in many areas of critical theory, which have examined the way the "regime of the normal" (Warner 1999) has come to shape the lives of those whose sexualities, genders, and/or bodies do not conform to normative assumptions about them. Beginning with Michael Warner's landmark identification of queer as that which opposes "not just the normal behavior of the social but the *idea* of normal behavior" (1993: xxvii), critiques of the normal and of normativity have occupied a central position in queer studies (e.g., Halperin 1997; Halberstam 2005), critical disability studies (e.g., Garland Thomson 1996; Davis 1995), studies of bodily difference (e.g., Dreger 2004), gender variance (e.g., Halberstam 2012), transgender studies (e.g., Spade 2011), and postcolonialism (e.g., Carter 2007). The ongoing proliferation of such critiques is a reflection of how privileged the idea of normality remains. For Warner, the desire for normality is one of the definitive characteristics of the late twentieth century: "Everyone, it seems, wants to be normal. . . . What immortality was to the Greeks, what *virtù* was to Machiavelli's prince, what faith was to the martyrs, what honor was to the slave owners, what glamor is to drag queens, normalcy is to the contemporary American" (1999: 53).

Given its cultural ubiquity and its centrality to contemporary studies of embodiment, it is curious that the term *normal* and the history of which it is a part have been subject to so little critical interrogation. What has been overlooked, in consequence, is that the history of the normal is much more recent, and its meaning much more unstable, than generally recognized. The word *normal* first appears in the *Oxford English Dictionary* in 1848. However, at the end of the century its meaning is still so unfamiliar that it is described in the *Grand Larousse du XIXe siécle* as "new in the language," and requiring "from the person who hears it for the first time a certain effort of attention" (quoted in Warman 2010: 203). Etymological antecedents of the nineteenth-century *normal* can be dated to the mid-eighteenth century, when the word first appeared in two highly specialized and apparently distinct discursive locations: geometry, in which it was used as a less common synonym for a perpendicular line; and, second, anatomy, in which it was paired with, and used in opposition to, the "pathological." What these instances have in common is an association of the normal with the regular: it is "that which conforms to the rule (*norma*)" (Canguilhem 1991: 125), and that which is seen to be morally as well as geometrically upright (Warman 2010: 206–7).

For Georges Canguilhem: "To set a norm (*normer*), to normalise, is to impose a requirement on an existence" (1991: 239), and it is this the understanding of the normal that informs Michel Foucault's influential theory of normalization in *Discipline and Punish*. Foucault describes normalization as a practice of standardization and identifies it as "one of the great instruments of power at the end of the classical age" (1991: 184). Like all forms of power, Foucault argues, normalization is both repressive and productive: while it "imposes homogeneity" (184), it is also that which constitutes the modern subject as an "individual" (170). Normalization does this not simply by moving subjects toward a norm— by making them more normal—but by measuring the gaps and differences by which they deviate from that norm. The purpose of the norm is thus to serve as an ideal that can never be embodied but around which minutely differentiated distances can be charted: "When one wishes to individualise the healthy, normal and law-abiding adult, it is always by asking him how much of the child he has in him, what secret madness lies within him, what fundamental crime he has dreamt of committing" (Foucault 1991: 193).

Although Foucault dates the end of the eighteenth century as the period in which "the power of the Norm becomes the new law of modern society" (1991: 184), it should be remembered that the word *normal* is still so unfamiliar a century later that it is identified as linguistically new and conceptually difficult, and the concept of "a norm" itself did not yet exist. The term *norm* dates only from the very end of the nineteenth century, emerging subsequent to the theory of "normal distribution" in statistics, which is usually attributed to Francis Galton (Kevles 1985; Porter 1986). Normal distribution describes the mathematical law in which the greater the variance from a given mean, the lower the frequency with which it will occur (Galton 1869). Galton's statistical research was undertaken in conjunction with his work on eugenics: biological evolution, he argued, was like numerical variation in that it "follows certain statistical laws, of which the best known is the Normal Law of Frequency" (Galton 1909: 3). For Galton, the normal is what is both statistically most common and socially preferable; it is the average and also an ideal.

This is the double meaning of the normal that Canguilhem examines in *The Normal and the Pathological*, which focuses on the conceptual incoherence of this term. In biology, Canguilhem notes: "the normal state designates" both "the habitual state" of the body and its "ideal" (1991: 152). Canguilhem's great contribution to a critical genealogy of normality—one that is of great potential application to transgender studies—is to see the normal as a dynamic relation rather than a static quality: "The living being and its environment are not normal," he argues; "it is their relationship that makes them such" (143). In consequence: "There is no fact which is normal or pathological in itself. An anomaly or a mutation is not in itself pathological. These two express other possible norms of life" (144).

We might bear this in mind when considering the context in which the concept "normal subject" first emerges: in and through the work of the biologist and sexologist Alfred Kinsey (Igo 2007). A few short decades later, the idea of "normal" sexuality and gender occupy such a privileged role in John Money's writing on gender roles and reassignment that it constitutes a form of paraphilia itself, Lisa Downing argues, which we might term "normophilia" (Downing 2010). This instability in the concept of the normal—in which it is both the average and the ideal, a habitual state and the object of excess or obsession—underpins its ambiguous role in contemporary studies of sexuality and gender, in which it continues to mark an important fault line between queer and transgender studies (Stryker 2004). For this reason, we might productively return to the apparently obsolete original meaning of the normal in geometry: a perpendicular line. Here, as in Canguilhem's critique of theories of biological normativity, the "normal" is ontologically relational, describing not a fixed thing but an orientation of one thing in relation to another.

Elizabeth Stephens is an ARC Senior Research Fellow and deputy director of the Centre for the History of European Discourses at the University of Queensland. Her publications include *Anatomy as Spectacle: Public Exhibitions of the Body from 1700 to the Present* (2011 and 2013) and *Queer Writing: Homoeroticism in Jean Genet's Fiction* (2009).

References

Adams, Mary Louise. 1997. *The Trouble With Normal: Postwar Youth and the Making of Hetero-sexuality.* Toronto: University of Toronto Press.

Canguilhem, Georges. 1991. *The Normal and the Pathological.* With an introduction by Michel Foucault. London: Zone.

Carter, Julian. 2007. *The Heart of Whiteness: Normal Sexuality and Race in America, 1880–1940.* Durham, NC: Duke University Press.

Creadick, Anna. 2010. *Perfectly Average: The Pursuit of Normality in Postwar America.* Amherst: University of Massachusetts Press.

Davis, Lennard. 1995. *Enforcing Normalcy: Disability, Deafness, and the Body.* London: Verso.

Downing, Lisa. 2010. "John Money's 'Normophilia': Diagnosing Sexual Normality in Late-Twentieth-Century Anglo-American Sexology." *Psychology and Sexuality* 1, no. 3: 275–87.

Dreger, Alice Domurat. 2004. *One of Us: Conjoined Twins and the Future of Normal.* Cambridge, MA: Harvard University Press.

Foucault, Michel. 1991. *Discipline and Punish: The Birth of the Prison.* London: Penguin.

Galton, Francis. 1869. *Hereditary Genius: An Inquiry into Its Laws and Consequences.* London: Macmillan.

———. 1909. *Essays in Eugenics.* London: Eugenics Education Society.

Garland Thomson, Rosemarie. 1996. *Extraordinary Bodies: Figuring Physical Disability in American Culture and Literature.* New York: Columbia University Press.

Halberstam, Judith. 2005. *In a Queer Time and Place: Transgender Bodies, Subcultural Lives.* New York: New York University Press.

———. 2012. *Gaga Feminism: Sex, Gender, and the End of Normal.* Boston: Beacon.

Halperin, David. 1997. *Saint Foucault: Towards a Gay Hagiography.* New York: Oxford University Press.

Igo, Sarah. 2007. *The Averaged American: Surveys, Citizens, and the Making of a Mass Public.* Cambridge, MA: Harvard University Press.

Kevles, Daniel. 1985. *In the Name of Eugenics: Genetics and the Uses of Human Heredity.* Berkeley: University of California Press.

Porter, Theodor. 1986. *The Rise of Statistical Thinking, 1820–1900.* Princeton, NJ: Princeton University Press.

Spade, Dean. 2011. *Normal Life: Administrative Violence, Critical Trans Politics, and the Limits of Law.* Brooklyn, NY: South End.

Susan Stryker. 2004. "Transgender Studies: Queer Theory's Evil Twin." *GLQ* 10, no. 2: 212–15.

Warman, Caroline. 2010. "From Pre-normal to Abnormal: The Emergence of a Concept in Late Eighteenth-Century France." *Psychology and Sexuality* 1, no. 3: 200–213.

Warner, Michael, ed. 1993. *Fear of a Queer Planet: Queer Politics and Social Theory*. Minneapolis: University of Minnesota Press.
———. 1999. *The Trouble with Normal: Sex, Politics, and Ethics of Queer Life*. Cambridge, MA: Harvard University Press.

DOI 10.1215/23289252-2399848

Pedagogy

FRANCISCO J. GALARTE

Pedagogy, narrowly construed, is the study of teaching and learning; more generally, it pertains to the social construction of knowledge, values, and experiences. The common assumption that the classroom is the exclusive site where pedagogy transpires is challenged by educational theorists such as Henry A. Giroux (2004), Antonia Darder (2002), and bell hooks (1994), whose definitions of pedagogy extend it beyond the classroom and who, like Paolo Freire, advance a conception of pedagogy as a "practice of freedom" (Freire 2000: 80). Freire similarly redefines "educator" to mean more than a mere classroom instructor; for him, being an educator should encompass the multiple perspectives of "border intellectual, social activist, critical researcher, moral agent, radical philosopher, and political revolutionary" (Darder 2002: 249). Pedagogy, broadly defined in this way, engages questions of teaching and learning with questions of culture and power, of democracy and citizenship. It points to the multiplicity of sites (corporeal, spatial, temporal, psychic) in which education takes place and where, most importantly, knowledge is produced.

Transgender studies, as a framework or lens through which to theorize the myriad ways in which people understand, name, experience, and claim gender in relationship to such other processes as racialization, class, nationalism, and globalization, needs to incorporate a critical pedagogical perspective. In the 2008 *Women's Studies Quarterly* special "Trans-" issue, Vic Muñoz and Ednie Kaeh Garrison coined the term *transpedagogies* (291), seeking a word to capture the dialogic relationship between trans subjects and pedagogical practices. They envisioned the term as a "coalitional concept" that encompassed transsexual, transgender, and gender/queer perspectives, through which an analysis of the production of knowledge could be linked conceptually to varying experiences of gender socialization or gender identity in diverse contexts.

What might such a transpedagogy encompass? A pedagogical perspective on transgender studies should, at a minimum, note that teaching and learning about transgender phenomena take place across a spectrum of social practices and locations and that transpedagogies are part of a broader public politics not solely limited to what goes on in schools. But more expansively, a pedagogical perspective on transgender phenomena can also help unsettle historically and contextually specific knowledge(s) that shape understandings of normative gender. Transpedagogies should offer students the tools they need to participate in the political and economic power structures that shape the boundaries of gender categories, with the goal of changing those structures in ways that create greater freedom. In a transpedagogical approach, processes of learning become political mechanisms through which identities can be shaped and desires mobilized and through which the experience of bodily materiality and everyday life can take form and acquire meaning.

Transpedagogies supply a discursive mode of critique for challenging the production of social hierarchies, identities, and ideologies across local and national boundaries. They represent both a mode of cultural production and a type of cultural criticism for questioning the conditions under which knowledge of gendered embodiment is produced. They provide a space for affective engagement, for the affirmation or rejection of values, and for the inhabitation, negotiation, or refusal of culturally prescribed gendered subject positions. Understanding pedagogy as a mode of cultural production in this way underscores its performative nature. It is how theory becomes practice.

The proliferation of culture via new communication technologies and social media further shifts the production, reception, and consumption of knowledge about gender diversity. It allows for new and alternative modes of access to knowledge and for fresh ways of knowing that purposefully resist normative bodily comportment and that confound the boundaries of gender. Such technologies of the self create a space for what Chela Sandoval has called "differential maneuvering," where "the transcultural, transgendered, transsexual, transnational leaps necessary to the play of effective stratagems of oppositional praxis" can begin articulating themselves (2000: 63).

Stratagems of oppositional praxis are precisely what critical transpedagogical practices should aim to produce: they must shift the framework available for understanding, describing, and addressing the multiple and varying vulnerabilities to violence faced by transgender subjects. As Dean Spade notes, there is an uneven distribution of vulnerability and violence across trans populations, and such harms are not fully described or addressed by the single vector of transphobia (2010: 447). Paying attention to the highly variable and sometimes contradictory narratives that transgender subjects actually use to describe and explain their experiences of classist, racist, sexist, and ableist exploitation is a necessary pedagogical practice. It situates knowledge production in specific or local "acts of knowing."

Centering the transgender body as a site of knowledge production is a crucial transpedagogy. It creates new opportunities for teaching and learning by working to understand how transfolk critically understand their places in the world and tactically maneuver through it (i.e., how they negotiate relations of power, privilege, and subordination) as well as how they actively participate in the transformation of their world(s). This type of transpedagogy is radical to the extent that it critiques, and can potentially transform, how power and authority construct and organize knowledge—including knowledge of gendered desires, values, and identities (Giroux 2004: 69). Transpedagogies are indeed "practices of freedom" that can link teaching and learning to social change.

Transpedagogies must keep up with the continually shifting terms and conditions through which gender is named, imagined, and theorized as well as with the ongoing neoliberal depoliticization of public life and the impoverishment of public discourse. Transpedagogical perspectives and approaches need to ask how knowledge of transgender phenomena is constructed through this absence as well as through its presence and circulation in the public sphere. Proliferating trans-knowledges in the public sphere is only the first step of a radical educational agenda. The heart of effective transpedagogy, buttressed by rigorous intellectual work and political courage, is to link theory and praxis to create new modes of resistance and collective struggle.

Francisco J. Galarte is an assistant professor of gender and women's studies at the University of Arizona, where he teaches Chicana/Latina studies and transgender studies.

References

Darder, Antonia. 2002. *Reinventing Paulo Freire: A Pedagogy of Love*. Boulder, CO: Westview Press.
Freire, Paulo. 2000. *Pedagogy of the Oppressed*. New York: Continuum.
Giroux, Henry A. 2004. "Cultural Studies, Public Pedagogy, and the Responsibility of Intellectuals." *Communication and Critical/Cultural Studies* 1, no. 1: 59–79.
hooks, bell. 1994. *Teaching to Transgress: Education as the Practice of Freedom*. New York: Routledge.

Muñoz, Vic, and Ednie Kaeh Garrison, moderators. 2008. "Transpedagogies: A Roundtable Dialogue." *Women's Studies Quarterly* 36, no. 3–4: 288–308.

Sandoval, Chela. 2000. *Methodology of the Oppressed*. Minneapolis: University of Minnesota Press.

Spade, Dean. 2010. "Introduction: Transgender Issues and the Law." *Seattle Journal for Social Justice* 8, no. 2: 445–52.

DOI 10.1215/23289252-2399857

Performativity

KENDALL GERDES

In her 1990 *Gender Trouble: Feminism and the Subversion of Identity*, Judith Butler connected the conceptual category of performativity to the formation of the gendered subject. A *performative*, in its early usage by speech act theorist J. L. Austin, names a type of utterance (such as "I do" or "shame on you") that, by virtue of a felicitous context and relation to authority, accomplishes the action that it also announces (Austin [1962] 1975; Felman 2003; Sedgwick 1993). In a collection of lectures first published in 1962 as *How to Do Things with Words*, the terms of Austin's classifying system proliferate and repeatedly break down in a demonstration of how even descriptive language's performativity—what it does—calls into question its referentiality—what it seems to point to in the world (Austin 1975). *Gender Trouble* braids speech act theory's insight into the scandalous power of language to posit what it describes together with strands of Lacanian psychoanalysis and poststructuralism that show that this positing power belongs to language, to "discourse" in a Foucauldian register, and precisely *not* to the authority of the intending subject employing language that Austin started with.

Yet a rhetoric of performativity has developed that strips it of this theoretical heritage and turns it into a tool for defending the power of the subject, through the conscious presence of agential intention, to intervene in the discourse of gender and so to free that discourse of its injurious potential. To paraphrase the argument: "Because I *choose* my gendered practices, I subvert their harmful functions."[1] This rhetoric of performativity is a much-weakened strain of the one articulated in *Gender Trouble* and across Butler's subsequent work. In a sense, it reduces performativity to *performance*: that is, it focuses on a single instance of a gendered practice and so forgets the historical chain of repetitions that makes each instance possible. Moreover, this weakened rhetoric of performativity allocates the positing power of the performative (whether speech act or gendering practice) back to an impenetrable, invulnerable, and independent subject that Butler went to psychoanalytic theory and deconstruction precisely to expose—as already pierced, already vulnerable, and already conditioned by a linguistic and therefore rhetorical relation. The subject does not wield the discursive power of the performative. Discourse, language itself, first en-genders the subject as an effect of language's positing power.

Transgender studies is inextricably invested in the question of intentionality: is the subject of gender in charge or not? For some, to answer in the negative runs the risk of also negating the "experience of gender identity's profound ontological claim . . . about the realness and inalienability of that identity" (Stryker and Whittle 2006: 183). And yet, as Sandy Stone argues in her 1987 field-inaugurating essay, "The *Empire* Strikes Back: A Posttranssexual Manifesto," to treat (trans)sexuality as an *esse*ntial component of one's being actually forecloses the analysis of the complex and even contradictory "chaos of lived gendered experience" ([1987] 2006: 230). Treating sex *or* gender as if they were unalterable facts of our being, or, on the other hand, treating them as if they were the radically alterable selections of a freely choosing subject, or even treating them as the culturally determined products of a socially constructed reality—each of these alternatives misses the significance of performativity for any theory of gender. The subject of gender is not in charge, but exposed, addressed by the performative power of gender rather than the addresser of it. Stone points our attention both beyond an essentialist understanding of gender and directly at its lived embodiment. The performative power of gender is its ceaseless materialization of gender in the flesh. It is the power not only to make bodies legible as having gendered characteristics but also to make gender itself *take place* through bodies. Gender is performative because it inscribes itself as a discourse each time it inscribes itself on a body, as a lived experience. As Susan Stryker argues in a 1998 special transgender issue of *GLQ*, lived experience "provide[s] a site for grappling with the problematic relation between principles of performativity and a materiality that, while inescapable, defies stable representation" (147). Through the rich yield of lived experience, transgender studies must pursue the question of performativity *beyond* representation. Transgender studies is positioned, at the intersection of gender's discursivity and its materiality, to open vital questions about the (re)formation of gender, subjectivity, bodies, and the body. These questions demand a performative theory that can also account for the unrepresentable experience of gender, of being addressed by gender, and so being tossed into a rhetorical relation with it. Performativity is the connection between gendered embodiment, gendered experience, and gender's discursive force.

Kendall Gerdes is a PhD student in English with an emphasis in rhetoric at the University of Texas at Austin. Her research interests include rhetorical theory, queer theory, feminisms, and ethics; her work has been published in *Kairos* and in the *E3W Review of Books*.

Note

1.   For two exemplary refutations of such claims, see J. Halberstam 1998 (303, 306) and 2011.

References

Austin, J. L. (1962) 1975. *How to Do Things with Words*. 2nd ed. Edited by J. O. Urmson and Marina Sbisà. Cambridge, MA: Harvard University Press.

Butler, Judith. (1990) 2006. *Gender Trouble: Feminism and the Subversion of Identity*. 2nd ed. New York: Routledge.

Felman, Shoshana. 2003. *The Scandal of the Speaking Body: Don Juan with J. L. Austin, or Seduction in Two Languages*. Translated by Catherine Porter. Stanford, CA: Stanford University Press. Originally published as *The Literary Speech Act* (Ithaca, NY: Cornell University Press, 1983).

Halberstam, J. 1998. "Transgender Butch: Butch/FTM Border Wars and the Masculine Continuum." *GLQ* 4, no. 2: 287–310.

———. 2011. " 'The Killer in Me Is the Killer in You': Homosexuality and Fascism." In *The Queer Art of Failure*. Durham, NC: Duke University Press.

Sedgwick, Eve Kosofsky. 1993. "Queer Performativity: Henry James's *The Art of the Novel*." *GLQ* 1, no. 1: 1–16.

Stone, Sandy. (1987) 2006. "The *Empire* Strikes Back: A Posttranssexual Manifesto." In Stryker and Whittle, *Transgender Studies Reader*, 221–35.

Stryker, Susan. 1998. "The Transgender Issue: An Introduction." *GLQ* 4, no. 2: 145–58.

Stryker, Susan, and Stephen Whittle, eds. 2006. *The Transgender Studies Reader*. New York: Routledge.

DOI 10.1215/23289252-2399866

Perfume

LUCAS CRAWFORD

Transgender studies has ignored perfume—that simulation of "essence," that cheap man-musk that occupies busy-subway-space, that elixir that vaults old lovers and dead grandmothers into the present—perhaps because of an occasionally "occularcentric" approach (Prosser 1998: 43). To better sense that which eludes vision, can we follow our noses with three pungent imperatives? First: reclaim bodily decadence as a transing art of gender. Consider T. S. Eliot's forceful association of perfume with wasteful confusion (2011: 86–89):

> In vials of ivory and coloured glass
> Unstoppered, lurked her strange synthetic perfumes,
> Unguent, powdered, or liquid—troubled, confused
> And drowned the sense in odours

This admonishment of decadent artifice is located in an open—"unstoppered"—vial of perfume, which Eliot describes disapprovingly as a genderqueer aesthetic object: it revels in synthetics, décor, and flash, while its contents "trouble," confuse, and drown the habits of others. By reclaiming rather than refuting Eliot's judgments, we can acknowledge the artifice of olfactory norms and try to change them. For instance, we can reject the sense of wealth that Eliot attributes to perfume by revaluing the many perfumes of labour. We can eschew middle-class norms of bodily control and hyper-hygiene in order to waft ourselves in uncontrollable trajectories toward the other.

Second: critique the centrality of pheromones to gender and desire. "Super-Primal Human Female Pheromones" is a pheromone perfume marketed to MTF (male-to-female) women. The website states: "Pheromones define us to the opposite sex. . . . Instinct tells another person that though everything looks fine, there is 'something' odd. It may be the male pheromone message the TG/CD is radiating" ("Female Pheromones"). Here, smell is the sense that cannot be "fooled." Even though research on human pheromones is preliminary at best, this advertisement asserts that MTF women smell "like men." The resultant binary economy of smell implies that heterosexuality is hardwired, as if the role of perfume is to solicit more heterosexual interaction through the sneaky manipulation of instinct.

Finally, use fragrance to build a new praxis of connection and memory. Against the binary economy described above, queer perfumer Christopher Brosius has offered scents such as "Faggot" and "Lipstick" as well as a series called "Metamorphosis." Brosius describes these scents as distilled motion that can be reanimated by bodies: one scent, for instance, replicates "the moment when one simple beautiful gesture can transform an entire life" (Brosius). To Brosius, the perfumed body can activate memories that belong to others or are yet to happen to us. The perfumative gesture can trigger such transformations of olfactory expectation by turning time into vapor. Smells can even cloud and combine above and around us, creating a smelled version of what Susan Stryker calls the nonsovereign "transsubjective ensemble" (2008: 41). This is the transing potential of perfume: it disrupts our sense that we live only in the present; it uses the body as an archive that moves people; it clouds our separations; it communicates to those who would never think of talking to us; it is gender in motion, midair and inhaled.

Lucas Crawford is Ruth Wynn Woodward Lecturer in Gender Studies at Simon Fraser University. Lucas's poetry is forthcoming in *Rattle, Rampike, PRISM International*, and *Between: New Gay Poetry*. Lucas's forthcoming scholarship includes articles in the *Journal of Homosexuality* and *English Studies in Canada*.

References

Brosius, Christopher. CB I Hate Perfume. www.cbihateperfume.com (accessed November 14, 2012).

Eliot, T. S. 2011. *The Waste Land*. In *The Waste Land and Other Poems*, 63–83. Toronto: Broadview.

Female Pheromones. "The Little Bit of Magic No Girl Can Be Without." www.thebreastformstore .com/Pheromones.aspx (accessed November 15, 2012).

Prosser, Jay. 1998. *Second Skins: The Body Narratives of Transsexuality*. New York: Columbia University Press.

Stryker, Susan. 2008. "Dungeon Intimacies: The Poetics of Transsexual Sadomasochism." *Parallax* 14, no. 1: 36–47.

DOI 10.1215/23289252-2399875

Phenomenology

GAYLE SALAMON

Phenomenology is that branch of philosophy concerned with the way in which things in the world give themselves to consciousness and with the structures through which we experience that givenness. Phenomenological philosophy is understood as originating with Edmund Husserl and developing throughout the twentieth century, though as a movement in philosophy it is something more diffuse than a coherent school of thought or an agreed-upon set of tenets, in no small part because phenomenology was a reaction against philosophy's tradition of grand system building. Phenomenology thus names a number of philosophers concerned variously with the way in which the world presents itself to consciousness, the fundamentally ambiguous nature of human existence and meaning, and the shared nature of the lifeworld. It also includes branches in the social sciences that emphasize the lifeworld in its externality and the specificity of the social world in which individual experience is necessarily embedded, focusing more squarely on social contexts and human relations, as in the work of Alfred Schutz (1972). What might be said to unite these philosophers is a careful attention to how the world appears to us and an endeavor to see anew that which we move through everyday, a breaking out of our habitual and customary way of perceiving, categorizing, and understanding our world. It is that endeavor to see the familiar with new eyes—that phenomenological principle of holding in abeyance what we know about any object, situation, or person in order to see it freshly and more precisely—that offers itself as an incitement to reinterrogate that which we think we know about gender and thus to radically open up the traditional categories through which it is understood.

The prefix *trans-* has, within phenomenology, most often referred to transcendental phenomenology, Husserl's endeavor to craft philosophy as a scientific inquiry into phenomena and essences. But phenomenology can also be understood as receptive to trans in its gendered sense, through insistence on the importance of embodied experience to understanding the nature of self, others, and the world. This emphasis on lived experience proves helpful in two ways. First is the thesis that the body is fundamentally important to subjectivity, vital and essential to it rather than a distraction from it. This might initially seem like a position that is at odds with some variants of trans studies; one could imagine the objection that gender is precisely *not* found or determined at the level of the body. But phenomenology offers an expansive conception of the body in which it is more than merely its materiality, emphasizing the importance of how one feels in and senses with and inhabits one's body. The phenomenological claim that the body is not just something I have or use, not merely an object I haul around, but is rather something that I *am* allows an understanding of the body as defined and constituted by *what I feel* and not simply *what others see*. In this phenomenological view, drawn largely from Maurice Merleau-Ponty, gender and sex can be understood as delivered to the subject through a felt sense rather than determined by the external contours of the body, thus circumventing a view of sex or gender that understands either to be a matter of bodily morphology as given. Merleau-Ponty (2010) spends little time ruminating on gender as such, and that within a squarely normative framework. However, his account of gender, binary and normative though it may be, understands it to be gestural rather than morphological, an articulation that anticipates Judith Butler's account of gender as performative.

Henry S. Rubin's foundational 1998 article "Phenomenology as Method in Trans Studies" was the first piece to explore the ways in which phenomenology offered methodological resources to the newly emerging field of trans studies. Rubin argues that phenomenology is uniquely suited to the study of trans lives because it privileges the unique perspective of subjects in describing their own subjectivity. Rubin draws on Merleau-Ponty's phenomenology to argue that one's own account of one's own positioning is more accurate exactly because one is the only person who can inhabit that individual position. The enunciating subject's own account, then, will be more precisely located than anyone else's ostensibly more "objective" assessment, privileged rather than suspiciously subjective or biased, as the traditional charge against such narratives would have it. In his book *Self-Made Men* (2003), Rubin suggests that the phenomenologically grounded "I" has a favored relation to truth.

Though Merleau-Ponty's emphasis on the centrality of the *corps propre* to subjectivity and relation has perhaps the most obvious connection with trans studies, phenomenology has been drawn on otherwise and variously regarding trans issues. Emmanuel Levinas has written on our necessarily ethical relation to the face of the other, and Nikki Sullivan (2006) has drawn on a Levinasian ethics in her concept of the transmogrification of the other. Heidegger, too, has been used as a resource; Das Janssen (2011) has suggested that Heidegger's concept of Dasein can be used as a resource for thinking about trans embodiment in a philosophical context. Simone de Beauvoir's (1948) ethics of ambiguity and work on gender offers another potentially fruitful philosophy of ethics for trans studies, and Frantz Fanon (1967) has theorized the social consequences of racial difference and the perception and the effect of racism in phenomenological terms. Even Husserl, for all his abstraction, has been usefully mobilized by Sarah Ahmed (2006) for queer studies, and his concepts of internal and external horizons show future promise for trans studies.[1]

Gayle Salamon is assistant professor of English and gender and sexuality studies at Princeton University. She is the author of *Assuming a Body: Transgender and Rhetorics of Materiality* (2010), winner of the 2011 Lambda Literary Award in LGBT Studies.

Note

1.   For a more in-depth discussion of issues presented here, see "The Sexual Schema: Transposition and Transgender in *Phenomenology of Perception*" in *Assuming a Body: Transgender and Rhetorics of Materiality* (Salamon 2010).

References

Ahmed, Sara. 2006. *Queer Phenomenology*. Durham, NC: Duke University Press.

Beauvoir, Simone de. 1948. *The Ethics of Ambiguity*. Translated by Bernard Frechtman. Secaucus, NJ: Citadel Press.

Fanon, Frantz. 1967. *Black Skin, White Masks*. Translated by Charles Lam Markmann. New York: Grove Weidenfeld.

Janssen, Das. 2011. "Transgender Dasein: Stuck in the Wrong Theory of Embodiment," paper presented at the Society for Phenomenology and Existential Philosophy Annual Meeting, Philadelphia, October 19.

Merleau-Ponty, Maurice. 2010. *Phenomenology of Perception*. Translated by Don Landes. New York: Routledge.

Rubin, Henry S. 1998. "Phenomenology as Method in Trans Studies." *GLQ* 4, no. 2: 263–81.

———. 2003. *Self-Made Men: Identity and Embodiment among Transsexual Men*. Nashville: Vanderbilt University Press.

Salamon, Gayle. 2010. *Assuming a Body: Transgender and Rhetorics of Materiality*. New York: Columbia University Press.

Schutz, Alfred. 1972. *Phenomenology of the Social World*. Chicago: Northwestern University Press.

Sullivan, Nikki. 2006. "Transmogrification: (Un)becoming Other(s)." In *The Transgender Studies Reader*, ed. Susan Stryker and Stephen Whittle, 553–63. New York: Routledge.

DOI 10.1215/23289252-2399884

Pornography

ELIZA STEINBOCK

Pornography was famously defined by Judge Potter Stewart's maxim, "I know it when I see it" (*Jacobellis v. Ohio* 1964, quoted in Williams 1999), highlighting its subjective, visual status and its political kinship to obscenity. The production and consumption of pornographic materials forms a major transnational economy, demonstrating capitalism's uneven development and circulation of images.[1] Porn in its various forms and niches can also be considered highly localized, personalized even, as evidenced by specific mail-order and online digital cultures. It signifies the apotheosis of Western confession culture in which the declaration of sexuality anchors the self in the social order (Foucault 1978).

My penis is like a wart. Trans bodies and identities are equally solicited to participate in "speaking sex." However, the sexological histories that prefigure the sexual in a transsexual diagnosis (gender identity disorder, gender dysphoria) fasten desire onto the transition itself. The criteria in the *Diagnostic Standards and Procedure Manual* V seek statements of disgust with one's sexed embodiment. Any potential eroticism of a trans body by and for the trans individual is supplanted by the necessity to state a desire to change one's genitals. The construction of the monolithic transsexual reduces the heteroglossia of sexual experience to a whisper of secrets (Stone [1991] 2006).

My sexuality is not dysfunctional. Popular pornographies of so-called dysfunctional "trans sexualities" (Steinbock and Davy 2012) continue to involve forced feminization narratives and tribadism. With mass video accessibility, previously niche she-male/*travestie* fantasies entered the mainstream market. At the same time, transwomen filmmakers like Mirah-Soliel Ross and Stephanie Anne Lloyd as well as transmen Les Nichols and Chance Ryder began making porn addressed to the emerging transgender community. These works challenge the dominant imaginary by claiming erotic space and flirting with becoming fetishes for a cisgender *or* transgender gaze.

"Look! No, Don't!" With the aspiration to appear in a sexual imaginary, but not as a freak, came a community backlash. Feared repercussions for self-sexualization were setbacks in the political gains of medical access and social tolerance. Jamison Green describes this reflex in the phrase "Look! No, Don't!": to want political recognition but not social scrutiny (1999). Sexual representation was a key

problem for early trans activism; at issue was who would be a "good representative" for the community. Pornographic materials for trans communities, like for feminist camps, figured large in the war of identity politics. Claims for and against porn assume that the image transparently represents the real identity of the performer, collapsing visual realism into a "visual essentialism" of identity (Steinbock 2013).

Hard core is hard work. The political strategy of countering stereotyped images with more diverse images of trans sexuality has been championed by various organizations: Adult Video News Awards acknowledged the pioneering work of Buck Angel and Allanah Starr; the Feminist Porn Awards honors trans* and genderqueer performers like Drew Deveaux and Jiz Lee; and the Berlin Porn Film Festival actively supports trans (post)pornographies. Film directors focusing on trans sexuality from within the community include Christopher Lee, Hans Scheirl, Cary Cronenwett, Tobaron Waxman, Morty Diamond, T-wood team, and Tobi Hill-Meyer.

We have hit the cotton ceiling. The new wave of queer pornography, creating a professional and accessible DVD and online alt.porn world, has swept along trans sexualities. Notably, Courtney Trouble's "Queer Porn.TV" and Shine Louise Houston's queer-lesbian "Crash Pad Series" regularly include trans performers. However, the trans pornographic ideal appearing in most queer porn has become mainly aligned with either transmasculine or post-operative transfeminine bodies. The marginalization of transwomen in queer sex scenes echoes the status of transfeminity in queer erotic communities, which has been dubbed the "cotton ceiling." A new queer normativity set by porn conventions continues to exclude certain forms of trans sexuality. The "productive disruption of structured sexuality and spectra of desire" (Stone [1991] 2006: 231) engendered by trans embodiments has yet to be fully explored in pornography.

Eliza Steinbock is lecturer in literature and art at the University of Maastricht. Her recent publications include work featured in *Journal of Homosexuality* (2014), *The Transgender Studies Reader 2* (2013), *Violence and Agency: Queer and Feminist Perspectives* (2013), and *Somatechnics: Queering the Technologisation of Bodies* (2009).

Note

1. For trans porn, this means the major markets for sourcing she-male pornography for the global North are in Latin America. The alternative community pornographies mainly derive from the United Kingdom and North America. I have tried to indicate the diversity of porn cultures through the examples given of cultural workers, which I encourage the reader to explore further. For a post-Foucauldian analysis of pornography's transnational flows in relation to gender, see Beatriz Preciado 2008.

References

Foucault, Michel. 1978. *An Introduction*. Vol. 1 of *The History of Sexuality*. Translated by Robert Hurley. New York: Vintage.

Green, Jamison. 1999. "Look! No, Don't! The Visibility Dilemma for Transsexual Men." In *Reclaiming Genders: Transsexual Grammars at the* Fin de Siècle, ed. Stephen Whittle and Kate More, 117–31. London: Cassell.

Preciado, Beatriz. 2008. "Pharmaco-pornographic Politics: Towards a New Gender Ecology." *Parallax* 14, no. 1: 105–17.

Steinbock, Eliza. 2013. " 'Look!' but Also, 'Touch!': Theorizing Images of Trans-Eroticism beyond a Politics of Visual Essentialism." In "Porno-Graphics and Porno-Tactics: Desire, Affect, and Representation in Pornography." Special issue, *Re-public: Re-imagining Democracy*. www.re-public.gr/en/?p=5514 (accessed October 28, 2013).

Steinbock, Eliza, and Zowie Davy. 2012. " 'Sexing Up' Bodily Aesthetics: Notes towards Theorizing Trans Sexuality." In *Sexualities: Past Reflections and Future Directions*, ed. Sally Hines and Yvette Taylor, 266–85. Basingstoke, UK: Palgrave Macmillan.

Stone, Sandy. (1991) 2006. "The *Empire* Strikes Back: A Posttranssexual Manifesto." In *The Transgender Studies Reader*, ed. Stephen Whittle and Susan Stryker, 221–35. New York: Routledge.

Williams, Linda. 1999. *Hard Core: Power, Pleasure, and the "Frenzy of the Visible."* Berkeley: University of California Press.

DOI 10.1215/23289252-2399893

Postmodernism

JAMES SARES

For Jean Baudrillard, transsexuality symbolizes alienating postmodern transformations across economics, aesthetics, and politics. "We are all transsexuals *symbolically*," he argues, as the body is reduced to a mere canvas on which the traffic of gendered signs is grafted or torn in antipolitical play (2009: 23). Baudrillard understands the postmodern body as the extended site of integration into networks and circuits of superficial political action and cybernetic capitalist complicity. Similarly to Fredric Jameson, he employs the spatial metaphors of depthlessness and flattening to emphasize the subject's reduction to artifice. These metaphors reveal postmodern cultural production as underpinned by the disruption of mere appearance from identity or inner desire. The disruptive element of postmodern aesthetics underlies the denaturalization of sign from referent, such that the technologies of gendered and sexed transformation reveal the symbolic systems through which categories of gender and sex gain meaning. Thus the modernist aesthetic is put into crisis when the body, moving through time and space, is no longer the site of a stable, natural, and objective referential truth of gender or sex, despite the search for new relationalities constructed out of that very ontological denaturalization (Stryker 1999: 170–71).

Baudrillard's analysis falls into unsubstantiated fatalism because he emphasizes meaning's liquidation, while postmodern aesthetics shifts the grounds for understanding meaning through subjective rupture itself. The technologies and discourses of transsexuality reveal the tensions of transforming the body and its adornments across, between, or outside the policed confines of a gender/sex binary while also being reinscribed into multiple discourses of fractured referentiality. Some discourses appeal to an unchanging sense of gender identity and relocate a "truth" of gender to be revealed from within the body, while others emphasize dialectical movements of identity and embodiment or otherwise challenge the ontologized terms of gender identity and desire. Tensions among these multiple narratives are salient in the uneven ethical-material topographies of corporeal transformation across which conflicts of late capitalist modernity play out, including state and medical apparatuses and other trans community spaces. In these spaces, the boundaries of authentic transness are often policed by appeals to deep relationality between materiality and inner desire or identity, regardless of its stasis or dynamism, against merely superficial drag or the unfettered play of gendered signs. Yet all of these references to corporeal mutability emerge from particular conceptual constellations that reveal sex/gender as regimes of coding and producing bodies. These possibilities appear with the production of the subject as a form of rupture.

The postmodern aesthetic must be itself denaturalized as a particular regime of meaning-production rather than as meaning's mere liquidation or as the revelation of meaning's true form. The multiple articulations of subjective rupture become myth when concepts are ontologically essentialized rather than revealed as historical and social productions and abstractions that mediate each other. The denaturalization of both sex and gender as social constructions offers possibilities to refigure embodiment, but the conceptual disjunctures between materiality and symbolism, being and thinking, or body and desire threaten to ontologize and reinscribe authenticity through rupture itself. The conceptual mediation and latent unfolding of such categories denaturalizes rupture as a tenuously policed construction between concepts: sex's referent as body meets the body's materiality as symbolic, aesthetic, and interpersonal; gender's referent as social action, role, or symbolism meets the materiality of these processes produced out of and on to the body; identity's referent as inner desire or mind meets these terms as interpersonal and corporeal. Appeals to trans authenticity through statically constructed bounds of sex, gender identity, and gender performance thus encounter the body as site and product of deep relationality and that relationality's own latent unraveling. The deployments and subversions of these ontological layerings reveal tensions in ascribing through them authenticity of corporeality and embodiment.

The production and unraveling of this relationality constitutes the dialectic between nonconceptual materiality and its signification into concepts. Baudrillard's reduction of transsexuality to the symbolic realm presumes appearance as domineering the essence of the subject, such that the subject is hollowed of authentic content. Yet Baudrillard produces the very meaninglessness he critiques by hypostatizing the concept of the subject as form of rupture without reflexive critique of its historical and social construction. He thus ignores, as Theodor Adorno emphasizes throughout *Negative Dialectics*, the inadequacy of concepts in fully capturing the nonconceptual experiences and materiality to which they refer. The referents of concepts are irreducible to their conceptual signification, as concepts are abstracted *moments* of the dialectic of meaning-production; in self-critique, the very concepts of concept and nonconceptual materiality pass into each other rather than reduce to each other. Thus rather than being objective descriptions or symbolic reflections of reality, concepts of gender, sex, and subjective rupture are deployed as power-laced abstractions constituted through various discourses and technologies. The struggle to produce meaning in the face of meaning's own conceptual inadequacy and consequent mediated liquidation engenders political confrontation around life as somatic/technological structure and life as ethical question. Contrary to Baudrillard's lamentations, the "deep" political questions about meaning thrive through these tensions: What is the very nature of being gendered/sexed? Should sex and gender remain categories through which to classify and produce bodies? How do uneven conditions of meaning-production open possibilities for resistance, change, or integration into various political and economic apparatuses?

In imagining queered forms of labor, value, and materiality, it is necessary to confront spatial metaphors of superficiality that continue to haunt analyses of postmodernism. Thus far critical queer responses to the projects of Jameson and Baudrillard have left these metaphors unchallenged, perhaps in fear of slipping back into *modernist* aesthetics of authenticity based on the "mimetic reproduction for subjectivity of a stable, material objectivity that lies outside the subject" (Stryker 1999: 164). The tension between critique and appropriation of postmodernism synthesizes, in Jack Halberstam's work, as the reclamation of superficiality, which he claims "may not be a symptom of a diseased political culture but a marvelously flat and uninhibited repudiation of the normativity inherent in 'deep' political projects" (Halberstam 2005: 124). Halberstam explores two-dimensional transgender art as anticapitalist resistance but, in assuming the unidirectional gaze of the surgeon or the artist, flattens the body to a mere mimetic canvas on which technologies operate. He thus objectifies and alienates representations of the body from the shifting acts of embodiment and performance that catalyze conflict over the very terms and alignments of identity, aesthetics, and politics. Against such static analysis, it is necessary to reveal the competing metaphysics of desire, ontological layering, and appeals to authenticity that enable dynamic conflict over trans subjectivities. Moving forward, we do not need to "reclaim" superficiality from such analysis as much as recognize that depth has never left these struggles in the first place, manifesting instead in the debate over superficiality itself.

James Sares completed his AB degree from Harvard University in 2012.

References

Baudrillard, Jean. 2009. *The Transparency of Evil: Essays on Extreme Phenomena*. New York: Verso.

Halberstam, Jack. 2005. *In a Queer Time and Place: Transgender Bodies, Subcultural Lives*. New York: New York University Press.

Stryker, Susan. 1999. "Christine Jorgensen's Atom Bomb: Transsexuality and the Emergence of Postmodernity." In *Playing Dolly: Technocultural Formations, Fantasies, and Fictions of Assisted Reproduction*, ed. E. Anne Kaplan and Susan Squier, 157–71. New Brunswick, NJ: Rutgers University Press.

DOI 10.1215/23289252-2399902

Prison-Industrial Complex in the United States

ELIAS WALKER VITULLI

One night in June 2011, as they walked through a South Minneapolis neighborhood to the grocery store, CeCe McDonald, a young African American trans woman, and a group of her friends, all also African American and queer, were attacked by a group of white people who yelled racist and transphobic slurs at them, including "faggots," "niggers," and "chicks with dicks." When one of their attackers smashed a glass into McDonald's face, the attack escalated into a physical fight, during which one of her attackers was fatally stabbed. When police arrived on the scene, they arrested only McDonald.[1]

McDonald was later charged with two counts of second-degree murder. Initially, she was placed in solitary confinement at the Hennepin County men's jail, and she received insufficient medical care for a serious cut on her face, which eventually became infected. In May 2012, McDonald accepted a plea agreement in which she pleaded guilty to second-degree manslaughter and was sentenced to prison for forty-one months. In June, she was transferred to the men's prison in St. Cloud, Minnesota. In January 2014, McDonald was released from prison after serving nineteen months.

McDonald's experiences stitch together a web of racialized, gendered, and sexualized violence and criminalization that many trans people, especially trans women of color, experience daily. Her story is emblematic of the experiences of trans people whose lives come in contact with the prison-industrial complex. Over the past decade, some scholars and activists have begun to use the term *prison-industrial complex* to describe the mutually beneficial and far-reaching relationship between state and private interests that promotes the prison system as a central response to social, economic, and racial problems (see, e.g., Davis 2003; Gilmore 2007; Rodríguez 2006). The prison-industrial complex is a dynamic and productive web of white supremacist, neoliberal, heteropatriarchal, and gender-normative power that targets social deviance for criminalization and imprisonment and secures normativity. In practice, certain populations marked as racially, sexually, gender, and/or class deviant—such as low-income African American men, trans women of color, and gender-nonconforming queer women of color or aggressives—are criminalized, portrayed as suspicious and dangerous, disproportionately incarcerated, and subjected to violence, while whiteness, heterosexuality, and non-trans status are *de*criminalized. In other words, policing, prisons, and punishment are organized by and help construct race, gender, sexuality, and class in the United States.

While throughout its history the prison system has been a central site of social, racial, gender, and sexual formation and control, it has taken on new importance since the 1970s. Responding to the needs of globalization and deindustrialization and as part of the backlash against racial justice movements of the 1950s to 1970s, the United States began to rapidly grow its prison population from an average daily population of about 300,000 at the beginning of the 1970s to nearly 2.3 million today. This rise in prison population has been fueled by racialized law enforcement, prosecution, and sentencing that have produced a prison population that is approximately 70 percent people of color. The new mass scale of the prison system has been termed "mass incarceration" to mark how certain populations are targeted for systematic imprisonment and to describe its devastating impacts on targeted communities, most centrally low-income black communities but also many trans and queer communities.

Law enforcement's targeting of queer, gender-nonconforming, and transgender people is not new. The history of trans people in the United States has been a history of criminalization. Throughout most of the nineteenth and twentieth centuries, gender nonconformity, cross-dressing, and homosexuality were criminalized through laws and policing practices. Susan Stryker (2008) argues that trans communities and identities often formed and coalesced in response to experiences of persistent police scrutiny, harassment, and violence. This history produced what Joey L. Mogul, Andrea J. Ritchie, and Kay Whitlock (2010) call "queer criminal archetypes," which persist into the present.

Today, people who are visibly gender nonconforming, especially those who are also marked as racially and/or economically deviant, are often viewed by police as particularly suspicious and subject to intense surveillance, violence, and arrest. Trans women often report being stopped by police under the suspicion that they are sex workers, an experience so common it has been labeled "walking while trans." Queer criminal archetypes affect policing and also prosecution, sentencing, and treatment within penal institutions. This criminalization, coupled with endemic employment discrimination, poverty, homelessness, racism, and family rejection, has led to the disproportionate incarceration of trans and gender-nonconforming people. Within jails and prisons, trans people are almost always placed in a sex-segregated institution based on their genitals and are expected to conform to the norms of the sex of the institutions. Prison administrators often view gender-nonconforming and trans prisoners as security threats and subject them to increased surveillance and punishment, denial of medical care and appropriately gendered clothing and grooming products, isolation in segregation, and verbal, physical, and sexual harassment and assault.

Imprisoned trans and gender-nonconforming people, like McDonald, have fought against their criminalization and the prison-industrial complex's attacks on their gender identities and expressions for more than a century (Kunzel 2008; Stanley and Smith 2011). Yet their words, lives, and experiences are rarely part of trans studies conversations. As criminalization and disproportionate incarceration continue and as trans people continue to experience harassment and violence throughout the prison-industrial complex, the experiences and life chances of significant segments of our communities will be intimately bound to the prison-industrial complex.

Elias Walker Vitulli is a doctoral candidate in American studies at the University of Minnesota. His dissertation examines the history of the incarceration of gender-nonconforming and trans people in the United States. His article, "'A Means of Assuring the Safe and Efficient Operation of a Prison': Administrative Segregation, Security, and Gender Nonconformity," is forthcoming in *GLQ*.

Note

1.   For more on McDonald's case and to read some of her writing, go to supportcece .wordpress.com.

References

Davis, Angela Y. 2003. *Are Prisons Obsolete?* New York: Seven Stories.

Gilmore, Ruth Wilson. 2007. *Golden Gulag: Prisons, Surplus, Crisis, and Opposition in Globalizing California*. Berkeley: University of California Press.

Kunzel, Regina. 2008. *Criminal Intimacy: Prison and the Uneven History of Modern American Sexuality*. Chicago: University of Chicago Press.

Mogul, Joey L., Andrea J. Ritchie, and Kay Whitlock. 2010. *Queer (In)Justice: The Criminalization of LGBT People in the United States*. Boston: Beacon.

Rodríguez, Dylan. 2006. *Forced Passages: Imprisoned Radical Intellectuals and the U.S. Prison Regime*. Minneapolis: University of Minnesota Press.

Stanley, Eric A., and Nat Smith, eds. 2011. *Captive Genders: Trans Embodiment and the Prison Industrial Complex*. Oakland, CA: AK.

Stryker, Susan. 2008. *Transgender History*. Berkeley, CA: Seal.

DOI 10.1215/23289252-2399911

Psychoanalysis

PATRICIA ELLIOT

Psychoanalysis is a theory and practice of interpretation directed to making sense of otherwise unconscious sexual desire, sexual pleasure, and the gender identities of human beings. Neither a biological nor a social determinist theory, psycho-analysis theorizes human subjects as psychic entities inscribed in language, dis-course, and social relationships, all of which are primarily unconscious either necessarily or through a process of repression. Despite its justifiably contested history with regard to transsexuality, many psychoanalytic thinkers argue that psychoanalysis offers tools for thinking about the complexity and particularly of *any* subjectivity, including transsexual subjectivity (Elliot 2010). They do so in full awareness that trans persons have been negatively affected by transphobic atti-tudes and practices, especially when psychoanalysis adopts normative models of interpretation.

The history of the relationship of psychoanalysis to transsexuals is one that is exceedingly fraught, and trans persons have good reason to be sceptical about the potential for reconciliation. For those seeking surgery, the dependence on psychiatric approval already introduces a foreign element into the therapeutic relationship that compromises the relationship from the outset. But even in the absence of this element, resistance on the part of trans persons to psychoanalysis is a reasonable response to patronizing, moralizing, and stigmatizing attitudes held toward them by many analysts. Although this observation was made in 1974 (Person and Ovsey 1974), it has recently been reiterated by psychoanalyst and theorist Patricia Gherovici (2011: 3): "In both subtle and brutal ways, psycho-analysis has a history of coercive heteronormatization and pathologization of non-normative sexualities and genders." Indeed, as Gherovici points out, until very recently, many analysts have been either threatened or puzzled by trans-sexuals and often have been unsuccessful in concealing their transphobic views. Moreover, she suggests that this transphobic history is "based on a selective reinterpretation of the Freudian texts" or, more forcefully, one based not only on selective rereadings but on "reductive distortions" born of a "homophobic and transphobic history" (ibid.). Her point is that psychoanalysis has much to offer when it manages to divest itself of its normalizing and discriminatory history. It is to these often neglected but more valuable aspects that contemporary theorists turn in order to develop a more promising understanding of trans embodiments and identities.

Several psychoanalytic theorists have turned to Jacques Lacan's theory of sexuation to investigate sexuality, subjectivity, and desire in relation to transsexuality (Carlson 2010; Dean 2000; Elliot 2001, 2010; Gherovici 2010, 2011; Gozlan 2011; Salamon 2010; Shepherdson 1994). These theorists support Lacan's reading of sexuality as rooted in the polymorphous perversity of infantile sexuality and in the sexual drives that are *not* gender specific as well as his view that sexual positions of masculinity and femininity are taken up based on unconscious fantasy and not anatomy. While Freud took reproductive genitality as the ideal model of sexuality, Lacan (1998) rejected this norm in claiming that there is no sexual relation as such but that sexuality comes to attach itself to relations of love and gender identity that are socially constructed. Asserting a complex relationship between body and psyche, Lacanian theorists emphasize the instability and uncertainty of sexual identity, arguing that the normalizing constructions of gender imposed by the social must be understood as something other than sexual difference.

Recently, Shanna T. Carlson locates the rift between gender studies and psychoanalysis regarding the question of transgender precisely where the logic of sexual difference is concerned. Where gender refers to conventional meanings attributed to masculinity and femininity based on a belief that such meanings become attached to the body, sexual difference refers to "two different logics . . . two different approaches to the Other, two different stances with respect to desire, and (at least) two different types of *jouissance*" (Carlson 2010: 64). For Carlson, the only difference between transsexual and cisgender subjects is that the latter claim a "false monopoly on gender certainty" (ibid.: 65) and have the power to exclude and oppress transsexuals. Moreover, she suggests that transgendered persons who pose the questions "Am I a man, or am I a woman, and what does that mean?" have the potential to expose, through their suffering, what discourses of gender mask: not a "liberating multiplicity" but a "discursive flexibility" based on lack and on exclusion (ibid.: 66).

In a similar spirit, Gherovici (2011: 10–11) agrees with trans theorists Kate Bornstein (1994) and Patrick Califia (1997) that transsexual desires for gender certainty must not be simplistically reduced to a fantasy of being outside sex. Gherovici takes issue with Catherine Millot's (1990) assumption that transsexuals occupy a "psychotic" position based on the fantasy of a sex that is not lacking, a sex that is complete and outside sexual difference. Charles Shepherdson (1994) clarified what was at stake in this fantasy of psychic redemption, a concern anticipated by Sandy Stone (1991) and discussed by Patricia Elliot (2001) and Gayle Salamon (2004) with respect to aspects of Jay Prosser's (1998) theory of trans embodiment. Although some argued in the late 1990s against Millot's view that surgery is a harmful confirmation of the fantasy (Elliot and Roen 1998), it was not until a decade later that a practicing Lacanian analyst explicitly challenged her colleagues to abandon Millot's "generalized assumption that most transsexuals are psychotic" (Gherovici 2011: 12).

Gherovici creatively extends Lacan's concept of the "sinthome"—a kind of generalized model of the symptom that is a way to deal with what Lacan calls the absence of sexual relation—to trans desires for reembodiment or transition. A symptom is a compromise formation between a repressed drive element and a repressing agency. For Lacan, the ego structured by the compromise of id and superego is the typical symptom of humans. The sinthome suggests that it is possible through analysis or through writing to bring about a subjective change that replaces a dysfunctional symptom with a new compromise that better favors life, love, and work. Gherovici (2011: 14) endorses Lacan's view that there is "no subject without a sinthome," a construction of the subject's position in relation to discourses of the social. Moreover, because sexual positions are not based on anatomy but on uncertainty, transsexual transition is a sinthome that establishes "a workable consistency for the subject" (ibid.: 12). With reference to Prosser and others, Gherovici contends it is the trans narrative, the writing of one's transformation, that marks the sinthome for transsexual subjects.

Psychoanalyst Oren Gozlan applies Gherovici's concept of the sinthome to transsexuality as well. As the place "where surgery and writing intersect," the transsexual sinthome is a solution to suffering that goes beyond a defensive illusion of unity that would deny lack, subjectivity, and desire (Gozlan 2011: 48). Differing from the symptomatic idealization of the other sex that represses sexual difference, the sinthome offers a way to understand transsexual surgery as "a means to claim one's desire" through giving meaning to one's embodiment (ibid.: 46). Gozlan describes transitioning as a "rebirthing of oneself," but one that "accepts failure as inevitable and is willing to live creatively with the 'between zone'" (ibid.: 48). For him, the scar becomes an important "remainder" and "reminder" of separation from the Other, and surgery "becomes an act—it traverses a phantasy of union, giving up the phantasized Other, but having to live with a scar" (ibid.: 49). Like Gherovici, Gozlan recasts the process of transitioning as a creative project that includes both surgery and narration—an affirmation that mirrors the experience of many transsexual authors.

As the psychoanalytic work of Gherovici and others aims to depathologize transsexuality, there may be a new beginning for the relationship between psychoanalysis and trans as well. There is certainly some hope in Gherovici's observation that "transgender people are actually changing the clinical praxis, advancing new ideas for the clinic" (2011: 9), ideas that, if heeded, promise to transform the relationship altogether.

Patricia Elliot is a professor of sociology at Wilfrid Laurier University. She is author of *Debates in Transgender, Queer, and Feminist Theory: Contested Sites* (2010).

References

Bornstein, Kate. 1994. *Gender Outlaw: On Men, Women, and the Rest of Us*. New York: Routledge.

Califia, Patrick. 1997. *Sex Changes: The Politics of Transgenderism*. San Francisco: Cleis.

Carlson, Shanna T. 2010. "Transgender Subjectivity and the Logic of Sexual Difference." *differences* 21, no. 2: 46–72.

Dean, Tim. 2000. *Beyond Sexuality*. Chicago: University of Chicago Press.

Elliot, Patricia. 2001. "A Psychoanalytic Reading of Transsexual Embodiment." *Studies in Gender and Sexuality* 2, no. 4: 295–325.

———. 2010. *Debates in Transgender, Queer, and Feminist Theory: Contested Sites*. Surrey, UK: Ashgate.

Elliot, Patricia, and Katrina Roen. 1998. "Transgenderism and the Question of Embodiment: Promising Queer Politics?" *GLQ* 4, no. 2: 231–61.

Gherovici, Patricia. 2010. *Please Select Your Gender: From the Invention of Hysteria to the Democratizing of Transgenderism*. New York: Routledge.

———. 2011. "Psychoanalysis Needs a Sex Change." *Gay and Lesbian Issues and Psychology Review* 7, no. 1: 3–18.

Gozlan, Oren. 2011. "Transsexual Surgery: A Novel Reminder and a Navel Remainder." *International Forum of Psychoanalysis* 20, no. 1: 45–52.

Lacan, Jacques. 1998. *The Seminar of Jacques Lacan, Book XX, Encore: On Feminine Sexuality: The Limits of Love and Knowledge, 1972–1973*. Edited by Jacques-Alain Miller. Translated by Bruce Fink. New York: Norton.

Millot, Catherine. 1990. *Horsexe: Essay on Transsexuality*. Translated by K. Hylton. New York: Autonomedia.

Person, Ethel Spector, and Lionel Ovesey. 1974. "The Transsexual Syndrome in Males. II. Secondary Transsexualism." *American Journal of Psychotherapy* 28, no. 2: 174–93.

Prosser, Jay. 1998. *Second Skins: The Body Narratives of Transsexuality*. New York: Columbia University Press.

Salamon, Gayle. 2004. "The Bodily Ego and the Contested Domain of the Material." *differences* 15, no. 3: 95–122.

———. 2010. *Assuming a Body: Transgender and Rhetorics of Materiality*. New York: Columbia University Press.

Shepherdson, Charles. 1994. "The *Role* of Gender and the *Imperative* of Sex." In *Supposing the Subject*, ed. Joan Copjec, 158–84. London: Verso.

Stone, Sandy. 1991. "The *Empire* Strikes Back: A Posttranssexual Manifesto." In *Body Guards: The Cultural Politics of Gender Ambiguity*, ed. J. Epstein and K. Straub, 280–304. New York: Routledge.

DOI 10.1215/23289252-2399920

Psychoanalytic

SHANNA T. CARLSON

The failures of psychoanalysis with respect to transgender people are somewhat—
and sadly—familiar. Perhaps the most famous example is Lacanian psychoanalyst Catherine Millot's *Horsexe: Essay on Transsexuality*, a text whose precision
explaining Lacanian terminology is matched only by its tendency to sensationalize
and generalize about transgender experience. Mostly, however, Lacanians are
strikingly silent on the subject of transgender phenomena—striking, given that
Lacanian psychoanalysis is fundamentally preoccupied with the question of
"sexual difference."[1] Yet is there not something trans about psychoanalysis? Might
there be something psychoanalytic about trans? Which "trans" and which "psychoanalysis"? And what is the relation between "sex" and "gender"?

It was Anna O., a "hysterical"[2] analysand of Joseph Breuer, who coined the
term *the talking cure* and thereby—in a sense—invented psychoanalysis. The
invention of psychoanalysis by a hysterical analysand is not simply anecdotal,
for hysteria is at the heart of psychoanalysis in other ways, too. The "truth" with
which Lacanian psychoanalysis concerns itself is the idea that the subject is
divided from itself; this truth goes by various names, including subjective division and, controversially, castration. In Lacanian terminology, hysteria is that
psychic structure most preoccupied with subjective division. As the structure
most preoccupied with the truth that Lacanian psychoanalysis wishes to support,
it stands to reason that hysteria should possess a fundamental position in the
discourse.

Hysteria's centrality to Lacanian psychoanalysis is relevant here because
one form that the preoccupation with subjective division takes involves the critique
and questioning of ways in which gender identities fail to encapsulate the body. This
is one sense in which psychoanalysis itself may be trans, for various lines of inquiry
in transgender studies also involve the critique and questioning of ways in which
gender identities fail to encapsulate the body. These lines of inquiry are motivated
by diverse objectives and arrive at diverse conclusions. Some, however—like psychoanalysis—explore the limits of language itself: "What about those messy spaces
between words and around their borders?" (Wilchins 2002: 46). Some confront the
unverifiable character of sex and gender, as in the words of Bo Luengsuraswat:

"What proof do I have to secure my masculinity at this point?" (2010: 245). Some locate in an impasse the site from which to invent something new, as in Matt Richardson's essay on Jackie Kay's novel *Trumpet*: "Joss [the protagonist] advises us to 'make it up,' leaving us with the burden of decision: To keep chasing the genders of white society that we are excluded from or to embrace other possibilities" (2012: 376). These examples have differing points to make, but in moments like these they converge with Lacanian psychoanalysis, articulating singular accounts of the idea that "the body will never find in language a harmonious home" (Gherovici 2010: 212) and proposing solutions as to how to make do in proximity to that limit.

Near the end of his career, Lacan (1998: 78–89) articulates a new way of thinking sexual difference. His "formulas of sexuation" use the vocabulary of logic to map two positions that subjects take in language. These positions—to be "not-all" or "all" inscribed within the phallic function—are "sexes," but there is nothing *necessarily* gendered about them; neither do they refer to biological sex.[3] Instead, they describe stances a subject takes with respect to subjective division. According to this view, language "sexes" us in that it demands that we take a position with respect to our own division.

What happens when we take a trans look at the formulas, not expecting the formulas' positions to be occupied by (only) the "men" and "women" of normative imaginings? The formulas rely for their coordinates on neither biological theories of sex nor normative understandings of gender; instead, the positions they map are oriented around the un-gendered (but very sexy) notion of subjective division. As such, I would submit that these positions are—like the "genders" described here—"each capable of supporting rich and rapidly proliferating ecologies of embodied difference" (Stryker, Currah, and Moore 2008: 12).

Part of what Lacanian psychoanalysis has to offer the field of transgender studies can be located in the language it has developed for thinking about that suffering of the subject that eludes the social. However, the drive to support the subject in this capacity also limits Lacanian psychoanalysis's usefulness to the field—that is, to the extent that "transgender is an expansive and complicated social category" (Currah, Juang, and Price Minter 2006: xv). The meeting spaces between the psychic and the social have always been vexed for psychoanalysis, and necessarily so.

Still: what if Lacanian psychoanalysis and transgender studies could forge an understanding of sex capable of conjugating multiplicity with division, self-determination with limits, and empowerment with "castration"? This sex need not be inhabited only by norm-abiding "men" and "women" who have bowed to the "real"; it could be inhabited by the rest of us, too.

Shanna T. Carlson is a Collegiate Assistant Professor/Harper Schmidt Fellow at the University of Chicago, where she teaches literature. Her publications include "Transgender Subjectivity and the Logic of Sexual Difference" (*differences*, summer 2010), "In Defense of Queer Kinships: Oedipus Recast" (*Subjectivity*, September 2010), and "Symbolic Deliveries: Logic, the Act, and *The Case of the Young Homosexual*" (*(a): The Journal of Culture and the Unconscious*, forthcoming).

Notes

1. The notable exception is Patricia Gherovici.
2. *Hysteria* is a term with baggage. I am not suggesting there is any necessary link between hysteria and transgender; instead, I am interested in the possibility that certain ways of *thinking* about transgender may converge with features of Lacanian psychoanalysis that are radical, generous, even hope filled.
3. There are limitations here, too. For instance, while Lacan is clear that gender does not dictate one's unconscious sexuation, he uses gender-normative language to name the bodies that occupy these sites. Additionally, work needs to be done with the "phallic function," perhaps beginning with radical rereadings of the phallus as the signifier for the subject's lack-in-being.

References

Currah, Paisley, Richard M. Juang, and Shannon Price Minter. 2006. Introduction to *Transgender Rights*, xiii–xxiv. Minneapolis: University of Minnesota Press.

Gherovici, Patricia. 2010. *Please Select Your Gender*. New York: Routledge.

Lacan, Jacques. 1998. *On Feminine Sexuality: The Limits of Love and Knowledge, 1972–1973*. Book 20 of *Encore: The Seminar of Jacques Lacan*. Edited by Jacques-Alain Miller. Translated by Bruce Fink. New York: Norton.

Luengsuraswat, Bo. 2010. "Proof." In *Gender Outlaws: The Next Generation*, ed. Kate Bornstein and S. Bear Bergman, 242–46. Berkeley, CA: Seal.

Richardson, Matt. 2012. " 'My Father Didn't Have a Dick': Social Death and Jackie Kay's *Trumpet*." *GLQ* 18, no. 2–3: 361–79.

Stryker, Susan, Paisley Currah, and Lisa Jean Moore. 2008. "Introduction: Trans-, Trans, or Transgender? The Stakes for Women's Studies." *WSQ* 36, no. 3–4: 11–22.

Wilchins, Riki. 2002. "Queerer Bodies." In *Genderqueer: Voices from beyond the Sexual Binary*, ed. Joan Nestle, Clare Howell, and Riki Wilchins, 33–46. Los Angeles: Alyson Books.

DOI 10.1215/23289252-2399929

Queer

HEATHER LOVE

What is the place of *queer* in transgender studies? The fields of queer studies and transgender studies are linked through shared histories, methods, and commitments to transforming the situation of gender and sexual outsiders. While *queer* is associated primarily with nonnormative desires and sexual practices, and *transgender* is associated primarily with nonnormative gender identifications and embodiments, it is both theoretically and practically difficult to draw a clear line between them. In distinction to both gay and lesbian studies and sexuality studies, queer studies defines itself as a critical field that questions stable categories of identity. Transgender studies also defines itself against identity, offering a challenge to the perceived stability of the two-gender system. Whether and in what context these fields should be seen as distinct is a live question; however, *queer* and *transgender* are linked in their activist investments, their dissident methodologies, and their critical interrogation of and resistance to gender and sexual norms.

Challenging discrete categories of identity has been central to the work of both queer and transgender studies from the start. In the late 1980s and early 1990s, *queer* emerged as an activist slogan that sought to capture the radical energies of struggles for sexual and gender freedom in the face of the AIDS crisis. By reclaiming a homophobic slur as the name for a movement and, soon after, a field of study, queer activists and scholars indicated the significance of violence and stigma in the experience of gender and sexual outsiders. Queer, with its valences of strange, odd, and perplexing, was also meant to indicate a range of nonnormative sexual practices and gender identifications beyond gay and lesbian. Forwarding a model of coalition among the marginalized and the excluded, queer as at its most capacious was imagined as a rallying cry against "the regimes of the normal" (Warner 1993: xxvi), poised to address "the fractal intricacies of language, skin, migration, state" (Sedgwick 1993: 9).

Transgender is also a term that emerged in an activist context in order to challenge the rule of identity. If *queer* can be understood as refusing the stabilizations of both gender and sexuality implied by the categories gay and lesbian and opening onto a wider spectrum of sexual nonnormativity, *transgender* emerged as a term to capture a range of gendered embodiments, practices, and community formations that cannot be accounted for by the traditional binary. Although the precise origins of the term are contested, it has taken root over the past couple of decades as an activist, scholarly, and vernacular term that refuses normalizing and clinical views of gender in favor of a more capacious and mobile account. In *Transgender History*, Susan Stryker (2008: 1) defines the concept of transgender as "the movement across a socially imposed boundary from an unchosen starting place," capturing the critical force and flexibility of the term. While *transgender* functions as an umbrella term, able to conjure a spectrum that can include trans-sexuals, cross-dressers, and butches and femmes, it also signals a resistance to the taxonomic framework implied by the model of the spectrum (even as it "overcomes" it). Such a critical impulse—the refusal of all categories of sexual and gender identity—might be called *genderqueer*, a term that suggests the intimacy between *transgender* and *queer*.

Queer and transgender studies are linked not only in their shared critique of sexual and gender normativity but also in their resistance to disciplinary and methodological norms. The counterdisciplinary thought of Michel Foucault has been crucial for the development of both fields. Foucault's (1978) account of the disciplinary force of the modern regime of sexuality informs the antinormative, anti-identity politics of transgender and queer studies. In addition, Foucault's genealogical approach to history allowed him to consider a range of genders and sexualities—for instance, in the story of the complex nineteenth-century figure Herculine Barbin (Barbin and Foucault 1980)—outside modern categories of identity. Such unsettled and unsettling instances of embodiment, practice, and identification threaten not only discrete categories of sexual and gender identity but the very distinction between gender and sexuality. Finally, Foucault's critique of the will to knowledge masquerading as scientific objectivity is crucial to the methodology of both queer and transgender studies. Since those with nonstandard embodiments and sexual practices have been disproportionately subjected to the clinical gaze, Foucault's (2003) critical history of the human sciences has led to an insistence in both fields on queer and trans people as the subjects rather than the objects of knowledge. Such insistence points to a shared commitment to the politics of knowledge, to the idea that new ways of being in the world depend on new ways of thinking and new critical frameworks.

Despite historical, methodological, and political overlaps, queer and transgender studies have not always traveled in tandem, and it is not clear, as these fields age, to what extent they should. It is clear that the anti-identitarian, anti-normalizing, and coalitional aspects of queer have been useful in articulating and furthering transgender scholarship and politics; and indeed this shared commitment to crossing disciplinary and identity boundaries can make it hard to distinguish sharply between queer and transgender studies or to sort out these lines of influence. However, while *queer* at its most capacious is understood to indicate a wide range of differences and social exclusions, it has often been critiqued for functioning more narrowly in practice. In her important account of the exclusions of queer politics, "Punks, Bulldaggers, and Welfare Queens," Cathy J. Cohen (2005) indicts *queer* as a false universal, one that claims to address the situation of all marginal subjects but in fact is focused on the concerns of gays and lesbians. One can see a similar critique of *queer* among some trans scholars, who have argued that queer studies has not engaged fully with the material conditions of transgender people but has rather used gender nonnormativity as a sign or allegory of queerness.

Such tensions about the status and inclusiveness of queer do not take place in a vacuum but rather in fraught material, professional, and institutional contexts. Queer studies, despite some notable successes, remains an understaffed and underfunded venture. Nonetheless, the field is in a stronger position than transgender studies, which is often taught as an addendum to queer studies or gender studies. How women's and gender studies programs and LGBT studies programs can best support institutional initiatives in the field of transgender studies is a crucial question in the present. Inclusion of transgender material in courses and curricula is a double-edged sword, since it advances knowledge of the field and meets considerable student demand, but it arguably forestalls the most crucial step in the institutionalization of transgender studies: the hiring of scholars primarily situated in transgender studies and of trans-identified scholars to tenure-track positions in the university.

Furthermore, despite significant overlap in the intellectual formations of queer and transgender studies, the conceptual fit between them is not seamless. Queer has proven less useful than transgender studies in accounting for embodiment. Trans studies makes accounting for material experience and making space for new forms and experiences of embodiment central (in this aspect, one sees significant links between transgender and disability studies). Queer is deeply tied to the intellectual formation of poststructuralism, particularly as it developed in literary theory and psychoanalysis. The field of transgender studies also was influenced by this framework—particularly in canonical texts such as Sandy Stone's "The *Empire* Strikes Back" (1991)—but it has tended to be more methodologically inclusive and diverse. While queer studies continues to resist social science methodologies in favor of a more humanistic version of interdisciplinary or cultural studies, trans studies has stronger ties to legal studies, transnational analysis, the history of medicine, architecture and design, ethnography, and political economy.

It is not clear whether *queer* is best understood as a substantial term with historical links to communities marked as gender and sexual deviants or as a more abstract theoretical term, one that describes a capacious nonnormativity, political critique, and resistance to identity. A similar ambiguity marks *transgender*, which can refer to particular modes of embodiment or communities of people but can also be understood as a theoretical term that points to the crossing and dena- turalizing of identity categories. The powerful destabilizations that both queer and transgender have effected are crucial, but in the present they may need to be balanced by an awareness of the continuing force of identity. Etymologically, both *trans* and *queer* refer to crossing, and in that sense both terms invoke mobility as well as its limits. Given that more and more gender-normative, economically and racially privileged, coupled, and metropolitan gays and lesbians are crossing into the mainstream, these fields may need to turn their attention in the present to crossing in the sense of being crossed or thwarted in one's desires, ambitions, or life chances. Social class, race, region, ability, and gender presentation play a crucial role in determining rights, access to resources, and freedom from violence; and transgender, transsexual, and genderqueer people suffer disproportionately from what Amber Hollibaugh and Cherríe Moraga, writing in 1981, called "queer attack" (403). If *queer* has political force in the context of struggles for gender and sexual freedom, it is because of its ability to convey the ongoing realities of stigma, violence, and exclusion.

Heather Love teaches gender studies and twentieth-century literature and culture at the University of Pennsylvania. She is the author of *Feeling Backward: Loss and the Politics of Queer History* (2007) and the editor of a special issue of *GLQ* on Gayle Rubin ("Rethinking Sex").

References

Barbin, Herculine, and Michel Foucault. 1980. *Herculine Barbin: Being the Recently Discovered Memoirs of a Nineteenth-Century French Hermaphrodite.* New York: Pantheon Books.

Cohen, Cathy J. 2005. "Punks, Bulldaggers, and Welfare Queens: The Radical Potential of Queer Politics?" In *Black Queer Studies: A Critical Anthology,* ed. E. Patrick Johnson and Mae G. Henderson, 21–51. Durham, NC: Duke University Press.

Foucault, Michel. 1978. *An Introduction.* Vol. 1 of *The History of Sexuality.* New York: Vintage.

———. 2003. *The Birth of the Clinic: An Archaeology of Medical Perception.* London: Routledge.

Hollibaugh, Amber, and Cherríe Moraga. 1981. "What We're Rollin around in Bed With: Sexual Silences in Feminism." *Heresies,* no. 12: 58–62.

Sedgwick, Eve Kosofsky. 1993. "Queer and Now." In *Tendencies,* 1–20. Durham, NC: Duke University Press.

Stone, Sandy. 1991. "The *Empire* Strikes Back: A Posttranssexual Manifesto." In *Body Guards: The Cultural Politics of Gender Ambiguity*, ed. Julia Epstein and Kristina Straub, 280–304. New York: Routledge.

Stryker, Susan. 2008. *Transgender History*. Berkeley, CA: Seal.

Warner, Michael. 1993. Introduction to *Fear of a Queer Planet*, ed. Michael Warner, vii–xxxi. Minneapolis: University of Minnesota Press.

DOI 10.1215/23289252-2399938

Reveal

DANIELLE M. SEID

The reveal is a moment in a trans person's life when the trans person is subjected to the pressures of a pervasive gender/sex system that seeks to make public the "truth" of the trans person's gendered and sexed body. While the reveal is frequently used as a narrative technique in literature and film, it also profoundly impacts trans people's actual lives, as seen in media event reveals, like Christine Jorgensen's, and as experienced by trans people in a variety of situations in daily life—such as border crossings, doctor's visits, and job interviews.

At stake in reveals is the issue of agency. Inextricably bound to narrative, the reveal can be seized upon by a trans person as a moment to exert agency and reveal oneself, to determine the meaning of one's own life and body. Unlike the act of coming out for gays, lesbians, and bisexuals, which can have the effect of affirming an "identity," the reveal results in a predicament in which the meaning of the trans body is contested, and competing "truths" vie for dominance. And yet such a "performance," of revealing instead of being revealed, frequently demands that trans persons continuously reassert and defend their truth.

When used as a narrative technique in literature and film, the reveal presents previously "hidden" or unknown information to the audience, often in a manner that twists the plot or produces a climax. In popular narrative fiction and film representations of transgender people, the moment in which a trans character's trans status is discovered by the audience, or by another character, typically functions as a reveal. This reveal is often highly sensationalized, dramatized, or eroticized, though it is also sometimes depicted as comic. Reveals involving trans women, like those in *The Crying Game* (dir. Neil Jordan, 1992) and *Transamerica* (dir. Duncan Tucker, 2005), often display the trans woman's genitals, as an excitatory practice which, projected at a presumably heteronormative, cissexual audience, increases the likelihood that the audience will react with shock and revulsion. Film reveals of trans men generally shy away from an explicit genital reveal, though "female" body parts are often highlighted, as with the display of chests between one trans man and another in *Albert Nobbs* (dir. Rodrigo García, 2011).

In mainstream film, the reveal stages a denaturalization of widespread assumptions about gender and sex—namely that one's gender must match one's sexed body—but it typically does so in a manner that regulates and corrects gender noncompliance, narratively reinscribing a binary gender system as "natural" and desirable. Structuring an audience's knowledge of a character's transgender status as a reveal can contribute to the perception that living a transgender life involves concealing "the truth" of sexed bodies. The moment of the reveal provokes a struggle over the meaning of the trans body, a struggle in which the trans person often "loses" to dominant discourses about trans lives, the conclusion being: that's *really* a man. As such, the reveal places many trans people in a vexed situation in which the terms that would make a trans person intelligible are already predetermined.

Danielle M. Seid is a PhD student at the University of Oregon, where she specializes in film/TV, queer studies, and critical race theory.

DOI 10.1215/23289252-2399947

Revolution

GABRIELA CANO

A revolution is generally understood as the violent upheaval of the established order. The Mexican Revolution of 1910 destroyed the oligarchic state and created a new constitutional order that promised land reform to the peasants, welfare and labor rights to the working class, and a national direction to the economy. Like other revolutionary processes, it also produced a nationalist culture and a narrative that celebrated the political and military contributions of male revolutionaries as well as their violent masculinity set to defend the goals of social emancipation. At the same time, postrevolutionary culture was set to stabilize traditional gender hierarchies and the masculine/feminine binary.

However, the instability and disorder of wartime also dismantled social hierarchies and Victorian respectability and provoked ruptures of gender conventions, opening the space for gender transitions that would perform masculinity in the armed struggle (Monsiváis 1984). Some women took up male attire and masculine identities in order to pass as men to protect themselves from the sexual violence that commonly intensifies during armed conflicts or simply to fight as soldiers without the social gender restrictions that usually burden women in combat. In most cases it was a temporary, strategic masculinization that often included taking up a male mode of attire and name; for example, Angela Jiménez fought under the name of Angel Jiménez. At the end of the war, Jiménez and several other women gave up their masculine identities and went back to their feminine names, to wearing women's clothing, and to female roles in society as mothers and wives. The documented exception is Amelio Robles (1889–1984). Born Amelia Robles, he preserved the masculine identity he forged within the rough environs of war until his death, even through old age and illness (Cano 2006). His masculinization during war did not simply respond to the pragmatic purpose of enjoying the social privileges reserved to men, but rather it was the product of a deeper, more vital desire to radically transform the female identity assigned at birth in order to make himself male in every aspect of life (Fig. 1).

Interest in Amelio Robles's story goes beyond its particulars: his story is the only documented case of a gender transition that occurred during a Latin American revolution and was accepted by the institutions of the postrevolutionary state. Practically all of his identification papers are issued in the masculine, and he was even decorated as a veteran of the Mexican Revolution by the Ministry of War, the highest military authority of the country. Such recognition was possible because his comrades in arms admired the masculinity—machismo—that Robles displayed on the battlefield. Personal qualities such as his courage and capacity for responding to aggression immediately and violently, his skills with guns and horses, and his enjoyment of heavy drinking and womanizing won him the appreciation of fellow men in the army. In the face of death and living through the horrors of the battlefield, Amelio Robles made good friends among guerrilla fighters. Such strong bonds and complicities

Figure 1. Letter submitted by Amelio Robles to the Mexican Ministry of Defense in 1970. Courtesy of Archivo Histórico de la Secretaría de la Defensa Nacional, Mexico

would be instrumental for the official recognition of his masculinity. Once the war was over, some of Robles's comrades moved up to high offices in the postrevolutionary state, and they were complicit in extending official letters of recommendation to Robles referring to him in the masculine.

In the days of combat, moral reserves and gender conventions were often abandoned, creating spaces of subversion such as the one that made Robles's masculinization possible. However, such acceptance was not granted to other forms of gender transgression; effeminacy and male homosexuality drew extreme rejection. Fellow soldiers, on the other hand, admired and recognized Amelio Robles's masculinity because he took the stereotype of machismo. This stereotype eventually became central to the heroic nationalist narrative of the Mexican revolution.

At a time when surgical procedures and hormone therapies for sex change had not been developed, Amelio Robles constructed a very convincing masculine social identity and body image through performance, attire, and the skillful handling of studio photography, the cultural resources available in an isolated rural area of Mexico in the early twentieth century. A carefully selected wardrobe featuring the pants, shirts, jackets, and hats common in rural environments complemented the poses, gestures, and attitudes involved in this daily performance. He chose shirts with large chest pockets that concealed his small breasts. With enduring portraits of Robles's perfectly credible masculine poses, gestures, and mode of dress, studio photography contributed as well to the establishment of his masculine appearance.

The scant historical evidence available—photographs and official documents—suggests that Amelio Robles felt nothing but a man. However, even if the term *transgender* did not exist in his day (it was coined as an umbrella term in the late twentieth century in a context of reclaiming rights and visibility for diverse cross-gender identities), Robles's masculinity can be better understood, and acquires wide significance, as the result of a successful transgendering process that made the most of the cultural resources of his time and benefited from the breaking of conventions during revolutionary war and from the nationalist narratives that worked to stabilized the gender binary that prevailed in the postrevolutionary Mexican state.

Gabriela Cano is a professor at El Colegio de México in Mexico City. She is the author of *Se llamaba Elena Arizmendi* (2010) and coeditor of *Sex in Revolution: Gender, Power, and Politics in Modern Mexico* (2006). Her book *Gender Battles in the Mexican Revolution, or The Intimate Joy of Colonel Robles* is forthcoming.

References

Cano, Gabriela. 2006. "Unconcealable Realities of Desire: Amelio Robles's (Transgender) Masculinity in the Mexican Revolution." In *Sex in Revolution: Gender, Power, and Politics in Modern Mexico*, ed. Jocelyn Olcott, Mary Kay Vaughan, and Gabriela Cano, 35–56. Durham, NC: Duke University Press.

Monsiváis, Carlos. 1984. "La aparición del subsuelo: Sobre la cultura de la Revolución Mexicana." *Historias*, no. 8–9, 159–77.

DOI 10.1215/23289252-2399956

Sick

MICHA CÁRDENAS

They say we're sick.
The year I gained a breast, my mother lost one to breast cancer.
The year I gained my voice, my mother was losing hers to dementia,
brought on by chemo and twenty years of anti-psychotics for her schizophrenia.
The doctors say we're sick
Myself and my mom.
We each take our pills everyday from little amber bottles.
But I don't feel sick
and that gives me some feeling of
solidarity, empathy, something I can't find words for,
for my mother.
It makes me wonder if my mom feels sick?
I remember her smile when I last visited her, in North Carolina,
which I can't do often.
Laughing with her, I started to relate to her in a new way,
as a person, as a femme who wore poodle skirts and now uses a wheelchair,
who loved my Colombian father and his thick accent.
Getting in the car, my mom held my hand in hers and said
we have almost the same color of nail polish on,
the day was beautiful and so painful
I struggled not to cry, for her.
In a way we're all sick, but we're all also caretakers,
family members, chosen and biological,
and we are all there for one another,
in need or to offer help,
in a society that would leave each of us in isolation,
we are finding ways of existing together, interdependent,
and however difficult it may be at times, with love.

In an article discussing Lea T's fall advertising campaign for Givenchy and Lady Gaga's fashion shoot as Joe Calderone in *Vogue Hommes*, the *New York Times* declared "2010 will be remembered as the year of the transsexual" (Van Meter 2010). In *Gaga Feminism*, J. Jack Halberstam describes "the very recent rise in popularity of the term 'transgender'" and states that "the tendency to read gender variance in non-Western contexts as a sign of anachronism has not been particularly productive, nor has the tendency to read all gender variance as 'transgenderism'" (2012: 81). Following this claim, one can ask: What is lost in the transgender movement's increasing mainstream success, and who is left behind? How does the media's representation of transgender people in a positive light serve to normalize and regulate the image of gender nonconformance and limit the range of political possibility?

A news article describing Lana Wachowski's speech at the Human Rights Campaign awards illustrates this limiting in action. The *Hollywood Reporter* article is titled "Lana Wachowski Reveals Suicide Plan, Painful Past in Emotional Speech (Exclusive Video)" (Abramovitch 2012). The title performs the common narrative surrounding transgender people, the narrative that supports the model of medical intervention: we are sick, mentally ill, and without medical intervention we are suicidal. A disability studies critique is useful here when philosopher of disability Abby L. Wilkerson states, "Intersexualization illustrates the ways in which sexual disabilities are constituted in and through social environments" (2012: 193). One can ask, is being suicidal our condition, or is that condition created by the violence of a transphobic society?

The Wachowski article goes on to describe an image of transgender people that fits well within what Wilkerson describes as "normate sex": married, white, thin, financially successful, monogamous. Wilkerson points to the "desperate need for alliance building" between the disability rights movement and the transgender/intersex/genderqueer movements. She calls for "a sexual-political interdependence: a politics, that is, that emphasizes our interdependence as allies" (ibid.: 204). Such an alliance allows for a transgender movement that does not only follow a normative model of medical transition but that openly questions the narrative of pathologization placed on transgender and gender-nonconforming people and that questions the Western biomedical model of medicine, which only treats illness instead of focusing on healing and well being. While transgender people can claim a disabled status based on our medical diagnoses and frequent interactions with the medical-industrial complex, such a claim risks appropriation and the diluting of claims for justice from other disabled people. Transgender people can work in solidarity, or interdependence, with disabled people by joining the disability movement's strategy of critiquing the authority that defines illness, opening up a decolonization of medicine that can imagine other models of health based in desire and liberation, not illness and correction to norms. At the same time, transgender people who identify as disabled should be supported by their communities when they publicly identify as disabled and speak out in solidarity with other kinds of disabilities. I am sick too. On top of having the diagnosis of "transsexualism," I was diagnosed with ADHD as a child, and it persists in having a major influence on my life.

The transgender rights movement can learn from women of color feminism that not only are coalitions essential for success, but recognizing and embracing difference within our movements is key to creating movements that perform the world we want now. The risk of not building solidarity between disability rights and transgender politics is demonstrated by movements such as Occupy Wall Street, whose focus on an economically reductive definition of the 99 percent versus the 1 percent created a movement in which sexual assault occurred (Newcomb 2011) and camps were divided into racial and class ghettoes. Queer of color critique builds on women of color feminism to demonstrate how these issues are inseparable. Roderick A. Ferguson, in *Aberrations in Black*, states: "The decisive intervention of queer of color analysis is that racist practice articulates itself generally as gender and sexual regulation, and that gender and sexual differences variegate racial fomations" (2003: 3) One could transpose this to state that abelist practice articulates itself as gender and sexual regulation, or transphobic practice articulates itself as the regulation of illness. Either way, such a conjunction helps one understand that the need for solidarity between disability activists and gender-nonconforming activists is not just strategic; it connects the roots of our struggles, deepening our claims for liberation and opening the way to a decolonial vision of healing justice.

micha cárdenas is a PhD student in media arts and practice (iMAP) and Provost Fellow at the University of Southern California and a member of the art collective Electronic Disturbance Theater 2.0. micha's coauthored book *The Transreal: Political Aesthetics of Crossing Realities* was published in 2012.

References

Abramovitch, Seth. 2012. "Lana Wachowski Reveals Suicide Plan, Painful Past in Emotional Speech (Exclusive Video)." *Hollywood Reporter*, October 24. www.hollywoodreporter .com/news/lana-wachowski-reveals-suicide-plan-382169.

Ferguson, Roderick A. 2003. *Aberrations in Black: Toward a Queer of Color Critique.* Minneapolis: University of Minnesota Press.

Halberstam, J. Jack. 2012. *Gaga Feminism: Sex, Gender, and the End of Normal.* Boston: Beacon.

Newcomb, Alyssa. 2011. "Sexual Assaults Reported in 'Occupy' Camps," November 3. abcnews.go .com/US/sexual-assaults-occupy-wall-street-camps/story?id=14873014.

Van Meter, William. 2010. "Transsexuals Are Edging into the Mainstream: Is 2010 the Year of the Transsexual?" *New York Times*, December 8. www.nytimes.com/2010/12/09/fashion/09TRANS.html.

Wilkerson, Abby L. 2012. "Normate Sex and Its Discontents." In *Sex and Disability*, ed. Robert McRuer and Anna Mollow. Durham, NC: Duke University Press.

DOI 10.1215/23289252-2399965

Sinophone

HOWARD CHIANG

Pioneered by the literary scholar Shu-mei Shih (2007), *sinophone* is an analytic category that provides a long-overdue alternative to the discourses of "Chinese" and "Chinese diaspora" that have traditionally defined Chinese studies. The sinophone world refers to Sinitic-language communities and cultures outside China or on the margins of the hegemonic productions of the Chinese nation-state and Chineseness. As such, Sinophone communities and cultures bear a historically contested and politically embedded relationship to China, similar to the relationships between the anglophone world and Britain, for example, or the francophone world and France, or the hispanophone world and Spain. Sinophone studies therefore presents a radical break from traditional approaches to Chinese studies in that it disrupts the chain of equivalence established, since the rise of nation-states, among language, culture, ethnicity, and nationality as meaningful categories of analysis.

The concept of the sinophone is important for transgender studies because the first case of transsexuality in Chinese-speaking communities was reported not in mainland China but in post–World War II Taiwan (Chiang 2012). In 1953, four years after Mao Zedong's political regime took over the mainland and the Nationalist government was forced to relocate its base, news of the success of native doctors in converting a man into a woman made headlines in Taiwan. The story first came to public attention on August 14, when the *United Daily News* (*Lianhebao*) surprised the public by announcing the discovery of an intersexed soldier, Xie Jianshun, in Tainan, Taiwan (*Lianhebao* 1953b). Within a week, the characterization of Xie in the Taiwanese press changed from that of an average citizen whose ambiguous sex provoked uncertainty and anxiety to that of being considered the "first" Chinese transsexual.

Xie was frequently dubbed the "Chinese Christine." This allusion to the contemporaneous American ex-GI transsexual celebrity Christine Jorgensen, who had traveled to Denmark for her sex reassignment surgery and gained worldwide familiarity immediately afterward due to her personality and glamorous looks, reflected the growing influence of American culture on the Republic of China at the peak of the Cold War. One newspaper headline on Xie's case, "Christine Will Not Be America's Exclusive: Soldier Destined to Become a Lady," exemplifies Xie's transformation into a transsexual cultural icon whose status would put Taiwan on a par with the United States on the global stage as a modern and technologically sophisticated nation (*Lianbebao* 1953a). As was the case with Jorgensen in the United States, extensive popular press coverage in Taiwan of Xie's transition shifted common understandings of sexuality and gender, introduced the concept of transsexuality as something distinct from intersex conditions, and amplified the roles of both medical science and mass media in the construction of modern identity.

Of significance in both national and trans-Pacific contexts, Xie's experience made *bianxingren* (transsexual) a household term in sinophone cultures of the 1950s. She served as a focal point for numerous news stories that broached the topics of changing sex, human intersexuality, and other atypical conditions of the body. People who wrote about her debated whether she qualified as a woman, whether medical technology could transform sex, and whether the two "Christines" were more similar or different. These persistent comparisons of Taiwan with the United States, through the comparisons of two versions of transsexuality, became an important arena for articulating a sense of sinophone difference from anglophone culture as well as of Taiwanese nationalism. Xie's story highlighted issues that pervaded postwar sinophone society in Taiwan: the censorship of public culture by the state, the unique social status of men serving in the armed forces, the limit of individualism, the promise and pitfalls of science, the normative behaviors expected of men and women, and the boundaries of acceptable sexual expression. Xie Jianshun's saga, and those of other reported cases of sex change that followed in her wake, attest to the emergence of transsexuality as a modern form of sexual embodiment in sinophone society. Xie's story in particular became a lightning rod for many post–World War II anxieties about gender and sexuality and called dramatic attention to issues that would later drive the feminist and gay and lesbian movements in the decades ahead.

Press stories of Xie and other transsexuals illustrate how the Republican government claimed sovereignty in postwar Taiwan in part by deploying and demonstrating its mastery of the Western biomedical epistemology of sex. Wide-ranging debates on sex transformation had preoccupied sexologists and popular writers in mainland China during the Republican era (1912–49) in response to scientific thought's global dissemination, and these debates migrated to Taiwan along with the Nationalist government (Chiang 2012). The Republican government in Taiwan also drew on the island's history of Japan colonization. As did Britain in Hong Kong, Japan institutionalized in Taiwan a highly Westernized biomedical infrastructure. After Mao "nationalized" Chinese medicine in mainland China in the 1950s, Taiwan and Hong Kong became the two locations within sinophone cultures where Western medicine was most "advanced." These historical legacies informed the immense media publicity showered on Xie Jianshun—and sex change more generally—first in Taiwan and afterward in Hong Kong. The rapid transfer of Western biomedical technology to these locations during the Cold War, coupled with their relatively open social and cultural milieus, enabled the sinophone articulations of transsexuality to emerge first and foremost along the postcolonial East Asian Pacific Rim.

The story of Xie Jianshun helps illuminate the broader contours of sinophone culture, because its epistemological and historical underpinnings are rooted outside "China" as conceived in a narrow geopolitical sense. It touches on legacies of both Japanese postcolonialism and American neo-imperialism; it involves the recontextualization of scientific internationalism, the Republic's nationalist state projects, and it touches as well on Taiwan's cultural, political, and economic affiliations with Hong Kong and Japan as anticommunist subregions of Cold War East Asia. Considering Xie's celebrity and influence as a sinophone (re)production of transsexuality can help push postcolonial queer studies beyond its overwhelming preoccupation with "the West" and recenter attention on China specifically and Asia more generally. Tracing the dispersed circuits of knowledge that condensed in the public representations of Xie Jianshun allows us to see the "Chinese Christine" not as a cheap knock-off of a Western original but rather as a figure through which to read inter- and intra-Asian regional dynamics and conditions of subjectivity.

Howard Chiang is an assistant professor of history at the University of Warwick. He is the editor of *Transgender China* (2012), *Queer Sinophone Cultures* (2013, with Ari Larissa Heinrich), *Psychiatry and Chinese History* (forthcoming), and *Historical Epistemology and the Making of Modern Chinese Medicine* (forthcoming). He is currently working on a manuscript tentatively titled "Sex Changed China: Science, Medicine, and Visions of Transformation."

References

Chiang, Howard. 2012. "Why Sex Mattered: Science and Visions of Transformation in Modern China." PhD diss., Princeton University.

Lianhebao 聯合報 (*United Daily News*). 1953a. "Burang Kelisiding zhuanmei yuqian dabing jiang bianchen xiaojie" 不讓克麗絲汀專美於前 大兵將變成小姐 ("Christine Will Not Be America's Exclusive: Soldier Destined to Become a Lady"). August 21, 3.

———. 1953b. "Nanshi faxian yinyangren jiangdong shoushu bian nannü" 南市發現陰陽人 將 動手術辨男女 ("A Hermaphrodite Discovered in Tainan: Sex to Be Determined after Surgery"). August 21, 3.

Shih, Shu-mei. 2007. *Visuality and Identity: Sinophone Articulations across the Pacific*. Berkeley: University of California Press.

DOI 10.1215/23289252-2399974

Somatechnics

NIKKI SULLIVAN

In 2003 a group of academics at Macquarie University organized a conference on body modification. The aim of the event was to articulate the diverse ways in which all bodies—not simply those that are tattooed or those that have undergone some sort of transformative surgical procedure—are always already modified. One of the keynote speakers at the conference was Susan Stryker, whose work in the field of transgender studies problematized the "common-sense" understanding of technology, which, at the time, underpinned the dominant model of the transsexual body as either requiring or having undergone technological intervention. Following the conference, Stryker and her colleagues at Macquarie coined the term *somatechnics* in an attempt to highlight what they saw as the inextricability of *soma* and *techné*, of the body (as a culturally intelligible construct) and the techniques (*dispositifs* and hard technologies) in and through which corporealities are formed and transformed. From the outset, then, somatechnics has addressed and been shaped by transgender issues, and this connection was explicitly articulated at the Transsomatechnics conference held at Simon Fraser University in 2008.

The term *somatechnics*, derived from the Greek *soma* (body) and *techné* (craftsmanship), supplants the logic of the "and," indicating that *techné* is not something we add or apply to the already constituted body (as object), nor is it a tool that the embodied self employs to its own ends. Rather, *technés* are the dynamic means in and through which corporealities are crafted: that is, continuously engendered in relation to others and to a world. What we see here, then, is a chiasmatic interdependence of *soma* and *techné*: of bodily being (or corporealities) as always already technologized and technologies (which are never simply "machinic") as always already enfleshed. Anna Munster nicely articulates this vision when she writes that technologies are "always in a dynamic relation to the matter which gives [them their] substance and to the other machines—aesthetic, social, economic—which substantiate [them] as . . . ensemble[s]" (1999: 121). To put it slightly differently, the categories of being that are integral to our (un)becoming-with, and the orientation(s) that shape them, are somatechnological (rather than simply natural or cultural, internal or external to us, enabling or oppressive). For example, transgender, like forms of bodily being commonly presumed *not* to be technologically produced, is a heterogeneous somatechnological construct that comes to matter in contextually specific ways and in relation to other discursive formations. In making this claim, I am not suggesting that modes and practices of embodiment (such as those we call transgender) are not "real." Indeed, they are the matter(ialization) of being, but this materialization takes place through certain highly regulated (situated) somatechnologies. Given this, the primary aim of somatechnics as a critical orientation is—at least as I understand it—to queer orderability by bringing to light the operations of power, the soma-techno-logic, that constitute(s) (un)becoming-with in situated ways. I will return to this point in due course.

The history of Western thought is, as Elizabeth Grosz and others have argued, subtended by "a profound somatophobia" (1994: 1). From the ancient Greeks, to Enlightenment thinkers (Descartes, Rousseau, Kant, Hobbes), to the common-sense fictions that shape contemporary life, the body has been conceived (and thus constituted) as a natural, biological entity, the fleshly shell of a soul, a self, and/or a mind that is superior to it. Given its status as both prison and property, the brute matter of the body (as object) is constituted in and through this particular imaginary as that which the subject must transcend, transform, master, and/or shape, and nowhere is this more apparent than in autobiographical transsexual narratives published in the west in the twentieth century. There have, of course, been various challenges posed, particularly from the mid-twentieth century on, to the kind of determinism associated with this model of the body, the self, and the relation between them, but all too often such attempts reiterate—albeit inadvertently—a sort of naive materialism in which the body appears as a fleshly substrate that simply *is* prior to its regulation. This ontological tendency is apparent, for example, in accounts of selfhood (often found in discussions of transgender) that rely on a presumed distinction between sex and gender—the idea that the sexed body is a natural biological substrate onto which contextually specific (that is, culturally determined) attributes, roles, and capacities are imposed—as well as in dominant conceptions of, and debates about, technology.

Technology, claimed Martin Heidegger in his influential essay, "The Question Concerning Technology," is commonly conceived both as a human activity and as a means to an end. The effect of this instrumentalist conception is that debates about technology tend to revolve around "our manipulating technology in the proper manner as a means" ([1954] 1977: 5). In other words, the primary focus of discussions of particular technologies tends to be on whether, how, and to what extent they might be used to enhance life, to achieve integrity, to enable one to realize one's true self. Little has changed, it seems, in the sixty years since Heidegger first made these claims, and this is clear if one looks at accounts of so-called gender reassignment surgeries. In brief, such practices are framed by some as medical treatments that will enhance the lives of those who undergo them, while others have argued that such practices are (for a variety of reasons) unethical and/or immoral; that they constitute a misuse of technology. Some argue that individuals have a right to bodily self-determination, and others argue (variously) that such a right, if it exists, is never absolute and that therefore the use of technologies that (re)shape the body requires strict regulation. Despite the differences of opinion expressed in these claims, what they share is an instrumentalist view of technology, one in which technology is (constituted as) an object external to and manipulable by the subject(s) who deploy it to their own ends (whether those ends be a sense of bodily integrity, the fulfilment of a religious obligation, the construction of the self as altruistic, appropriately professional, morally responsible, or whatever). Indeed, each is subtended by a will to mastery which, Heidegger and Foucault would argue, is itself technological. Technology, suggests Heidegger in his critique of instrumentalist logic, is less a thing that is external to the self than an orientation, a way of thinking/knowing/seeing that brings forth (or engenders, shapes, and "orders") being, or, more accurately, (un)becoming. Technology, then, is at once the (contextually specific) means by which we order the world and the ways of thinking/knowing/seeing that precede us and make us be(come). Given this, the problem with instrumentalism as an orientation, and thus with the instrumentalist view of technology as separate from the self who deploys it as a means to an identifiable and achievable end, is that it veils over the coindebtedness, coresponsibility, coarticulation, and movement of (un)becoming-with.[1] Critiques of this view of technology and the ethicopolitical effects that such a way of thinking produces have been articulated at length by theorists as diverse as Donna Haraway, Jean-Luc Nancy, Maurice Merleau-Ponty, Luce Irigaray, Gilles Deleuze, and Félix Guattari, to name but a few. Somatechnics adds another (heterogeneous) voice to these attempts to think otherwise, but it does so from the possibly unique position of having always already been shaped by trans*.

Nikki Sullivan is an associate professor of critical and cultural studies in the Department of Media, Music, Communication, and Cultural Studies at Macquarie University. She is coeditor (with Samantha Murray) of *Somatechnics: Queering the Technologisation of Bodies* (2009) and cofounder and co–chief editor (with Jane Simon) of the *Somatechnics* journal.

Note

1. Elsewhere I speak of the movement of (un)becoming-with as "transing" (Sullivan 2009).

References

Grosz, Elizabeth. 1994. *Volatile Bodies*. Bloomington: Indiana University Press.

Heidegger, Martin. (1954) 1977. "The Question Concerning Technology." In *The Question Concerning Technology and Other Essays*, trans. W. Lovitt, 3–35. New York: Harper Perennial.

Munster, Anna. 1999. "Is There Postlife after Postfeminism? Tropes of Technics and Life in Cyberfeminism." *Australian Feminist Studies* 14, no. 29: 119–29.

Sullivan, Nikki. 2009. "Transsomatechnics and the Matter of 'Genital Modifications.'" *Australian Feminist Studies* 24, no. 60: 275–86.

DOI 10.1215/23289252-2399983

Somatomorph

TARYNN M. WITTEN

Somatomorph. *Sō-ma?tō´-mōrf.* Despite a century of linguistic history that charts our cultural-political efforts to satisfactorily capture the complexity inherent in the matrix of human sex, gender, and sexuality, we remain hindered by an inadequate lexicon. The generally accepted meme "trans" originates from early medical language adopted in the late 1800s to describe people now referred to as "transdressers" (Williams 2012). As first coined, it established a lexicon of "difference" for those who failed to align with traditional biomedical and sociocultural expectations of sex and gender. Despite its origins, the word *trans* has evolved as the result of desires among those in both the trans-identified political community and the medical community to derive a more sufficient, meta-inclusive meme. Despite these good intentions, however, the unfortunate result continues to be an insufficiently complex meme, resulting in the exclusion of those who live beyond the expected Western biomedical, sexed, gendered, and sexual identity. This continued exclusion creates social and political inequalities and disparities in numerous aspects of daily life that translate into long-term, negative biomedical and psycho-socioeconomic impacts on those identified for various reasons as "trans" (Ettner, Monstrey, and Eyler 2007; Grant, Mottet, and Tanis 2011; Redman 2011; Witten and Eyler 2012).

For many individuals who would claim the identity transsexual, the root of their challenge is an inherent disconnection (lack of harmony) between the internalized perception of self and the embodied, corporal representation of themselves to others. Thus while sex, gender, and sexuality may be important ingredients in the identity recipe, they are sociolinguistic constructs that emerge from the physical corpus and its subsequent window dressing embedded within the totality of the sociocultural politics of a person's environment. In the language of complexity theory, the corpus is core and thus primary; the rest—including *perceived* sex, *depicted* sex, and *representations* of gender—is emergence.

Words like *trans*sexual and *trans*gender fail to accurately describe the core relationship to the body because they originate from the external, social perspective rather than from the inherent, material root: the body. While the language of "trans" may imply a transformation in the material being of the body or in the projection of sexed identity, it fails to capture the complexity of transfor-mation. Moreover, the meme "trans sexuality" inadvertently and unfortunately implies connection with sexual identity that is simply incorrect. Given that the corpus is core in the complex identity being, the word trans*sexual* should be replaced with a more accurate term so as to indicate that the challenge is around genital sex rather than sexuality or sexual identity. The word *transgender* fails to capture the now accepted multidimensionality of "gender" and does not speak to the corporal aspects of trans-identity. In addition, prefixes such as *cis* and *trans*— prefixes that emerged from the field of organic chemistry as descriptors of molecular conformation states—when used as modifiers of words like *sex* and *gender*, continue to promote a binary. That is, one's identity becomes either cis or trans rather than understood to be a continuum in which cis and trans coexist as descriptors within a larger semantic range.

In a frustrated effort to neutralize some of the stigma around the various trans identities, I first coined the word *transcorporal* (Witten 2007a, 2007b). This word offsets the stigma around the juxtaposition of trans and sex/gender/sexuality by replacing the emergent constructs of sex, gender, and sexuality with the core construct of the corporal nature of trans identity. In doing so, it somewhat levels the playing field with respect to discussions around trans versus non-trans bodies. However, it does not engage the larger queer population that chooses to bend, blend, and blur or to alternatively define the semiotics of the body and its myriad, complex representations. Nor does it extend its inclusion to a multicultural sensibility. Though the historical evolution of the meme "trans" reached for an inclusiveness for the breadth of the "condition" of trans, the actual effect was to reiterate the non-normality once again, even in the guise of *trans-corporal* being.

The larger question then becomes, how do we queer the insufficient meme "trans" to simultaneously escape the recapitulation of difference and fully encompass the complexity of human sexed, gendered, and sexual being? Can the meme "trans" be queered enough to embrace those who claim such identities as genderqueer, gender-bending, gender-blending, gender-variant, gender non-conforming, XTX, WBM, MBW, cross-dresser, transvestite, and a host of other descriptors? And given the organic, grassroots emergence of the concept of trans being, how do we preserve the sanctity of the historical language that other population members find more relevant to their state of being? Finally, how do we create a linguistic landscape that nullifies, to a greater extent, the significant negativity associated with the historical as well as the political semantics currently used to describe the Western trans community?

To address these questions, we revisit the idea that the core challenges or objectives faced by trans-identified individuals revolve around manipulations of the body, or soma, and what emerges through the body into the public as representations of sex, gender, and sexuality. Some of the biophysical manipulations incurred in transformation of the soma may be permanent; others may not. Some of the changes may be subtle, while others may be flagrant and readily apparent to those beyond the self. In our way of thinking, an individual who has chosen to morph the body, the soma, and to then engage in the sociolinguistic and evidentiary representation of the soma beyond the self has become a "somatomorph" or ought to be somatomorphically identified.

The phrase "somatomorphically identified" is semantically more inclusive of the complex human matrix of sex, gender, and sexualized being (Witten and Eyler 2012: ch. 6). *Somatomorph* is a continuum descriptor rather than a binary term; *morphing* is a continuum construct, while *trans* implies a discrete relationship between one state of being an another. Use of the term *soma* refocuses our sociolinguistic understanding of those we understand now to be trans back to the prime root—the body—while still acknowledging the emergent relevance of sexuality and gender. Because somatomorph implies a dynamic, continuum sexed-being, it encompasses additional continuum identities such as gender-bending, and gender-blending—identities made comprehensible through somatic change. Similarly, for those who choose to physically change their bodies in a permanent way, somatomorph is equally appropriate because these individuals are changing their soma. Various cultural gender identities can also fall under the aegis of somatomorphic identity, as gender is a sociocultural consequence of morphing the soma either through actual physical interventions such as surgery and/or hormones or through less permanent means such as makeup and dress.

Tarynn M. Witten is an associate professor of biological complexity and physics at the Virginia Commonwealth University. She is the author of *The Tao of Gender* (2002) and an editor/author of *Gay, Lesbian, Bisexual, and Transgender Aging: Challenges in Research, Practice, and Policy* (2012).

References

Ettner, Randi, Stanley Monstrey, and A. Evan Eyler, eds. 2007. *Principles of Transgender Medicine and Surgery.* Binghamton, NY: Haworth.

Grant, Jamie M., Lisa A. Mottet, and Justin Tanis. 2011. "Injustice at Every Turn: A Report of the National Transgender Discrimination Survey." Washington, DC: National Center for Transgender Equality and National Gay and Lesbian Task Force. www.thetaskforce.org/downloads/reports/reports/ntds_full.pdf (accessed October 29, 2013).

Redman, Daniel. 2011. "Fear, Discrimination, and Abuse: Transgender Elders and the Perils of Long-Term Care." *Aging Today* 32, no. 2: 1–2.

Williams, Cristan. 2012. "Tracking Transgender: The Historical Truth." *The TransAdvocate* (blog), March 28. www.transadvocate.com/tracking-transgender.htm.

Witten, Tarynn M. 2007a. "Transcorporality and Aging." Invited talk presented to the Center for the Study of Human Sexuality, New York University.

———. 2007b. "I'm Rubber, You're Glue—Words, Meaning, and Identity in Transgender." Invited plenary presentation to the Fifth Annual Translating Identity Conference, Burlington, Vermont.

Witten, Tarynn M., and A. Evan Eyler, eds. 2012. *Gay, Lesbian, Bisexual, Transgender, and Intersex Aging: Challenges in Research, Practice, and Policy.* Baltimore: Johns Hopkins University Press.

DOI 10.1215/23289252-2399992

Sports

ANN TRAVERS

Modern sport, which emerged in Europe and its colonies in the late nineteenth and early twentieth centuries, was a male-supremacist as well as a "civilizing" project that represented a backlash against the increasing power of middle- and upper-class white women; it was designed to emphasize sex difference, to socialize boys and men into orthodox masculinity, and to further the goal of white middle- and upper-class morality and leadership within Western imperialist projects (Pronger 1990; Carrington and McDonald 2009). Mainstream competitive and amateur sport in North America still plays a central role in naturalizing the ideology of a two-sex system while normalizing white cisgendered heterosexual masculinity and class privilege (Hill Collins 2005).

Sport has also been the site of resistance to oppressive systems of domination organized around categories of race and sex; in recent years, transsexual and transgender athletes and activists have challenged simplistic notions of binary-based biological sex difference (Travers and Deri 2010; Griffin and Carroll 2010). Reneé Richards, a transsexual woman, set an important precedent in 1977 when she successfully sued the Women's Tennis Association for barring her participation (Birrell and Cole 1990). Other ground-breaking trans athletes include Michelle Dumaresq (women's mountain biking), Lana Lawless and Mianne Bagger (Ladies Professional Golf Association), Kai Allums (NCAA women's basketball), Keelin Godsey (two-time NCAA women's hammer throw champion), and the Indian runner Shanti Soundarajan.

The International Olympic Committee (IOC) and its affiliates finally discontinued the long-reviled, scientifically unfounded practice of gender verification testing for women athletes prior to the 2000 Olympic Games (Cavanagh and Sykes 2006), but the IOC's role in normalizing the two-sex system and male superiority continues—most dramatically, in recent years, in the case of the gender-troubling figure of South African runner Caster Semenya, whose "masculine" appearance became a subject of concern among her competitors and sporting officials (Nyong'o 2010). The IOC enacted a policy on transsexual participation in 2003; known as the Stockholm Consensus, the policy requires transsexual athletes to complete hormonal transition at least two years prior to competing in an Olympic event, to undergo genital transformation surgery, and to have legally changed sex. While widely lauded as a first step, the Stockholm Consensus has also been broadly criticized on the grounds that genitals have no bearing on athletic performance, that the expense of surgery is a barrier for many athletes, and that many governments refuse to supply legal documents designating the appropriate legal sex identity (Cavanagh and Sykes 2006).

A 2010 report, *On the Team: Equal Opportunity for Transgender Student Athletes* (Griffin and Carroll 2010), proposed important policy recommendations that subsequently have been adopted in both the United States and Canada. Citing the broad overlap between male and female adolescent athletic performance, the report recommends that transgender high school students should be eligible to compete on whatever team they choose without medicalized "sex change." At the college level, participation by transgender athletes requires a formal diagnosis of gender identity disorder. Early-transitioning athletes who used hormone blockers during adolescence and who currently take "cross-sex" hormones are immediately eligible to participate in college sports; athletes who transitioned after puberty must undergo one year of cross-hormone therapy prior to participation. This protocol was adopted by the National Collegiate Atheltics Association (NCAA) in September 2011 (Lawrence 2011).

Transgender participation in college sports under these guidelines does not significantly affect the ideology of two sexes that undergirds modern sport, nor does it challenge assumptions about male athletic superiority. Male-to-female athletes are required to follow a hormone regime that negates the performance-enhancing effects of testosterone, considered normal in the "male" body, in order to participate as women in women's sports; in contrast, FTM (female-to-male) transgender athletes are not required to submit to any hormonal regime in order to participate as men in men's sports. Once they have undergone testosterone therapy as part of their transition, however, FTM athletes may no longer compete in women's sports. No current policy debate on transgender participation in mainstream sport questions the sex-segregated structure of sporting spaces.

Ann Travers is an associate professor of sociology in the Department of Sociology and Anthropology at Simon Fraser University. Recent articles include "The Sport Nexus and Gender Injustice" (*Studies in Social Justice*, 2008), "Women's Ski Jumping, the 2010 Olympic Games, and the Deafening Silences of Sex Segregation, Whiteness, and Wealth" (*Journal of Sport and Social Issues*, May 2011), and "Thinking the Unthinkable: Imagining an 'Un-American,' Girl-Friendly, Women- and Trans-Inclusive Alternative for Baseball" (*Journal of Sport and Social Issues*, February 2013).

References

Birrell, Susan, and Cheryl L. Cole. 1990. "Double Fault: Renee Richards and the Construction and Naturalization of Difference." *Sociology of Sport Journal* 7, no. 1: 1–21.

Carrington, Ben, and Ian McDonald, eds. 2009. *Marxism, Cultural Studies, and Sport*. Boston: Taylor and Francis.

Cavanagh, Sheila L., and Heather Sykes. 2006. "Transsexual Bodies at the Olympics: The International Olympic Committee's Policy on Transsexual Athletes at the 2004 Athens Summer Games." *Body and Society* 12, no. 3: 75–102.

Griffin, Pat, and Helen J. Carroll. 2010. *On the Team: Equal Opportunity for Transgender Student Athletes*. www.nclrights.org/press-room/press-release/groundbreaking-report-urges-high -school-and-college-athletics-to-establish-standard-national-policies-for-transgender -student-athletes/ (accessed December 13, 2013).

Hill Collins, Patricia. 2005. *Black Sexual Politics: African Americans, Gender, and the New Racism*. New York: Routledge.

Lawrence, M. 2011. Transgender Policy Approved. www.ncaa.org/wps/wcm/connect/public/NCAA /Resources/Latest+News/2011/September/Transgender+policy+approved (accessed December 13, 2013).

Nyong'o, Tavia. 2010. "The Unforgivable Transgression of Being Caster Semenya." *Women and Performance* 20, no. 1: 95–100.

Pronger, Brian. 1990. *The Arena of Masculinity: Sports, Homosexuality, and the Meaning of Sex*. New York: St Martin's.

Travers, Ann, and Jillian Deri. 2010. "Transgender Inclusion and the Changing Face of Lesbian Softball Leagues." *International Review for the Sociology of Sport* 46, no. 4: 488–507.

DOI 10.1215/23289252-2400001

The State

PAISLEY CURRAH

States do many things. They test students, imprison individuals, make roads, adjudicate property disputes, track the health of populations, issue identity documents, provide benefits to those deemed deserving, safeguard markets, regulate the poor, drop bombs, and patrol borders. Imaging "the state" as an entity, an institution, a unitary thing gives an intelligible shape to the countless activities carried out under the force of law. The idea of the state smuggles within it certain expectations: an ordered hierarchy, a comprehensive rationality, a unity of purpose and execution. Conceptions of the state differ depending on their particular historical or theoretical genealogies, and each one calls forth its commensurate form of political contestation or critical analysis. Those differences are visible in the range of political positions represented by trans movements. Examining the issue of sex classification can help illustrate them.

In the classical liberal tradition, the state is thought to be a neutral umpire, meting out judgment according to the rule of law, which Locke described as "settled standing rules, indifferent, and the same to all parties." Governments brought into being by this social compact should not treat people differently because of arbitrary particularities of identity. According to this tradition's contemporary script, that governments have denied rights based on distinctions of race and gender, among others, in the past is an unfortunate historical contingency, one that betrayed the principle of equality and that has now been, or soon will be, rectified. Because individuals exist before and outside the political community they decide to form or join, the characteristics they brought into the social state should not become the basis for treating them differently. In the United States, this view of the state is enshrined in constitutional jurisprudence and legal doctrine and provides the backdrop for most legal challenges to state-sponsored discrimination against trans people. For example, in framing arguments to jurists and policy makers, trans rights advocates are often forced to argue that it is not birth sex that is immutable but gender identity. The goal of what might be called the mainstream trans rights movement is to install gender identity as the basis for sex *re*-classification, rather than the sex assigned at birth or on the surgically modified body. This would do much to improve the day-to-day lives of transgender people.

For the Left, however, the liberal state and the principles of political equality it celebrates conceal the maldistribution of equality. A certain domesticated form of selfhood is reproduced when individuals petition the government for recognition of their particular selves and, in turn, recognize themselves when they are hailed by various state apparatuses—*interpolation* is the term of art used to describe this relationship. From this more radical perspective, then, the transgender rights movement is merely insisting that the hailing be more accurate. A transgender man will now have an *M* on his driver's license, and the police officer who stops him on the street may call him "sir" rather than "ma'am." But the power of the state to surveil individuals and to regulate gender remains intact. While the political approach of many trans legal advocates requires them to naturalize gender identity, the more radical trans Left recognizes that "sex" cannot be made to fit into a rigid presocial biological schema of male and female. On the question of sex classification, the goal should not be to install the "right" definition of sex in the regulatory architecture to make the legal recognition of transition possible but to get the state out of the business of defining sex in the first place.

Both the classical liberal theory of the state and the Left's critical rejoinder, however, lack the capacity or perhaps the flexibility to account for contradictions in policies for sex reclassification. Perhaps what underlies the inability to account for contradictions in sex classification is the belief that the state actions should manifest an underlying coherence. In fact, the hope—or fear—that we are governed by a single, rational legal structure is belied by the existence of a virtually uncountable number of state institutions, processes, offices, and political jurisdictions. In the United States, for example, when some individuals cross borders, walk into a government office to apply for benefits, get a driver's license, go to jail or prison, sign up for selective service, try to get married, or have any interaction with any state actor, the sex classification of some people can and often does switch. Even within a single jurisdiction, almost every particular state agency—from federal to municipal—has the authority to decide its own rules for sex classification. To complicate matters even more, both state and federal judges have found that one's sex classification for one social function may not hold for others. These include legislatures, courts, departments, agencies, elected officials, political appointees, public servants, constitutions, laws, regulations, administrative rules, and informal norms and practices. These intertwined and sprawling apparatuses all rest, sometimes uneasily, on diachronous layers of sedimented yet still active historical state formations. Given this disarray, it is not surprising that different state entities might sometimes advance different, even incommensurate, projects. Indeed, how could they not?

According to Gilles Deleuze, a concept "should express an event rather than an essence" (1995: 14). Molar, large-scale accounts of sex and the state have assumed a sameness to sex and a singular rationality to state actors, decisions, and projects. If the state is not unitary, coordinated, and hierarchically organized in an ultimately rational way—if, as Michel Foucault suggests, "the state is only a composite reality and a mythicized abstraction whose importance is much less than we think" (1991: 103)—then it should come as no surprise that state definitions of sex are also plural. A contradiction is something that does not make sense, a position that is logically inconsistent. To begin by letting go of the assumption that there is any "there there," any *whatness*, to (legal) sex apart from what an agency says it is, the contradiction evaporates. The official sex designation—or, more precisely, the *M* or the *F*—stamped on documents or coded in records becomes the starting point. Then an analysis can focus not on what sex *is*, or what it should *be*, but on what it does, what it accomplishes, what it produces. Indeed, if the only thing we know for sure about sex is what any of these many state actors say it is in any particular instance, sex will turn out to be as messy and diffuse a concept as the state. Entering into the analysis without a firm sense of what sex is or what the state is—as a priori facts, as edifices—makes the processes through which they come into being more visible. It might be better to defer attempts to resolve—theoretically or politically—the messiness in order to understand what a particular system of sex designation does for a particular state project such as recognition or redistribution (Currah, forthcoming).

Of course, states should not only or always be imagined as messy, scattered nodes of local and arbitrary power arrangements. The Leviathan state's terrible concentrated authority to impose sanctions (death, imprisonment, fines) has been the subject of theories of sovereignty for centuries. For this purpose, the most apt definition of the state begins with the simple description from Max Weber: "A human community that (successfully) claims the *monopoly of the legitimate physical violence* within a particular given territory" (1991: 78). To create a truly compelling account of sovereign violence and the paradox of sovereignty, one must take Weber's definition, put question marks around "legitimate," and add the observation made by scholars such as Walter Benjamin, Carl Schmitt, Hannah Arendt, Jacques Derrida, and Giorgio Agamben that the force that creates the law and makes it legitimate cannot be justified by a law that does not yet exist. Still, much of what states do—regulating the health, safety, and public welfare through myriad regulations, rules, decisions, practices—does not reach the threshold of juridical violence, even if those actions are ultimately undergirded by its threat. Fetishizing a generalized idea of the state and its terrifying or redemptive power (depending on one's perspective) can obscure what is actually happening in the local, micro, particular sites where most public authority is exercised. While it is crucial to theorize the singular finality of state violence, neglecting to examine the messiness of actually existing and potentially incommensurate policies, practices, rules, and norms risks substituting the conceptual for the concrete and gets in the way of understanding what might actually be going on (Latour 1995: 48).

Paisley Currah teaches political science and gender studies at Brooklyn College and the Graduate Center of the City University of New York. His recent publications include "Homonationalism, State Rationalities, and Sex Contradictions" (*Theory and Event*, 2013) and "Securitizing Gender: Identity, Biometrics, and Gender Non-conforming Bodies at the Airport," coauthored with Tara Mulqueen (*Social Research*, summer 2011).

References

Currah, Paisley. Forthcoming. *States of Sex*. New York: New York University Press.

Deleuze, Gilles. 1995. *Negotiations 1972–1990*. Translated by Martin Joughin. New York: Columbia University Press.

Foucault, Michel. 1991. "Governmentality." In *The Foucault Effect*, ed. Graham Burchell, Colin Gordon, and Peter Miller, 87–104. Chicago: University of Chicago Press.

Latour, Bruno. 2005. *Reassembling the Social*. New York: Oxford University Press.

Weber, Max. 1991. "Politics as a Vocation." In *From Max Weber: Essays in Sociology*, ed. Hans Heinrich Gerth and C. Wright Mills, 77–128. London: Routledge.

DOI 10.1215/23289252-2400010

Subaltern

TRISH SALAH

From a military term designating a subordinate officer, *the subaltern* entered social and cultural theory via the *Prison Notebooks* of Italian Marxist Antonio Gramsci. Gramsci used the term to designate proletarian and peasant classes denied access to political representation or voice within government by the fascist Italian state. More broadly, Gramsci (1971) used the term to designate classes excluded from political hegemony by ruling elites. The subaltern's contemporary usage in cultural and political theory dates from the rise of the Subaltern Studies Group, who redefined the term to describe the subordinated population of the South Asian subcontinent on the basis of their distance from economic and political elites and who developed an anti-imperial historiography from the point of view of those dispossessed under colonization (Louai 2012).

Postcolonial critic Gayatri Chakravorty Spivak reframed the term to foreground gendered, caste, class, and colonial constitutive elements barring the subaltern from speaking or from being heard by Western poststructuralist and feminist theorists as well as by diasporic intellectuals (1988). Troubling what might be seen, in the work of the Subaltern Studies Group, as the essentializing of the subaltern as a specific population, Spivak located the subaltern at the interstices of competing or conflicting discursive formations striated by class differentiation (1987). She argued that between the competing discursive claims of an imperial Western feminism and an anticolonial and sexist Hindu nationalism, the subjective and speaking position of a resistant Hindu woman was barred (1988). In *A Critique of Postcolonial Reason*, Spivak further queried progressives' insistence on the availability of subaltern speech given its location "on the other side of a difference, or epistemic fracture, even from other groupings of the colonized," and highlighted "our" implication as interpreters. She reiterated that the subaltern may be silenced by "her own more emancipated granddaughters: a new mainstream . . . [or] the liberal multiculturalist metropolitan academy" (1999: 309).

There are several senses in which the term *subaltern* speaks to and within trans studies. Drawing upon poststructuralist, feminist, and anticolonial discourses (Anzaldúa 1987; Derrida 1980; Foucault 1980, Spivak 1988; Haraway 1985, 1991), Sandy Stone's "The *Empire* Strikes Back: A Posttranssexual Manifesto" ([1991] 1996) theorized the ways in which transsexuals had been subalterned by both feminist transphobia and medical discourses. Stone both rebutted the antitranssexual polemic of Janice Raymond's *The Transsexual Empire: The Making of the She-Male* and critiqued a medical model in which, to be recognized as subjects eligible for medical care, transsexuals were enjoined to produce personal histories within the restrictive conventions of a diagnostic portrait. These conventions required "prospective transsexuals" to signify as highly gender normative within their sex of identification, as intensely body dysphoric, and as heterosexual. As well, they implicitly privileged middle-class and white subjects. While J. Meyerowitz (2002), Jay Prosser (1998), Henry Rubin (2003), and others have documented transsexual agency in forging diagnostic criteria as a way of securing access to transition-related healthcare, the erasures and coercive productivities of the diagnosis subalterned both transsexual and nontranssexual transgender subjects, subjecting both to institutional regulation and administrative violence. For example, for transsexuals validated by the medical model, the recognized program of care involved erasing or rewriting one's pretransition history and disappearing "into the woodwork." As Stone has noted: "It is difficult to articulate a counter-discourse if one is programmed to disappear" (1996: 295).

The meaning and political valences of such woodworking are, however, contested in queer, feminist, and trans studies. In *Changing Sex*, Bernice Hausman (1995) draws upon Michel Foucault to propose that transsexual subjects speak only through the demand for surgery and are duped into reproducing conservative gender norms. For Hausman, trans subjects are less excluded from meaningful speech than definitively constructed by hegemonic articulations. However, Prosser argues that Hausman obscures her own gendered embodiment and subjective investments to tacitly justify her nontranssexual authorial location as "the authoritative site from which to speak" (Prosser 1998: 132–33). Indeed, Viviane Namaste (2000, 2005), Prosser (1998), and Rubin (2003) all challenge queer feminist deployments of poststructuralism that mobilize transgender figures in the service of theoretical projects that paradoxically deny transsexual experience and speech.

Namaste's and Rubin's assessments of the discursive conditions of possibility underwriting transsexual speech within "queerly-paradigmed" transgenderism (Rubin 2003: 276) echo Spivak's concern with subalterning dynamics within progressive movements as well as within liberal, multicultural, metropolitan institutions. Demonstrating the exclusion of sex workers, prisoners, substance users, the poor, the racialized, and nonstatus people, Aizura (2011), Namaste (2000, 2005), Ross (2005), and Spade (2011) expose practices of erasure (of the excluded subaltern) in the contemporary production of the rights-bearing transgender subject.

Subaltern trans positions also appear at the interstice of transnational sexualities and genders, modernization and globalization, and through the networks of global gay human rights discourse and Anglo-American transgender liberation. How these English language forms encounter, appropriate, or are translated by globally local "trans" constituencies raises questions of the political economy of identity movements and discourses. Reflecting upon the situation of francophone *travesties* and *transsexuelles*, Namaste draws upon Spivak to critique as linguistic imperialism the export of US anglophone sexual minority nomenclature and politics (such as transgender and queer), arguing that they do not translate conceptually or culturally into Quebec (Namaste 2005). Similarly, David Valentine highlights differentials of class, race, education, and employment in the normative prescription of acceptable language in LGBT service provision, which effectively require gay-identified subjects to "speak transgender" in order to be legible (2006: 417). Meanwhile, Katrina Roen (2001) queries how, within capitalist globalization, transgender and transsexual rhetorics are valued as modern and metropolitan in opposition to non-Western and indigenous gender-variant identities. Conversely, genderqueer and transgender writers contest the terms of inscription within medically sanctioned transsexual discourses, arguing that they produce hierarchies of authenticity, reproduce class- and race-based privilege, and require that gender-nonconforming subjects enlist within binary gendered positions to be recognized (Halberstam 1998, Wilchins 2002).

Ewa Ziareck's recent application of Jean-François Lyotard's (1999) differend to progressive formations, including feminist movements and radical democracy theory, suggests some of the stakes of coercively homogenizing progressive discourses and raises the issue as one of constitutive as well as contingent violence (Ziareck 2001). There may be an affinity between the subaltern and Lyotard's notion of the differend, the trace or remainder of discursive battles, which must be resolved for a discourse, even a counterdiscourse, to emerge. Such traces of "border wars" attest to the violence by which transsexuality, transgenderism, and other kinds of gender and sex variance are repeatedly buried or erased from the social world.

Trish Salah is an assistant professor of women's and gender studies at the University of Winnipeg. Her recent publications include "Notes towards Thinking Transsexual Institutional Poetics" in *Trans/acting Culture, Writing, and Memory: Essays in Honour of Barbara Godard* (2013), *Wanting in Arabic: Poems*$^{&}$ (2nd ed., 2013), and *Lyric Sexology, Vol. 1* (2014).

References

Aizura, Aren. 2011. "The Persistence of Transsexual Travel Narratives." In *Trans Gender Migrations: Bodies, Borders, and the (Geo)politics of Gender Trans-ing*, ed. Trystan Cotton, 139–56. New York: Routledge.

Anzaldúa, Gloria. 1987. *Borderlands/La Frontera: The New Mestiza*. San Francisco: Spinsters/Aunt Lute.

Derrida, Jacques. 1980. "La loi du genre" ("The Law of Genre"). Translated by Avital Ronell. *Glyph*, no. 7: 176 (French), 202 (English).

Foucault, Michel. 1980. *Herculine Barbin: Being the Recently Discovered Memoirs of a Nineteenth-Century Hermaphrodite*. New York: Pantheon.

Gramsci, Antonio. 1971. *Selections from the Prison Notebooks*. New York: International.

Halberstam, Judith. 1998. "Transgender Butch: Butch/FTM Border Wars and the Masculine Continuum." In "The Transgender Issue," ed. Susan Stryker. Special issue, *GLQ* 4, no. 2: 287–310.

Haraway, Donna. 1985. "A Manifesto for Cyborgs: Science, Technology, and Socialist Feminism in the 1980s." *Socialist Review*, no. 80: 65–107.

———. 1991. "The Promises of Monsters: A Regenerative Politics for Inappropriate/d Others." In *Cultural Studies*, ed. Lawrence Grossberg, Cary Nelson, and Paula A. Treichler, 295–337. New York: Routledge.

Hausman, Bernice. 1995. *Changing Sex: Transsexualism, Technology, and the Idea of Gender*. Durham, NC: Duke University Press.

Louai, El Habib. 2012. "Retracing the Concept of the Subaltern from Gramsci to Spivak: Historical Developments and New Applications." *African Journal of History and Culture* 4, no. 1: 4–8.

Lyotard, Jean-François. 1999. *The Differend: Phrases in Dispute*. Translated by Georges van den Abbeele. Minneapolis: University of Minnesota Press.

Meyerowitz, J. 2002. *How Sex Changed: A History of Transsexuality in the United States*. Cambridge, MA: Harvard University Press.

Namaste, Viviane. 2000. *Invisible Lives: The Erasure of Transsexual and Transgendered People*. Chicago: University of Chicago Press.

———. 2005. *Sex Change, Social Change: Reflections on Identity, Institutions, and Imperialism*. Toronto: Women's Press.

Prosser, Jay. 1998. *Second Skins: Body Narratives of Transsexuality*. New York: Columbia University Press.

Roen, Katrina. 2001. "Transgender Theory and Embodiment: The Risk of Racial Marginalisation." *Journal of Gender Studies* 10, no. 3: 253–63.

Ross, Mirha-Soleil. 2005. "Interview with Mirha-Soleil Ross." In Namaste, *Sex Change, Social Change*, 86–102.

Rubin, Henry. 2003. *Self-Made Men: Identity and Embodiment among Transsexual Men*. Nashville: Vanderbilt University Press.

Spade, Dean. 2011. *Normal Life: Administrative Violence, Critical Trans Politics, and the Limits of Law*. Cambridge, MA: South End.

Spivak, Gayatri Chakravorty. 1987. "Subaltern Studies: Deconstructing Historiography." In *In Other Worlds: Essays in Cultural Politics*, 197–221. New York: Routledge.

———. 1988. "Can the Subaltern Speak?" In *Marxism and the Interpretation of Culture*, ed. C. Nelson and L. Grossberg, 271–313. Basingstoke, UK: Macmillan Education.

———. 1999. *A Critique of Postcolonial Reason: Toward a History of the Vanishing Present*. Cambridge, MA: Harvard University Press.

Stone, Sandy (1991) 1996. "The *Empire* Strikes Back: A Posttranssexual Manifesto." In *Body Guards: The Cultural Politics of Sexual Ambiguity*, ed. K. Straub and J. Epstein, 280–304. New York: Routledge.

Valentine, David. 2006. " 'I Went to Bed with My Own Kind Once': The Erasure of Desire in the Name of Identity." In *Transgender Studies Reader*, ed. Susan Stryker and Stephen Whittle, 407–19. New York: Routledge.

Wilchins, R. 2002. "Queerer Bodies." In *GenderQueer: Voices from beyond the Sexual Binary*, ed. R. Wilchins, C. Howell, and J. Nestle, 33–46. Boston: Alyson Books.

Ziarek, Ewa. 2001. *An Ethics of Dissensus: Postmodernity, Feminism, and the Politics of Radical Democracy*. Stanford: Stanford University Press.

DOI 10.1215/23289252-2400019

Surgery

TRYSTAN T. COTTEN

Redrawing the body's sex contours affirms the feminist mantra that biology is not destiny. Surgery has been an important part of trans agency and medical transitioning since Michael Dhillon began the first of thirteen operations to reconstruct his morphological sex in 1946. Trans surgery is any surgery that alters the body's primary and secondary sex characteristics, but this was not always the case when surgery was institutionalized in the gender clinics of large research universities like Johns Hopkins and Stanford in the 1950s and 1960s. The desire for surgery not only became a definitive characteristic of transsexuality, distinguishing it from other so-called disorders like cross-dressing, transvestism, and homosexuality. But it was also narrowly conceived as the reconstruction of morphological sex, which excluded trans people who wanted to keep their genitals intact from treatment. The formalization of the Harry Benjamin Standards of Care in 1979 liberalized trans people's access to surgery by extending diagnostic powers to clinicians and doctors outside the university gender clinics and opening up additional avenues of medical transitioning for trans people. Many trans people began having surgeries to masculinize or feminize parts of their body while leaving their genitalia intact. In turn, this helped produce a proliferation of transition trajectories in a multitude of directions, enabling (in part) the emergence of a critical transgender movement in the 1990s and debunking clinical assumptions that binary gender was the end goal of transitioning.

A "somatechnology" perspective views trans surgery as part of a larger *techne* of discursive and institutional practices (law, medicine/science, art, education, information and surveillance technologies) through which trans bodies are constituted, positioned, and lived. Sometimes more weight is given to structural practices in the substantiation of trans identities, which has been critiqued for its lack of emphasis on the role of trans people's agency as coconstitutive with technology and *dispositifs* in the making (and remaking) of trans bodies. While the former perspective sheds important light on somatechniques of trans identities, the emphasis is nonetheless on how trans bodies/identities are affected by discursive and nondiscursive practices. Equally important is understanding how trans people affect the evolution of discourses and technologies through individual/personal as well as collective resistance, organization, and struggle.

A good example of balancing both perspectives is that of Dr. Harold Gillies and Michael Dhillon. Gillies had been performing pedicle-flap phalloplasty to reconstruct the maimed genitals of war veterans for more than three decades, since inventing the surgery during WWI. Yet it was not until a transsexual man, Dhillon, contacted him that Gillies realized the more extensive potential of his surgical technique to assist not only cisgender but also transsexual males. Dhillon's transsexual body was both a fleshly and symbolic catalyst and field for Gillies's surgical imagination to extend and develop further. Cutting, splicing, pulling, tucking, and transplanting nerves, arteries, blood vessels, skin, fat, and muscle tissues, trans surgeries rewrite the functional and phenomenological circuitry of human bodies and change how subjects experience and express gender and sexuality. In doing so, trans bodies not only rewrite normative scripts of binary sex and gender. They are also (re)writing medical knowledge of human bodies and surgical practice, as surgeons, spurred by the needs of their patients, continue experimenting with new technologies and practices to produce better results.

Trans people seek sex reassignment surgery for many reasons, all of which highlight the significance of the body's fleshy contours and chemistry to gender identity and expression. Some form of surgical modification of sex characteristics is usually required in most countries to legally change the gender marker of identification documents, which is essential to trans people's mobility—social, economic, and geographical. Surgery gives fleshly form to proprioceptive gender, bringing bodily matter into alignment with gender self-image, and allows trans people new embodiments of experiencing/expressing gender and sexuality that were not possible before surgery. Some trans people's pursuit of surgery indicates how the performance of gender (e.g., cross-dressing, gait, mannerisms, motility, verbal expression, etc.) falls short in regards to some people's ability to fully embody and express their preferred gender identity. Trans people suffer discrimination, abuse, and even death when their morphological sex is discovered to be different from their visible gender. Depending on the context, for example, genital surgery might prevent trans women from being sentenced to male prisons where they would likely be sexually harassed and assaulted on a daily basis. Surgery can also remove barriers of exclusion from certain gender-specific spaces (e.g., locker rooms/bathrooms and bathhouses), social and medical services (e.g., shelters for homeless and/or battered women), or social events that privilege morphological sex over gender presentation as the definitive criterion for access. Some trans people are also hesitant to pursue romantic and sexual relationships, as the prospect of explaining their body's fleshly difference to potential lovers can bring up feelings of shame and fear of rejection. Surgery helps minimize some of these anxieties and opens up opportunities of romantic and social bonding for trans people.

While sex reassignment surgery can function as a vehicle of trans agency, it can also be deployed to police nonnormative trans bodies that transgress and challenge gender and sexual normativity. This is most evident in social policies requiring sex reassignment surgery for a legal change of sex on identification documents, for example, or bureaucratic rules making sterilization mandatory for gender transitioning. A biopolitical analysis emphasizes how these mandates are part of a larger administrative apparatus of managing bodies and their productive and reproductive capacities for state interests. Pregnant men, men with breasts, and females with penises all unhinge the sex/gender binary and heterosexuality as socially engineered contrivances, while bureaucracies are erected to reel these transgressive bodies back in for biopolitical management. Despite the attempt at containing trans bodies, many people still find ways (depending on their economic and political situation) to circumvent the system and exercise some modicum of control of their transition trajectory.

Trystan T. Cotten is an associate professor of gender studies at California State University, Stanislaus. His areas of research are in transgender surgery and medicine and transgender identities in Africa and the Diaspora. His latest book is *Hung Jury: Testimonies of Genital Surgery by Transsexual Men* (2012).

DOI 10.1215/23289252-2400028

Surveillance

TOBY BEAUCHAMP

Surveillance is built into the production of the very category of transgender. The Harry Benjamin International Gender Dysphoria Association's *Standards of Care* (1979) formally defined the category of transsexual in a list of behaviors and life narratives, formalizing the diagnosis of gender identity disorder as one of the first steps in a standardized process for managing transgender lives. Following these guidelines, medical professionals approved surgery or hormones for clients fitting the standardized criteria and expected these clients to eventually eliminate all references to their former gendered lives and fully assimilate into a normatively gendered world (see Stone 1991; Califia 2003). Indeed, in many cases the possibility of medical transition depended on one's perceived potential to pass as nontransgender, an assessment process typically grounded in the regulatory norms of whiteness, class privilege, and heterosexuality.

Thus two major forms of surveillance operate through medical and psychiatric institutions: first, the monitoring of individuals in terms of their ability to conform to a particular medicalized understanding of transgender identity; and second, the expectation that medical transition should enable those individuals to withstand any scrutiny that would reveal their transgender status. These forms of surveillance also reach beyond medical contexts to influence law, policy, and social relations. For instance, legal changes of gender on identification documents typically rely on medical evidence as proof of gender identity, and the data collected as part of these legal processes (along with any form requiring one to identify as a specific gender) form a paper trail through which state agencies may track, assess, and manage transgender people. Similarly, the policing of gendered spaces ranging from public bathrooms to homeless shelters disproportionately affects gender-nonconforming people (Spade 2011). And representations of transgender people in popular media such as police dramas and daytime talk shows often encourage viewers to uncover gendered truths by scrutinizing certain bodies and identities. All of these practices reinforce the discursive and material links between the category transgender and various forms of surveillance, from the systemic to the quotidian.

Yet surveillance practices need not specifically name transgender as a category of concern in order to be intimately connected to transgender politics or to affect the material lives of gender-nonconforming people. For instance, in the years following 9/11, the US Department of Homeland Security advanced new security policies as part of the war on terror, including increased scrutiny of identification documents at airports and national borders, that almost never explicitly mention transgender populations. But transgender people, particularly trans people of color, poor trans people, trans youth, and trans immigrants, are especially targeted by such scrutiny because they are more likely to have inconsistent identification documents. Related security measures, including increased restrictions on immigration and asylum, new forms of state scrutiny of those perceived to be undocumented immigrants, and the implementation of x-ray scanning technologies in airports and prisons typically do not cite explicit concerns with transgender populations. But because these policing practices are often concerned with individuals who appear to be fraudulent or deceptive, gender-nonconforming people—culturally constructed as concealing something—disproportionately feel their effects.

Even while surveillance mechanisms discipline transgender people, the very efforts made to police and manage gender nonconformity reveal productive contradictions and fissures in surveillance practices. By seemingly displacing gender regulation onto only transgender people, nontransgender bodies and identities appear both naturally gender normative and free from scrutiny. Yet the difficulty these systems encounter in trying to classify gender-nonconforming people demonstrates how regulatory norms of gender affect all bodies and identities by enforcing categories that are made to seem natural. For example, in cases such as medical requirements for changing identification documents, contradictory requirements put forward by different regions or jurisdictions point out the state's own confusion about how gender is defined and reveal gendered categories to be contingent rather than unchanging. In this sense, the category transgender can usefully problematize the narrow, immutable taxonomies on which surveillance programs and technologies tend to rely, showing how the state's own classification systems fail to account for the complexities of bodies and identities.

Toby Beauchamp is an assistant professor of gender and women's studies at Oklahoma State University. He is currently completing a book manuscript titled "Going Stealth: Transgender Politics and US Surveillance Practices."

References

Califia, Patrick. 2003. *Sex Changes: Transgender Politics*. San Francisco: Cleis.

Harry Benjamin International Gender Dysphoria Association. 1979. *Standards of Care: The Hormonal and Surgical Sex Reassignment of Gender Dysphoric Persons*. Galveston: Janus Information Facility, University of Texas Medical Branch.

Spade, Dean. 2011. *Normal Life: Administrative Violence, Critical Trans Politics, and the Limits of Law*. Brooklyn, NY: South End.

Stone, Sandy. 1991. "The *Empire* Strikes Back: A Posttranssexual Manifesto." In *Body Guards: The Cultural Politics of Gender Ambiguity*, ed. Julia Epstein and Kristina Straub, 280–304. New York: Routledge.

DOI 10.1215/23289252-2400037

Symbolic Subversion

SASKIA E. WIERINGA

Heteronormativity is imposed with the help of a sliding scale of violence: from material (economic and legal), structural, and physical to symbolic. *Symbolic violence* refers to the almost unconscious, internalized modes of cultural of social domination (Bourdieu 1991). Gender relations is a prime field of symbolic power (Butler 1990). *Heteronormativity* refers to a system in which sexual conduct and kinship relations are organized in such a way that a specific form of heterosexuality becomes the culturally accepted "natural" order. Thus biological sex, sexuality, gender identity and expression and normative gender roles are aligned in such a way that a dominant view on sexual and gender relations, identities, and expressions is produced. The forms of resistance to the effects of heteronormativity can likewise be located on a sliding scale of subversion. The forms of subversion range from struggles for sexual rights (political struggles for legal reform and social policies) to material (economic) resistance and to symbolic forms of subversion. Symbolic subversion extends from self-defeating strategies, via various forms of adaptation, to more or less public forms of rebellion. Along its path we find secrecy, partial acceptance of the codes of normalcy, denial of one's own needs, and the secret search for sexual pleasure, but we also find hard work, sacrifice, and defiance.

In a comparative research project on three categories of abjected women in India and Indonesia (widows/divorced women, sex workers, and lesbians; some individuals were included who identified as transgender and were in a same-sex relationship), we found that far from being passive victims of heteronormative (symbolic) violence, they demonstrated multiple forms of resistance ranging from outright defiance to more subtle accommodations (Wieringa 2012). Just as cultural and religious norms determine the particular construct of heteronormativity in a given society, they also shape the salience of particular types of resistance and make certain forms of subversion intelligible.

Subversions may be divided into manifest rebellions and symbolic forms of subversion; the latter range from self-defeating yet defiant actions of (self) destruction to ostensible adaptations to the current heteronormative model. Open, physical, and visible struggles include outright rejection of the model and the claims of sexual agency and citizenship. In situations where transgender people are stigmatized, lonely, and legally, economically, and psychologically vulnerable, searches for economic stability, social respect, friendship, and/or sexual partners constitute forms of symbolic subversion of the dominant gender order. Even if they ostensibly or publicly accept its hegemony, their very actions and search for accommodation within the system reveal subversion, or what James C. Scott (1990: 137) referred to as the "hidden transcripts, the disguised ideological resistance" to the dominant order.

Symbolic subversion can be seen as a continuum, its form ranging from outright resistance to (partial) compliance and even to defiant defeat. In the case of a double suicide of a lesbian couple, when they publicly go to their death together, usually because they are denied the possibility of staying together, the ultimate unmasking of heteronormativity is acted out. The myth of the "harmonious patriarchal family" is uncovered for what it means to those who are unable to live by its norms: a cruel power ploy that may end in death for those who experience this form of "happiness" as a travesty of the bliss they had found for themselves.

Some transgender people may perform their masculinity or femininity so convincingly that they are seen to be "normal" men or women, which is often also how they prefer to see themselves. Others are more likely to be perceived as rupturing the sex-gender nexus and subverting heteronormative norms, even though they may embrace certain aspects of them.

The subversion of heteronormativity covers a wide range from open forms of defiance and rebellion to more covert methods, rooted in daily practices and more or less subconscious strategies for survival. There is often a thin line between defiance and defeat. The risks of defeat are multiple. A certain amount of defiance is needed to survive—socially, economically, emotionally, and even physically.

But too much defiance carries enormous risks such as social isolation, economic hardship, or physical and psychological violence. Subversion should be seen as a continuum of practices and motivations—from visible, physical forms of resistance to more invisible, symbolic forms.

Saskia E. Wieringa is an honorary professor at the University of Amsterdam, holding the chair of women's cross-cultural same-sex relations. Her latest (coedited) books include *Women's Sexualities and Masculinities in a Globalizing Asia* (2007), *The Future of Asian Feminisms* (2012), *The Sexual History of the Global South* (2013), and *Family Ambiguity and Domestic Violence in Asia* (2013).

References

Bourdieu, Pierre. 1991. *Language and Symbolic Power.* Cambridge, MA: Harvard University Press.

Butler, Judith. 1990. *Gender Trouble: Feminism and the Subversion of Identity.* New York: Routledge.

Scott, James C. 1990. *Domination and the Arts of Resistance: Hidden Transcripts.* New Haven, CT: Yale University Press.

Wieringa, Saskia. 2012. "Passionate Aesthetics and Symbolic Subversion: Heteronormativity in India and Indonesia." In "Queer Asian Subjects: Transgressive Sexualities and Heteronormative Meanings," ed. Evelyn Blackwood and Mark Johnson. Special Issue, *Asian Studies Review* 36, no. 4: 515–31.

DOI 10.1215/23289252-2400046

Tatume

VIC MUÑOZ

Tatume or tatuma or calabacita (genus *Cucurbita*) is a keyword (Williams 1983) for transing land, decolonization, diaspora, the meaning of seasons, and growing food.[1] Tatume has made that steady bargain with the way things are (see Rich 1989); displaced to *el norte*, here in the garden, it grows southward toward the brightest sunlight. Tatume addresses my location on Cayuga Nation Territory, one of the Six Nations of the Haudenosaunee, as central to what it means to me to be a diaspora Boricua queer, trans-/gender-nonconforming in this queer decolonial time and Indigenous place (Halberstam 2005).

The intersections of diaspora and decolonization are what I attempt to trans—through a juxtaposing of the vocabulary of growing tatume and the challenges of definition it poses within a binary view of growing seasons and the concepts of immature (summer squash) and mature (winter squash). Growing through these narrow spaces is something that tatume knows how to do. Tatume is a search for an imagined home after forced displacement.

One of the earliest references to squash, in English, that I could locate is attributed to R. Boyle's 1661 *Sceptical Chymist* (ii. 107): "A selected seed of . . . Squash, which is an Indian kind of Pompion, that Growes a pace."[2] Growing quickly. Adapting.

Squash is one of "The Three Sisters" (squash, corn, and beans) planted together by the Haudenosaunee. Squash *becomes* zucchini through a process of colonization. The practice of interplanting, for example, the Three Sisters is a fundamental indigenous growing practice. To plant only one crop, to genetically engineer seeds to grow the sweetest vegetable, to create a tomato that can be picked green and shipped thousands of miles, is the continued imperialism of the fifteenth century; we are not postcolonial. Genetic modification is sold through the ideology of feeding the world; saving the hungry. But in fact, indigenous cultural property is stolen through the process of patenting. Traditional Ecological Knowledge (Salmón 2012: 82) is patented through a process of biocolonialism (Howard 2001). The ideology of saving the other fuels a colonizing mission that has not stopped (Smith 2012). The growing of only one kind of food, exemplified by Monsanto's genetically modified corn, can only be sustained through genetic engineering, because *nothing grows alone*. Organisms are inter-dependent as are concepts, such as trans- and gender.

Last year, I saved tatume seeds. This year I planted them. They are growing. Saving seeds, not souls. Rooting decolonization in the place where I live; I live on stolen land.

To understand tatume—and the vocabulary that surrounds its Western explanations—is to confront colonization and the struggle for land. The word, *squash*, is cut from the Narragansett word, *askutasquash*. What we eat tells of who has been colonized and by whom. How we "eat the other" (hooks 1992). Language cuts by those who have difficulty saying the "foreign" words but no difficulty colonizing land, bodies, and sexualities (Hutchins and Aspin 2007).

While looking for calabaza seeds among heirloom growers in the United States, I found tatume. The descriptions of the squash were appealing to me because the writers could not settle on whether the squash was a "summer" or "winter" squash. This complication with where to place the squash revealed not just that these gardeners had only two categories for squash but that there are only two possible growing seasons—summer and winter—and depending on when they are harvested, they are "mature" or "immature." Tatume was bound to confuse these categories.

Descriptions of tatume on blogs and websites highlight its difference within a binary framework of growth and harvest. Here are two illustrative examples:

> Most of the squash that we are familiar with come from the species *Cucurbita pepo*. "Tatume" is a variety of this species. *C. pepo* is a native of Meso-America and archeological evidence shows that gardeners there have been growing varieties of *C. pepo* for the past 8,000 to 10,000 years. In America, squash is generally divided into two categories based on when they are harvested. . . . "Tatume" is one the rare varieties of squash that can be harvested as either a summer or winter type. (White 2010)

> I said, "That's one of them? It doesn't look anything like the ones earlier in the season," and she remarked, "Yes that's one of them. They are actually a type of WINTER SQUASH. We just pick them when they are really young and immature and have no seeds." That is why we don't see them later on in summer—if you let it keep growing; it will become a mature winter squash. There were several there at her booth with different colors. Some were green with orange stripes and some were salmon-colored with green-grey stripes. ("Mystery" 2012)

I plant vegetables and herbs from home here, on Haudenosaunee lands. I am committed to non–genetically modified foods and seeds (Navazio

2012). When I listened to Onondaga Faith Keeper Oren Lyons say that we need to grow our own food, I understood this as food sovereignty, which is part of decolonization.

Tatume, an *askutasquash*, confuses Western binaries: summer or winter, mature or immature. It grows close to the ground, able to take up water from the morning dew and keep growing in hot, dry weather. When the zucchini plants wilt and need the scarce resource of water, tatume continues to grow its tendrils, seeking out moisture. It has adapted to the harsh, dry weather by growing in many directions. The growth habit is exponential, from one vine, others, then more from those: the shape of survival.

Tatume unsettles categories of summer and winter squash because it is both and neither. Tatume grows against predetermined categories, sprawling with strategic abandon across the dry ground, perhaps trying to find a way home. For me, the process of understanding this queer squash and what it tells about land, colonization, and diaspora is part of a process toward decolonial trans-gender sovereignty (Muñoz 2012). Transing Tatume is a conceptual interplanting. A negotiation with the way things are; changing ourselves through a constant study of what could be.

Vic Muñoz is a professor of psychology and gender studies and coordinator of the First Nations and Indigenous Studies Program at Wells College.

Notes

1.   I use "trans-" and "transing" in alliance with what Susan Stryker, Paisley Currah, and Lisa Jean Moore (2008) beautifully articulate:

> Neither "-gender" nor any of the other suffixes of "trans-" can be understood in isolation—that the lines implied by the very concept of "trans-" are moving targets, simultaneously composed of multiple determinants. "Transing," in short, is a practice that takes place within, as well as across or between, gendered spaces. . . . Those of us schooled in the humanities and social sciences have become familiar, over the last twenty years or so, with queering things; how might we likewise begin to critically trans- our world" (13).

2.   *Oxford English Dictionary Online*, s.v. "squash," accessed 7 January 2014, www.oed.com.

References

Halberstam, Judith. 2005. *In a Queer Time and Place: Transgender Bodies, Subcultural Lives*. New York: New York University Press.

hooks, bell. 1992. "Eating the Other: Desire and Resistance." In *Black Looks: Race and Representation*, 21–39. Boston: South End.

Howard, Stephanie. 2001. *Life, Lineage, and Sustenance: Indigenous Peoples and Genetic Engineering: Threats to Food, Agriculture, and the Environment.* Edited by Debra Harry and Brett Lee Shelton. Wadsworth, NV: Indigenous Peoples Council on Biocolonialism. www.ipcb.org/pdf_files/LifeLineageandSustenance.pdf.

Hutchins, Jessica, and Clive Aspin. 2007. *Sexuality and the Stories of Indigenous People.* Wellington, Aotearoa, NZ: Huia.

"The Mystery of the Calabacita Squash." 2012. *Blogcritics* (blog), January 15. blogcritics.org/tastes /article/the-mystery-of-the-calabacita-squash.

Muñoz, Vic. 2012. "Gender/Sovereignty." In *Transfeminist Perspectives in and beyond Transgender and Gender Studies,* ed. Anne Enke, 23–33. Philadelphia: Temple University Press.

Navazio, John. 2012. *The Organic Seed Grower: A Farmer's Guide to Vegetable Seed Production.* White River Junction, VT: Chelsea Green.

Rich, Adrienne. 1989. "The Desert as Garden of Paradise." In *Time's Power: Poems 1985–1988,* 25–31. New York: Norton.

Salmón, Enrique. 2012. *Eating the Landscape: American Indian Stories of Food, Identity, and Resilience.* Tucson: University of Arizona Press.

Smith, Linda Tuhiwai. 2012. *Decolonizing Methodologies: Research and Indigenous Peoples.* London: Zed.

Stryker, Susan, Paisley Currah, and Lisa Jean Moore. 2008. "Introduction: Trans-, Trans, or Transgender?" *WSQ* 36, no. 3–4: 11–22.

White, Jay. 2010. "'Tatume': The Squash of Many Names." *Aggie Horticulture* (blog), June. aggie-horticulture.tamu.edu/newsletters/hortupdate/2010/jun/tatume.html.

Williams, Raymond. 1983. *Keywords: A Vocabulary of Culture and Society.* New York: Oxford University Press.

DOI 10.1215/23289252-2400055

Television

QUINN MILLER

Transgender histories and TV intertwine. *RuPaul's All Stars Drag Race* (2012) resurrects Thelma Harper (Vicki Lawrence) of *The Carol Burnett Show*, a series that, in its original run, included a skit set at a trans person's class reunion. In *Gender Outlaws: The Next Generation* (2010: 10–11), Kate Bornstein and S. Bear Bergman point to *Star Trek* and *Star Trek: The Next Generation* as shared cultural touchstones. References to TV in scholars' accounts of their self-recognition as trans signal further connections between television and trans history. Milton

Berle's drag performances, Leslie Feinberg recalls, "hit too close to home. I longed to wear the boys' clothing I saw in the Sears catalog" (1996: 4). Jamison Green's viewing of NBC's 1955 broadcast of *Peter Pan* starring Mary Martin as the title character instigated "one of those lucid moments" of early male identification. "I clearly remember thinking," he writes, " 'if she can be a boy, then so can I' " (2004: 11–12).

An abundance of trans TV content makes the medium an important component of trans studies. Personal histories of gender regulation, gender nonconformity, and gender transition may develop in relation to the national and transnational star trajectories of televisual icons like Turkey's Bülent Ersoy and Kuwait's Shjoon Alhajri or through the circulation and aesthetics of series like *The Jack Benny Show*; *Soap*; *Bosom Buddies*; *Quantum Leap*; *Ask Harriet*; *Ugly Betty*; *All My Children*; *Degrassi: The Next Generation*; *Dirty, Sexy, Money*; *America's Next Top Model*; *The Glee Project*; *Work It*; and *Drop Dead Diva*. José B. Capino's study of Philippine TV's movie talk shows, a genre prominent from the mid-1980s through the present, illuminates another trans dimension of TV programming, that of production, showing how the medium has allowed drag queens, faux drag queens, and a variety of gender "outcasts" to "openly . . . party on television" in unexpected ways (2002: 273). Mary L. Gray (2009: 158) has argued that rural youth use "the portability and the 'realness'" of scientific TV specials to understand and articulate their gender identities and trans experiences.

In commercial TV systems, advertisers drive content, making decisions based on demographics and ciscentric market research strategies. Yet as Alexander Doty (1993) has shown, even within capitalism, television not only reinforces norms but also provides tools for nonconformity that people use to queer and feminist ends. The technologies of television and medical transition debuted publicly contemporaneously in the mid-twentieth century. Since then, the everyday flow of TV, like trans history, has remained highly ephemeral and egregiously undocumented. Consider a sitcom proposal I came across in the Bob Cummings Papers at Brigham Young University while deep into specialized research around genderqueer sitcom camp. As part of the backstory presented in this document—one I have yet to place chronologically but that Cummings, the star of two eponymous post–World War II series and the sitcoms *My Hero* and *My Living Doll*, appears to have penned—Christine Jorgensen shows up alongside Elizabeth Taylor, Ava Gardner, and other "divinely endowed international female luminaries," revealing a television history complex with respect to trans culture.

While the fields of TV studies and trans studies have not as yet intersected much, they actually have a lot in common. Television studies examines the ways in which TV takes on a wide range of competing and conflicting meanings through its characteristic discourse of multiplicity. Mark Williams, in arguing for "the significance of television" in cultural history, has encouraged scholars to empha-size the "fissures, occlusions, [and] discontinuities" of media by analyzing "borders that exist at the levels of technology/industry/mode of address, borders that appear to have inspired or enabled an attention to spatial/social/historical borders" (2009: 47). The commonality in trans studies' and TV's attention to borders and border crossings is evident in Julia Serano's *Whipping Girl: A Transsexual Woman on Sexism and the Scapegoating of Femininity* (2007). While television appears as an object of pro forma critique in the book's discussion of the print comic *Hothead Paisan*, with sitcom writing offered as the barometer for instrumentalist uses of gender and sexual minorities in genre fiction, TV also assists with critique, as when Serano describes how the narrational strategies of medical makeover reality shows on non-trans-specific topics helped her understand the workings of transphobic tropes in other mediums (203, 55).

New research trajectories in TV studies offer exciting opportunities for scholars in trans studies. Exploring synesthesia and sense memory through advertising content during the 1950s, Marsha F. Cassidy (2009: 43) argues for a "telesthetic" history, bringing "the full sensorium back to critical consciousness." TV studies' recovery of embodiment would benefit immensely from a broader awareness of trans people as a part of history, particularly as cultural workers. With postwar public intellectuals like Marshall McLuhan theorizing television as a prosthetic extension and technology of the self, the medium surely played a more crucial role in the early psychic and somatic dimensions of trans experience than we realize. Television offers things quite helpful for many trans people: gender performance, dysphoria relief, artistic expression, and queer family.

Quinn Miller is an assistant professor of English at the University of Oregon, where he teaches queer media studies. His recent publications include "How to Queer Television" (in *How to Watch Television*, 2013) and "Queer Exteriors" (in *Transgender Migrations*, 2011).

References

Bornstein, Kate, and S. Bear Bergman, eds. 2010. *Gender Outlaws: The Next Generation*. Berkeley, CA: Seal.

Capino, Jose B. 2002. "Soothsayers, Politicians, Lesbian Scribes: The Philippine Movie Talk Show." In *Planet TV: A Global Television Studies Reader*, ed. Lisa Parks and Shanti Kumar, 262–74. New York: New York University Press.

Cassidy, Marsha F. 2009. "Touch, Taste, Breath: Synaesthesia, Sense Memory, and the Selling of Cigarettes on Television, 1948–1971." In *Convergence Media History*, ed. Janet Staiger and Sabine Hake, 34–45. New York: Taylor and Francis.

Doty, Alexander. 1993. *Making Things Perfectly Queer: Interpreting Mass Culture*. Minneapolis: University of Minnesota Press.

Feinberg, Leslie. 1996. *Transgender Warriors: Making History from Joan of Arc to Dennis Rodman*. Boston: Beacon.

Gray, Mary L. 2009. *Out in the Country: Youth, Media, and Queer Visibility in Rural America*. New York: New York University Press.

Green, Jamison. 2004. *Becoming a Visible Man*. Nashville: Vanderbilt University Press.

"RuPaul's Gaff-In." 2012. Directed by Nick Murray. *RuPaul's All Stars Drag Race*. Logo (MTV/Viacom). October 29.

Serano, Julia. 2007. *Whipping Girl: A Transsexual Woman on Sexism and the Scapegoating of Femininity*. Emeryville, CA: Seal.

Williams, Mark. 2009. "Rewiring Media History: Intermedial Borders." In Staiger and Hake, *Convergence Media History*, 46–56.

DOI 10.1215/23289252-2400064

Temporality

KADJI AMIN

"Temporality" refers to the social patterning of experiences and understandings of time. Attending to the ways in which transgender experiences are constituted by yet exceed normative temporalities promises to do justice to the complex ways in which people inhabit gender variance. A critical focus on the temporal under-pinnings of transgender as a historical category, on the other hand, may open the way toward a more transformative politics of justice.

Transsexual autobiography, which narrates the transsexual subject's self-actualization through surgical and hormonal transformation, has been an impor-tant genre for the dissemination of transsexuals' understandings of their own life narratives; it is also a fraught practice, since the narration of a transsexual life in conformity to the diagnostic "narratemes" of gender identity disorder (GID) has been *the* medical criterion of transsexuality and thus the determining factor in accessing hormonal and surgical treatments (Prosser 1998: 104). Jay Prosser has argued that the value of autobiography to transsexuals must be understood according to its capacity, as a genre, to construct transsexual experience in and through time. Autobiography is a diachronic narrative form that retrospectively bestows an illusion of teleological progression upon the aleatory chaos of life experience. If some transsexuals return to the genre of autobiographical narrative post–medical transition, Prosser proposes that it is precisely because the genre's constitutive tension between retrospection and progression—between the self at the time of writing and the self of the past—contains the potential to heal the sexed and temporal splits in transsexual experience by producing "continuity in the face of change" (1998: 120). Prosser does not consider the fact that if the retrospective construction of a coherent transsexual plot narrative proves healing to some, it is at the expense of episodes, or even fleeting moments, that would fracture or exceed it. To transsexual or transgender people for whom such episodes are critical and thus impossible to excise or reinterpret without doing violence to experience, the generic and temporal conventions of autobiography may prove singularly confining and distorting, and the genre itself may replicate, rather than heal, the coercions of the medical demand for "proper" transsexual narrativization.

We might understand the construction of transsexual subjectivity according to an organized, progressivist temporality that joins both continuity and change as a form of what queer theorist Elizabeth Freeman has termed "chrononormativity," a social patterning of experiences of time in conformity with normative frameworks. Freeman proposes that chrononormativity is established via "a mode of implantation, a technique by which institutional forces come to seem like somatic facts" (2010: 3). The medical criteria for diagnosing transsexuality, the therapeutic confessional discourses of talk shows and the press, and the generic conventions of written autobiography might all be thought of as authorizing transsexual subjects by implanting normative narratives of sexed development, continuity, and coherence. To say that transsexual autobiography is chrononormative is not necessarily to say that it is bad but rather to illuminate the ways in which it produces an experience of healing and empowerment for certain trans subjectivities and one of fragmentation and invalidation for others. Attending to the vagaries of transgender and transsexual experience, on the other hand, may necessitate a recognition of what some theorists have described as a "queer"—that is, nonchronological and nonnormative—form of temporality. The emergent literature on queer temporalities explores the patterning of time according to social modes of power and the potential alliance between asynchronic temporalities and queer sexual and social practices (Freeman 2007). J. Halberstam (2005) in particular associates ambiguously gendered bodies and noncontinuously gendered life narratives with the experience of being out of sync, a sense of rupture between past, present, and future, and split subjectivities. His work suggests that transgender lives may require mixed strategies—not only healing and an achieved coherence but also the ability to represent and to inhabit temporal, gendered, and conceptual discontinuities.

Any inquiry into the social patterning of temporality must, however, broaden the lens beyond individual transgender experiences of time to scrutinize the temporal underpinnings of transgender as a historically produced category. David Valentine (2007) has argued that through US activism that led to the simultaneous removal of homosexuality and inclusion of gender identity disorder in the *Diagnostic and Statistical Manual of Mental Disorders*, third edition (*DSM*-III) in 1980—followed by the promotion by the mainstream US gay and lesbian movement of an account of homosexuals as essentially *the same* as heterosexuals but for an essentially "private" difference of sexual practice—homosexuality has been normalized, stabilized, and privatized by being purged of gender transitivity, which has been displaced onto the separate category of transgender. Although, according to Valentine, this particular historical relation between homosexuality and transgender *produced* gender and sexuality as separate categories of analysis, this history is increasingly erased as the separation of gender and sexuality—and of homosexuality and transgender—is institutionalized as a matter of ontology, not historical process. Since this ontological conceptual separation is seen as a mark of modernist progress, the self-understandings of those gender-variant subjects who do not experience their gender as separate from their sexuality are increasingly dismissed as atavistic modes of false consciousness.

Given that each deployment of the term *transgender* risks reifying the notions of the at once ontological and progressive distinction between gender and sexuality, a critical transgender studies must work actively against transgender's historical baggage and temporal underpinnings. Strategies for doing this might include foregrounding modes of gender variance inseparable from homosexuality; returning to a feminist understanding of gender not simply as a neutral category of social difference but as a site invested with relations of power; and capitalizing on transgender's associations with public sex, economic marginality, racialized inequality, and policing to promote a politics of structural transformation rather than identity. Since a modernist progress narrative is being institutionalized along with the category of transgender, an attentiveness to nonchronological, nonprogressivist temporalities of gender variance across the registers of experience, history, and geography could prove critical to contesting a normative organization of temporality and identity that blocks transformative justice politics and distorts the experiences of many gender-variant people.

Kadji Amin is an assistant professor of queer studies in the Department of Cultural Analysis and Theory at Stony Brook University. His book *Untimely Genet* is forthcoming.

Works Cited

Freeman, Elizabeth, ed. 2007. "Queer Temporalities." Special issue, *GLQ* 13, no. 2–3.

———. 2010. *Time Binds: Queer Temporalities, Queer Histories*. Durham, NC: Duke University Press.

Halberstam, Judith. 2005. *In a Queer Time and Place: Transgender Bodies, Subcultural Lives*. Sexual Cultures. New York: New York University Press.

Prosser, Jay. 1998. *Second Skins: The Body Narratives of Transsexuality*. New York: Columbia University Press.

Valentine, David. 2007. *Imagining Transgender: An Ethnography of a Category*. Durham, NC: Duke University Press.

DOI 10.1215/23289252-2400073

Tranifest

KAI M. GREEN and TREVA ELLISON

"Tranifesting" (transformative manifesting) calls attention to the epistemologies, sites of struggle, rituals, and modes of consciousness, representation, and embodiment that summon into being flexible collectivities. Flexible collectivities are those that are capable of operating across normativizing and violative configurations of race, gender, class, sex, and sexuality. Our first encounter with *tranifest* as a term was at a June 2011 gathering for black radical warrior/healers that took place in Durham, North Carolina, called Indigo Days. *Tranifest* circulated as a part of an experimental lexicon created by Indigo Days participants to think and dialogue about gender and sexuality across generational, class, and gender differences in order to build collective capacity for bodily, emotional, and structural healing. To tranifest is to mobilize across the contradictions, divisions, and containment strategies produced by the state and other such large-scale organizations of power that work to limit our capacity to align ourselves across differences in ways that are necessary for social transformation.

The need for such flexible new collectivities is underscored for us by our observation, working as we do within the contemporary United States, that the hierarchical stratifications of race, gender, and sexuality that work against our survival are in part reproduced by institutionalizing within the academy the very political-intellectual projects that seem most capable, through their intersectional analyses, of articulating the necessary preconditions of deep social transformation

(Ferguson 2012: 28). Tranifesting enacts a resistance to the political and epistemic operations that would encapsulate, and capitalize for others, the fruits of our labor. It is a form of radical political and intellectual production that takes place at the crossroads of trauma, injury, and the potential for material transformation and healing.

We draw inspiration from the history of US black women's struggles—which we believe is underengaged by transgender studies—in, for example, the 1969 decision by members of the six-month-old Black Women's Alliance to rename themselves the Third World Women's Alliance in order to acknowledge the shared experiences and goals of black and Puerto Rican women with regard to forced sterilization and reproductive self-determination. This act of renaming and refiguring exemplifies precisely that sense of a flexible epistemology, in which ruptures are mobilized as generative sites for solidarity and transformation, that we seek to address by tranifesting. Similarly, tranifesting, we contend, to borrow language from Sylvia Wynter, is "the ceremony that must be found," the "re-writing of knowledge such that it is 'availing to the needs of mankind,' de-structuring the ratiomorphic apparatus" in ways that clear the ground for dreaming a different future, a future that keeps alive the liberatory potential of black feminism and Third World solidarity and liberation (Wynter 1984: 21).

Tranifesting, as an epistemic operation, is meant to call attention to the ways in which black feminism and transgender studies are similarly yet differentially capable of mediating particular individual experiences and operationalizing identity—not as ends in themselves but as places from which to generate transformative politics. The aim of doing so is to encourage a deeper and more intentional engagement between these two fields of study. Both transgender studies and black feminism enter the white feminist/women's studies terrain by marking its conceptual limits, its inability to account for those who are disappeared, or who are only taken up as marginalized tokens of diversity (Enke 2012; Salamon 2010). Also, black feminism and transgender studies scholarship both challenge the categories of man and woman as ontological givens by naming the logics, relations, forces, and developments that have been productive of multiple gendered and sexual discourses, expressions, and embodiments. As early as 1851, when Sojourner Truth confronted an audience of mostly white women with her famous question, "Ain't I a woman?," she was pointing out how gender emerges as much from such contingent social formations as plantation capitalism as from the biological body. Subsequent generations of black feminist scholars—Hortense Spillers, Denise Riley, Toni Cade Bambara, and Frances Beal, to name but a few—have furthered this fundamental insight into gender's sociohistorical contingency and its imbrication with constructions of race and class (Bambara 1970; Riley 2003).

Transgender studies has also emerged as a product and project of trani-festing. Scholars and activists like Leslie Feinberg and Marsha P. Johnson politicized gender-nonconforming expression and embodiment through the term *transgender* in order to call into being a collectivity centered on gender self-determination that reveals and challenges the social production and state-sanctioned contain-ment and regulation of gender and sexual deviancy. Transgender studies scholars have also theorized how racism, gender discrimination, and transphobia are coconstituted, calling on transgender studies and political organizing to deal with unmarked privileges in order to "face our own contradictions" (Juang 2006; Koyama 2006). Our formulation of tranifesting, as a political-intellectual endeavor, proceeds from these types of engagements as well as more recent work situated at the intersections of transgender studies and black feminism (Snorton 2011; Sudbury 2009; Walcott 2009).

The political urgency of this "inter-inter-disciplinary" engagement is underscored by the increasing access to visibility, rights, and citizenship afforded to some transgender subjects alongside the simultaneous expansion of penal democracy in the United States and beyond that ensnares transgender and gen-der-nonconforming subjects whose vulnerability is produced around other axes of difference, including race, poverty, and legal citizenship status (Aizura 2012; Shelley 2011).

Black feminism and transgender studies share an investment in destabi-lizing the gender and sexual normativities through which such injustices are perpetrated. Let us use their tools to move beyond mere theorizing, to tranifest the forms of collective life that can enliven and sustain us in a future worth living in. Let us tranifest a new world order!

Kai M. Green is a PhD candidate in the Department of American Studies and Ethnicity at the University of Southern California. His dissertation manuscript is titled "Into the Darkness: A Black Queer (Re)Membering of Los Angeles in a Time of Crises."

Treva C. Ellison is a PhD candidate in the Department of American Studies and Ethnicity at the University of Southern California. Treva's forthcoming dissertation, "Towards a Politics of Perfect Disorder: Carceral Geographies, Queer Criminality, and Other Ways to Be," gives an account of LGBT and queer organizing and advocacy in Los Angeles around issues of surveil-lance, policing, and incarceration between 1949 and 2012.

References

Aizura, Aren. 2012. "Transnational Transgender Rights and Immigration Law." In Enke, *Transfeminist Perspectives*, 133–52.

Bambara, Toni Cade. 1970. *The Black Woman: An Anthology*. New York: New American Library.

Enke, Anne. 2012. *Transfeminist Perspectives in and beyond Transgender and Gender Studies*. Philadelphia: Temple University Press.

Ferguson, Roderick A. 2012. *The Reorder of Things: The University and Its Pedagogies of Minority Difference*. Minneapolis: University of Minnesota Press.

Juang, Richard. 2006. "Transgendering the Politics of Recognition." In *The Transgender Studies Reader*, ed. Susan Stryker and Stephen Whittle, 706–20. New York: Routledge.

Koyama, Emi. 2006. "Whose Feminism Is It Anyway? The Unspoken Racism of the Trans Inclusion Debate." In Stryker and Whittle, *Transgender Studies Reader*, 698–705.

Riley, Denise. 2003. *Am I That Name: Feminism and the Category of Women in History*. Minneapolis: University of Minnesota Press.

Salamon, Gayle. 2010. *Assuming a Body: Transgender Theory and Rhetorics of Materiality*. New York: Columbia University Press.

Shelley, Kristopher, "Krystal." 2011. "Krystal Is Kristopher and Vice Versa." In *Captive Genders: Trans Embodiment and the Prison Industrial Complex*, ed. Nat Smith and Eric A. Stanley, 165–69. Oakland, CA: AK.

Snorton, C. Riley. 2011. "Transfiguring Masculinities in Black Women's Studies." The Feminist Wire. May 18. thefeministwire.com/2011/05/transfiguring-masculinities-in-black-womens-studies/.

Sudbury, Julia. 2009. "Maroon Abolitionists: Black Gender-Oppressed Activists in the Anti-prison Movement in the U.S. and Canada." *Meridians* 9, no. 1: 1–29.

Walcott, Rinaldo. 2009. "Reconstructing Manhood; or, The Drag of Black Masculinity." *Small Axe* 13, no. 1: 75–89.

Wynter, Sylvia. 1984. "The Ceremony Must Be Found: After Humanism." *Boundary 2* 12–13: 19–70. doi:10.2307/302808.

DOI 10.1215/23289252-2400082

Tranimals

LINDSAY KELLEY

The prefix *trans-* engulfs *animal*, making the singular animal plural: *tranimals*.[1] This portmanteau word articulates the labor and biocapital of cross-species organisms. Animals become tranimals through the prefixial materiality of genetic modification (Hansen 2008; Kelley and Hayward 2013), digital distribution (King 2010), and aural affinity (Prabhakar 2009). Tranimals turn "sex-bending trick[s]" (Helmreich 2011); their procreations are interstitial, decorative, and discursive. Transdisciplinary in their pluralities, these indeterminate, disordered forms secrete traces across disciplines and pollute categories.

Trans- extends beyond animal to microbial, even molecular, forms of life. Trans- implies interchange between both gender expression and genetic expression (tranimals are said to "express" their modifications). Their movement across categories coupled with their vulnerable position as experimental subjects binds tranimals to other forms of trans- life, including humans. Trans- organisms are under the same knife, compelled to navigate diagnostic and pharmacological landscapes. This shared terrain troubles "animacy hierarchies" that would limit opportunities along species lines (Chen 2012: 98).[2] Within the imagined correspondence between trans- and animal, nonhuman and human, fragile lives are set adrift on currents of biomedical capital.

Consider the "tranimal[s]-forming agent" (Helmreich 2011) green fluorescent protein (GFP), a reporter gene first harvested and synthesized from the jellyfish *Aequorea victoria* in the 1960s (Shimomura 1995; Baille Gerritsen 2001). Following GFP, we find jellyfish proteins drifting through the bodies of other species. A GFP bestiary works to carry transgenic bioluminescence: GFP-expressing rhesus monkey ANDi has siblings who glow in stillborn death while ANDi's date of death remains unknown (Trivedi 2001). Eduardo Kac's *GFP Bunny*, Alba, frames the laboratory rabbit as both conceptual art and domestic companion (Kac 2005). Developed in Taiwan for commercial purposes, multicolored GFP fish are sterile and decorative (Whitehouse 2003; Taikong Group). GFP expression in domestic kittens marks a protein that resists feline immunodeficiency virus: glowing paws point to clinical intervention into human-cat disease (Wongsrikeao et al. 2011). Transgenic pig flesh follows stem cells like breadcrumbs (Hsiao et al. 2011). Countless other organisms labor to express GFP for biomedical science, including bacteria, microbes, and flies.

Tranimals-forming agents like GFP suggest a fluid exchange of tissue and sensation, mediated by the constraints of the laboratory. Technoscience has transformed the jellyfish's localized flash in response to external stimulus into a steady, diffuse glow. Even as *Aequorea victoria* populations diminish at sea, their synthesized flesh multiplies and flourishes. Yet, the fleeting, responsive biolu-minescence of jellyfish becomes uninteresting if not invisible compared to the constant visual excitement of GFP tranimals. As the watery bodies of *Aequorea victoria* haunt the celebrated lives of ANDi and Alba, we begin to understand and become tranimals by finding their flesh in our own.

Lindsay Kelley's art practice and scholarship explore how the experience of eating changes when technologies are being eaten. She is an associate lecturer in the College of Fine Arts, University of New South Wales. Her book, *The Bioart Kitchen*, is forthcoming. She has also published numerous essays and coedited an issue of *parallax*, "bon appétit."

Notes

1. The term *tranimals* debuted at the 2009 annual meeting of the Society for Science, Literature, and Art panel "TRANimalS: Theorizing the Trans- in Zoontology" (Kelley and Hayward 2009), and was presented again in the "Somatic Sociality of Tranimals" panel at the 2010 Zoontotechnics (Animality/Technicity) Conference (Kelley and Turner 2010).
2. Borrowing from linguistics, Mel Chen critically engages the term "animacy hierarchy" ("the tenuous hierarchy of human-animal-vegetable-mineral") to question assumptions about race, sexuality, and liveliness (Chen 2012: 98).

References

Baille Gerritsen, Vivienne. 2001. "The Greenest of Us All?" *Protein Spotlight* 11. web.expasy.org /spotlight/pdf/sptlto11.pdf (accessed December 1, 2012).

Chen, Mel. 2012. *Animacies: Biopolitics, Racial Mattering, and Queer Affect*. Durham, NC: Duke University Press.

Hansen, Natalie. 2008. "Humans, Horses, and Hormones: (Trans) Gendering Cross-Species Relationships." *Women's Studies Quarterly* 36, no. 3–4: 87–105.

Helmreich, Stefan. 2011. "*Homo microbis* and the Figure of the Literal." Fieldsights—Theorizing the Contemporary. *Cultural Anthropology Online*, April 24. culanth.org/fieldsights/259 -homo-microbis-and-the-figure-of-the-literal.

Hsiao, F. S. H., et. al. 2011. "Toward an Ideal Animal Model to Trace Donor Cell Fates after Stem Cell Therapy: Production of Stably Labeled Multipotent Mesenchymal Stem Cells from Bone Marrow of Transgenic Pigs Harboring Enhanced Green Fluorescence Protein Gene." *Journal of Animal Science* 89, no. 11: 3460–72. doi:10.2527/jas.2011-3889.

Kac, Eduardo. 2005. *Telepresence and Bio Art: Networking Humans, Rabbits, and Robots*. Ann Arbor: University of Michigan Press.

Kelley, Lindsay, and Eva Hayward, panel cochairs. 2009. "TRANimalS: Theorizing the Trans- in Zoontology," panel at the annual meeting of the Society for Science, Literature, and Art, Atlanta, November 5–8.

———. 2013. "Carnal Light." *parallax* 19, no. 1: 114–27.

Kelley, Lindsay, and Lynn Turner, panel cochairs. 2010. "Somatic Sociality of Tranimals," panel at the Zoontotechnics (Animality/Technicity) Conference, Cardiff University, May 12–14.

King, Katie. 2010. "My Distributed Animality." *SL Tranimal* (blog). sltranimal.blogspot.com (accessed December 1, 2012).

Prabhakar, Prema. 2009. "'Do Not Rest in Peace': The Obsessional Mediumship of Diamanda Galas." Paper presented at the annual meeting for the Society for Science, Literature, and Art, Atlanta, November 5–8.

Shimomura, Osamu. 1995. "A Short Story of Aequorin." *Biological Bulletin* 189, no. 1: 1–5. doi:10.2307/1542194.

Taikong Group. Taikong Group Ornamental Fish. www.tkfish.com.tw/en/about/about-tk (accessed December 1, 2012).

Trivedi, Bijal P. 2001. "Introducing ANDi: The First Genetically Modified Monkey." *Genome News Network*, January 16. www.genomenewsnetwork.org/articles/01_01/ANDi.shtml.

Whitehouse, David. 2003. "GM Fish Glows in the Bowl." BBC News. news.bbc.co.uk/2/hi/science/nature/3026104.stm (accessed October 15, 2012).

Wongsrikeao, Pimprapar, et al. 2011. "Antiviral Restriction Factor Transgenesis in the Domestic Cat." *Nature Methods* 8, no. 10: 853–59. doi:10.1038/nmeth.1703.

DOI 10.1215/23289252-2400091

Transability

ELISA A. G. ARFINI

"Transability" denotes the persistent desire to acquire a physical disability and/or to seek the actual elective transition of the body from abled to disabled. It can be understood as the cultural translation of the diagnostic category BIID (body integrity identity disorder), which, albeit not currently listed in the World Health Organization's International Classification of Diseases or in the American Psychiatric Association's *Diagnostic and Statistical Manual of Mental Disorders*, frames the desire for disability as a mental disease. Relevant biomedical literature on the condition was inaugurated by John Money (Money, Jobaris, and Furth 1977), who reported two case studies of individuals desiring amputation.

Transability is an umbrella term developed within the community of individuals who identify as transabled. It mirrors the term *transsexuality*. In particular, the term is meant to echo the "wrong body" metaphor and what is perceived to be a trajectory of successful recognition, one that transsexual individuals gained after obtaining regulated access to medical technologies of sex reassignment. Transability thus constructs a narrative of transsexuality, one that understands the goal of transition as passing, accepts a prediscursive origin of trans desire, and defers to a regulated process that proceeds from medical diagnosis to legal name change. Although it is currently deprecated in favor of a more counternormative model of transgender embodiment, transsexual narrative as constructed by transability is naturalized as the figural model of transition from deviancy to normality, from suffering to reconciliation, and as an exemplary history of social acceptance and cultural recognition.

An analysis of transabled narratives (Arfini 2010) demonstrates how regimes of justification (Boltanski and Thévenot 1999) and autobiographics (Gilmore 1994) are carefully orchestrated in order to achieve a similar naturalization of transabled desires. The struggle for recognition of transabled politics rests its modern and liberal claims on the right for self-determination (Stryker and Sullivan 2009). The goal of this politics thus relies on constructing an autonomous and compos mentis subject rather than on the construction of a certain body.

Transabled agendas can be evaluated in terms of antagonism and/or conformity to normative discourse. However, a deconstructive reading can also expose how transability reveals crucial processes regulating the binary opposition between ability and disability. If, despite its assimilationist goals, transability remains a desire for malfunction, aberration, deformity, this is due not to the nature of transabled desire but to the social construction of body standards. Normative body standards, in fact, construct sovereign subjects by conflating difference with lack and integrity with autonomy. Legitimate membership in the class of able bodied is thus revealed as a highly policed social determination.

Elisa A. G. Arfini is a postdoctoral fellow in sociology in the Department of Philosophy and Communication at the University of Bologna, Italy. She is the author of *Scrivere il sesso. Retoriche e narrative della transessualità* (2007).

References

Arfini, Elisa A. G. 2010. "Istruzioni per diventare disabili: Un'analisi narrativa del progetto sul corpo transabile." *Studi Culturali* 7, no. 3: 343–64.

Boltanski, Luc, and Laurent Thévenot. 1999. "The Sociology of Critical Capacity." *European Journal of Social Theory* 2, no. 3: 359–77.

Gilmore, Leigh. 1994. *Autobiographics: A Feminist Theory of Women's Self-Representation*. Ithaca, NY: Cornell University Press.

Money, John, Russell Jobaris, and Gregg Furth. 1977. "Apotemnophilia: Two Cases of Self-Demand Amputation as a Paraphilia." *Journal of Sex Research* 13, no. 2: 115–25.

Stryker, Susan, and Nikki Sullivan. 2009. "King's Member, Queen's Body: Transsexual Surgery, Self-Demand Amputation, and the Somatechnics of Sovereign Power." In *Somatechnics: Queering the Technologisation of Bodies*, ed. Nikki Sullivan and Samantha Murray, 49–61. Farnham, UK: Ashgate.

DOI 10.1215/23289252-2400118

Transbutch

JEN MANION

The vast possibilities for gender variance manifested by the category of transgender have been precluded by a dominant narrative of crossing from one clear gender to another (Meyerowitz, 2002). As the categories "transman" and "transwoman" become increasingly stable, other transgressive gender identities are obscured and separated from the category of transgender (Feinberg 1996; Stryker and Whittle 2006). "Transbutch" signifies a gendered embodiment that is both butch and trans, not tied to any singular definition of butch or trans but rather falling somewhere in between. Transbutch marks a liminal space that embraces both the historical legacies of the category of butch and the more expansive possibilities created by the transgender rights movement for recognition, community, and empowerment.

The category of transbutch is a response to the hostility and misunderstanding displayed by some butches and lesbians toward transmen (Halberstam 1998). As many lesbians mourned the alleged loss of the butch and felt they needed to defend the boundaries of their "woman identified woman" communities, butches became increasingly reappropriated with an emphasis on their sex (female) rather than their gender (masculine). Some have promoted the use of the phrase "butch women" to emphasize that butches are not transgender and love being women (Bergman 2010). Transbutches embody a third space (with others) between the uncritical celebration of "womanhood" and its rejection entirely.

Transbutches embrace aspects of masculinity without denouncing their social affiliation with an oppressed group of people who were predominantly raised and socialized as girls.

The category of transbutch has emerged from trans* discourses, activism, and communities that challenge people to claim conscious gender identities. This is a departure from the historic butch code of silence that required masculine women to avoid, downplay, or deny their gender deviance. Requests for preferred pronouns and the emergence of the category of cisgender have compelled butches to figure out where they fit in this new gendered order. While butches or even transbutches might not identify as transgendered, they are not cisgendered either.

Transbutches relate to transmen and embrace their status as gender outlaws. Both share many of the following: identifying as more masculine than androgynous, taking pleasure from passing as male, assuming a male sexual identity, and rejecting the notion that biology is destiny. Like most butches and transmen, transbutches do not embrace a chief marker of female embodiment—the breast—and seek to minimize its presence through baggy clothes, binding, or top surgery (Rubin [1992] 2011). Top surgery (or the desire for it) has historically distinguished transsexuals from butches, but this is changing. As more transmen embrace top surgery and share powerful stories of pleasure and relief, butches are following their lead. This further blurs the line between transmen and butches.

In a group of transmen, the transbutch may or may not be accepted as a peer. In society, transmen and transbutches are treated to similar forms of judgment and misunderstanding that also vary depending on region, race, ethnicity, class, ability, and body type. Despite these variations, however, the nuances of these complicated gender identifications are largely meaningless to the masses. Transbutches might retain some social privilege by not fully claiming a male identity (as many transmen do) in a world where so many people still believe that one needs to be born with a penis to really be a man.

Jen Manion is an associate professor of history at Connecticut College. Jen is coeditor of *Taking Back the Academy: History of Activism, History as Activism* (2004). Jen's book *Liberty's Prisoners: Gender, Sexuality, and Punishment in Early America* is forthcoming. Jen's new project is titled "Early American Transgender Histories: From Revolution to Civil War."

References
Bergman, S. Bear. 2010. *Butch Is a Noun*. Vancouver: Arsenal Pulp.
Feinberg, Leslie. 1996. *Transgender Warriors: Making History from Joan of Arc to RuPaul*. Boston: Beacon.

Halberstam, Judith. 1998. *Female Masculinity*. Durham, NC: Duke University Press.

Meyerowitz, Joanne. 2002. *How Sex Changed: A History of Transsexuality in the United States*. Chicago: University of Chicago Press.

Rubin, Gayle. (1992) 2011. "Of Catamites and Kings: Reflections on Butch, Gender, and Boundaries." In *The Gayle Rubin Reader*, 241–53. Durham, NC: Duke University Press.

Stryker, Susan, and Stephen Whittle, eds. 2006. *The Transgender Studies Reader*. New York: Routledge.

DOI 10.1215/23289252-2400127

Transgender

CRISTAN WILLIAMS

The word *transgender* entered widespread use as an umbrella term for describing a range of gender-variant identities and communities within the United States in the early 1990s.[1] At that time, Virginia Prince (1913–2009), a self-identified heterosexual cross-dresser from Los Angeles who later started living socially as a woman full time and who played an indisputably important role in the formation of gender-variant communities, organizations, and identities within the United States in the mid-twentieth century, was often credited with coining the term (Feinberg 1996). Her role in this regard has been overstated, and the history of the word itself is far more complex than has been previously understood.

Prince did describe herself with such terms as *transgenderal* as early as 1969 and *transgenderist* as early as 1978, as a means to name the specific behavior of living full time in a chosen social gender role different from that typically associated with birth-assigned sex, without undergoing genital sex-reassignment surgery (see Ekins and King 2006). In 1975, *FI News* featured an article about the term *transgenderist* (Mesics 1975), defining it in the manner Prince would later use, and in 1976, Ari Kane, a contemporaneous gender-variant community leader on the East Coast, used the term in a similar fashion (see Mesics 1975). Prince and Kane, however, did not use the word "transgender" in its contemporary all-inclusive sense, nor were they first in coining words involving some compound of trans + gender. More importantly, the earliest documented uses of "transgender" do not distinguish cross-dressing or living full time without surgery from transsexual identities.

In 1965, for example, Dr. John Oliven proposed that the term *transsexualism* be replaced by the term *transgenderism*, arguing that the concept of sexuality could not account for the "all consuming belief that [transsexuals] are women who by some incredible error were given the bodies of men" (1965: 514). On April 26, 1970, a *TV Guide* newspaper insert used the term "transgendered" to describe the transsexual title character of Gore Vidal's sex-change farce *Myra Breckinridge* ("Sunday Highlights" 1970). In 1974, Drs. Robert Hatcher and Joseph Pearson used "transgender" as a term for operative transsexuals, writing, "The transvestite rarely seeks transgender surgery" (1974: 176). During that same year, Oliven again used "transgender" but this time as a term inclusive of both transvestites and transsexuals (1974). By 1975, transvestite/transsexual groups began using "transgenderism" as a term inclusive of transsexuals and transvestites (Dowell 1975). In 1979, 1982, and 1985, Christine Jorgensen, then perhaps the world's most famous transsexual, publicly rejected the term *transsexual* in favor of the term *transgender* (Parker 1979; Associated Press 1982; Canadian Press 1985). In 1984, *TV-TS Tapestry* magazine featured an article recounting the importance of a "transgender community," in which "transgender" was used as an umbrella term inclusive of transsexuals and cross-dressers (Peo 1984). By the mid-1980s, "transgender" had been used multiple times—in medical, pop-culture, and trans community sources alike—as an umbrella term inclusive of transsexuals, cross-dressers, and other gender-variant people.[2] The dramatic rise in the term's popularity in the early 1990s, therefore, should be seen as the acceleration of a longer trend rather than the creation of a new meaning for an existing term that originally meant something else. The coinage, uptake, and diffusion of "transgender" was an organic, grass-roots process that emerged from many sources, in many conversations happening in many different social locations.

This new understanding of *transgender*'s etymology not only has important implications for tracing the complex recent history of gender and sexuality; it can also intervene in contentious identitarian disputes within and among various contemporary trans communities. One common polemical use of what might be called the "Virginia Prince Fountainhead Narrative" of *transgender*'s origin is that a motley movement of various gender-nonconformists, transsexuals, and queers commandeered a term that referred specifically to heterosexual cross-dressers who chose to cross-dress full time—*transgenderists*—thereby colonizing the identity label of another group and forcibly assimilating them into political and social formations they wanted nothing to do with.[3] Prince herself felt this way; she claimed ownership of the term and objected to the broader use of "transgender" (Prince 1991).

Etymological research clearly documents, however, that since the 1970s, "transgender" has in fact been used with a variety of meanings. One important use has been to group together different kinds of people who might otherwise have virtually no social contact with one another. This grouping together across fine gradations of trans experience and identity can facilitate communication and hence build the experienced reality of a shared community, with overlapping and intersectional social needs and political goals. It is this expansive, rather than narrow, use of the term that encompasses the intellectual and political promise of a *transgender studies*.

Cristan Williams is the founder of the Transgender Archives in Houston, Texas, and is the executive director of the Transgender Foundation of America.

Notes

1.   See the chart documenting the rising popularity of *transgender* in Stryker and Aizura 2013 (2).
2.   See the extensive citations published in Williams 2012.
3.   See, for example, the opinion of Billie Jean Jones (1992), publisher of cross-dresser magazine *TV Guise*.

References

Associated Press. 1982. "Transgender." *Appeal-Democrat*, May 11.

Canadian Press. 1985. "She Gave Spark to Sexual Revolution." *Regina Leader-Post*, December 18.

Dowell, Frances. 1975. "Salmacis Offer Lectures." *Female Impersonator News* 1, no. 6: 2.

Ekins, Richard, and Dave King. 2006. *The Transgender Phenomenon*. London: Sage.

Feinberg, Leslie. 1996. *Transgender Warriors: Making History from Joan of Arc to Dennis Rodman*. Boston: Beacon.

Hatcher, Robert, and Joseph Pearson. 1974. "Psychiatric Evaluation for Transgender Surgery." In *A Practical Handbook of Psychiatry*, ed. Joseph R. Novello, 176–78. Springfield, IL: Charles C. Thomas.

Jones, Billie Jean. 1992. "Readers Write. . . . " *Gender EUPHORIA* 6, no. 2: 9.

Mesics, Sandy. 1975. "The Transgenderist Explains." *Female Impersonator News* 1, no. 6: 4.

Oliven, John F. 1965. *Sexual Hygiene and Pathology*. Philadelphia: Lippincott.

———. 1974. *Clinical Sexology*. Philadelphia: Lippincott.

Parker, Jerry. 1979. "Christine Recalls Life as Boy from the Bronx." *Winnipeg Free Press*, October 18.

Peo, Roger. 1984. "The 'Origins' and 'Cures' for Transgender Behavior." *TV-TS Tapestry*, no. 42: 40.

Prince, Virginia. 1991. "VIEWPOINT!!!" *Gender EUPHORIA* 5, no. 11: 7.

Stryker, Susan, and Aren Aizura. 2013. "Transgender Studies 2.0." In *Transgender Studies Reader 2*, ed. Susan Stryker and Aren Aizura, 1–12. New York: Routledge.

"Sunday Highlights." 1970. *TV Guide. Des Moines Register*, April 26.

Williams, Cristan. 2012. "Tracking Transgender: The Historical Truth." *Ehipassiko* (blog). cristanwilliams .com/b/tracking-transgender-the-historical-truth (accessed November 1, 2013).

DOI 10.1215/23289252-2400136

Transition

JULIAN CARTER

In the late twentieth century, *transition* became the vernacular term of choice in anglophone North America for describing the process or experience of changing gender. Initially, "transition" denoted a standardized trajectory of "sex reassignment" in which people were shuttled from the psychiatrist, through the endocrinologist, to the surgeon, to the judge (Cooke 1998; Rubin 2003). While any individual element of this sequence may be passionately desired, its trajectory through batteries of expert gatekeepers can be alienating even for those who most closely conform to those experts' standards. The sequence itself materializes the discomforting biopolitical requirement that trans-people must literally embody a particular set of psychiatric perspectives and medical practices.

Transition thus weighs especially heavily on people who lack the resources or the wish to conform to its polarized definitions of sexed embodiment, such as poor and/or uninsured people and those whose gender expression is not formed in relation to dominant white European American conventions. This is why many North American trans- communities insist that "everyone transitions in their own way": open-ended refusal to define "transition" is a principled stance against institutionalizing any given form of trans- being. Such resistance reflects decades of struggle over who decides what counts as legitimate trans-/gender expression—struggle that clings to the word itself.

Despite its affective complexity and political freight, "transition" is frequently deployed to refer to the ways in which people move across socially defined boundaries away from an unchosen gender category. Such actions, and the language denoting them, have varied over time and place. For instance, in the nineteenth-century US West, people "assumed the dress" of their preferred gender (Boag 2011). In the mid-twentieth century, one had "the operation" that accomplished a "sex change." Late 1960s San Francisco queens "came out," submerging references to specific strategies in a wider celebration of social emergence as a member of one's chosen sex while echoing the self-affirmative language of gay liberation (Cooke 1998). "Transition" became widely used only in the mid-1990s. "Transition" differs from "sex change" in its inherent reference to duration rather than event, from "assuming a dress" in its attention to the embodied self who dresses, and from "coming out" in its disengagement from politically radical and street subcultures; yet conceptual residue from these earlier vocabularies adheres to the term as the activities it encompasses expand. Thus in common usage, "transition" conjoins expectations of ongoing, indeterminate process with expectations of eventual arrival and implies some shift in bodily self-presentation that is both central to, and inadequate to describe, the interpersonal/psychic experience of altering one's social gender.

Multiple technical definitions of *transition* preexisted the word's application to gender, and we might well consider how the resonances of these earlier usages could perhaps linger in the new transgender context. In rhetoric, transitions function as the ramps and bridges over which audiences are guided from one point to the next; they are evaluated as successful when our presentation seamlessly supports our claims, weak when the seams show. In physics, transition refers to a state of matter in which different phases of the same substance (as solid, liquid, or gas) achieve a temporary, unstable equilibrium that allows them to coexist. In dance, transitions are strategies for redirecting embodied energies; they can change the quality or the direction of movement, increase or decrease momentum, cover space, and/or occupy time. In parturition, transition names the shift from active labor to pushing the baby out. Transitions are brave work. Like birth, like writing, gender transition is when hopes take material form and in doing so take on a life of their own.

Transition is a list of trial names on the fridge, initials doodled on notepads. It is wearing a dress every day for a year, even though you imagine yourself as a rocker chick in torn jeans. It is searching for your name and photograph on your company's website so you can compile a list to send through HR to the IT people who will, you hope, be consistent about updating them. It is borrowing your brother's clothes. Transition is a misnomer because you were here, like this, all along. Transition is calling 911 before you cut off your dick so they can get you to the hospital before you bleed out. It is never having to reassure an embarrassed checkout clerk again. It is when you stop—or maybe start—avoiding mirrors, and bathrooms. It is like being slowly flayed in public. It is a rush of romantic feeling when you touch your own skin. Transition is a revised interface with agents of the security state. Transition is your secret self made available for social relationships.

Transition is thousands of little gestures of protest and presence, adding up and getting some momentum behind them so that you finally achieve escape velocity from the category you were stuck in all those years ago. But how do you know when you have arrived? "Transition" is not like "the operation" in this sense, though "the operation" often serves as an imagined conclusion. At some point, for many people, changes become less pronounced, less socially and affectively intense. We may stop celebrating every sign of our revised movement in the world. We are on the other side. Still when we pass, if we are unlucky in our relatives, we may be buried in clothes and under a name that suit someone else's idea of authentic gender, and none of us control how we are remembered. When we are not aware of the days getting longer, have the seasons stopped changing? This is the promise of transition, as the term continues to expand from its psychiatric and surgical usage: that we can live in the time of our own becoming and that possible change is not restricted to the narrow sphere of our conscious intention.

Julian Carter is associate professor of critical studies at California College of the Arts in Oakland and San Francisco. He is the author of *The Heart of Whiteness: Normal Sexuality and Race in America, 1880–1940* (2007) and is currently writing about transformation and transition in contemporary dance.

References

Boag, Peter. 2011. *Re-dressing America's Frontier Past*. Berkeley: University of California Press.

Cooke, Suzan. 1998. Interview by Susan Stryker. San Francisco, CA, Jan 10. Tape recording. San Francisco: GLBT Historical Society.

Rubin, Henry. 2003. *Self-Made Men: Identity and Embodiment among Transsexual Men*. Nashville: Vanderbilt University Press.

DOI 10.1215/23289252-2400145

Translatinas/os

LAWRENCE LA FOUNTAIN-STOKES

The neologism *translatinas/os* is of recent coinage and has been employed to identify transgender, transsexual, and transvestite individuals in Spanish-speaking parts of Latin America and elsewhere.[1] The term brings together the prefix *trans-* and the noun *Latina/o*, employed as a gender-inflected synonym for Latin American or as an ethnic or racial marker for a person of Latin American descent who lives elsewhere, for example in Australia, Canada, Europe, or the United States. Given that the prefix *trans-* is used to indicate individuals who might have migrated (or whose family histories might include migration) and who might have transnational connections, it acquires a double valence, referring to geography and physical displacement as much as to gender identity and expression. The expansive use of the root word *Latina/o* is quite notable, as this term is more associated in recent times with US populations, who use it in contradistinction to *Hispanic* but also to *Latin American* (or *latinoamericana/o*) (see Oboler 1995). The term *translatina/o* is not coterminous with or representative of the entire Latina/o trans population—a broader and more diverse group, as Marcia Ochoa (2010) has discussed—and can be juxtaposed to vernacular Latin American terms explored by others, such as Don Kulick's (1998) analysis of the word *travesti* in Brazil and Annick Prieur's (1998) discussion of *jota* and *vestida* in Mexico.[2] Ochoa actually proposes the terms "Latina/o transpopulations" and "US trans-Latina/os" (with a hyphen), and protests the dominant practice of marginalizing female to male (FTM) transgender Latinos. In his own work on Latina trans performers on Australian television (specifically on the Mexican transsexual Miriam), Vek Lewis (2009) proposes the term "translatinidad" to convey "the idea of a uniform, colossal Latin American type that traverses national borders and celluloid memory, tinged with the connotations of a colonially inscribed, phallic femininity, which [the performer's] transsexuality is positioned to represent" (240). Lewis (in Namaste 2011) also criticizes the use of English-language terms and neologisms and privileges the use of vernacular Spanish and Portuguese-language categories.

"Translatina" has been employed in the Unites States to name community support groups such as El/La para Translatinas, an AIDS-prevention and social support group for Latina trans women located in the Mission District of San Francisco. The name of this group plays with the standard third-person singular female pronoun in the Spanish language, *ella* (she), and breaks it down into two elements with a slash: the first word, *el* (the), is the singular male article in Spanish and also references the third person singular male pronoun *él* (he), while the second word, *la* (the) is the singular female article. As such, "El/La" can be read in many ways, for example as He/She, S/he, or "He who is intrinsically part of She." Leading trans figures in El/La have included Alexandra Byerly (now known as Alexandra Rodríguez de Ruiz), who is originally from Mexico.

A variation of "translatina" appears in the name of a national US organization established in 2009, the Coalición TransLatin@ (TransLatin@ Coalition), which uses the at symbol to indicate double gender valence in the Spanish language, following very recent linguistic innovations (other new spellings in Spanish include the use of a/o and o/a to mark female and male). The TransLatin@ Coalition identifies itself as "La voz de inmigrantes TransLatin@s/The voice of TransLatin@ Immigrants." There appear to be no transmen in positions of leadership in this organization, based on the names included as members of the board of directors on its website.

Translatina is also the title of a feature-length documentary by the Peruvian director Felipe Degregori (2010). This 93-minute film was funded by the Pan American Health Organization (a Regional Office of the World Health Organization), UNAIDS (the Joint United Nations Program on HIV/AIDS), the United Nations Development Program, RedLacTrans (Red Latinoamericana y del Caribe de Personas Trans [Latin American and Caribbean Network of Trans People]), and ILGA-LAC (the Latin American and Caribbean Region of the International Lesbian and Gay Association), with additional support from the Spanish Agency for International Development Cooperation (AECID). The documentary focuses mostly on the Peruvian experience, including interviews with trans individuals, government officials, members of the police, LGBT activists, and health professionals. It also includes interviews with a large number of trans women and LGBT leaders from throughout Latin America and the Caribbean (fifteen nationalities), including trans rights pioneers such as Marcela Romero, Claudia Baudracco, and María Belén Correa (Argentina), Liza Minnelli (Brazil), Raiza Torriani (Bolivia), Valentina Riasco (Colombia), Bianca Vidal (Chile), Rashell Erazo (Ecuador), Paty Betancourt and Amaranta Gómez (Mexico), Silvia Martínez (Nicaragua), Venus Tejada (Panama), Jana Villayzan (Peru), and Gloria Mariño (Uruguay), most of whom are involved with RedLacTrans. The film also highlights the role of nongovernmental organizations and of trans organizations at the national level, for example the Association of Transgenders, Transsexuals, and Transvestites of Argentina (ATTTA). Topics addressed include police brutality, lack of employment opportunities outside traditional fields such as sex work and beauty salons, educational and family discrimination, health challenges (particularly HIV/AIDS), body modification (particularly through the use of injectable biopolymers), legal challenges (including name change legislation), personal relationships, dreams of migration (particularly to Italy) and of sex-reassignment surgery, testimonials about the difficulties of living abroad, and activism. Many of the interviewees discuss the incipient state of trans activism in the region. The term *Latina* is not discussed and is offered simply as a synonym for Latin American; there is no mention of Latina women in the United States.

Finally, *translatina* can be associated with other Spanish-language neologisms such as *translocas* and *transmachas*, which have been used by scholars to refer to transnational Latin American feminism (Álvarez 2009; Costa and Álvarez 2009) and to transnational or translocal trans performers and activists, including drag queens, drag kings, and performance artists (La Fountain-Stokes 2011). Sonia Álvarez highlights the usage of the term *loca* as "madwoman" in Spanish and proposes a resistant reinterpretation for contemporary feminists who explore the transnational dimensions of Latin American women's experience. In my own work, I have also used the term *translocas* but embraced the alternate, vernacular, and highly stigmatized meaning of *loca* as effeminate male and seen this epithet (which is widely used among gay men and trans women as a term of endearment) as a potential site for resignification in a translocal and transnational performance framework. I have also been interested in the linguistic gender shifts entailed in the feminized use of the term *macha* as a variant of macho, already common in epithets such as *marimacha* (masculine woman, lesbian, butch), following up on queer and feminist theorizations by individuals such as Ana Castillo (1995) to see its connection to contemporary performance artists such as Elizabeth Marrero (particularly her drag king character of Macha in the Bronx, New York City) (La Fountain-Stokes 2009) and Gisela Rosario, best known in Puerto Rico for her punk rock persona of Macha Colón.

Lawrence La Fountain-Stokes is an associate professor of American culture, Romance languages and literatures, and women's studies at the University of Michigan. He is the author of *Queer Ricans: Cultures and Sexualities in the Diaspora* (2009), *Uñas pintadas de azul/Blue Fingernails* (2009), and *Abolición del pato* (2013).

Notes

1. Roger Lancaster (1998) discusses the wide variety and heterogeneity of trans categories and practices in Latin America.
2. Vek Lewis (2006) offers a critique of Kulick and Prieur, privileging the research of César O. González Pérez (*Travestidos al desnudo: Homosexualidad, identidades y luchas territoriales en Colima*) and Josefina Fernández (*Cuerpos desobedientes: Travestismo e identidad de género*). Also see Viviane Namaste 2011.

References

Álvarez, Sonia. 2009. "Construindo uma política feminista translocal da tradução." *Revista Estudos Feministas* 17, no. 3: 743–53.

Castillo, Ana. 1995. "La Macha: Toward an Erotic Whole Self." In *Massacre of the Dreamers: Essays on Xicanisma*, 121–43. New York: Plume.

Costa, Claudia de Lima, and Sonia Álvarez. 2009. "Translocalidades: Por uma política feminista da tradução." *Revista Estudos Feministas* 17, no. 3: 739–42.

Degregori, Felipe. 2010. *Translatina*, DVD (93 min.). Lima, Peru: Buenaletra Producciones.

Kulick, Don. 1998. *Travesti: Sex, Gender, and Culture among Brazilian Transgendered Prostitutes.* Chicago: University of Chicago Press.

La Fountain-Stokes, Lawrence. 2009. *Queer Ricans: Cultures and Sexualities in the Diaspora.* Minneapolis: University of Minnesota Press.

———. 2011. "Translocas: Migration, Homosexuality, and Transvestism in Recent Puerto Rican Performance." *e-misférica* 8, no. 1. hemisphericinstitute.org/hemi/en/e-misferica-81 /lafountain.

Lancaster, Roger. 1998. "Transgenderism in Latin America: Some Critical Introductory Remarks on Identities and Practices." *Sexualities* 1, no. 3: 261–74.

Lewis, Vek. 2006. "Sociological Work on Transgender in Latin America: Some Considerations." *Journal of Iberian and Latin American Research* 12, no. 2: 77–89.

———. 2009. "Performing Translatinidad: Miriam the Mexican Transsexual Reality Show Star and the Tropicalization of Difference in Anglo-Australian Media." *Sexualities* 12, no. 2: 225–50.

Namaste, Viviane. 2011. "Critical Research and Activisms on Trans Issues in Latin America: An Interview with Vek Lewis." In *Sex Change, Social Change: Reflections on Identity, Institutions, and Imperialism*, 2nd ed., 181–203. Toronto: Women's Press.

Oboler, Suzanne. 1995. *Ethnic Labels, Latino Lives: Identity and the Politics of (Re)presentation in the United States*. Minneapolis: University of Minnesota Press.

Ochoa, Marcia. 2010. "Latina/o Transpopulations." In *Latina/o Sexualities: Probing Powers, Passions, Practices, and Policies*, ed. Marysol Asencio, 230–42. New Brunswick, NJ: Rutgers University Press.

Prieur, Annick. 1998. *Mema's House, Mexico City: On Transvestites, Queens, and Machos*. Chicago: University of Chicago Press.

DOI 10.1215/23289252-2400154

Translation

A. FINN ENKE

Our telling reaches across chasms of power and privilege. Struggles with willful unknowing. Stands on fault lines between people most similar. Insists upon wholeness. This is the work of translation.
—Eli Clare, *The Marrow's Telling: Words in Motion*

Translation, from Latin: to carry or bring across.

Translation is a necessary and profoundly hopeful act for those who trans gender, for we have been taught that transgender is marked by dysphoria, a word from Greek that means difficult to bear, difficult to carry. In order to carry or bring across, we become poets, storytellers, and artists.

Sandy Stone, a founder of trans studies, tells this story: it is 1972 at the Stanford Gender Dysphoria Clinic, and Sandy is waiting for her appointment, one of many that she hopes will establish her eligibility for sex reassignment support.

Another trans woman also waiting pulls a clay pipe out of her purse. Sandy says, "tell me, if you think of yourself as a woman, why have you chosen to smoke a pipe?" The woman responds, "I am a woman. This is my pipe. Therefore, this is a woman's pipe." Sandy suddenly understands something new (Gabriel 1995: 16). Meanings collide across time and space, and the definition of "pipe" has changed. Still, let us not forget that in many parts of the world for at least four centuries, "pipe" has acted as a polite translation for "penis." Translation transforms us.

Much is lost in translation. With what do we replace the parts we let go? From one language to another, translators of poetry must decide: what demands unwavering loyalty? The meter, the rhyme, the literal word, or the use of space on the page? Translation creates two things: first, something new; and second, the illusion that there was an original from which the translation sprang. But there is no original: the poem is a medium, a conveyance. We ask, should our translations conform to audience expectations or transform them? We dance between, always doing both, by the very act of being.

Translation traffics in power. As Hala Kamal reminds us, "translation is not merely an act of transferring information, but a process of knowledge production" (Kamal 2008: 274; also see Wieringa, Blackwood, and Bhaiya 2007). In a world in which gay, queer, and transgender all comingle with imperialist institutions, translators carry the burden of destruction and creation. Choices must be made. In Arabic, neither "gender" nor "queer" has an explanatory equivalent. In Taiwan, *T-Po* is not equivalent to the American *butch-femme;* both pairings are multilingual and both require further contextualization. In Mandarin, *tongzhi* conventionally means common cause, commitment, or comrade; it carries a concept of affinity across Chinese socio-temporal contexts, specifically using the tensions of homosexual in/visibilities to arrive at a new meaning commonly translated into English as "gay." Translators of Japanese *manga* into English usually choose to completely obliterate the self-gendering signifiers within Japanese first-person singular pronouns. Who, then, is the author, and to whom does the translated text belong?

We remake and even exceed language, but we do not escape it. In English alone, we constitute ourselves within grammar. To paraphrase Judith Butler, "I" still cannot speak "apart from the grammar that establishes my availability to you" (1999: xxiv; see also Stone 1991). Grammar signs gender as well as race, age, dis/ability, social status. The speaker is never indigenous, pure, or even original. Communication depends on translation. Yet what happens in the turbulent distance between mouth and ear?

Gender becomes legible through acts of translation that betray disciplinary success and failure simultaneously. Perhaps few things point out the failure of words to convey our arrival in this social body quite so well as transgender.

Transgender highlights the labors of translation, inhering an implied "before" and "from which." The present moment does not tell the story, only that there is one worth telling.

Transgender—an explicitly imperfect translation—itself carries institutional and imperial discipline: to be named and to name oneself transgender is to enter into disciplinary regimes that distribute recognition and resources according to imperial logics. As a term, *transgender* translates an infinite multiplicity into a single disciplinary body. But this project fails, and its failure incites creative elaboration, the proliferation of stories. Transgender demands above all the need for more context, more story, and thus the translation *into* transgender never arrives and rests. Instead, it begs that we continuously translate *from* transgender, provide new contextual elaborations that include time and place and all the disciplinary regimes through we which have named and been named, the names that are the precondition of our passing.

The Skin of Transgender

Translation is the skin of transgender,
gender's carriage, its conveyance:
>   we carry it
>   we bring it
across time from one place to another
as if there is no friction
>   in between.

Translation like law does not carry
>   does not bind
>   documents across borders:
birth certificate SSN driver's license passport doctor's note if lucky green card.

Translation like pronoun fails
becomes interpretation, imposition, the transposition of one body on to an other
not one, not two: it multiplies with each border crossed or
not crossed.

There is always friction: meaning not like an object transported
and dropped into a new place, but meaning
like skin
>   it bears scars, rips and tears, hydrated nourished and
worn.

It's the story we make of our lives
to get a job to get
hormones to get a ride to get across time to get
      home.

It's how we make our name make ourselves
make sense
      how we find
      how we invent
common language
      not just words
      not just voice
your hands my hands
sign language
      act it out
      show me
      point
skin flexes over adam's apple: whose sign?

A. Finn Enke is an associate professor of history, gender and women's studies, and LGBT studies at the University of Wisconsin–Madison. Enke edited the collection *Transfeminist Perspectives in and beyond Transgender and Gender Studies* (2012) and is working on a graphic novel titled "With Finn and Wing: Growing Up Amphibious in a Nuclear Age."

References

Butler, Judith. 1999. *Gender Trouble: Feminism and the Subversion of Identity*. New York: Routledge.

Gabriel, Davina Ann. 1995. "Interview with the Transsexual Vampire: Sandy Stone's Dark Gift." *Trans Sisters*, no. 8: 14–27.

Kamal, Hala. 2008. "Translating Women and Gender: The Experience of Translating *The Encyclopedia of Women and Islamic Cultures* into Arabic." *Women's Studies Quarterly* 36, no. 3–4: 254–68.

Stone, Sandy. 1991. "The *Empire* Strikes Back: A Posttranssexual Manifesto." In *Body Guards: The Cultural Politics of Gender Ambiguity*, ed. Julia Epstein and Kristina Straub, 280–304. London: Routledge.

Wieringa, Saskia, Evelyn Blackwood, and Abha Bhaiya, eds. 2007. *Women's Sexualities and Masculinities in a Globalizing Asia*. New York: Palgrave.

DOI 10.1215/23289252-2400163

Transmedia

JIAN CHEN and LISSETTE OLIVARES

Transmedia, as it is activated in this inaugural issue of *TSQ: Transgender Studies Quarterly*, focuses on subversive uses and conceptualizations of media by and for transgender and gender-defiant people in the transnational "post-digital" age. Media activists, artists, and cultural workers, including Allucquère Rosanne "Sandy" Stone, Cheang Shu Lea, IRANTI-ORG, Tanwarin Sukkhapisit, Beatriz Preciado, Dees Rees, Yozmit, Micha Cárdenas, Ignacio Rivera, Kit Yan, Wu Tsang, Felix Endara, Shawna Virago, Sean Dorsey, Sin Kabeza Productions and Coco Rico, Leeroy K. Y. Kang, Tobaron Waxman, the Electronic Disturbance Theater, Chris Vargas, Cayden Mak, and Jacolby Satterwhite, have created works that express dimensions of transgender and gender-nonconforming experience while also transforming the relationship between the aesthetics, politics, and technologies of cultural representation. In their transmedia productions, bodies, images, sounds, materialities, politics, and informatics offer points of social contact and expressive meaning making rather than static representations and theories. These practitioners engage transmedia critically by paying attention to shifting networks of interrelated references, such as masculine and feminine, surface and essence, migrant and citizen; race, region, ethnicity, and nationality; urban, suburban, and rural; post- and nonindustrial; human, animal, plant, and thing. Their moving, networked aesthetics visualize and exploit the linked media forms (performance, video, film, painting, print, games, television, photography, music) and technologies (computer, typewriter, pen, brush, camera, projector, stage, body, audio recorder and player, radio, phone) enabled by the globally networked electronic infrastructure (cables, towers, satellites, and devices), built on the US Cold War's Internet. Like the illegitimate cyborg offspring envisioned in Donna Haraway's famous manifesto, these transmedia practitioners are unfaithful to imperial technological origins (Haraway 1990). For example, Cheang Shu Lea's net videos, installations, and performances visualize the Internet and the "digital revolution" as partially embodied and materialized spaces where racially gendered bit-bodies morph according to programmed desires and mutating viruses. In Cheang's media worlds, sex, pleasure, and play are never freed from techno-economies of labor or the histories of American and Japanese imperial militarism, science, industry, and culture that shape the origins of high-tech global networks (Cheang 2001, 2009–12).

Allucquère Rosanne "Sandy" Stone's "The *Empire* Strikes Back" has been foundational in assembling transgender archives and discourses in opposition to medical, academic, and mainstream feminist "technolog[ies] of inscription" (Stone [1991] 2006). Stone's attention to the mediation of transgender lives by dominant institutions and her convergent practices as theorist, artist, and activist offer interlocking modalities for critical transmedia approaches. In *The War of Desire and Technology at the Close of the Mechanical Age* (1996), Stone explains how the act of listening to a public lecture by Stephen Hawking, amplified through microphone, computer, and speakers, can create a communicative intimacy that trespasses the presumed boundaries of the body and internal self. For Stone, communications technology and the gendered body itself are virtual "prostheses" that provide zones of active social interaction, boundary shifting, and communicated meaning (ibid.). In response to the epistemic violence of academic knowledge production, Stone has turned to performance as her primary medium of knowledge transmission, emphasizing the impact of sharing space, time, and physical presence in specific contexts (Stone 2010). During one of her recent performances, Stone arranged for the simultaneous closure of ActLab's digital archives, stored on the University of Austin's web servers. This real-time action in performance produced a layered media insurgency that destabilized academic paradigms of knowledge production and ownership.

Subversive transmedia exploits, undermines, and overwrites corporate uses of the same term by "post"-industrial transnational Hollywood. As a commercial concept, transmedia describes contemporary media products that are created *through* models of production and *for* models of consumption that differ from mass industrial modes. Transmedia products are hybrids that cross and connect multiple media narrative threads, genres, and forms. They are produced, circulated, and consumed across interconnected media industries and technologies within the United States and transnationally. The hybridity of transmedia products is the result of the economic consolidation of different national, regional, and international media industries into linked units in the US transnational entertainment chain (Miller et al. 2008). While decentralized networks of media units allow for diversified, time-compressed, audience-responsive, and cost-flexible content production and delivery, US entertainment conglomerate bases maintain administrative control over hierarchies of creative labor, technologies, and capital. The hybrid products created through managed transnational media networks promise diverse yet coordinated entertainment experiences for different audiences—and greater profit for media corporations—through multiple avenues of consumption. With total cost estimated at US$400–$500 million and film production scattered across Los Angeles, Hawaii, and New Zealand, James Cameron's *Avatar* (2009) illustrates the concentrated wealth and decentralized control needed to produce today's Hollywood blockbuster. New Zealand was an outsourced and economically incentivized filming location for *Avatar*. The location was also a source of labor and an ecological resource (the basis for the virtual world of Pandora) for the film. As *Avatar*'s multinational base for digital production, Peter Jackson's Weta Digital in New Zealand provided the technological labor and effects that allowed *Avatar* to remake film itself into a 3-D portal of immersion for weary American audiences and new international audiences. *Avatar*'s makeup of 80 percent computer-generated special effects, 20 percent live action grossed US$2.7 billion worldwide in ticket sales alone and provided a transition into other routes for immersion and consumption, such as DVD, Blu-ray Disc, video, games, toys, and web tourism. As shown by *Avatar*, US corporate-based transmedia resurrects the controlled techno-aesthetic environments of nineteenth-century commodity culture embodied in the Parisian arcades. The interpenetration of media industries and technologies produces phantasmagorias, or simulated sensory connections between products that overload and alienate the senses so that consumption becomes passive (Buck-Morss 1991). A reclaimed transmedia approach recognizes that commercial intoxication relies on sustaining the out-of-world feeling of having been transported across space and time. Becoming aware of our participation in these time-space warps, or "wormholing dynamics," can jolt us out of sensory alienation (King 2012). Trans and genderqueer rebels mobilize transmedia to recover the deleted material conditions that have enabled the current technological and economic networking of media. What has been called the "digital revolution" describes the transformation of late nineteenth- to mid-twentieth-century mass media technologies, including newspapers, magazines, radio, television, and film, by new media technologies that rely on computational devices and the Internet as a backbone for communicative networking (Chun and Keenan 2005). The shift from "old" to "new" media has helped to facilitate a broad transition from mass industrial economies based in manufacturing in the global North to a new global economy based on services, leisure, and entertainment. This technological shift has also supported the expansion of US political and military institutions beyond the geographic borders of the nation-state (Castells 2009). Critical transmedia approaches interrupt corporate and state narratives on the purely democratizing effects of new media and the new "weightless" political economy that it has created. Digital forms are materially grounded in the globally networked electronic infrastructure that builds on the architecture of the US-born Internet, which was coinvented by the military, government, scientific researchers, universities, and private companies by the 1970s and then given over to privatized popular use in the 1990s. The "virtual" network infrastructure does not only rely on conductors (cables, towers, satellites), nodes (connecting points, protocols, packet switching), and devices (computers, mobile phones, digital cameras). It also depends on a labor-intensive economy that includes creative work along with cassiterite mining, semiconductor manufacturing, the the production and laying of fiber-optic cables in regions of Africa, Latin America, and Asia (Ekine 2010). Revealing the hidden labor of the transnational bodies found on the integrated circuit is mandatory for a critical understanding of global media networks and commerce.

Jian Chen is an assistant professor of English and affiliate faculty of sexuality studies, Asian American studies, women's, gender, and sexuality studies, and film studies at the Ohio State University. Their/his research focuses on new strategies for transgender, queer, and gender and sexual nonconforming cultural activism at the turn of the twenty-first century, with the transition from cultural politics to cultural economies facilitated by networked media technologies.

Lissette Olivares is a PhD candidate in the History of Consciousness Department at the University of California, Santa Cruz, where she investigates the role of new media in social movements from a transnational and transhistorical perspective. Olivares's work has been exhibited in dOCUMENTA(13), Institute of Cultural Inquiry-Berlin, Mix Queer Experimental Film Festival (NY), Berlin Porn Film Festival, and DonauFestival (Austria), among others.

References

Buck-Morss, Susan. 1991. *The Dialectics of Seeing: Walter Benjamin and the Arcades Project.* Cambridge, MA: MIT Press.

Castells, Manuel. 2009. *Communication Power.* Oxford: Oxford University Press.

Cheang Shu Lea, director. 2001. *I.K.U.* Tokyo: Aries, Uplink.

———. 2009–12. *U.K.I.* www.u-k-i.co (accessed November 14, 2012).

Chun, Wendy Hui Kyong, and Thomas Keenan. 2005. *New Media, Old Media: A History and Theory Reader.* New York: Routledge.

Ekine, Sokari, ed. 2010. *SMS Uprising: Mobile Activism in Africa.* Oxford: Pambazuka.

Haraway, Donna. 1990. "A Cyborg Manifesto: Science, Technology, and Socialist-Feminism in the Late Twentieth Century." In *Simians, Cyborgs, and Women: The Reinvention of Nature,* 149–82. New York: Routledge.

King, Katie. 2012. "Wormholed Critique and Design." *SF Ecologies: Speculative, Feminist, Science as Knowledges* (blog). ecosfking.blogspot.com/2012/04/wormholed.html (accessed November 2, 2013).

Miller, Toby, et al. 2008. *Global Hollywood 2.* London: British Film Institute.

Stone, Allucquère Rosanne. 1996. *The War of Desire and Technology at the Close of the Mechanical Age.* Cambridge, MA: MIT Press.

Stone, Allucquère Sandy. 2010. "Curating Academic Insurgencies." Performance at The Task of the Curator Conference, University of California, Santa Cruz, May 14–15.

Stone, Sandy. (1991) 2006. "The *Empire* Strikes Back: A Posttranssexual Manifesto." In *The Transgender Studies Reader,* ed. Stephen Whittle and Susan Stryker, 221–35. New York: Routledge.

DOI 10.1215/23289252-2400172

Transphobia

TALIA MAE BETTCHER

That transphobia exists is uncontroversial. Almost any trans person can attest to the existence of it based on personal experiences or the experiences of acquaintances. And there is documented evidence of sexual violence, physical violence, and verbal harassment of trans people, and at least the self-reports of trans people indicate that such behavior often arises from hostile attitudes toward them as trans. However, the exact rates, nature, and extent of violence are difficult to determine, in part because there are no reliable statistics on how many trans people there are and because the various methods for collecting these data have specific limitations (Stotzer 2009).

While it is clear transphobia exists, however, it is far from evident what transphobia *is*. Provisionally, the term can be defined to mean any negative attitudes (hate, contempt, disapproval) directed toward trans people because of their being trans. When taken literally, the word means a kind of fear. But like *homophobia* (on which the word is modeled), it is used more broadly. And while *transphobia* suggests an analogy with terms like *agoraphobia* and therefore implies irrationality (*Merriam-Webster's Collegiate Dictionary* defines *homophobia* as "an irrational fear of, aversion to, or discrimination against homosexuality or homosexuals"[1]; most dictionaries do not define *transphobia* at all), this implication ought to be rejected. Transphobia occurs in a broader social context that systematically disadvantages trans people and promotes and rewards antitrans sentiment. It therefore has a kind of rationality to it, grounded in a larger cisgenderist social context (Hopkins 1996).[2]

The question, however, is how much such a definition can tell us about the nature of transphobia. I have defined *transphobia* as directed toward *trans people*. In doing this, I have tried to avoid smuggling an actual account of the underlying nature of transphobia into the definition. But much depends upon how the expression *trans people* is itself defined. If it is defined as "those who violate gender norms," or as "those who are problematically positioned with respect to the gender binary," then a very general account of the nature of transphobia *is* immediately forthcoming—namely, transphobia is a hostile response to perceived violations of gender norms and/or to challenges to the gender binary.

It is not wise, however, to build a robust account of transphobia into the definition. A trans woman may not view herself as violating norms of gender, and she may not view herself as beyond the binary. Rather, she may see herself as a woman living *within* the binary and in accordance with norms of womanhood. A robust definition of this type ironically invalidates her gender identity in order to function as an account of transphobia. That is, it perversely enacts a verbal hostility that it fails to explain. I therefore prefer to leave *trans people* undefined and open to the multiple, contested meanings. Consequently, while *transphobia* is provisionally defined, one of the central components of that definition (*trans people*) is not only undefined but left open to multiple interpretations.

Underlying the attempt to build a robust account of transphobia within the definition of the term is the problematic assumption that there *is* a singular phenomenon of which there *can be* a uniform account. Consider that while the pronoun *it* can be used to deny the personhood of individuals deemed outside the binary categories, the expression *really a man disguised as a woman* effectively accuses a trans person of pretense by deeming them *within* one of the binary categories. Both are instances of verbal harassment, and both can function as "justifications" for physical violence. But that the latter concerns a response to perceived violations of the binary is surely controversial. Both trans woman and transphobe may agree that she belongs in the binary. The question, on the contrary, is *where*. Whether there is a singular phenomenon here (hostile responses to perceived violations of the binary) is therefore far from clear.

And transphobia can be manifested differently in different cultures. For example, Latin American representations of trans people as deceivers may include stronger associations with criminality (Lewis 2010). Indeed transphobia can occur differently in different types of social contexts within a culture. In therapeutic contexts it is not uncommon for trans people to be viewed as mentally ill. Yet this representation need not be found in other contexts (say, sex work). The view that "mental illness" is *the* paradigmatic stigma elides different forms of stigma applied to trans people for whom access to medico-psycho-therapeutic narratives is irrelevant. And the controversial expectation that there is a single phenomenon is precisely what helps promote treatment of specific kinds of transphobia as somehow exemplary.

Finally, the view that transphobia can be separated from other enactments of power (such as sexism, classism, racism) is a nonstarter. This means that not all acts of violence against trans people need be transphobic in nature. A trans woman might be targeted not because of her trans status but because she is simply viewed as a sex worker (Namaste 2005). Moreover, at least in some cases, transphobia may be inseparably blended with misogyny or racism in ways that challenge a single-axis model of power (Juang 2006). Such inseparabilities undermine the attempt to account for transphobia in a way that excludes or marginalizes considerations of sexism, racism, classism, ableism, and so forth. This consideration is important because it questions why certain instances of violence should be characterized as instances of transphobia (as opposed to instances of racism or sexism) in the first place and what the underlying political agenda sustaining such characterization is. My conclusion, at any rate, is that while we might have a definition of *transphobia*, the term is not much more than a convenient (and not altogether innocent) placeholder for the real intellectual work that remains to be done.

Talia Mae Bettcher is a professor of philosophy at California State University, Los Angeles. Her research is located at the intersections of transgender studies and feminist philosophy. She is currently working on a book about the nature of gendered personhood and its relationship to transphobic violence. Some of her articles include "Evil Deceivers and Make-Believers: On Transphobic Violence and the Politics of Illusion" (*Hypatia*, summer 2007) and "Trapped in the Wrong Theory: Rethinking Trans Oppression and Resistance (*Signs*, winter 2014). With Ann Garry, she coauthored the *Hypatia* special issue "Transgender Studies and Feminism: Theory, Politics, and Gender Realities" (summer 2009).

Notes

1. *Merriam-Webster's Collegiate Dictionary Online*, s.v. "homophobia," accessed December 13, 2013, www.merriam-webster.com/dictionary/homophobia.
2. While Hopkins discusses homophobia, not transphobia, his idea is useful in this context.

References

Hopkins, Patrick. 1996. "Gender Treachery: Homophobia, Masculinity, and Threatened Identities." In *Rethinking Masculinity: Philosophical Explorations in Light of Feminism*, ed. Larry May and Robert A. Strikwerda, 95–116. Lanham, MD: Rowman and Littlefield.

Juang, Richard. 2006. "Transgendering the Politics of Recognition." In *The Transgender Studies Reader*, ed. Susan Stryker and Steven Whittle, 706–19. New York: Routledge.

Lewis, Vek. 2010. *Crossing Sex and Gender in Latin America*. New York: Palgrave MacMillan.

Namaste, Viviane. 2005. *Sex Change, Social Change: Reflections on Identity, Institutions, and Imperialism*. Toronto: Women's Press.

Stotzer, Rebecca. 2009. "Violence against Transgender People: A Review of United States Data." *Aggression and Violent Behavior* 14, no. 3: 170–79.

DOI 10.1215/23289252-2400181

Trans-poetics

REBEKAH EDWARDS

Where "trans-" animates the suffixes to which it is attached and "poetics" explores "how meaning is possible, by whom and at what cost" (Barthes 1999: 218), "trans-poetics" refers to techniques for communicating "complex, unstable, contradictory relations between body and soul, social self and psyche" (Ladin 2013: 306). Trans-poetic projects often seek to navigate the limits of the (im)possible, writing the "resistance of the inarticulate, in a language that situates" (edwards 2013: 325) or lending poetic form to "a body that has been historically illegible" (Shipley 2013: 197). Such projects may engage relations between the textual and the corporeal, between content and form, between "signifiers and the world they configure" (Holbrook 1999: 753).

An example of a trans-poetics relevant to transgender studies is one articulated in feminist translation studies regarding the inevitability and potentiality of error. As translation is imbricated with cultural/political oppressions, silences, repressions, and reiterations, the error produced in the discord between two languages offers clues to the limits of the self: within these errors one encounters and disrupts the boundaries between self and another (author, text, language) (Spivak 1993). In the context of gender performativity, error is also conceived as generative, as the imperfect iteration that allows for the possibility of the "improper" (Butler 1993). A trans-poetics making use of both of these understandings of error draws on the discord, contingencies, and multiplicities possible in language in order to narrate and subvert cultural and critical attempts to fix gender and sexual boundaries.

"Trans-poetics" refers to the art and the labor of transgender poets, and it refers to diverse interpretative and compositional strategies attentive to relational movements between/across/within linguistic, embodied, affective, and political domains.

Rebekah Edwards teaches in the Departments of English and Women, Gender and Sexuality Studies at Mills College and Visual and Critical Studies at the California College of Arts. Edwards is the author of *Then's Elsewhere* (2010).

References

Barthes, Roland. 1999. "The Structuralist Activity." In *Criticism: Major Statements*, 4th ed., ed. Charles Kaplan and William Anderson, 487–92. New York: Macmillan.

Butler, Judith. 1993. "Imitation and Gender Insubordination." In *The Lesbian and Gay Studies Reader*, ed. Henry Abalone, Michele Aina Barale, and David M. Halprin, 307–20. New York: Routledge.

edwards, keri. 2013. "A Narrative of Resistance." In *Troubling the Line: Trans and Genderqueer Poetry and Poetics*, ed. T. C. Tolbert and Time Race Peterson, 317–25. Callicoon, NY: Nightboat Books.

Holbrook, Susan. 1999. "Lifting Bellies, Filling Petunias, and Making Meanings through the Trans-Poetic." *American Literature* 71, no. 4: 751–71.

Ladin, Joy. 2013. "Trans Poetics Manifesto." In Tolbert and Peterson, *Troubling the Line*, 299–307.

Shipley, Ely. 2013. "The Transformative and Queer Language of Poetry." In Tolbert and Peterson, *Troubling the Line*, 187–198.

Spavik, Gayatri Chakravorty. 1993. "The Politics of Translation." *Outside in the Teaching Machine*, 179–200. New York: Routledge.

DOI 10.1215/23289252-2400109

Trans Species

HARLAN WEAVER

Trans species highlights the ways in which trans formations are connected to and made possible by relationships among humans and nonhuman animals that productively disrupt heterosexual gender norms and kinship formations.

From the Latin *speciē*—appearance, form, kind—*species* has long been caught up in racisms, colonialisms, and sexual and gender norms. For example, the eighteenth-century notion of species as interfertility—the ability to produce viable offspring—introduced by Georges-Louis Leclerc, Comte de Buffon, was central to nineteenth-century eugenicists' assertions of race as species (Nott 1843). More recently, Ernst Mayr's well-known 1942 biological definition of species as "actually or potentially interbreeding natural populations, which are reproductively isolated from other such groups" (120), while contested, helped solidify heterosexuality's starring role in species debates. Trans species challenges these intersecting stories of nature that culture tells itself.

Myra Hird notes that nonhuman living organisms "display a wide diversity of sex" (2008: 235), a diversity evident in examples such as the platypus's five X and five Y chromosomes and the coral goby's environment-dependent sex changes. Indeed, for many species, heterosexual sex is impossible, as with fungi whose thousands of sexes make of propagation a nonheterosexual flourishing. The many species of trans are species disruptors.

Trans species also describes connections integral to human processes of being and doing trans. Premarin, a hormonal treatment derived from the urine of pregnant mares and often used for human feminization, involves "horses kept in cycles of gestation and impregnation so as to collect their urine" (Hayward 2010: 228); this entwining of bodies and violences makes many trans embodiments possible. Trans species encounters also commingle ontologies and identities. Eva Hayward describes the ways in which "a transitioning woman is enfleshing, enfolding elements of her environment within herself . . . a spider in her web" (ibid.: 238–39), while Harlan Weaver writes about how his relationship with his pit bull–type dog facilitated his safety in public spaces when he was "vulnerable as a visibly transgender person," helping to make his gender possible (2013: 689). Trans species reveals how these coconstitutive identities and ways of being happen through species differences.

Imbricated ontologies and mutually constitutive identities reveal trans species as a mode of connection. Trans species promotes hybrid fruit and rhizomatic extensions that make new becomings possible, becomings that reveal intimacies inconceivable under the genus regime. Trans species is trans making, in that it demonstrates how the illicit tendrils of trans formations weave new webs that join multiple and diverse bodies and beings, making them kin in spite of kind.

Harlan Weaver is a visiting research scholar at the Center for Science, Technology, Medicine, and Society at the University of California, Berkeley. Recent publications include "Becoming in Kind: Race, Gender, and Nation in Cultures of Dog Fighting and Dog Rescue" (*American Quarterly*, September 2013) and "Monster Trans: Diffracting Affect, Reading Rage" (*Somatechnics*, September 2013).

References

Hayward, Eva. 2010. "Spider City Sex." *Women and Performance* 20, no. 3: 225–51.

Hird, Myra. 2008. "Animal Trans." In *Queering the Non/Human*, ed. Myra Hird and Noreen Giffney, 227–48. London: Ashgate.

Mayr, Ernst. 1942. *Systematics and the Origin of Species*. New York: Columbia University Press.

Nott, J. C. 1843. "The Mulatto a Hybrid—Probable Extermination of the Two Races if Whites and Blacks Are Allowed to Intermarry." *Boston Medical and Surgical Journal* 29, no. 2: 29–32.

Weaver, Harlan. 2013. "Becoming in Kind: Race, Gender, and Nation in Cultures of Dog Fighting and Dog Rescue." *American Quarterly* 65, no. 2: 689–709.

DOI 10.1215/23289252-2400100

Transxenoestrogenesis

EVA HAYWARD

Trans-: Latin *trans*, across; through; transversal.

Xeno-: Greek *xénos*, a strange guest; other; a different kind of difference; divergence; see Octavia Butler's *Xenogenesis*, an Afro-futurist science fiction trilogy about the interbreeding of humans and aliens.

Estrogen: Greek *oistros*, literally a gadfly—a biting insect; and hence, by extension, a provoking person; figuratively, a provocation of passion and sexual desire, as in the condition of estrus, the cyclical female animal's attraction of rutting males for coitus; with suffix *-gen*, meaning "producer of."

Genesis: Greek *gignesthai*, produced; a mode of formation: symbiogenesis; root.
—*New Oxford American Dictionary*

Xenoestrogenic, even without the prefix *trans-*, is already an overgrown, weedy keyword sinking heterogeneous taproots into the histories, politics, and embodiments of life on planet Earth. Hence my recourse to etymology. It is an adjective form of *xenoestrogen*: that is, an estrogen anthropocentrically and racially marked as "foreign" or "alien," which includes those estrogens belonging to plants (phytoestrogens) and fungi (mycoestrogens) as well as various kinds of synthetic estrogens (e.g., Bisphenol A). The *xenoestrogenic* tangles with the more familiar rootstock of steroidal estrogens—estrone, estradiol, and estriol—that have come to define the female sex hormone. It therefore twines itself with the lives of transwomen who situate themselves within the milieu of hormonal transition or "hormone replacement therapy" (HRT).

   Prefixing *trans-* to *xeno-* produces fruitful tension. *Trans-* further concatenates the oversimplified alienations and *-phobias* connected to *xeno-* by enacting "movements-across-into-strangeness" that foster new conjugations, allowing *xeno-* to suggest alternate worldings rather than marking a discontinuous zone of incommensurable and inaccessible difference (King 2012). *Trans-*ing *xeno-* unsettles the oversimplified Others necessary for the production of stratification and disallowance, without in the process destroying difference and the ethics of encounter. *Transxenoestrogenesis*, a word with prefixes like nerve endings, recapitulates the syntax of sensate life folding over itself, invaginating itself, to encounter its own materiality.

Premarin, the brand name of a popular and widely prescribed *xenoestrogen* first introduced to the market in 1941, is a portmanteau word derived from PREgnant MARes' urINe, because the hormone is manufactured from "conjugated equine estrogens" (CEE) isolated from the urine of female horses that are gestating fetuses. Used in the treatment of postmenopausal and post-hysterectomy symptoms, regulation of the female reproductive cycle, osteoporosis, ovarian failure, prostate cancer, and certain intersex conditions, Premarin also has been used *transxenoestrogenically* by transwomen following the now antiquated yet nevertheless still employed Standards of Care for hormonal transition issued by the World Professional Association for Transgender Health and its predecessor organization, the Harry Benjamin Gender Dysphoria Association. The manufacture of Premarin remains controversial, because it relies on the forced use, suffering, and dying of horses. Cramped in small stalls, kept indoors for six months of the year, mares are forcibly impregnated so that their urine can be collected for the manufacture of Premarin. Animal rights groups have protested these conditions, influencing policy and compelling changes in industrial practice that have benefited the well-being of horses exploited for Premarin production while not yet winning their liberation.

Attending to the roots of *conjugate*, Donna Haraway notes that the "yoking together" of "molecules and species to each other in consequential ways" is fundamentally constitutive of Premarin (2012: 307). In Haraway's conceptualization, the singular—for instance, subject, species, or woman—is necessarily conjoined (conjugated) with the multiple through corporeal involvements that place demands on the social. Kinship, relationality, and affect are always already "naturecultural." Conjugating with Haraway, *transxenoestrogenesis* can be considered a hothouse of filiations and accountabilities. The cultivation and exploitation of equines has been built into the biopolitics of transwomen. Thus, historically, human bodies hormonally sex-transitioning from male to female have always been trans-species ("tranimal") bodies (Kelley 2014 [in this issue]). This is a more general state of affairs than commonly recognized, given that estrogens—produced by most vertebrates, some insects, and a number of plants— trans (an active verb, like *queer*) the boundaries of species, phyla, and kingdoms. For example, phytoestrogens in red clover (*Trifolium prantense*) affect testosterone levels in grazers, resulting in changes to herd fecundity. There is nothing particularly novel about Premarin's trans-conjugating sex transition for transwomen as a kind of becoming-with-horse.

Premarin refigures morphology and sensoria in transwomen: olfactory nerves, optical lens, and the body's haptic and acoustic registers are altered; fingers touch differently; transxenoestrogenated breasts begin to lactate, leaking estrogen-dense milk. Some transwomen feed their breast milk to their infants, further unleashing Premarin's effects along human lineages. We transwomen are not alone in experiencing transxenoestrogenic effects. Premarin and its many xenoestrogenic kin found in foods, medicines, fertilizers, cosmetics, sanitary products, and other elements of material culture leak into habitats, environments, and ecosystems. They pass through the bodies of human consumers and non-human foodstuff animals into urine, milk, vomit, feces, and blood, seeping into septic waters and leeching into fields, fertilizing vegetal and bacterial growth, entering into new biochemical conjugations that make their ways into the bodies of others that, in turn, consume them. Here, in the regenerative bowels of natureculture, Octavia Butler's *Xenogenesis* is well underway.

National Geographic deploys the rhetoric of moral sex-panic in a spate of recent articles with titles such as "Sex-Changing Chemicals Found in Potomac River" and "Animals' Sexual Changes Linked to Waste, Chemicals," that connect xenoestrogenic pollution to the apocalyptic undermining of sexual differences (see Kier 2010). Rhetoric aside, polar bears, alligators, frogs, mollusks, fish, and birds are numbered among more than two hundred animal species around the world that are indeed already responding physically to hormone-altering xenoestrogenic pollutants in their environments (Ah-King 2013). A joint report issued by the Scientific Committee on Problems in the Environment (SCOPE) and the International Union of Pure and Applied Chemistry (IUPAC) concludes that endocrine disruption eventually can be expected in all animals in which hormones initiate physical changes, including humans (see Hayward 2011).

Transestrogenic xenogenesis outpaces Darwinian natural and sexual selection and in so doing reinvigorates the promise of transgender politics. Sexual difference—already a "difference engine" driving change—is monkey-wrenched by toxicity and pollution to propagate different differences rather than difference as usual (Chen 2012; Helmreich and Greenforst 2012). Neither utopic nor dystopic, *transxenoestrogenesis* invites the realization that bodies are lively and practical responses to environments that change over time, even when those environmental changes involve exposure to carcinogens, neurotoxins, asthmagens, and mutagens, to possibilities of cancer, diabetes, immune system failure, and heart disease. But where danger lies, promise might also be found: in the double binds of biochemistry, some phytoestrogens and mycoestrogens promote heart health and cancer prevention in humans; such is the emergent nature of the conditions of life and death.

Is there a way for transgender studies to reevaluate ecological destruction—such as the sex-changing response—in order for us to greet the future organisms that we are all already (and have always been) becoming? *Transxeno-estrogenesis*, a purposely unmetabolizable term proposed as a key concept for a twenty-first-century transgender studies, can be characterized as a toxic, expressive, resilient, and ethico-politically problematic form of species symbiosis that undoes sex and embodiment as we know it. It names both a threshold of emergence and a mode of upheaval. As much an environmental concern as a transgender one, transxenoestrogenesis is not a forecast of disaster but rather a reminder that we are already living in ruination. Transgender is noninnocent; *xeno-* still gives rise to *-phobias*; estrogens are unavoidable; genesis remains biblical, and Eden is dirty—Adam and Eve are increasingly undone as industrialism continues to release its effluvient progeny into our garden states. Things can get worse, and probably will; but life for earthlings is already precarious. *Transxenoestrogenesis* names but one form of our shared vulnerability to one another, our bodies open to the planet.

Eva Hayward teaches in the College of Design, Architecture, Art, and Planning at the University of Cincinnati. Her essays have appeared in *Cultural Anthropology*, *differences*, *Women's Studies Quarterly*, and *Women and Performance*.

References

Ah-King, Malin, and Eva Hayward. 2013. "Toxic Sexes: Perverting Pollution and Queering Hormone Disruption." *O-Zone* 1: 1–14.

Chen, Mel. 2012. *Animacies: Biopolitics, Racial Mattering, and Queer Affect*. Durham, NC: Duke University Press.

Haraway, Donna J. 2012. "Awash in Urine: DES and Premarin in Multispecies Response-ability." *Women's Studies Quarterly* 40, no. 1–2: 301–16.

Hayward, Eva. 2011. "When Fish and Frogs Change Gender." *Independent Weekly*, August 3. www.indyweek.com/indyweek/when-fish-and-frogs-change-gender/Content?oid=2626271.

Helmreich, Stefan, and Tue Greenforst. 2012. "Species." *Frieze d/e*, no. 6. frieze-magazin.de/archiv/kolumnen/species/.

Kelley, Lindsay. 2014. "Tranimals." *TSQ* 1, no. 1–2: 226–28.

Kier, Bailey. 2010. "Interdependent Ecological Transsex: Notes on Re/production, 'Transgender' Fish, and the Management of Populations, Species, and Resources." *Women and Performance* 20, no. 3: 299–319.

King, Katie. 2012. *Networked Reenactments: Stories Transdisciplinary Knowledges Tell*. Durham, NC: Duke University Press.

DOI 10.1215/23289252-2400190

Umbrella

T. BENJAMIN SINGER

The umbrella metaphor emerged along with the category transgender in the United States in the 1990s. An early version of the "transgender umbrella" is found in a Human Rights Commission of San Francisco report on the *Investigation into the Discrimination against Transgender People* (Green 1994), a document drafted to educate city officials adjudicating a "gender identity" civil rights ordinance. Conceived by the San Francisco–based therapist Luanna Rodgers, this model consisted of a hand-drawn umbrella with an open canopy stretched over a now dated set of terms: "crossdresser ('drag')," "transvestic fetishist," "transvestite," "transgenderist," "transsexual," and "man/woman." As the product of classifica-tory imaginaries produced by "trans-101" trainers, nonprofits, government-funded social service programs, and international human rights organizations, all transgender umbrellas contain terminology that reflects generational, geographic, political, social, and cultural differences. The contexts of use for this heuristic also vary; they include trans-101 trainings, public health programming and reports, legal policy documents, community conference workshops, children's books, and more.

In the two past decades, the umbrella diagram has spread nationally (United States) and internationally to become a widely utilized educational tool. Given that its original purpose was for political advocacy, the image suggests sheltering trans-identified and gender-nonconforming individuals from the hard rain of discrimination. By gathering nonnormative sex and gender terms underneath its canopy, the umbrella visually casts an aggregative categorical imaginary that includes all sex/ual and gender-nonconforming identities and expressions. In so doing, the umbrella implies that *all* formations of sex and gender are not only possible but also taxonomically containable. While it draws upon the appearance of a "natural" or ontologically prior grouping, the umbrella is produced through a classificatory imaginary that constitutes the population it purports simply to represent.

The aggregating aspect of the transgender umbrella is predicated upon historically shifting understandings of the category transgender. This history is complicated because the term references both a specific identity and a con-solidation of various sex- and gender-nonconforming individuals. With the publication of Leslie Feinberg's influential pamphlet *Transgender Liberation: A Movement Whose Time Has Come* (1992), the collective architecture for transgender was solidified. Feinberg's manifesto resonated with an early 1990s social imaginary that infused the category transgender with the collective energy of social *movement*—enabling a range of different bodies to congregate underneath a single umbrella. Without this sense of political collectivity, it would not have been possible to visually render transgender as an umbrella instead of as a continuum of gender-nonconforming identities and behaviors or as a particular mode of being.

The umbrella that sorts and classifies all sexual and gender nonconformity underneath a singular canopy is not without controversy. As anthropologist David Valentine argues, the very "flexibility" of the category transgender constitutes its "capacity to stand in for an unspecified group of people" and to encompass "individual identity and simultaneously [to represent] gendered transgressions of many kinds" (2007: 39). Realignments of identities via this particular transgender imaginary can productively differentiate trans-identified people from those who are nontrans gay or queer. However, these same "flexible" sorting practices sometimes obscure the specific intersections of classed, raced, geographic, and cultural dimensions of personhood. As anthropologist Megan Davidson explains: "Different constructions of the category transgender, who it includes and excludes, are not simply negotiations of a collective identity but . . . negotiations about the boundaries of a social movement and that movement's efforts toward social change" (2007: 61). Such negotiations around inclusion, exclusion, and erasure occur in and through differing conceptions of the category transgender, even as those differences are often "elided in public consciousness by the category transgender and the notion of a unified umbrella implied within it" (ibid.).

Erasures happen when individuals who are placed under the umbrella do not imagine themselves to belong (e.g., some gay men in drag). Erasures also occur through colonizing impulses that include culturally specific terms like hijra or waria. Such categorical appropriations constitute what Evan B. Towle and Lynn M. Morgan call "the transgender native," a figure that collapses historical and cross-cultural specificities of sex and gender into a catch-all "third gender" category (2006: 469). This move obscures the differential contexts of historically situated or non-Western subjects; it also ensures that coercive mechanisms of Western sex/gender systems remain unexamined in exchange for a reassuring fantasy that gendered utopias exist elsewhere.

The umbrella is no different from other models sutured to the visibility and erasure problematic that shadows all emergent categorical formations. As such, the transgender umbrella and its aggregative imaginary is useful in that it enables disparate sexual- and gender-nonconforming people to coalesce for individual and political identification, community mobilization, resource accrual, and the harnessing of social power. But given the potential exclusions and erasures produced by an all-encompassing classificatory practice, a caution remains. Umbrellas should arrive with a disclaimer: *One size does not fit all.* Umbrella politics necessitates a mindfulness of categorical sorting practices itself in that it differentially, and sometimes detrimentally, impacts upon personal and political identity formation in addition to social movement building.

T. Benjamin Singer is a Mellon Visiting Assistant Professor of Women's and Gender Studies at Vanderbilt University. His work has appeared in *The Transgender Studies Reader*, the *Journal of Medical Humanities,* and *Discourse*.

References

Davidson, Megan. 2007. "Seeking Refuge under the Umbrella: Inclusion, Exclusion, and Organizing within the Category Transgender." *Sexuality Research and Social Policy* 4, no. 4: 60–80.

Feinberg, Leslie. 1992. *Transgender Liberation: A Movement Whose Time Has Come.* New York: World View Forum.

Green, James. 1994. *Investigation into Discrimination against Transgendered People.* San Francisco: Human Rights Commission of San Francisco.

Towle, Evan B., and Lynne M. Morgan. 2006. "Romancing the Transgender Native." In *The Transgender Studies Reader*, ed. Susan Stryker and Stephen Whittle, 666–84. New York: Routledge.

Valentine, David. 2007. *Imagining Transgender: An Ethnography of a Category.* Durham, NC: Duke University Press.

DOI 10.1215/23289252-2400199

Voice

ANDREW ANASTASIA

Voice is an apropos keyword for transgender studies, as the field rests on the demand that "the embodied experience of the speaking subject" subtend any analysis of transgender phenomena (Stryker 2006a: 12). Speech is propelled into the world through bodily actions, which is why a more metaphorical effort to "claim our voice" is synonymous with agential self-definition. "Voice," used metaphorically, signifies multiple meanings at once: a sound that represents a person, the agency by which an opinion is expressed, and the expressed will of a people. This is why the keyword is frequently invoked to narrate the struggles of transgender studies' formation as a field. For example, in one of multiple figurative uses of "voice" in the forward to the 2006 *Transgender Studies Reader*, Stephen Whittle (2006: xv) notes that trans scholars "have enabled the coherent voices of trans people to be heard throughout the academy." This discursive coherence has been a necessary strategy to combat logics of pathologization, through which trans* voices have sounded like "confused ranting of a diseased mind" (Stryker 2006b: 249). In the struggle for coherence, however, metaphorical references to "voice" privilege its discursive connotations, which relegates the embodied voice to a service role of rendering audible the coherent thought.

As transgender studies approaches its second iteration, claiming our discursive voice is less urgent. *Voice*, as a keyword for the next generation, demands that we listen, like musicians, to the voice qua voice—not merely as the message. This is not to say that our trans* voices can or wish to escape the gridding act of "making sense"; the voice certainly has something to say about the body's age, sex, race, nationality, or ability. How others make sense of a trans* voice, especially relative to one's physical appearance, can provoke great anxiety or pleasure. The voice, however, does not always vector toward the word; it can pierce us in unexpected ways, turning us toward (or away from) another in an acoustic and affective register. Voices enter our bodies through the ear and/or as felt vibrations and act as vocal vectors—means of escape from stratification and suppression. These vectors project outward toward the ear of another. One can never predict how our voices will be heard, and unpredictable reception is part of the voice's value.

In 2005, music critic John Hodgman interviewed trans-identified artist Antony Hegarty for a *New York Times* article he titled "Antony Finds His Voice." In the piece, Hodgman attempts to make sense of Hegarty's voice, which he admits "is difficult to describe," with a sound that "keens in the upper registers, somewhere between male and female." Hegarty's voice is often likened to that of an angel (Hodgman 2005) or described as belonging to another world (see Currin 2009). These attributions use metaphor to get at the affective experience of hearing a voice one cannot quite recognize (as male, female, or human). Hegarty's trans* voice is a powerful instance of nondiscursive ways to trouble and blur normative assumptions about sex and gender, human and creature. Trans* voices can fail to make sense in spectacular ways when our voices no longer provide adequate evidence for the bodies that emit them. In those spectacular failures, our ghostly utterances, we find the forms of resistance that beckon from the future of transgender studies.

Andrew Anastasia is a doctoral candidate in rhetoric and composition studies at the University of Wisconsin–Milwaukee. His dissertation is a qualitative, multicase investigation of teachers' and students' descriptions of "teaching discomfort" in first-year writing classrooms.

References

Currin, Grayson. 2009. "Another World." *Pitchfork*, August 4. pitchfork.com/features/articles/7634-another-world.

Hodgman, John. 2005. "Antony Finds His Voice." *New York Times*, September 4. www.nytimes.com/2005/09/04/magazine/04ANTONY.html?pagewanted=all&_r=0.

Stryker, Susan. 2006a. "(De)Subjugated Knowledges: An Introduction to Transgender Studies." In *The Transgender Studies Reader*, ed. Susan Stryker and Stephen Whittle, 1–17. New York: Routledge.

———. 2006b. "My Words to Victor Frankenstein above the Village of Chamounix: Performing Transgender Rage." In Stryker and Whittle, *Transgender Studies Reader*, 244–56.

Whittle, Stephen. 2006. Foreword to Stryker and Whittle, *Transgender Studies Reader*, xi–xv.

DOI 10.1215/23289252-2400208

Whiteness

SALVADOR VIDAL-ORTIZ

Constructions of whiteness are geopolitical, hierarchically placed, and structured around class and status. To insert the study of whiteness into trans studies means to develop a critical lens of seemingly disparate elements, like beauty, access, visibility, and acceptance within, for instance, the history of transgender people seeking services and gaining access to them (in the mid-twentieth century) and leadership and activism (at the present time). Furthermore, to think of it on a global scale demands a recognition that gendered attributes of maleness or femaleness are intercepted by whiteness. In many instances, constructions of gender are about being white, being perceived to be white, or sometimes they are deeply ingrained in perceptions of beauty as white. We can see this in cosmetic interventions for trans women, for instance.

Whiteness is evident in transgender communities, transgender studies, and transgender history not only in terms of color (particularly notions of whiteness as lightness or paleness) but also, and more importantly, in terms of how "color" sustains hierarchies of leadership, authority, and credibility. In other words, while it is tempting to see whiteness as skin color, whiteness is a structuring and structured form of power that, through its operations, crystallizes inequality while enforcing its own invisibility. In US society, an economy of value around light-skinned trans people is often noticeable in contemporary scholarship or activism. Scholars like Avery Tompkins, who bring whiteness studies and trans studies together, note that it is through the silences in which whiteness operates that trans* communities, representations, and thus visibility retain a white homogeneous perception—both among members of such communities and to observers (Tompkins 2011: 155–56.).

Since the study of whiteness coincided very much with the development of transgender studies, the two are intertwined in this given cultural moment (Stryker 1998; Roediger 1999). Both intend to show previously unmarked social locations—albeit with different weights of power. Whiteness turned the eye back into racial formation systems by shifting from multicultural, abstract discussions of race into discussions about white dominance and its reproduction. Meanwhile, the emergence of transgender studies sometimes noted the normative (white, heterosexual, and cisgender male privilege) position of those defining transsexuality and gender reassignment procedures (thus limiting those who would have access to sociomedical services). But most importantly, trans studies also revealed the unmarked position of the gender normative: the group once called non-transsexual people is referred to now as cisgender people. Both studies based on transgender issues and whiteness studies help to indicate the need for thinking of race and gender/sexuality as axes of power. White privilege and cisgender privilege have received a lot of attention as social locations that run the risk of providing universalizing statements about their constituents—in whatever social movement they are located. Trans discussions in both academic and activist spaces voice an intent of diversity and inclusion or demands for the end of oppression based on racism and discrimination, while they simultaneously use language in everyday interaction (in tactics of recruitment, socialization, and scholarly writing) that construes such spaces as predominantly white (see Bérubé 2001). For instance, in contemporary trans* spaces, the perception of having the choice about being genderless, gender fluid, or genderqueer, is often tied to white privilege, especially when *some* members of communities of color may understand their trans experience as nonidentity, as expressions of gayness, or as in a space between gay and trans (Valentine 2007). I do not seek to establish an essentialist, oppositional view of trans* that splits people of color and whites but do so in order to illustrate the systemic forms of naming and sustaining trans* as something defined hierarchically, even if without a conscious intent.

Beauty is also a key, intertwined element of whiteness in transgender representations. Perceptions of being a legitimate transgender person were dutifully noted in the twentieth century (Meyerowitz 2002). In the 1950s and until the 1970s, it became evident that certain ethno-racial groups were not intelligible as trans, as for instance the perception that "Puerto Ricans" (a very heterogeneous group ethno-racially and in terms of socioeconomic status) did not look to be trans but "fags" (Billings and Urban 1982; Vidal-Ortiz 2008). Black constructions of beauty often fell outside the perception of beauty in transitioning as well, as African American transgender individuals enounced their desire for transition before Christine Jorgensen but did not achieve such recognition. For instance, today, being a Latina or Asian undocumented immigrant who is trans embodies a completely different experience from that of being a white trans person in academia or heading a NGO. While tokenistic efforts to mention trans people of color are often part of the production of whiteness in transgender studies (Vidal-Ortiz 2009), the leadership of most contemporary movements involving trans rights, studies, and activism is predominantly white. This is also evidenced at an international level, where forms of access to transitioning (surgical procedures in particular) and forms of visibility for trans* people operate with whiteness as an ideal (Aizura 2009, 2011).

A lens on whiteness forces contemporary transgender politics to confront transgender normativity (and citizenship), in which whiteness is imbricated in complex ways. Critically encountering whiteness in trans movements and studies has direct-action and social-movement implications in that it forces the discourse of community and membership to levels that surpass liberal multicultural attempts for inclusion and diversity.

Salvador Vidal-Ortiz is an associate professor of sociology at American University in Washington, DC. He coedited *The Sexuality of Migration: Border Crossings and Mexican Immigrant Men* (2009).

References

Aizura, Aren Z. 2009. "Where Health and Beauty Meet: Femininity and Racialisation in Thai Cosmetic Surgery Clinics." *Asian Studies Review* 33, no. 3: 303–17.

———. 2011. "The Romance of the Amazing Scalpel: 'Race,' Labour, and Affect in Thai Gender Reassignment Clinics." In *Queer Bangkok*, ed. Peter A. Jackson, 143–62. Hong Kong: Hong Kong University Press.

Bérubé, Allan. 2001. "How Gay Stays White and What Kind of White It Stays." In *The Making and Unmaking of Whiteness*, ed. Birgit Brander Rasmussen et al., 234–65. Durham, NC: Duke University Press.

Billings, Dwight B., and Thomas Urban. 1982. "The Socio-Medical Construction of Transsexualism: An Interpretation and Critique." *Social Problems* 29, no. 3: 266–82.

Meyerowitz, Joanne. 2002. *How Sex Changed: A History of Transsexuality in the United States.* Cambridge, MA: Harvard University Press.

Roediger, David R., ed. 1999. *Black on White: Black Writers on What It Means to Be White.* New York: Schocken.

Stryker, Susan. 1998. "The Transgender Issue: An Introduction." *GLQ* 4, no. 2: 145–58.

Tompkins, Avery. 2011. "Intimate Allies: Identity, Community, and Everyday Activism among Cisgender People with Trans-Identified Partners." PhD diss., Syracuse University.

Valentine, David. 2007. *Imagining Transgender: An Ethnography of a Category.* Durham, NC: Duke University Press.

Vidal-Ortiz, Salvador. 2008. "Transgender and Transsexual Studies: Sociology's Influence and Future Steps." *Sociology Compass* 2, no. 2: 433–50.

———. 2009. "The Figure of the Transwoman of Color through the Lens of 'Doing Gender.'" *Gender and Society* 23, no. 1: 99–103.

DOI 10.1215/23289252-2400217

Wrong Body

ULRICA ENGDAHL

The notion of "wrong body" consists of a dichotomous explanation of the transgender experience as a state of "being in the wrong body." Wrongness is here understood in relation to how the body is gendered, connoting that the body is wrongly gendered in relation to a self-identified gender identity.

The wrong-body conception is criticized from feminist, queer, and trans political/theoretical points of view. The critique regards the gatekeeping consequences this conception has within a medical discourse of true transsexualism. The diagnosis is defined within the *International Statistical Classification of Diseases and Health Problems*, tenth ed. (*ICD*-10) as: "A desire to live and be accepted as a member of the opposite sex, usually accompanied by a sense of discomfort with, or inappropriateness of, one's anatomic sex, and a wish to have surgery and hormonal treatment to make one's body as congruent as possible with one's preferred sex" (World Health Organization 2010: F64.0 Transsexualism). And within the *Diagnostical and Statistical Manual of Mental Disorders*, fourth ed., text revision (*DSM*-IV-TR) as: "A strong and persistent identification with the opposite gender. There is a sense of discomfort in their own gender and may feel they were 'born the wrong sex.'" (American Psychiatric Association 2000: Gender identity disorder). Diagnostic criteria regulate access to treatment and legal recognition of self-identified gender identity. Although the recently published *DSM*-5 drops "gender identity disorder" in favor of "gender dysphoria," it still uses ideas of "wrong body," expressed, though, in a way that does not necessarily put the wrongness with the body but that does put it somewhere along the line between expectations from others and an inner experience and its expression: "For a person to be diagnosed with gender dysphoria, there must be a marked difference between the individual's expressed/experienced gender and the gender others would assign him or her" (American Psychiatric Association 2013: gender dysphoria).

The theoretical critique regards the assumption of essentialism that underlies the wrong-body conception. The body is assumed wrong in relation to an inner, real, and authentic gender identity, thus giving the impression of an essence that the body constrains, producing a reified image of both body and self as static and separate entities and thereby correlating an essentialism of genital materiality that disputes the realness of transgender experience. The idea of authenticity underlies essentialism and produces norms of naturalness and real-ness. Essentialism therefore reinforces the norms of a gender binary, resulting in misrecognition of gender-varied bodies and expressions, risking stigmatization, discrimination, and exclusion. Hence the critique mainly concerns: the master narrative of the wrong body that overshadows gender-variant body experiences as valid; the reference to gender and/or genital essentialism; the reification of body and self as static and separable entities; and the reproduction of gender binary norms.

The wrong body is envisioned as a state in which gender body and gender identity do not match; hence a disparity between body (materiality) and self (subjectivity) is embodied in the narrative, entertaining dichotomous disjunc-tions such as the body and its expression, the body and its perception, the body and surrounding gender norms, and sex and gender, which implicitly places sex with (material) genitalia and gender with its (social) expression. The underlying assumption lies with the gender binary imaginary, which is upheld by the elas-ticity of gender categories—that is, the tendency to understand gender expression as male or female by exclusionary interpretation, equalizing nonmale with female and vice versa (Halberstam 1998: 20, 27)—and by the pretense-reality dichotomy, interpreting transgender expression as pretense and genital status as reality, hence denying first-person authority to transgender identity experience (Bettcher 2009). Conceptualizing wrong body in this way involves making a distinction between materiality (the body) and subjectivity (the self), implying that these are sepa-rable things rather than being inherently inseparable. This in turn leads to other ways of speaking and thinking that reproduce this disjunctive dichotomy, such as "the body *and* its expressions and perceptions," or "the body *and* its surrounding gender norms." This dichotomy structures the very distinction we typically make between sex and gender, which implicitly places sex (genitalia) on the side of material reality and gender (identity or expression) on the side of immaterial-ity and, potentially, unreality—or worse, pretense, deception, or error. This framework ultimately denies first-person authority to the experience of trans-gender identity. (Bettcher 2009).

Phenomenology offers another explanation of trans body experience that builds from overlapping understandings of self, body, sex, and gender. One phenomenological way of reading the wrong-body narrative is through the concept of "the lived body": "a unified idea of a physical body acting and expe-riencing in a specific sociocultural context; it is body-in-situation" (Young 2005: 16). The emphasis on body-in-situation underlines the situatedness of a wrong-body experience, hence opposing a permanently fixed understanding, relating the wrongness to situations of misreadings. Gayle Salamon's concept, "a felt sense of a body" (2010: 2), emphasizes the impact that cultural interpretations have for the meaning of a specific bodily sensation. Materiality and discursivity, hence, are reciprocally dependent on each other's interpretative forces to make meaning. Neither exists outside the others' meaning (ibid.: 40). Embodiment is understood through an intertwining of subjectivity, materiality, and discursivity.

Wrong body as lived body expresses the situatedness of trans body experience as wrong, hence relativizing it. Wrong body as trans embodiment expresses subjectively felt bodily meaning interacting with cultural interpretations of bodies, where the subjective and the cultural are not always congruent. This way the gender binary is replaced with gender variance as a frame for understanding gender, offering a more fluid understanding of the trans body.

Ulrica Engdahl holds a PhD in gender studies. Her doctoral thesis concerns the concepts of justice, recognition, and identity in relation to a trans* context. Her research interests are transgender studies and ethics, in particular the ethics and politics of recognition, identity, and visibility.

References

American Psychiatric Association. 2000. *Diagnostic and Statistical Manual of Mental Disorders.* 4th. ed., text revision. Washington, DC: American Psychiatric Association.

———. 2013. *Diagnostic and Statistical Manual of Mental Disorders.* 5th ed. Arlington, VA: American Psychiatric Publishing.

Bettcher, Talia Mae. 2009. "Trans Identities and First Person Authority." In *"You've Changed": Sex Reassignment and Personal Identity*, ed. Laurie Shrage, 98–120. Oxford: Oxford University Press.

Halberstam, Judith. 1998. *Female Masculinity.* Durham, NC: Duke University Press.

Salamon, Gayle. 2010. *Assuming a Body: Transgender and Rhetorics of Materiality.* New York: Columbia University Press.

World Health Organization. 2012. "ICD-10 Version:2010." *International Statistical Classification of Diseases and Related Health Problems.* apps.who.int/classifications/icd10/browse/2010/en (accessed March 7, 2014).

Young, Iris Marion. 2005. *On Female Body Experience.* New York: Oxford University Press.

DOI 10.1215/23289252-2400226

X-jendā

S. P. F. DALE

The term *x-jendā* began appearing in the late 1990s in publications as well as in independently produced documentaries created by and featuring transgender individuals in the Kansai area of Japan (centered around the cities of Kyoto, Osaka, and Kobe).[1] Since then, the term has spread to the extent that it is now recognized within the Japanese (primarily online) queer community, is featured in write-ups about sexual minority/LGBT issues in Japan, and appears as a gender option on materials circulated at queer-focused events such as film festivals. The definition of *x-jendā* is one that although generally taken for granted remains ambiguous as well as open to individual interpretation. It is generally understood to refer to a gender identity that is neither female nor male, although how such an identity is conceived varies greatly.

X-jendā is ostensibly a loan word (a word of foreign origin) in Japanese, with *jendā* being the Japanese transliteration of the English "gender" and its use in an academic context highly mirroring that of the anglophone academic sphere. The term *jendā* has not, however, caught on at a popular level in Japan and tends to be used primarily in academic and political discourse. *Jendā* is not a term that one finds on forms requiring personal information; in such cases, *seibetsu* (often interpreted as referring to biological/physiological sex) is used. *X-jendā* can be taken to signify that one's gender is neither female nor male but "x." However, although an ostensible loan word is used, the term *x-gender* is not used (or rather, has not up to the present been used) in cultural contexts outside Japan. The difference in the connotations between the term *gender*, used in an anglophone context, and *jendā* in Japanese draws attention to the multiple meanings that translation can create and points to the differences in the reception of a term that cultural context fosters. This also goes for terms such as *toransujendā* (transgender) and applies not only to a Japanese context but to other nonanglophone contexts that utilize "universal" terms such as *queer*, *gay*, and so on, terms that seem universal but that are actually adapted to local contexts and as such are not as homogenous as we may presume them to be.

The term *x-jendā* first emerged after the concept of GID, or gender identity disorder, (*seidōitsu seishōgai*) was officially recognized in Japan in the late 1990s. GID has since become popularly recognized and has dramatically impacted not only how transgender identities are thought of but how gender as well as sexuality is seen. As a result of this, most inexplicitly female/male ways of being have been subsumed by the concept and reframed in a medical/psychological discourse. The medicalization of transgender ways of being in Japan as such came about relatively later than in European and North American countries, and this has impacted the path that transgender politics has come to take.

Most *x-jendā* individuals frame their identity using terms such as FTX (female to X), MTX (male to X), or XTX (used by intersex individuals or those who say that they have never identified as a specific gender), following the model of sex assigned at birth to sex transitioned to that is used by transgendered individuals (i.e., MTF, FTM). Some individuals who identify as *x-jendā* liken it to "genderqueer" or "gender bender" and describe *x-jendā* as a Japanese version of these concepts. Others view *x-jendā* as a convenient category that includes a variety of identities that do not conform to the male/female gender binary. There are also individuals who view *x-jendā* as a subset of GID and who push for the medical diagnosis of *x-jendā*. *X-jendā* is a modern identity construct, one that also takes as its basis global transgender discourses such as that of transgender and GID; in the online (Japanese) discourse, *x-jendā* is often framed within the global transgender or GID discourse. As such, it is not necessarily viewed as a local construct but rather as a universal identity. Websites such as Wikipedia do not always provide cultural context; a page about transgender in Japanese, for example, will list *x-jendā* as a sub-category, without stating the locality of the term (see Wikipedia 2013).

X-jendā symbolizes for some the rejection of a system that judges individuals based on their sex/gender. However, it also has the potential to reify stereotypical gender roles and expectations in its definition. What is woman/man/female/male—and how does *x-jendā* distinguish itself from these categories? The answer is one that has ramifications for personal as well as social conceptions of gender.

S. P. F. Dale is a postdoctoral research fellow in the department of global studies, Sophia University (Japan). Recent publications include "The Role of the 'Foreign': Examining the Use of the 'Foreign' in Japanese Transgender and Gender Identity Disorder Discourse" (in Japanese, *AGLOS*, October 2012).

Note

1.   This entry provides a very brief overview of *x-jendā*. For a more in-depth article, see Dale 2012.

References

Dale, S. P. F. 2012. "An Introduction to *X-Jendā*: Examining a New Gender Identity in Japan."
      Intersections, no. 31. intersections.anu.edu.au/issue31/dale.htm.

Wikipedia (Japanese). 2013. "Toransujendā." ja.wikipedia.org/wiki/%E3%83%88%E3%83%A9%
      E3%83%B3%E3%82%B9%E3%82%B8%E3%82%A7%E3%83%B3%E3%83%80%E3%
      83%BC (accessed December 12, 2013).

DOI 10.1215/23289252-2400235

Negotiating the Spectacle in Transgender Performances of Alexis Arquette, Zackary Drucker, DavEnd, niv Acosta, and Tobaron Waxman

Abstract This review looks at the work of five North American artists who tackle the prevailing social demand upon transgender subjects to make a spectacle of their bodies. They reflect upon the body as a social site in order to resist and redeploy the scrutiny under which transgender is drawn. In film, dance, and visual and relational performance, the artists contest conventional social constructions of transgender and articulate existential possibility in ways that contribute to and echo the development of new ideas about embodiment.

The relationship between Alexis Arquette and the British television station that funded her 2007 movie *She's My Brother* is emblematic for contemporary artists tackling the performance contexts in which they represent transgender.[1] The celebrity family member substantiated her on-screen identity by achieving legal, medical, and cultural agency while confounding Channel 4 expectations for a Hollywood surgical transition story. Due to her concern about side effects, she procured a therapist's letter for the right to vaginoplasty that precluded the usually compulsory course of hormone treatment. Yet Arquette denied the viewer a spectacle of surgical transition, which has come to dominate representation of transsexuality in mainstream culture. She achieved visibility for transgender bodily self-possession by fighting on camera for medical intervention on her own terms, and she insisted on her claim to female identity while keeping private whether she has undergone, is undergoing, or will undergo surgery. Arquette used

TSQ: Transgender Studies Quarterly ★ Volume 1, Numbers 1–2 ★ May 2014 **273**
DOI 10.1215/23289252-2400244 © 2014 Duke University Press

the spectacular conjunction of her gender identity and popular culture notoriety in a way that subverted the usual demands of performing reality television.

Contemporary artists are engaging transgender subjectivity to reflect upon the body as a social site. In the twenty-first century, critical transgender performance has exploded into a challenging field as part of the emergence of community, activist, and academic movements. Bodies from across the globe have increasingly come into view configured through the term *transgender*.[2] They are seen in focused festivals, the art world, and mainstream media. Artists are articulating a performing self that contests the conventional social construction of transgender and articulates existential possibility in ways that contribute to and echo the development of new ideas about embodiment. The terms by which such bodies achieve legibility are politically bound in ways that precede any performance intervention. But artists resignify the conditions under which their bodies come into view, stretching the significance that they are called upon to fulfill. I take a brief look here at how the conditions for performance are negotiated by a handful of American-based artists who critically embody transgender.

Zackary Drucker, like Arquette, is a Los Angeles artist screwing with the burden of spectacle that attends transgender bodies. In her performance "The Inability to Be Looked at and the Horror of Nothing to See" (2008), Drucker ritualizes and thereby exposes the misogynist construction of femininity.[3] Her "Live Art"[4] context is wildly different from the one in which Arquette performs; Live Art practitioners are from various fields and push against any given genre, foregrounding sociopolitical concerns in performance staged as provocation; and like off-off-Broadway, they play to small audiences. If the transitioning body is called upon to fulfill the demand for provocation, it becomes a spectacle.[5] But Drucker averts this tendency by cultivating audience complicity: spectators standing around her gagged supine body become participants as they are led through an ironic New Age guided meditation. The audience is instructed to approach and pluck hairs from Drucker's body using tweezers that surround her. Drucker's recorded voice instructs them to direct their negative energy into her: "This body is a receptacle for all of your guilt and shame and trauma."[6] The audience is prevented from anonymous consumption of a transgender spectacle, and through their collaborative act they are called upon to embody transphobia. Even while they apparently collectively enact part of Drucker's corporeal transition, her voice dismisses the activity in which they are engaged: "You will never be a woman," she insists.[7] Her voiceover suggests that her body is in a state of trauma, reflecting upon the social challenges of transition. Yet by implicating the audience in the process, Drucker resists the construction of a spectacular-heroic narrative of overcoming.[8]

Beyond the glare of Tinseltown, San Francisco–based DavEnd also critiques the spectacular construction of transgender. Gender variant identity and self-sufficient community are central concerns in her Bay Area art context.[9] DavEnd argues that unpaid performing is inescapable for trans/queer bodies in heterosexual culture, but she insists that invisible labor can be culturally remunerated through conscious acts of performance. She recuperates self-possession through collective methodology in which intimacy is cultivated behind a veil of spectacle. In the 2012 project "Intimasew," DavEnd staged an ideal vision of community through the catwalk-like presentation of ostentatious hand-made garments constructed directly onto queer/trans bodies, creating images of desirable and self-desiring superheroes (see fig. 1).[10] The spectacular construction of these bodies was made explicit and redeployed, yet it was underpinned for the subjects of DavEnd's sartorial artistry by interpersonal value generated through the tailoring process. DavEnd insisted that there is a relationship between theatrical and existential concerns by representing the creative process in the concert performance of "Intimasew": "I use collaborative garment construction to transform feelings of scarcity around style, options, intimacy, desire, time, and safety, into a world of custom-made abundance."[11] She articulates as aesthetics the interpersonal practices through which trans/queer bodies negotiate their spectacular conspicuousness.

On the other side of the country, spectacle seems like a handmaiden to the critique of representation staged by New York dancer niv Acosta. Experimental aesthetics define the postmodern dance community in which Acosta is choreographing. Small, well-informed audiences typically attend the dance concerts, in which playful, risky, implicit, and veiled references to political identity are often staged, while proselytizing is frowned upon.[12] Acosta achieves explicit reference to his identity while averting polemics by insisting that his subject exists in the relationship between subsequent works.[13] Across his dancing body, the artist contemplates the intersections of race and gender by layering references from film, musical, song, and dance forms such as classical ballet and vogueing, which first came to broad prominence through the film *Paris Is Burning* (dir. Jennie Livingston, 1991). For example, in "I shot denzel," Acosta juxtaposes dance and conversation, camp and seemingly authentic acts of personal frustration.[14] He refers to his masculinity and Black Dominican identity in "I shot denzel," but questions linger that may or may not be answered by four other related "denzel" dances. Like Arquette, he limits access to his embodiment of transgender, because the answers to Acosta's body and story are hinted at and obfuscated through references to absent performances and in the detritus of mainstream culture.

Tobaron Waxman also points toward and obscures the legibility of his body-identity. Performing primarily in visual art contexts and declaring his address as unfixed, Waxman references his gender and religion-ethnicity through ritual acts such as shaving his hair and beard as well as singing in Hebrew. Conscious that he can become an ethnic-religious transgender spectacle, he draws attention to the

Figure 1. Images from performance of "Intimasew." Photograph by Robbie Sweeny

looking process. For example, in "Fear of a Bearded Planet" (2012), the artist commissioned street portraits in various cities, which when viewed together draw attention to the way in which his ambiguously raced Semite appearance signifies in post-9/11 culture.[15] Waxman foregrounds his transgender Jewish-diasporic masculinity to critique heteronormative Zionist masculinity, which he argues is underpinned by the conventional idea of virility in nation building. At the same time, by exposing the multiple meanings embedded in a beard, he offers religious-ethnic critique within FTM (female to male) culture and thereby insists that gender transition must be understood as infused with other cultural references.

The artists whose work is touched on in this review deftly navigate the obstacle course created by the demand to make a spectacle of transgender visibility in film, performance, and dance. Arquette, Drucker, DavEnd, Acosta, and Waxman all critique prevailing two-dimensional representations, and in the process they generate aesthetics through which greater possibility for embodiment is achieved.

Doran George is a dance artist and scholar completing a PhD in late twentieth-century contemporary dance at the University of California, Los Angeles. Doran has chapters in the *Meanings and Makings in Queer Dance* and the *Handbook on Dance and Wellbeing*, both forthcoming.

Notes

1. I am using *transgender* as an umbrella term for artistic practices staged across bodies that disidentify with sex assigned at birth. I am not distinguishing between surgical and nonsurgical trajectories or grappling with the class and racial politics of the use of the term in academic and cultural spheres. While I acknowledge problems with glossing of the significance of "transgender," I am doing so in order to focus on other dimensions of artists' practice in the short review.

2. Both non-Western and Western, including indigenous, cultures have played a role in the emergence of *transgender* as an umbrella term. Gilbert Herdt's 1993 book *Third Sex Third Gender* is a good example. The anthology includes cross-cultural anthropological and historical examples of lifeworlds that contest the paradigm of male and female in a way that suggests a third identity is a universal phenomenon. Similarly, festivals such as the late 1990s London-based International Transgender Film and Video Festival and the twenty-first-century Netherlands Transgender Film Festival programmed cinema, performers, and speakers from non-Western and indigenous contexts. Nevertheless, activists and scholars have acknowledged that applying the term universally can flatten out differences and impose Western assumptions.

3. I first saw the performance as part of *PRAXIS Mojave* 2008, a performance art workshop showing in Morongo Valley, California. The work has subsequently been performed at *Resonate/Obliterate*, Sweeney Gallery, University of California, Riverside, 2009; at *Visions of Excess* at Spill Festival, London, 2009; at APF LAB, New York, 2009; and at Steve Turner Contemporary, Los Angeles, 2009.

4. Live Art became an important term in the United Kingdom. However, I am associating Drucker with this context because it has become transnational in scale both through an association with the academic area study of "performance" and also through a network of artists and venues that align themselves with either performance or Live Art. Drucker's work is increasingly becoming significant within this context, a fact to which the performances of the work detailed in note 3 attest.

5. I put forward the argument that Live Art privileges provocation as a critical strategy and articulate some of the problems with such a methodology for transgender among other bodies in "Forget Provocation Let's Have Sex" (George 2013).

6. Quoted directly from the performance text, courtesy of the artists.

7. Ibid.

8. A heroic narrative of transsexuality has begun to replace the figure of horror as transgender identity has been increasingly represented as a viable possibility in mainstream media. The difference between the main protagonist in the 2005 movie *Transamerica* (dir. Duncan Tucker) and the serial killer in *Silence of the Lambs* from 1991 (dir. Jonathan Demme) is a vivid illustration of this change.

9. I define some of the ideas and history of the artistic community in which DavEnd works in "Forget Provocation Let's Have Sex" (George 2013).

10. "Intimasew" was commissioned for the festival "This Is What I Want 2012," for which I was a cocurator. I saw the project at the festival in San Francisco in June of that year, at SoMa Arts.

11. Text courtesy of the artist, from DavEnd's proposal for "This Is What I Want."

12. I am situating Acosta's work within New York East Village dance. I trace the development of this artistic community in "Whose Queen Is It Anyway" (George, forthcoming). East Village refers not to its current location but to the origins of the artistic community, which is now in Brooklyn as much as on Manhattan's Lower East Side.

13. My understanding of Acosta's approach is informed by his artist statement published on his website (Acosta 2013).

14. I first encountered Acosta's "denzel" series at Pieter Performance Art, Space, and Dance, in Los Angeles in May 2012. The piece was "denzel minipetite bathtub happymeal." I have viewed "I shot denzel" online courtesy of the artists.

15. I have viewed "Fear of a Bearded Planet" online courtesy of the artist, and my reading is also informed by the interview transcript "Gender Diasporist," with Waxman, by Shawn Syms, also courtesy of the artist.

References

Acosta, niv. 2013. "Artist Statement." niv Acosta's website. www.nivacosta.com/artist-statement.

George, Doran. 2013. "Forget Provocation Let's Have Sex." *Dance Theatre Journal* 25, no. 2: 5–10.

———. Forthcoming. "Whose Queen Is It Anyway: History, Femininity, and Theatrical Display in the Choreographic Contestation of Heterosexual Gender," in *Meanings and Makings in Queer Dance*, ed. Clare Croft. Oxford: Oxford University Press.

Herdt, Gilbert. 1993. *Third Sex Third Gender: Beyond Sexual Dimorphism in Culture and History*. New York: Zone.

Interview with Kortney Ryan Ziegler of the Trans*H4CK Project

New media technologies—from the Web to social media to mobile apps—provide a platform for trans activism, identity formation, and community building outside the analog confines of space and time. The recurring New Media section will feature projects that examine how trans lives penetrate and are penetrated by the mediatization of culture.
—Editors

Abstract *TSQ* New Media editor Tobias Raun interviews Kortney Ryan Ziegler, the organizer of the Trans*H4CK hackathon, which took place in Oakland, California, in September 2013. The hackathon brought forty transgender, gender nonconforming, cisgender, and queer people together to create digital tools and content for trans communities. Raun and Ziegler discuss the usefulness of social entrepreneurship models to trans community formation, the importance of fostering digital activism by and for underrepresented communities, and the possibilities of circumventing traditional grant-making institutions by raising seed money for trans activism through crowd funding.

"Hackathons" started out as events exclusively for technophiles with interests in coding, data, and computer programming. Recently, however, hackathons have invited the participation of community members to address social issues. Created by Kortney Ryan Ziegler, Trans*H4CK is a social justice project that encourages the development of technology that will socially empower trans people. Trans*H4CK was the first transgender hackathon that aimed to address issues specific to the transgender community. To kick off the project, Trans*H4CK hosted a hackathon in September 2013. As the word hackathon suggests, this was an intense two-day hacking marathon during which programmers, developers, designers, entrepreneurs, thinkers, and community members brainstormed ideas and shared skills to create content or tools for trans communities.

TSQ: Transgender Studies Quarterly ★ Volume 1, Numbers 1–2 ★ May 2014
DOI 10.1215/23289252-2400253 © 2014 Duke University Press

The event took place at the Betti Ono Gallery in Oakland, California, and was attended by forty transgender, gender nonconforming, cisgender, and queer people. Ziegler decided to locate the event in Oakland, a majority nonwhite city, rather than San Francisco, to ensure that a diverse group of participants would be welcome. Over two days, participants got to know each other, formed teams, and heard a panel discussion about the social problems affecting trans and gender-nonconforming people, like high unemployment rates (especially for trans people of color), homelessness, overwhelming discrimination, and inadequate health care and legal services. And they hacked, some overnight. Set up as a competition, the event would award first prize to the individual or team who created the most innovative new use of technology for trans people. The judges were all trans social media producers and advocates: blogger Monica "The Transgriot" Roberts, YouTube vlogger Erin Armstrong, and artist, student, and trans youth advocate Benji Delgadillo.

The exchange between interviewer Tobias Raun, editor of the New Media section (identified here as TSQ) and the organizer of Trans*H4CK Kortney Ryan Ziegler (KRZ) took place over e-mail just before and after the Trans*H4CK hackathon. Using e-mail for the interview seemed both suitable and at the same time a little old school, considering the universe of new media communication technologies now easily available. But with constraints of space (between California and Denmark), time (a nine-hour difference in times zones), and a concussion (Tobias) as well as the all-consuming work of running the event itself (Kortney), e-mail was the obvious choice.

TSQ: *When and why did you get the idea to create the Trans*H4CK project?*

KRZ: I got the idea after participating in other hackathons concerned with social justice. Each time, myself along with a team of creative thinkers collectively made prototypes of mobile apps that had the potential to affect diverse communities. I felt that this model could be very applicable to transgender advocacy, since our community has historically created community through engaging various tech mediums.

TSQ: *What actually happened at the hackathon? Who came and who interacted with whom? What was the atmosphere like?*

KRZ: While the goal of Trans*H4CK was to collaborate on tech innovation, what happened over the weekend was pretty unique. There was an impressive turnout of trans people who work in tech, such as engineers from Twitter and Google, along with artists and activists from all types of backgrounds. There were also allies to the community who showed up to code and create community. Everyone felt accepted and safe and ready to work on improving the lives of those of us in the room and the extended trans community.

TSQ: *Reading your blog post "How Thinking Like a Social Entrepreneur Can Shift the Transgender Movement" (Ziegler 2013), I see you suggest new ways of thinking transgender advocacy that is not afraid to partner outside the LGBT umbrella. You mention self-financing instead of the constant cycle of fundraising and seeking out corporate partnerships. Can you elaborate on that, and on your own strategies in this respect developing Trans*H4CK?*

KRZ: We are living in a moment in which different sources of capital are more readily accessible due to the breaking down of boundaries that technology affords. For example, sending a simple tweet requesting philanthropic advice can open up the doors to venture capitalists, investors, and donors that are interested in financing socially driven projects. Because of this, I think it is important for all of us interested in LGBT advocacy to reach out to different sources beyond the expected grants and donations that are consistently dwindling.

TSQ: *Who have you partnered with to make Trans*H4CK a reality, socially and financially?*

KRZ: I have been very lucky to partner with Mozilla, a nonprofit tech company that privileges open-source data, and the Kapor Center for Social Impact, which funds early-stage tech ventures focused on underrepresented communities. With their help and a successfully run crowd-funding campaign, I was able to successfully finance Trans*H4CK. I also developed a way to leverage the power of Twitter networks through creating Social Media Partnership positions that provided official hackathon sponsorship in exchange for weekly promotion of the event. It helped tremendously with bringing notoriety to Trans*H4CK.

TSQ: *Has this been a perfect match so far?*

KRZ: It has been perfect, because the mission of everyone involved with Trans*H4CK was to elevate the voices of trans people, and that is exactly what we did.

TSQ: *What potentials and what risks do you see in, for instance, Google Inc. or Apple investing in "transgender empowerment"?*

KRZ: I think there are risks involved with any entity investing in trans empowerment that is not explicitly trans focused. But as an entrepreneur, I think those are risks worth taking when the benefit of sustaining trans lives outweighs the fear of potential disempowerment.

TSQ: *In your work as an academic and as a cultural producer making films and blogging, you focus on increasing awareness of and visibility for trans people of color. How do you see the utilization of technology as a way to help create further awareness and bridge race and class division?*

KRZ: I think that technology can foster many types of bridges across communities for the many reasons you expressed in this question. We can now connect with people we weren't able to before, we can hear their voices and see their faces, and that dramatically changes awareness.

TSQ: *Many researchers, myself included, agree that the rise in trans visibility and awareness is greatly amplified by the Internet. More and diverse trans narratives have surfaced, and community building and mobilization have advanced at speeds that were not possible in the era of print culture and face-to-face meetings. And the participants of the Trans*H4ckathon showed how technology can be a tool for empowering trans individuals. However, I wonder if we as trans activists, cultural producers, and researchers should pay more attention to who and how information technology might disempower within the trans community?"*

KRZ: I think one of the faults we have as cultural critics is to focus on things that might bring us harm in order to prevent it. In doing so, we block out the power inherent in seeing the bigger positive picture that expanding modes of communication through technology affords. I hope that we do continue to critique technology, especially as it concerns digital divides, but to also see how certain types of tech keep us alive.

TSQ: *Can you talk about a few specific programs or apps that came out of the hackathon?*

KRZ: All of the projects were creative and well designed given the short amount of time teams had to produce them. The first prize went to Trans*ResourceUS, a searchable and editable Web and mobile wiki that provides information on employment, housing, and health. Second place went to Dottify.me, a social media mapping service that streamlines and makes anonymous trans surveys to better curate data. The Trans Health Access Wiki collects information through the wiki model to give trans people information about the health coverage available in their state. You can see these projects and others online at www.hackerleague.org /hackathons/trans-star-h4ck/hacks.

Tobias Raun, New Media section editor, is an assistant professor of communication studies at the University of Roskilde (Denmark). He is the author of "DIY Therapy: Exploring Affective Self-Representations in Trans Video Blogs on YouTube," in A. Karatzogianni and A. Kuntsman's edited volume *Digital Cultures and the Politics of Emotion* (2012).

Kortney Ryan Ziegler, PhD, is a social entrepreneur who focuses on sustainability and scalability for transgender-led enterprises.

Reference

Ziegler, Kortney Ryan. 2013. "How Thinking Like a Social Entrepreneur Can Shift the Transgender Movement." *Huffington Post*, March 27. www.huffingtonpost.com/kortney-ryan-ziegler -phd/how-thinking-like-a-socia_b_2960690.html.

The Flourishing of Transgender Studies

REGINA KUNZEL

Transfeminist Perspectives in and beyond Transgender and Gender Studies
Edited by A. Finn Enke
Philadelphia: Temple University Press, 2012. 260 pp.

"Transgender France"
Edited by Todd W. Reeser
Special issue, *L'Espirit Createur* 53, no. 1 (2013). 172 pp.

"Race and Transgender"
Edited by Matt Richardson and Leisa Meyer
Special issue, *Feminist Studies* 37, no. 2 (2011). 147 pp.

The Transgender Studies Reader 2
Edited by Susan Stryker and Aren Z. Aizura
New York: Routledge, 2013. 694 pp.

For the past decade or so, "emergent" has often appeared alongside "transgender studies" to describe a growing scholarly field. As of 2014, transgender studies can boast several conferences, a number of edited collections and thematic journal issues, courses in some college curricula, and—with this inaugural issue of *TSQ: Transgender Studies Quarterly*—an academic journal with a premier university press. But while the scholarly trope of emergence conjures the cutting edge, it can also be an infantilizing temporality that communicates (and contributes to) perpetual marginalization. An emergent field is always on the verge of becoming, but it may never arrive.

The recent publication of several new edited collections and special issues of journals dedicated to transgender studies makes manifest the arrival of a vibrant, diverse, and flourishing interdisciplinary field. The work collected in these volumes follows agenda-setting scholarship by Susan Stryker, David Valentine, Joanne Meyerowitz, Paisley Currah, and others in the 1990s and early 2000s (Stryker and Whittle 2006; Stryker 2008; Meyerowitz 2004; Valentine 2007; Currah, Minter, and Juang 2006). What will now surely be known as the *Transgender Studies Reader 1*, edited by Susan Stryker and Stephen Whittle and published in 2006, gave a name to the field. With its door-stopping heft and 768 pages, it literally weighed in on the field's existence. The equally substantial and perhaps even more sweepingly ambitious *Transgender Studies Reader 2* (hereafter *TSR2*), coedited by Stryker and Aren Z. Aizura, follows and complements the first volume, collecting together new and recently published articles and book excerpts and charting the multiple directions of the flood of work published over the past several years. While *TSR1* traced the conceptualization of gender variance historically, from nineteenth-century sexology through foundational theoretical, autoethnographic, and political texts of a century later, *TSR2* charts the field's emerging trends and lines of analysis.

While *TSR2*, organized into ten thematic sections of five essays each, strives for broad coverage, other recent collections take more topical approaches. The past year also saw the publication of *Transfeminist Perspectives in and beyond Transgender and Gender Studies* (hereafter *TP*), edited by A. Finn Enke, which was honored with a Lambda Literary Award in 2013. *TP* assembles twelve essays that reflect on what Enke characterizes as "the productive and sometimes fraught potential" of the relationship between feminist studies and transgender studies (1). Two exciting journal special issues devoted to transgender studies have also appeared in the past couple of years. A thematic issue of *Feminist Studies* titled "Race and Transgender" (hereafter "RT"), edited by Matt Richardson and Leisa Meyer, includes seven essays, poetry, an art essay, and an interview that together bring transgender studies and critical race theory into dialogue. And a special issue of *L'Espirit Createur*, the international journal on French and francophone studies, titled "Transgender France" (hereafter "TF"), edited by Todd W. Reeser, makes note of the French theorists who have inspired transgender theorists (Maurice Merleau-Ponty, Michel Foucault, Gilles Deleuze, and Félix Guattari) and includes twelve essays, in English and French, that bring transgender analysis to French and francophone texts and contexts.

A review of these collections gives me the opportunity to take account of this exciting interdisciplinary field at this moment of its explosive growth and to consider the inspiring work taking place under its rubric. I cannot hope to do justice to these collections in their entirety and certainly cannot capture the richness and range of the eighty-two articles published in them. What follows is a selective tour through these new volumes, a series of transects through the field that maps its animating themes and questions.

Trans Optics

Pioneering activist Virginia Prince was perhaps the first to put the lexical compound of trans+gender to work, Robert Hill tells us in "Before Transgender: *Transvestia*'s Spectrum of Gender Variance, 1960–1980" (*TSR2*). Prince coined the term *transgenderist* in the 1970s, Hill observes, to distinguish heterosexual male cross-dressers from transsexuals and homosexuals. A few decades later, in the early 1990s, transgender took on a new and expansive life, first deployed by activists as an organizing principle to hail and connect a broad spectrum of gender-nonconforming people and then conceived and claimed as an identity.

Much of the early work in a field that would become known as transgender studies focused on transgender identity: pondering its embodiments, working to leverage its political utility, and debating its distinction from and/or inclusion of other gender and sexual identities, including transsexual, butch, queen, queer, and genderqueer. As Stryker and Aizura observe, "The first iteration of the field engaged in the kind of identity politics necessary to gain speaking positions within discourse, and consequently featured a good deal of autoethnographic and self-representational work by trans subjects" (*TSR2*: 3).

Given that history, perhaps the most striking development in transgender studies as represented in these new collections is the turn away from identity as a primary object of analysis and, in some work, the move to critique the notion of a coherent transgender identity or a master narrative of transgender identity formation. Indeed, much of the work in these collections is explicitly anti-identitarian. Aizura, for instance, in his essay in *TP*, "Transnational Transgender Rights and Immigration Law," argues that we need a theory "that turns 'trans' in an anti-identitarian direction," one more attentive to "where and how bodies escape or act clandestinely outside those categories—and at moments in which the categories of immigrant, transgender person, man, and woman become incoherent and inconsistent" (135). To Enke, transgender studies is limited by "a perception that [it] only or primarily concerns transgender-identified individuals" (*TP*: 2). Enke is eager to see "trans" and "feminist" "do more flexible work . . . opening broadly in all directions, . . . modify[ing] and . . . modified by participants whose names we may not even yet know" (3).

Several contributors to these volumes critique an emerging transnormativity, whereby certain transgender bodies are valued, counted, recognized, and folded into citizenship, while others are marginalized, rendered abject, excluded, and made vulnerable to violence and premature death. A biopolitics of transgender examines the processes by which some trans subjects gain rights and recognition at the expense of others. For instance, in "Convivial Relations between Gender Non-conformity and the French Nation-State," Todd Sekuler draws on Jasbir Puar's insights on homonationalism and sexual essentialism in the US context to analyze a move toward the depathologization of "medically legible" transsexual subjects in France and "a transformation in the relationship of the French nation-state with transgender subjects from one of neglect and sickness to one of health, integration, and productivity" ("TF": 15). In the process, however, Sekuler notes, the French state secures its status as a forward-thinking, human rights–protecting nation, and the non-French immigrant—usually a Muslim "other"—is cast as backward, rights-denying, and heterosexual. In "Elusive Subjects: Notes on the Relationship between Critical Political Economy and Trans Studies," Dan Irving asks, "How do neoliberal discourses mediate masculinities to enable select trans men to be assimilated into society while those positioned in the underlayers of the trans demographic remain abject?" (*TP*: 155). An emerging body of work poses a trans of color critique, included in all these collections and featured in "RT," the special issue of *Feminist Studies*, drawing our attention to the ways in which some white transgender subjects have become recognized as rights-deserving citizens while trans people of color often remain excluded. Bobby Noble explores the racial and class privileges of white transgender masculinities in "Our Bodies are Not Ourselves: Tranny Guys and the Racialized Class Politics of Incoherence" (*TSR2*). C. Riley Snorton and Jin Harithaworn's "Trans Necropolitics: A Transnational Reflection on Violence, Death, and the Trans of Color Afterlife" in *TSR2* draws on Achille Mbembe's concept of necropolitics to capture the systemic forms of violence experienced by trans people of color.

If transgender *identity* raises problems for many contributors to these collections—problems of false coherence that flattens out differences among transgender subjects, of required conformities for recognition as authentically transgender, of the implicit whiteness and middle-classness of the transgender subject—transgender *analysis* holds considerable promise. Many scholars in these collections put transgender to use as a mode of analysis rather than as an identity category. Transgender (and sometimes *trans-* as prefix or *trans* as verb—transing disciplinarity, citizenship, childhood, cisgender, nation, species, feminist and women's studies, pedagogy, and more) emerges in this new body of work as an illuminating analytical lens.

Scholars and activists who contribute to these four collections bring that optic to a wide range of topics. A transgender analytic allows Reeser to identify and critique what he terms the "omnipresent sexual binarism of the nation state" that defines and polices normative gender through its educational system, citizenship laws and passport regulations, carceral systems, and marriage ("TF": 9). Paisley Currah and Lisa Jean Moore's " 'We Won't Know Who You Are': Contesting Sex Designations in New York City Birth Certificates" (*TSR2*), a fascinating account of debates about the appropriate sex designation on birth certificates of transgender people in New York City between 1965 and 2006, reveals how post-9/11 anxiety about the fixity of identity has had particularly harmful consequences.

Others bring a transgender analytic to questions of political economy. For example, Irving argues for the importance of the socioeconomic logics of capitalism and neoliberalism to transgender subjectivity, embodiment, and politics. Those logics, Irving notes, promote the construction of "the active/proper/worthy/deserving neoliberal citizen, a construction that disrupts and further devastates the lives of trans people for whom the systemic barriers to emulating these ideals are insurmountable" (*TP*: 154).

Transgender is a way of seeing; it is also, in some new work, a way of knowing. Some contributors reflect upon transgender as an epistemological position from which new, dissident forms of knowledge are produced. An excellent example of this kind of analysis is Marlon M. Bailey's "Gender/Racial Realness: Theorizing the Gender System in Ballroom Culture," in which he details the epistemological inventiveness of poor Black queer communities in Detroit's ballroom scene ("RT"). There, Bailey explains, the category of "realness" functions both as a metric of competitive performance and as a creative survival strategy for people vulnerable to race-, sexuality-, and gender-based violence.

Trans Lives

Framed in universalizing terms (employing Eve Kosofsky Sedgwick's framework developed for queer studies [1990]), transgender is widely relevant to understanding the constructedness of gender and the normativizing power of the gender binary that governs everyone's lives (and, analytically, it is widely relevant to those who work in fields other than transgender studies). However, as Reeser astutely reminds us in his essay "*Trans*France," "We are all trans, and some of us are trans" ("TF": 13). A minoritizing framework highlights the distinctive vulnerabilities and world-making possibilities of transgender and gender-variant people (13). As Currah and Moore propose in their essay in *TSR2*, "Instead of asking what transgender activism does to/for gender," it remains important to "center the effects of the current gender regime on trans people" (609). While transgender studies has developed new analytics of gender normalization, regulation, and surveillance that affect everyone's lives, scholars and activists in the field remain attentive to the lived experiences and material circumstances of transgender and gender-nonconforming people.

Much of that work focuses on the encounter of transgender people with the violence of systems of normalization and on the cultural, legal, and state insistence on binary understandings of gender. If earlier work in transgender studies identified medicine as the disciplinary technology with most significance for trans and gender-variant people, new scholarship featured in these collections interrogates newer administrative, discursive, and surveillance regimes. In this shift, transgender studies reckons with the most important global geopolitical changes of the past ten years: new forms of state power with the tightening grip of neoliberalism and the post-9/11 expansion of surveillance, securitization, and border control. Toby Beauchamp offers perhaps the closest analysis of the links between the policing of transgender and securitization in "Artful Concealment and Strategic Visibility: Transgender Bodies and U.S. State Surveillance after 9/11," a critique of post-9/11 surveillance policies that are, Beauchamp argues, "deeply rooted in the maintenance and enforcement of normatively gendered bodies, behaviors, and identities" (*TSR2*: 47). For Beauchamp, transgender studies "provides an ideal point of entry for thinking through state surveillance of gendered bodies" (ibid.).

While no collection—even one as wide-ranging as *TSR2*—can cover everything, the relative lack of engagement of scholars in these collections with the continued expansion of mass incarceration and the experience of transgender people in prisons, jails, and other institutions of punitive confinement is a striking and surprising omission. There is a brief but powerful mention, in Che Gosset's "Silhouettes of Defiance: Memorializing Historical Sites of Queer and Transgender Resistance in an age of Neoliberal Inclusivity," of the "deadly telos of the prison regime, its threat to and destructive agenda for queer, trans and gender non-conforming people of color and our communities" (*TSR2*: 589). The prison distills many of the dynamics of most concern to this generation of transgender studies scholars and activists—strictly policed binary gender and the exposure of the most marginalized of trans and gender-variant people, especially people of color, to harassment, surveillance, violence, discrimination, and death—and there is ample opportunity here for future scholarship as well as an urgent need for activism.[1]

If the prison is a place of profound vulnerability and violence for transgender people, the academy is a contested site of struggle for recognition and inclusion. Enke's *TP* includes several essays that examine the place of transgender people in university infrastructures. Clark Pomerleau outlines a set of best practices to make universities more welcoming to transgender and gender-variant university students and staff in "College Transitions: Recommended Policies for Trans Students and Employees." Vic Muñoz elaborates a "decolonizing pedagogy of transing" that recovers historical and contemporary experiences of colonization and is based on a politics of location, in "Gender/Sovereignty" (23). In "'Do These Earrings Make Me Look Dumb?': Diversity, Privilege, and Heteronormative Perceptions of Competence within the Academy," Kate Forbes writes as a scholar in the natural sciences to critique heteronormative and sexist perceptions of competence, calling on the academy to address "how it views feminine people and all individuals who do not mirror the dominant paradigm" (34). Pat Griffin explores the consequences of sex segregation in collegiate sports for trans and gender-variant student-athletes. And in "Trans. Panic: Some Thoughts toward a Theory of Feminist Fundamentalism," Bobby Noble tracks the ambivalent, ghosting presence of transgender in women's studies.

Trans often functions as a metaphor of geographic movement, and several of the essays in a section of *TSR2* consider the movement of trans bodies in and across space. In a critique of the valorization of the urban in trans studies, Lucas Cassiday Crawford considers "new creative potentials" in trans lives in rural spaces and small towns and asks us to imagine "the very different affects and lives that could be realized there (475, 481). In his intriguing and thoughtful biographical essay "Longevity and Limits in Rae Bourbon's Life in Motion," Don Romesburg tracks the "multiple forms of mobility and migration"—across national borders, "shifting terrains of social attitudes, law enforcement, performance trends, . . . subcultures," performance genres, and racial, class, sex/gender, and sexual subject positions—undertaken by performer Rae Bourbon over her sixty-year career and impressively long life (484).

Much of the work in these collections responds to critiques of earlier limitations and blind spots of the field, taking aim, as Stryker and Aizura write, at "its implicit whiteness, U.S.-centricity, Anglophone bias, and sometimes the suspect ways in which the category *transgender* has been circulated transnationally" (*TSR2*: 4). Moving from the predominantly US-centered focus of earlier iterations of the field, these collections make visible what Todd A. Henry calls an "increasingly globalized transgender studies" (*TSR2*: 404). That global approach goes far beyond what Stryker in *TSR1* characterized as "around the world in eighty genders," to explore how geographic and geopolitical location and histories of empire, colonialism, displacement, and settlement shape different gender-variant subjectivities, identities, and embodiments (14).

The global and transnational scope of the field is on full display in *TSR2*, integrated in most of the volume's ten sections and in the other collections as well. That fascinating body of work includes Marcia Ochoa's "Perverse Citizenship: Divas, Marginality, and Participation in 'Loca-Lization,'" about the alternative political imaginaries that Venezuelan trans women articulate in the face of violence and marginalization. In "Unlikely Sex Change Capital of the World" ("RT"), Elizabeth Bucar and Enke explore the media-generated astonishment at the "unlikeliness" of "sex change capitals" in Tehran, Iran, and Trinidad, Colorado, spinning Tehran as the site of homophobic violence and coercion while representing Trinidad as a model of American liberalism. In "*Kaming Mga Talyada* (*We Who Are Sexy*): The Transsexual Whiteness of Christine Jorgensen in the (Post)Colonial Philippines" (*TSR2*), Stryker reflects on the appearance of

Jorgensen in a 1962 Filipino feature film to consider the encounter of white American privilege with postcolonial histories of Filipino sex and gender, producing "global mappings of disparate and differently subjugated assemblages of sex/gender/sexuality" (552). In "Reading Transsexuality in 'Gay' Tehran (Around 1979)" (*TSR2*), Afsaneh Najmabadi offers a tentative mapping of what she terms "non-heteronormative Tehran" in the 1970s (380). Aizura considers the political and affective economies of travel for sex reassignment in "The Romance of the Amazing Scalpel: 'Race,' Labor, and Affect in Thai Gender Reassignment Clinics" (*TSR2*). Aizura examines the orientalist discourse of tourist-marketing strategies aimed at white trans women and the emotional labor of Thai gender clinic workers to contribute to "a critique of economies of feminized and racialized transnational labor" (505). Kale Bantigue Fajardo explores the transformative nature of global markets and movement in his study of the complex and fluid masculinities forged by Filipino seamen in the global shipping industry through their "intimate relationalities" with tomboys (*TSR2*: 529).

While most work in transgender studies is understandably focused on the contemporary moment, I was excited to read new work on the historical possibilities of the concept of transgender in the past. Some use the concept of transgender to name gender-variant phenomena in the "pre-historical," ancient, medieval, and premodern record. In "Towards a Transgender Archaeology: A Queer Rampage through Prehistory" (*TSR2*), Mary Weismantel critiques the ways in which archaeological disciplinary practices have ignored or suppressed transgender phenomena. Deborah Miranda reconstructs the history of the genocidal extermination of gender-variant native people by Spanish colonizers in "Extermination of the Joyas: Gendercide in Spanish California" (*TSR2*). And Gary Ferguson examines stories of early modern gender change and ambiguities of the sexed body in late seventeenth- and early eighteenth-century France in "Early Modern Transitions: From Montaigne to Choisy" ("TF").

Others explore gender-variant lives in the more recent past. In "Elusive Subjects: Notes on the Relationship between Critical Political Economy and Trans Studies" (*TP*), Irving offers a fascinating reading of 1950s medical studies of transsexuality by sexologist David O. Cauldwell alongside early transsexual autobiographies to locate the roots of neoliberal discourses of the good transsexual as "a flexible, courageous, and physically/mentally and financially fit individual who displays productive potential" (169). Hill's exploration in *Transvestia* magazine of the identity terms used to distinguish MTF (male-to-female) heterosexual cross-dressers from homosexuals and transsexuals in the 1960s and 1970s looks at the period of "taxonomic revolution" after World War II, when doctors, sexologists, and people from across the gender spectrum "began to map and sort out the overlapping subcultures of gender and sexual variance and make ontological distinctions among the categories of 'sex,' 'gender,' and 'sexuality'" (*TSR2*: 366). *Transvestia*'s readers and writers, Hill finds, "engaged in a relentless and often-times vicious politics of respectability when classifying and differentiating types of (trans)gender embodiments, practices, and identities" (ibid.).

What are the temporal and conceptual borders of transgender history? Who are its subjects? Scholars who explore the portability of the contemporary concept of "transgender" to the past reflect on questions of temporality and sometimes bend and break the methods of disciplinary history. For Christy Wampole, the "impudence" of Claud Cahun's repudiation of gender norms in her 1920s self-portraiture signaled a self-styling in which history had not quite caught up, forecasting "with confidence the arrival and permanence of transgender as a category" and anticipating a future transgender subject ("TF"). Kadji Amin offers an intriguing reading of nonnormative genders and sexualities in Colette's *The Pure and the Impure*. Instead of reading Colette's texts for depictions of same-sex and cross-gender subcultures, Amin writes that they "demand a form of literary close reading attuned to the text's ellipses, limits, and contradictions . . . and its persistent soldering of a discourse on gender and sexuality to concerns about historicity and time" ("TF": 114).

Beginning in the early 1990s and accelerating with the turn of the twenty-first century, representations of transgender lives in films, novels, the Internet, and television have made transgender an increasingly familiar concept. Con-tributors to these collections consider transgender representation in narrative, experimental, and documentary film and literary texts. Darren Waldron offers an insightful reading of Celine Sciamma's 2011 feature film *Tomboy*, admiring the director's departure from the theatricalization of gender identity in a story focusing on a gender-nonconforming ten-year-old child. *Tomboy*, Waldron writes, "reveals the conditionality of all gendering by highlighting the perfor-mative strategies undertaken by boys to comply with compulsory masculinity" ("TF": 60). *TSR2* includes a chapter from Jack Halberstam's *In a Queer Time and Place*, which considers the operation of the "transgender gaze" in recent popular films and the multiple meanings of the transgender body to multiple audiences.

Trans Conversations
These collections showcase a deeply interdisciplinary and intersectional field in conversation with other disciplines and interdisciplines. Transgender studies as represented in these collections enters into and transforms multiple fields of study. The scholarly dialogue most fully developed in transgender studies is in some ways one of the most surprising: from a history of conflict, dismissal, and epistemic disconnect with feminist and women's studies, transgender studies scholars have developed a body of theoretical and empirical work under the

rubric of "transfeminism." Enke's excellent introduction to *TP* outlines a conversation between transgender studies and feminist studies, organized around their "mutually constituted but highly ambivalent relationship" (vi). As Enke elaborates, both trans studies and feminist studies are committed to the notion that gender is made; both are committed to "some version of gender self-determination and resistance to binary gender norms"; and both fields, at their best, are dedicated to an intersectional analysis (5). In *TP*, Enke argues that trans "might be central, not marginal to gender and women's studies" and offers models for the fields' integration and mutual transformation (2).

Richardson and Meyer's coedited special issue of *Feminist Studies* offers a series of essays that engage "the varied intersections and mutual constitutiveness of transgender and critical race theory" ("RT": 247). Work in that issue considers the "impact of race on transgender theory" and challenges critical race studies to think about "how our studies of racialized communities would be different if we put transgender subjects at the center of our work" (248). Contributors consider the mutual constitution of race and gender identity through a wide range of themes, including racial and ethnic cross-identification in gender performance, racialized meanings of media representations of transgender subjects, and subjugated knowledges shaped by gender difference and race. "RT" reprints Emily Skidmore's prizewinning article, "Constructing the 'Good Transsexual': Christine Jorgensen, Whiteness, and Heteronormativity in the Mid-Twentieth-Century Press." There, Skidmore shows how race mattered in mid-twentieth-century constructions of transsexuality, contrasting the public reception of three white transsexual women in the 1950s with that of three transwomen of color who appeared in the mainstream, tabloid, and African American press in the 1950s and 1960s. Transsexual women "with most proximity to white womanhood," Skidmore finds, gained visibility in mainstream press as "authentic"; their stories "therefore came to define the boundaries of 'transsexual' identity" (271).

A few articles in these collections suggest the possibility of an emerging conversation between transgender studies and disability studies. Enke draws on disability studies to pose an astute and provocative critical genealogy of the term *cisgender*, in "The Education of Little Cis: Cisgender and the Discipline" [*TP*; reprinted in *TSR2*]. Enke's critique of the embrace of the term *cisgender*—especially in the gender studies classroom—as reifying a cis/trans binary and for encouraging "investments in a gender stability that undermines feminist, trans*, queer, and related movements" is enabled by Enke's conversation with disability studies (*TP*: 62, 61). Both transgender and disability studies are about "movement and change," Enke writes, "but disability studies may do a better job of recognizing that bodies, abilities, and core identities change" (74). As Enke observes, disability studies would never reify ability as a static condition: "Cis-abled?!

Impossible" (ibid.). In "Body Shame, Body Pride: Lessons from the Disability Rights Movement," Eli Clare imagines "a disability politics of transness," described as "not one of simple analogy, but one that delves into the lived experiences of our bodies, that questions the idea of normal and the notion of cure, that values self-determination, that resists shame and the medicalization of identity—a politics that will help all of us come home to our bodies" (*TSR2*: 265). A disability studies analysis is implicit but powerfully enabling in Clare Sears's examination of the history of cross-dressing laws in late nineteenth-century San Francisco, alongside the history of the dime museum's freak shows, to explore their "similar disciplinary effects, producing and policing the boundaries of normative gender" (*TSR2*: 555).

Trans Visions

New work in transgender studies sharpens analytical critiques of technologies of power and regimes of normalization; it also strives to make the world more livable for transgender and gender-variant people. Contributors to these collections conjure a range of transgender political imaginaries and visions of justice and freedom. While some promote visions of rights and protections for transgender people, one of the most striking and challenging moves in the field is the turn away from a politics of recognition and inclusion and toward a critique of what Dean Spade and others have called "trickle-down" models of social justice, ones that prioritize neoliberal rights frameworks at the expense of interests of transgender populations most at risk: immigrants, undocumented people, people of color, low-income people, and youth (See also Cohen 1999; Strolovitch 2007). Sarah Lamble thus critiques the framing of Transgender Days of Remembrance, in "Retelling Racialized Violence, Remaking White Innocence: The Politics of Interlocking Oppressions in Transgender Day of Remembrance" (*TSR2*). Those memorialization practices, Lamble argues, deracialize violence against trans people and fail to engage white witnesses in their own complicity with the forces of racist violence. In "What's Wrong with Trans Rights?" (*TP*), Spade assails the mainstream LGBT political agenda that prioritizes antidiscrimination and hate crime legislation which, in Spade's analysis, tightens the grip of the carceral system that is so oppressive to trans and other people. Scanning more radical emancipatory horizons, Spade argues for shifting the framework of trans rights to "critical trans resistance," targeting "the sites of violence we see producing trans death" and promoting an explicitly redistributionist political agenda (193). In "Normalized Transgressions: Legitimizing the Transsexual Body as Productive," Irving promotes alliances with "other individuals who are understood as improperly sexed/gendered such as single mothers, women and men of color, those on social assistance, and those engaged in sex work" and with "anticapitalist and antiglobalization activists who engage in queering all facets of political economy" (*TSR2*: 27).

While a number of scholars and activists call for resistance to the forces of neoliberalism that bear down on and constrain transgender (and all) subjects, Michelle O'Brien underlines the inevitable complicity of transgender people with these forces in her remarkable essay "Tracing this Body: Transsexuality, Pharmaceuticals, and Capitalism" (*TSR2*). O'Brien tracks the connections of her own consumption of hormones to the pharmaceutical companies that produce them, to insurance companies that exclude transgender healthcare, to transnational free trade agreements that make buying them more affordable in Mexico and Canada than in the United States. She considers as well as the circulation, regulation, and criminalization of needles. Locating her own body within global flows of power and capital, O'Brien cautions against the impossibility of a politics of purity even as she enjoins us to "trace the possibilities of resistance and liberation" (64). "We are all in the midst of structures of tremendous violence, oppression, and exploitation," O'Brien writes. "There is no easy escape or pure distance from them. . . . But resist we do" (ibid.).

* * *

Read together, these collections make an impressive statement about the dynamism and diversity of transgender studies. The essays in these tightly edited and thoughtfully conceived volumes cut across many disciplines and interdisciplines, including history, philosophy, anthropology, evolutionary biology, critical race studies, public policy, feminist studies, geography, francophone studies, media studies, science studies, and more, staging conversations that will enrich scholarship within and beyond the borders of the field. While it is overly optimistic to think that the dazzling work in these volumes heralds the "transing" of academia, their publication will certainly make it harder to ignore the field. While transgender studies has clearly established a place in the academy, contributors to these collections go beyond academic conversations to venture world-changing claims about the urgencies of our present moment. Excellent introductions by Enke in *TP* and by Stryker and Aizura in *TSR2* map the field and point to its exciting futures.

Regina Kunzel is the Doris Stevens Chair of Women's Studies and a professor of history and gender and sexuality studies at Princeton University. She is the author of *Criminal Intimacy: Prison and the Uneven History of Modern American Sexuality* (2008).

Note

1.	For work on the carceral state, incarcerated people, and transgender, see Stanley and Smith 2011, Spade 2011, and Kunzel 2008.

References

Cohen, Cathy J. 1999. *The Boundaries of Blackness: AIDS and the Breakdown of Black Politics.* Chicago: University of Chicago Press.

Currah, Paisley, Shannon Minter, and Richard Juang. 2006. *Transgender Rights.* Minneapolis: University of Minnesota Press.

Kunzel, Regina. 2008. *Criminal Intimacy: Prison and the Uneven History of Modern American Sexuality.* Chicago: University of Chicago Press.

Meyerowitz, Joanne. 2004. *How Sex Changed: A History of Transsexuality in the United States.* Cambridge, MA: Harvard University Press.

Sedgwick, Eve Kosofsky. 1990. *Epistemology of the Closet.* Berkeley: University of California Press.

Spade, Dean. 2011. *Normal Life: Administrative Violence, Critical Trans Politics, and the Limits of Law.* Brooklyn, NY: South End.

Stanley, Eric, and Nat Smith, eds. 2011. *Captive Genders: Trans Embodiment and the Prison Industrial Complex.* Oakland, CA: AK.

Strolovitch, Dara Z. 2007. *Affirmative Advocacy: Race, Class, and Gender in Interest Group Politics.* Chicago: University of Chicago Press.

Stryker, Susan, and Stephen Whittle, eds. 2006. *The Transgender Studies Reader.* New York: Routledge.

Stryker, Susan. 2006. "(De)Subjugated Knowledges: An Introduction to Transgender Studies." In Stryker and Whittle, *Transgender Studies Reader.*

———. 2008. *Transgender History.* Berkeley, CA: Seal.

Valentine, David. 2007. *Imagining Transgender: An Ethnography of a Category.* Durham, NC: Duke University Press.

Supporters of *TSQ*

Institutional Supporters

Office of the Provost
Office of the Vice President for Research
College of Social and Behavioral Sciences
Institute for LGBT Studies
Department of Gender and Women's Studies
University of Arizona

The Williams Institute
University of California, Los Angeles, School of Law

Connecticut College

Wells College

Department of Gender and Women's Studies
University of California, Berkeley

Women's and Gender Studies Program
Brooklyn College, City University of New York

School of Law
Seattle University

Department of Gender, Sexuality, and Women's Studies
Simon Fraser University

LGBT Resource Center
University of California, San Diego

University of Victoria Libraries

Department of History
University of Warwick

TSQ: Transgender Studies Quarterly ★ Volume 1, Numbers 1–2 ★ May 2014 **298**
DOI 10.1215/23289252-2679896   © 2014 Duke University Press

Grassroots Supporters

Anonymous

Kayden Arias Sharky Althen

Rustem Ertug Altinay

Elisa A. G. Arfini

Caroline Arnold

Daniel Bao

Barbara A. Barnes

Jesse Bayker

Alyson Belcher

Caprice Bellefleur

Kile Bigbee

Mons Bissenbakker

Cooper Lee Bombadier

Marsha C. Botzer

Alison Boyd

T. Sharon Brackett

Jennifer Brier

Matt Brim

Denise E. Brogan-Kator

Tom Buchanan and Robert Bell

Jennifer Burney

Diana Cage

Megan Carrigy

Megan M. Carroll

Simone Chess

Hae Yeon Choo

Ann L. Clark

Tim Cochrane

Kathy Cole

nic connolly

Jeanette Cool

Kel Currah

Jamie Dailey

Christopher Daley

Kat Daniels

Steven F. Dansky

Carlos Ulises Decena

Guillermo de León

J. Michael Denton

Jenn De Roo

Monika Dryburgh

Kit Edgar

Patrick J. Egan

Harley Ehrman

Zillah Eisenstein

Juliette Valentin Emerson

Rose Ernst

Hélène FD

Sam Feder

Kathy E. Ferguson

Andrea Friedman

Ane Møller Gabrielsen

Ann Garry

Eric Geiger

Stacey Goguen

Alicia E. Goranson

Lorraine Coley Gray

Julie A. Greenberg

David Greene

Zach Hall

Mobina Hashmi

Benjamin Rousselle Herbert

E. L. Hill

Heather L. Hiscox

Moa Holmqvist

Laura Horak

Jim Hubbard

Olivia I. Hunt

Damien S. Hunter

David Inwood

Alice Izsak

Ada Jaarsma

Kaden Mark Jelsing

Abigail Jensen

Fenton Johnson

Jacob Kaagaard

J. Kēhaulani Kauanui
Liesl Koehler
Elias D. Krell
Christa J. Kriesel-Roth
Kam Wai Kui
Jessica Lauren
Anna Law
Antonia Leotsakos
Susan J. Leviton
M. Tyler Levy
Ana Laura Lopes
Eithne Luibheid
Laura Mamo
Jen Manion
Daniel C. Manuel
Nikiko Masumoto
Alysandra McCann
Sarah McCormic
Duffi McDermott
Karen McLaren
Tey Meadow
Cortney Mihulka
Christopher Moller
Parker Marie Molloy
Dawne Moon and Searah Deysach
Rusty Mae Moore
Tara Mulqueen
Kevin P. Murphy
Z Nicolazzo
Camille Nurka
Jenni Olson and Julie Dorf
Kathleen Nicole O'Neal
John Helle Otto
Katy Otto
Sara Pacelko
Andrew C. Parker
Greg Parkinson
Jezebel Parks
Gina Patterson
Roy Pérez

Melissa Minor Peters
Michael Nebeling Petersen
Laurel J. Popp
Lavelle Porter
Mary Purdey
Avery Radclyffe
Trystan Angel Reese
David Reichard
Hai Ren
Jeremy Reppy
Amanda R. Reyes
Casey Robertson
Richard T. Rodriguez
jules rosskam
Nina Rota
Lisa S. Salazar
Evren Savci
F. Allen Sawyer
Sima Shakhsari
Eve Shapiro
Russell Sheaffer
Sherri Shimansky
Lincoln Shlensky
Alexis Shotwell
John-Paul Smiley
K. Stevens
James and Maryann Stewart
Max Strassfeld
Celina Su
Daniel Scott Swenson
Noah Tamarkin
Charlotte Tan
Tawaen
Kathrin Thiele
S. P. Thompson
Transgender Michigan
Michael Trigilio
Robin Udell
Emmi Vähäpassi
Paul VanDeCarr

Iris van der Tuin
Tyrras Warren
Amy Widdifield
Rachel Miranda Wedig
Jamie Weil
Meredith L. Weiss
Evan Lutz Wells
Amy Wilhelm

Cristan Williams
Anna James Neuman Wipfler
Veronika Wöhrer
Marcy Wood
Regina Mariam Wright
Andie Wyatt
William Zimmerman

Founding Supporters

Anonymous
Richard K. Adler
Rabih Alameddine
Alexander | Carrillo Consulting
I. Alkalay
Bonnie S. Anderson
Anjali Arondekar
Kerry Ashforth
Marc B.
M. V. Lee Badgett
Dana Baitz
Karen Barad
M. Anthony Barreto-Neto
Toby Beauchamp
Anne Befu
Elspeth H. Brown
M. K. Bryson
Mary Bunch
Mauro Cabral
Terrilynn Cantlon
Shanna T. Carlson
Monica J. Casper
William Evin Chalmers
Shaun-Adrian F. Choflá
Dainna Cicotello
Valérie Robin Clayman
Jennifer Collins
Vincent and Teresa Cook

Cos
Paisley Currah
Cynthia Degnan
Aaron H. Devor
Susan Hope Dundas
Patricia Elliot
Finn Enke
Jennifer Evans
Deanna Leigh Fassett
Jamie Faye Fenton
Milton E. Ford
Holly Gaiman
Daniel Garcia
Patrizia Gentile
Miqqi Alicia Gilbert
Robin Diane Goldstein
Aden Hakimi
Sally Haslanger
Rose Hayes
Ryder Julian Henderson
Todd A. Henry
Henry Hohmann
James-Henry Holland
James Hotelling
Nat Hurley
Dan Irving
Lisa Jakobsen and Hanna Miller
Andrea James

Julia R. Johnson
Katherine Johnson
Meredith Jones
Chase Joynt
William Kapfer
Cael M. Keegan
Alexander Kelly
Maureen Kelly and Luca Maurer
Reese C. Kelly
Kim Klausner
Thamar Klein
Kyle Knight
Anson Koch-Rein
Katy Koonce
Regina Kunzel
Liz Loeb
Helen Hok-Sze Leung
Liina
Michael Lucey
Mickey R. Mahoney
Brandon Peter Masterman
Tim McCarthy
Adam M. McMahon
Jeremy Melius
Sandy Mesics
Alasdair Murrie-West
Elijah Nella
Jamie Nelson
Douglas Noffsinger
Oscar Wilde Cooperative, Berkeley,
    California
Lara Palombo
Scott Pask
Stephan Pennington
Carla A. Pfeffer
Emily Pitt
Katherine Prevost
Erica Rand
Holly Randell-Moon

Masha Raskolnikov
K. J. Rawson
Elizabeth Reis
Tamara Ritt
Amanda Roberts
Megan Rohrer
Jess Scott Rowell
Aviva Rubin
Noah Ryan
David Sacks
Trish Salah
Naomi Scheman
Celine Parreñas Shimizu
Victor Silverman
Melissa Sklarz
Ana Marie Smith
Spider
Marc Stein and Jorge Olivares
Eliza Steinbock
Devyn Stock
M. Dana Strauss
Dara Strolovitch
Denise Tse-Shang Tang
Denise Taylor
Jeanne Theoharis
Shaun Travers
Trembling Void Studios
Rebecca Turner
David Valentine
Sarah Anne Vestal
J. Keith Vincent
Georgina Voss
K. and L. Wachowski
Jane Ward
Sean Whelan
Tommie Whitaker
Joe Wilson and Dean Hamer
Stephanie R. Wilson
C. Michael Woodward

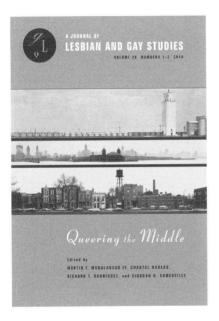